THE EDUCATION OF NICHOLAS PETROVICH

The Education of Nicholas Petrovich

A novel
by
EUGENE CHRISTY

Adelaide Books
New York / Lisbon
2021

THE EDUCATION OF NICHOLAS PETROVICH
A novel
By Eugene Christy

Copyright © by Eugene Christy
Cover design © 2020 David Holscher

Published by Adelaide Books, New York / Lisbon
adelaidebooks.org
Editor-in-Chief
Stevan V. Nikolic

All rights reserved. No part of this book may be reproduced in any manner whatsoever without written permission from the author except in the case of brief quotations embodied in critical articles and reviews.

For any information, please address Adelaide Books
at info@adelaidebooks.org
or write to:
Adelaide Books
244 Fifth Ave. Suite D27
New York, NY, 10001

ISBN: 978-1-955196-14-7

Printed in the United States of America

For Caitlín

Contents

Volume IV

    OF THE TWENTIETH CENTURY QUINTET *11*

Part 1 REVERE *15*

    Chapter 1 Descending to Eden *17*

    Chapter 2 The God in the Garden *25*

    Chapter 3 Achilles in the Camp of the Women *35*

    Chapter 4 The Angel of Mercy *48*

    Chapter 5 The Spartan Mothers *69*

    Chapter 6 Death of a Piano *90*

Part 2 SPICKET FALLS *115*

    Chapter 7 The Cat in the Hallway *117*

    Chapter 8 The Bronte Sisters *128*

    Chapter 9 The Railroad Yards of Milltown *141*

    Chapter 10 The Fieldstone House *159*

Chapter 11	The Shop	*180*
Chapter 12	Roseann	*191*
Chapter 13	The Wonder Bar	*202*
Chapter 14	Jimmy Dillard	*207*
Chapter 15	Guilt and Innocence	*218*
Chapter 16	Pershing, Pennsylvania	*224*
Chapter 17	Central Junior	*233*
Chapter 18	The Facts of Life	*240*
Chapter 19	Gently Down the Stream	*246*
Chapter 20	Lindy Bergan	*251*
Chapter 21	Victor Hugo	*254*
Chapter 22	The Stardust Lounge	*259*
Chapter 23	A Death in the Family	*264*
Chapter 24	Time is a River	*269*
Chapter 25	Playing Ball	*275*
Chapter 26	Molly Jones	*280*
Chapter 27	The Sixties Begin	*291*
Chapter 28	Molly, I Have to Go	*297*

Part 3   BOSTON   *307*

Chapter 29	College on a Hill	*309*
Chapter 30	Good Catholic Boys	*320*
Chapter 31	Something Had to Change	*328*
Chapter 32	Otherwise Known as Sheila Blake	*336*

Chapter 33 She Made Me Want To *350*

Chapter 34 Girl From the County Mayo *353*

Chapter 35 Sheila, I Have to Go *365*

Chapter 36 The Three Faces of Jealousy *368*

Chapter 37 A Shot at the Window *375*

Chapter 38 A Time to Every Purpose *381*

Chapter 39 Pinky and Jeanie *384*

Chapter 40 What's a Petrovich? *389*

Chapter 41 Life Doesn't Come in a Bottle *392*

Chapter 42 The Summer of '68 *398*

Chapter 43 Snake in the Grass *405*

Chapter 44 A Death in Vietnam *409*

Part 4 SOUTH COUNTY *417*

Chapter 45 Love on 250 Dollars a Month *419*

Chapter 46 Marshall Andrews *425*

Chapter 47 The Honest Truth *429*

Chapter 48 The Darling Month of May *434*

Chapter 49 Culchies, Jackeens and Ignorant Yanks *442*

Chapter 50 Catch You Later, Man *447*

Chapter 51 David and Susan *455*

Chapter 52 The 4th of May *461*

Part 5	MILLTOWN	**463**	
	Chapter 53	Leaves of Grass	**465**
	Chapter 54	Chickie and Phil	**473**
	Chapter 55	Eddie Domani	**476**
	Chapter 56	I Dreamed I Saw Joe Hill Last Night	**483**
	Chapter 57	Thanksgiving and Forgiveness	**489**
	Chapter 58	The War Comes Home	**498**
	Chapter 59	Nixon Strikes	**505**

About the Author **517**

VOLUME IV

OF THE TWENTIETH CENTURY QUINTET

Most people go to their graves with their music still locked up inside them . . .

Benjamin Disraeli

Part 1

REVERE

Chapter 1

Descending to Eden

Night drops down to the dark before dawn. I lower my body from my bed. There is no sleep for the anti-hero tonight. I pick my way through the aged room to the end of the empty hall, and I take my bones down the racking stair. I climb down the back steps, bang the trellis and stumble down the walk with the broken bricks and the leafless rosebush. The street is long and void. The lawns lie bitter with lime. In the eastern sky is a charred light.

Into this devastated world I was born, in the heart of the century, on Christmas Day, a year after the war ended.

This charred light, this eastern sky, are born again and again, in every dawn, in every birth.

Just as this war blasted humanity, yet it did not end hope, which is reborn in every heart that loves, every heart that seeks to question an answering heart, in every child that is born.

So it was with me. I was born, and with me, it all began all over again.

For the newborn babe is already an old, old man, and the night dropping down and the racking stair and the street long and void are within us, vying with the light and the love. *Everything happens at the same time* and we must plow our path between the mountains and the sea because we are neither animal nor god, but somehow, human.

The record will state that I was born on a certain date in a certain city in a certain country because that is how records work and we like to record everything.

For the record I was born, on Christmas Day, in 1946, in Revere, Massachusetts, a small resort city famous for its beach, a place, bordering on East Boston, which was a magnet for many, a popular escape.

At the moment I was born I had no categories, no labels, no language, but I had other things the record will not show.

I had a memory that I existed previously. That I had always existed. I came from somewhere else and I did not belong here. Not yet.

But I did not know who I was or what I was. I would have to find that out from others. They would tell me who I was.

That there *were* others, others who were *not me,* was a concept that I could not have grasped at the beginning, not for a long time, but I knew dramatically the pain of being rudely ripped from a place of benign oceanic floatation, and I wanted to go back. I wanted to go back because beyond that place was a vastness where I was one with all, and all with one.

My mother, too, knew awful pain when I was born because I was born by cesarean section at the Children's Hospital in Revere.

In the moment, she did not feel this pain as a physical hurt because she was under total anesthesia, but the minute she awoke, she was immediately overwhelmed with a deep sense of loss and felt unaccountably, alarmingly anxious.

This did not go away until they brought me to her and placed me in her arms as she lay prostrate in her hospital bed.

That is definition No. 9 in the dictionary. *Prostrate.* **9.** Physically weak or exhausted. 10. Submissive. 11. utterly dejected; disconsolate.

But then they placed me in her arms. My mother magically, immediately, felt a burst of powerful love envelop her, and me, with warm comfort, a blanket of proud desire, as she felt we were one again.

Everything my mother felt, I felt, too.

Her pride filled the room and bloomed in the faces of all her family members gathered there.

Her father, Antonio LaStoria, glowed with satisfaction. This birth meant to him a secret sense of accomplishment, a sign he shared only with God, that now his last daughter, Gerry, had joined the other three, Mary, Margaret and Anna, in bestowing upon him, as firstborn, a grandson, just as his own first child, Pasquale, had been a boy.

This was no accident. *It was God's approbation of his entire life.*

My mother's mother, Gigi LaStoria, felt immense relief that Gerardina, the last of her four daughters to be married, and the newborn, too, had survived the doctor's knife, for Gigi re-lived every one of her own seven pregnancies each time the Holy Mother bestowed another grandchild.

Besides, *this bambino had been born in a caul,* which everyone knew marked the boy as special, *as selected by fate,* and Gigi, the boy's grandmother, insisted that the veil must be kept, always, *and never, never thrown away,* or the good luck would go with it.

When Gerry made a face of disgust at this proclamation, her three sisters were quick to second their mother. They closed ranks in solidarity with superstition. Nothing was said, but it was written in their faces, in their heavenward looks, in their eyes downcast knowingly in the other direction.

Their mother had whispered her admonitions to her daughter Mary, who was standing next to her. All five LaStoria women shared Italian fluency and frequently used it as their private language, which reinforced the old traditional ways. Which their three brothers, who also were fluent, had passed beyond, now that the war had broken so many old ties to the things that came before.

Gerry's most modern sister, Anna, to break this spooked silence, spoke first, wanting to change the subject, so she asked, "What are you going to call him, *Andrew?*"

Anna stood there in the hospital room with her entire gathered clan surrounding her while she held in her arms her own first baby, her son Thomas, born just three weeks before. This boy was named after his father, Tommy DiPrima, so Anna, always so proper, expected Gerry to follow suit, and call her new baby boy 'Andrew,' after his father. But Gerry corrected her, saying, "Anna, that's not Andy's name," referring to the boy's proud papa. "My husband's name is Andrej."

Her sister Mary, who was well-acquainted with her saints, said, "What about Christopher? After all, he was born on Christmas day."

"I hate that name," said Gerry.

Her brother Patsy said, "Well, you can call him Patsy, after me!"

Patsy's face shone like a lightbulb. This was his attempt to lighten the mood, but his suggestion met with general derision, and the laughter it prompted was not exactly with him, but *più o meno* at him. Anna slugged him in the upper arm. "One Patsy in this family is enough!"

Patsy, everyone's older brother, the firstborn of Tony and Gigi LaStoria, always sensitive about receiving his due respect, said, "I don't know why none of you girls ever thinks of me. Pasquale's your grandfather's name, after all, may he rest in peace. Jesus, that's why Ma named me after her Dad, out of respect!"

But his father, Tony LaStoria, from the other side of the family, only said, one eyebrow raised, "Hey, watch your mouth, you're not directing traffic here."

His son Patsy had been an M.P. with Patton's Third Army in the war.

Patsy's sister Margaret now piped up, derisively. "Yeah, Staff-Sergeant Patsy, watch out, you're not too big in your britches to get a lickin' from your Pa!"

This sister, known to all as Peggy, was divorced, a cardinal sin. Peggy had two sons, Henry and Ronnie, whose names came from the family of her ex-husband, Henry Fabiano. Everyone knew it was no accident that Peggy had not named a son after her father. *No doubt she hadn't yet forgotten the lickin's she got from her Pa, and as for forgiving, well, that wasn't Peggy!*

Gerry's brother Gene, the sensible brother, the one who took after their father, right down to the hand gestures, now rode to the rescue. "What does Andy say?" He looked questioningly at Andy Petrovich, the baby's father, who was seated on the bed with one hip next to Gerry's pillow and his arm slung casually over the headboard.

"Well, I guess I'm it, since I'm the one handin' out the see-gars" said Andy, who, for once, was the center of attention.

Among the assembled LaStorias, Andy Petrovich, ex-coalminer, ex-US Navy, was, as yet, still the new boy in town, and his own family, 500 miles away, in Fayette County, Penna., was not about to stroll suddenly into this maternity room at the Children's Hospital in Revere, Mass. to join him in celebration of the happy event. So it was up to Andy, who called everybody 'buddy,' to assert his parental rights. He looked down with love on Gerry's uplifted face, and said, "Hon, I think we oughta call him Nicholas."

"Oh, that's cute," said Peggy. "Little Saint Nick."

Gerry frowned. *Why did Peggy always have to spoil everything?*

"It's a good saint's name," said Gigi, out loud. In spite of speaking only Italian, she often understood more than she cared to let on. Now she felt put upon to defend the daughter, Gerry, the newborn's mother, who had always stayed at home with her and never left her side. Then she realized her mistake. You weren't supposed to speak Italian in front of Andy, out of politeness, so he wouldn't feel left out.

Mary, known to be the family historian, said, "Did we ever have any Nicks in the family?" And answered herself, "Not that I ever heard of."

Eldest brother Patsy, always protective of male prerogative, said to Andy, "You're the Dad."

Andy smiled with obvious pleasure, and common-sense diplomacy. "Whatever Gerry wants, Gerry gets!" Nothing was going to spoil this moment for him.

Everyone liked Andy. He was a breath of fresh air. None of them had ever met anyone like him, except perhaps for the three LaStoria boys, Patsy, Gene, and Augie, who'd all been in the Service. Andy was easy-going, friendly, a real American kid, somebody who'd just walked off the set of the Andy Hardy series, a farm-fresh egg, like Mickey Rooney himself.

"Well, let's just wait one little minute here, 'cause I'm gonna explain why," said Andy, "why I wanna call him Nicholas. See, I know that you all say he was born on Christmas Day, and that's true, we all know that. But in my church, the Serbian Orthodox church, our Christmas hain't till January 7th. That's right, January the 7th. But we got a holiday on December 19th that you guys don't got in your calendar, and that's St Nicholas Day. And what do we do on St Nicholas Day, which is our Serbian Thanksgiving? Why, we put a shoe out on the windowsill. And by the morning, well, what do you think? We might find that shoe filled with nuts and candies, or little toys, or a new pencil-box for school, yes-sir-ee-bob. And then we'd know that St Nicholas came by and awarded us for bein' good little children all year. But if you was a bad boy, like Patsy here, all you'd get was an onion!"

Andy looked down with love into Gerry's eyes. "So, hon, have I been a good boy this year?"

Gerry looked around at her entire family, and for approval, to her brother Augie, who was standing there, and with whom she had a special connection, and as Augie nodded to her, she looked up at her husband Andy, and said, "I think little Nicholas Petrovich here says 'Yes!'"

They say that you cannot remember being born, but I do.

And on that day, in the Maternity Ward of the Children's Hospital in Revere, Massachusetts, in the late afternoon of December 25th, 1946, I looked on from my vantage point, perched as I was up in the corner of the ceiling, where three straight lines converged.

That's how I remember all this. I looked down upon it from my own exalted point of view. *From a point in space and time where three lines intersected with an invisible fourth.*

And I remember how it made me feel, too. That, especially.

These people were all strangers to me, nor did I know the object of their affections, wrapped in his mother's arms, down there, below, who now decided to break things up with a good angry crying jag. He certainly wasn't me. I certainly didn't belong in the midst of *this* family. I had other plans. I wanted out. I wanted to get back to where I came from.

To accomplish that, I wanted to burrow back the same way I came. I wanted to be inside that oceanic pool where I floated in bliss, floating back, back, in gentle wavelets till I washed up on the shore of the endless highway that led in the extreme distance to the point of infinity, where I dissolved, and emerged, back on the other side of the double vortex, into the cone of light. To burrow back I would have to climb back inside my mother and regress to a cellular size to fit through the infinite point. I would have to descend from my superior perch.

My mother's belly and breasts were warm and comforting and promised to open up like a blossoming flower, but somehow as I probed and pushed, she would not yield, and I was becoming more and more frustrated and furious, and afraid, afraid that I would never get back, and angry, angry that she would not let me in, fearful that I would be stranded in this terribly bright, alien white room, so angry that, to spite her, her, *her,* my mother, the one who would not let me back in, I wanted to destroy myself.

Chapter 2

The God in the Garden

"There's something wrong with this baby," my mother kept saying. She was panicked because I would not stop scratching at myself with tiny hands and nails. "Why is he bleeding from the scalp?"

"We don't know," said the nurse. "The doctors are consulting an allergist."

"When are you letting me out of here? I wanna go home."

Lying in her grasp, I could feel her heart pounding out of her bosom.

"If you ask me," said the nurse, "it's that caul he was born in. Do you know how rare that is? We've certainly never had one of those here. Now we're keeping you here till you get recovered from that cesarean."

"When's that gonna be?"

"Don't worry. Couple of days."

My mother thought this nurse was mean, and the nurse read her face and tried to reverse course. "Listen, dearie, if you could just try and relax and let yourself get better." The nurse was fluffing her pillow, and my mother was thinking *Irish bitch*.

"Have you seen the crook of his arms?" she said. "His eyelids?"

"We're doing everything we can. He's only been here one day. Now, dearie, you have to try to get him to take that whole bottle. Here's your call bell, right across your middle. Are you nice and comfy?"

I'm not your dearie, thought my mother, and I heard that. *I'm the most fair-complexioned of all of us, but I'm not parchment white, like you!*

My mother was never happy when she was not in complete control of the situation. Neither was the nurse. I was caught in the middle. Everything I was doing was by reflex and impulse. A nipple was thrust into my mouth and I sucked. I felt an itch and I scratched. I felt hunger gnawing at my belly and I screamed and cried and kicked. I saw my mother's face with her brown eyes full of love and trembling concern and I wanted to do anything to please her.

But mostly I was alone. My mother was too. We were abandoned. The cigars passed around, the congratulations, those were yesterday. The night was long and lonely, and bloody in the back of the knees. The only relief was to slip into sleep and dream of the soft walls of a protean cave.

Somewhere in the passing of these hospital days a wall of mud and tears, sludge, urine, feces and blood came sliding downhill, eradicating all memory of anything fine-spun or ethereal. A barrier of formidable blankness rose up between me and my birth. This river rolled over me with none of the cleansing or washing waters of Lethe, purported by the ancient Greeks to bring forgetfulness. Rather than being refreshed, I was clogged on the riverbank in the tangled roots of earth.

Perhaps I was fortunate that in future I would remember almost nothing of the actual torment of being born, that only vague rumors would rise up like wisps of trees in a riverbank of fog. Perhaps this was Mother Earth's way of loving, to overwhelm one with a clasp so powerful that one was buried alive in her choking embrace.

My mother was released from the hospital. I was not. My mother was a grown woman, strong and determined, fortified with her own stubbornness. I was newborn and frail. My mother wanted to be home. She wanted her own life, and I was the key who opened the door to that independence for her. *At last she was a person in her own right, with accomplishment, equal to her mother's, able to stand proud beside her father.*

But it hurt my mother to have to leave me behind in the care of strangers. And for years afterward she repeated the story to me of my first days, so often, so earnestly and urgently, even compulsively, that I learned not the facts of my beginnings, but the legend.

"It was a miracle you ever made it. I almost lost you, you know. They kept you in there a month. Nothing worked. They tried one thing after another. I used to go visit you every day and every day you got worse and worse. I thought you were going to scratch yourself to death. You were one bloody mess, head to toe. Finally, they had to tie you down in the bassinet. Tie your little hands so you couldn't get at yourself. Mamanonna was saying rosaries for you, they were lighting candles at St Anthony's. They kept changing your formula and nothing seemed to do the trick until finally they found that formula way out in Chicago. All the way from Chicago it had to come before you were saved at last. And when I got you home to your own crib, I still had to tie you down. It killed me to see you like that but I had to do it. So, you better be good, or else, after all I've been through with you."

I became convinced that but for a formula from Chicago I would not be here now.

And so in this manner I came eventually to be glad to be alive, on this earth, in this world, in this time and place, among these people; indeed, I was blessed, miraculous, a surpassing paragon.

And I remembered nothing else of the agony of being born.

The crisis over, I settled into a new world, a world made for me, where all I need do was to lie on my back and reach up above my head in order to pluck the grapes of paradise.

The ruler of this world was my Papanonni.

He was my mother's father, Antonio LaStoria, known to all, affectionately, as Tony.

Having been born in Italy in 1889, he was at this time in my life already almost sixty years old, and I remember him as being older than the stones in the ground, so ancient that he embodied eternity; in his person, he made eternity not a far-off fiction, but a thing intensely present and real. Standing in his shadow in the sun, I could reach out and touch the solid rock of the ages.

He was the ruler of this world made for me, because he was the man who made the garden.

The garden was the world into which I was born.

My Papanonni dug the garden with his own two hands. He wielded the spade and turned over the earth. He planted the tomatoes, the strawberries, the ears of corn, the potatoes, the flowering spinach; the red radishes with their white flesh, the green cucumbers, orange carrots, the peppers, green and red. Above all, he created the grape arbor.

My Papanonni was a powerful man with a mighty secret who knew how to make the stony soil grow. He was All-Powerful and All-Wise. He was loving and benign. He was the God who walked the Earth.

The garden was in the rear of the two-family house at 48 Payson Street in Revere, beyond the back porches, up and down. Papanonni could stand on his porch on the first floor leaning hands on the railing and survey his domain. He was the owner of the house, his name, and no other, was on the deed. His house was tall and wooden, the shingled exterior painted chocolate brown, with window and door trim cream-colored. I did not realize at the time, not until much later, that Papanonni had had the house repainted, when he first bought it, in this lush color. Once, in his own childhood, a beloved woman, the grandmother he had never had, had told him a tale of a house made out of chocolate. But that seminal story would have to wait for later explorations.

This house of Papanonni's was directly opposite the back of the Shurtleff School, a red-brick Victorian edifice whose granite cornerstone was inscribed *1898*. The front of the Shurtleff was on School Street, which ran parallel to Payson Street, but lower in elevation. Two houses down, on the bedroom side of our house, was the corner of Tree Valley Road, which rose steeply uphill.

This chocolate-colored house dwelt in both perpetual sun and permanent shadow. On the kitchen-and-parlor side was a vacant lot, coming between us and the Sullivan's two-family, rendering that side of the house open to the morning sun. The bedrooms ranging the other side of the house looked out in the afternoon shade on a narrow strip of lawn, a white picket fence, and, close to hand, the Merritts' house next door. The sun rose over the ocean each day, traversed Revere Beach, floated high overhead, flooding Mamanonna's flower garden with sunshine, ripening the good things growing in Papanonni's back garden, and descended in the west over the Shurtleff School, leaving the school shrouded in shadow and the world in twilight.

Payson Street was a quiet residential byway, continually lined on both sides with parked cars. After the schoolyard at the back of the Shurtleff, houses marched down to the corner of Beach Street, where the streetcar stop was. Beach Street and the trolley tracks took you in two directions: left to Bell Circle, and eventually, two miles from our house, Revere Beach itself; or right, leading to the corner of School Street, where Rupp Brothers butcher shop stood and the Central Ave. streetcar tracks, buried in cobblestone, branched off down to Broadway. Beach Street itself curved sibilantly away gently downhill till it ran past the First Baptist Church at the corner of Library Street, where the city baseball field lay, level, green and inviting; and after that came the Carnegie Library, and Revere High School.

On our street, there was barely enough room for one automobile to prowl between the lines of parked vehicles. When the ragman came by with his horse and wagon, nothing could pass.

Our house was open to the sky and the hectic world beyond. The broad Shurtleff schoolyard with its swings and jungle-gym, slide and see-saw, directly faced our front gate. Papanonni's long driveway ran the length of our house to the brown-and-cream garage at the end of it. To our secluded enclave, the noise of wooden trolleys and cobble-stoned traffic filtered in but faintly.

These were the boundaries of the world I was born into. Our house was in a place of peace and plenty.

Both the peace and the plenty were due to my grandfather.

You could say he ruled with an iron fist but you can't leave out the velvet glove. His touch was light and tender. His disapproval was so adamantine that he need not raise his voice. To say that he looked with love on his family was true, but it was true in equal measure with the absolute certainty that he was always right, and that his was the final word.

I remember him in those years as a terribly handsome, craggy version of his own misspent youth, with silken white hair parted always in the middle in a style belonging to the 1910s, and soft brown eyes that penetrated into the interior of whatever he looked at, whether the glove compartment of his big black Buick, or the bottom of the purse of your own soul. Only one actor of those Hollywood years could have played him, and that was Spencer Tracy, and only if he were in the role of a Mexicali patriarch in a film made from a Steinbeck novel.

The backyard at 48 Payson Street was commodious. The front of the lot was where our house full of spacious rooms stood squarely planted. The entire length of the driveway bordering the vacant lot on that side was closed in with a waist-high chain-link fence, and it was occupied by my grandmother's technicolor flower garden.

My grandmother grew flowers to nourish the souls of her children, and their children; my grandfather grew food, to feed their bellies, and in the cellar, made wine to ease their hearts.

The backyard was so spacious that Papanonni built his grape arbor right behind the garage, and there was still plenty of leeway to put all the good things to eat in the ground flanking the arbor, all the way over to the white picket fence on the other side.

At the back of the property was a concrete retaining wall holding back the lumpy hillside behind it. Nothing was up there but scraggly bushes and low trees. These were the long back lots of houses that were situated on top of the humpbacked hill of Cary Ave.

Between the concrete wall and the back of the two-car garage, Papanonni built a wooden box. This he filled with dirt and loam to form an elevated, shaded lawn, where the grass grew long and wavy as a woman's hair beneath the grape arbor with its overhead trellises. This carpet of green grass sported a bench on the afternoon side, which is where I used to lie on my back and pluck sweet grapes to pop into my mouth. There was a chicken-wire enclosure between the oblong of the grape arbor and the back of the garage. This was the dirt-floored kennel where Papanonni kept his well-fed, well-behaved dogs, all working bird-dogs, pointers and retrievers, often up to a dozen at a time.

There in the grape arbor I could nap and dream away my life. Behind my head, lying on one crooked arm, I was conscious of the dogs, breathing, tongues lolling, contented in the shade of the arbor.

My grandfather did not keep pets. Dogs were to earn their keep just as the people in the house had to. Nor were his dogs allowed at the kitchen or dining-room table.

In a closet in his bedroom he kept his shotgun, and outside, he kept his dogs, ready to take bird-hunting with him up in the Lynn marshes. A nice fat pheasant is a delicious bird to cook and eat.

Whenever Papanonni wanted to get out of the house, he had man's best friends to visit and frolic with, and often he took me, too. He believed that dogs and grandsons were his true companions. He treated me and them with kindness and pleasure and he enjoyed feeding treats to us both, sweet grapes for me and bones from the butcher shop for them.

I was the most fortunate of all Papanonni's grandchildren because I was the only one who lived in his own house. This gave me the unparalleled opportunity to become his favorite. And it bestowed upon me, without me having to do anything to merit it, the gifts of his wisdom and the bounty of his largesse.

Never in my life afterwards did I ever stand as near to God as when I stood outside with my grandfather and his dogs, my small hand in his big one, that hand with its roughened skin and earth-blackened nails.

"Okay, Nicky," said my grandfather. "Watch how we do this. We make a heaping little mound of dirt, so. Then, one finger, we put a hole in the top. See? It's like a volcano. A little Vesuvius. Then we drop the seeds inside, and *voila,* we grow the cucumber."

My grandfather was always sure to speak to me in English. He was teaching me not only how to grow cucumbers and tomatoes, but how to prepare for my life later on, in the world beyond the garden.

"Now—we water the garden. You can help with that. I'll show you how."

My grandfather spoke English with no trace of an accent— or rather, his accent was from New York, instead of Boston.

"Let's go. Be careful to walk on the boards."

In that life later on, I tried always to heed Papanonni's command, to be careful, to keep my balance, to walk on the boards, and not step on the rows, and it was the worse for me when I did not succeed. And no matter where I went, I walked behind him, no matter whose voice I listened to, his voice never left the hollow of my ear, nor did I need to know princes or presidents, colonels or kings, since I already knew my grandfather.

Chapter 3

Achilles in the Camp of the Women

Inside the house, there was another world where dirt was the enemy, not something you threw in the air with both hands, or sifted lovingly with your fingers. There, Mamanonna was the queen, and her throne was the straight-backed kitchen chair by the window where she sat all day, overlooking the top of the driveway and the length of her flower garden, issuing her commands in rapid, voluble Napolitano dialect, tinged with the hard g's and clipped endings of her native mountains and the town of Alta Villa where she was born and reared.

Mamanonna was the second daughter, and the favorite, of her fond father, the butcher Fabrizio, who called her by the pet name of Gigi, though her given name was Gioconda. My grandmother was spoiled by her indulgent father, and, when their mother was arranging her older daughter's marriage, with her papa's connivance, out-rivalled her older sister, Anna-Vittoria, for the hand of Antonio LaStoria. My grandparents married in 1913 when the Fabrizios were living on Prince Street in the North End of Boston. By that time my grandfather, having left

New York behind him for good, was starting his life all over again in Boston. These were seminal events which happened long before I was born, but their influence nevertheless haunted the atmosphere of the kitchen where my grandmother ruled and her daughter, my mother, resisted.

Just as a cloud of steam rises from a steep-sided bowl of freshly-boiled spaghetti, and then fades from sight as the dinner cools, (yet the memory of a delicious repast tantalizes you for days with the desire to taste it again) so the storms and rainbows of 1913 lingered on in the hearts of the women in the kitchen on Payson Street as they repeated their rounds of daily drudgery, 35 years later.

Somehow, in my infancy, along with the formula from Chicago, I imbibed all this ancient drama and poetic epic while cradled on my grandmother's broad lap when she was bottle-feeding me. Old battles and fierce emotions burst through Mamanonna's chest and were instilled into the fibers of my being right through the fabric of her purple dress, on the waves of her heaving heartbeats.

My mother was a woman of her new day and desired to do everything the right way, and the right way to her was to listen to her doctor, the obstetrician, Dr Fairburn, who after all, had saved her life by performing the cesarean section which delivered me, her firstborn, at the hospital.

My grandmother had given birth to my mother, and her six brothers and sisters, at home, and breastfed them all, as women of her day and her culture did.

My mother had been advised, counseled and coached all the way through her pregnancy, by Dr Fairburn, and now, with her baby at home, she wished, whenever in doubt, to consult her dog-eared paperback copy of Dr Spock, so as to be current, correct and up-to-date.

My grandmother, on the other hand, had a storehouse of age-old child-rearing practices, mother's wisdom handed down from countless generations, memorized in her head, and needed no stiff-necked Yankee doctor to tell her what was what; nor would she have deigned to look up an answer in a book. Nor would she brook one jot of disobedience in her grown daughter, for my Mamanonna's proclamations were to be taken as unbreakable law.

Somehow, in my toddler years, when I crawled, climbed and played among and over and around and underneath the carved, ornate, stout-footed, massive legs of the kitchen table, I was privy to a great debate, an endless argument, ongoing constantly, without interruption. I was a prisoner in a woman's world, subject to not one, but two, domineering voices, continually contesting for my obedience and loyalty.

I judged them both right. I heard them both. I wanted to comfort both and ease their agitation, I wanted to crawl into their arms, sit on their laps, reach up to their cheeks and wipe away their tears; I wanted to love them so that finally I would see them smile.

I also wanted to be attended to immediately whenever I felt hungry or in the least uncomfortable whether I was wet or tired or simply aggravated that they were not paying attention to me, me, *me*, right now—*subito*.

And so I learned to manipulate them by crying, making faces, acting out; I got in between them, and sure enough, one or the other of them always rushed to my relief.

As I grew older I responded to my grandmother, who spoke only Italian, in her native tongue, and to my mother, who used both languages, and rendered each into baby-talk, according to her mood of the moment; but to me, there was no difference, it was all one babbling river of *conversazione.*

But when we heard the back door crack open, or the screendoor bang, when we heard his voice, coughing in the hallway, or talking to himself, when the doorknob to the kitchen door turned, and in he walked—all debate ceased, all was hushed and respectful, waiting for his wishes to be stated, in order to rush to fulfill them.

My mother, like her mother before her, was in adoration of her father, devoted to his image, worshipping at the altar of his presence, bolstered and augmented by the benediction of his favor, glorying in her exalted status as her daddy's girl. Unlike her three sisters, my mother had never left home, had never left her father's side, except that one time when her new husband, my father, during the war, had called her up from San Diego, where he was then stationed at the naval base, to come out there and join him, and my mother had crossed the country by train to be with him.

My grandmother, who wanted all her children to look upon their father as she had upon hers, with eyes of love, but, above all, and more importantly, respect, had taken the utmost care to make sure that the children never glimpsed one moment of discord between their parents, no matter what went on between them in hushed voices alone in their bedroom. Always she presented a determined, united front—to keep peace and a semblance of order among seven unruly children, this was absolutely mandatory, in her estimation—and so, long before my time, Mamanonna adopted the facade of subservience in my grandfather's presence.

So that when he opened that kitchen door, the women conspired to have *all go silent.*

Into this kitchen-stew of baby formula, boiling water, and wine in gallon jugs made of glass, the other men of the house walked on tiptoe.

For there were more people living on the first floor of the house on Payson Street than me and my mother, and her mother and father.

There were also my father and my uncle. That made six in all.

Now to fit all six at the kitchen table you had to pull out the leaves.

This table was either a monstrosity or a masterpiece. The tabletop was made of smooth steel ingrained with a pattern around the four edges of the rectangle resembling, to me, railroad tracks, so that when I was old enough, I used to reach up and run my toy cars on the track, racing round and round the table till somebody made me stop. Because the leaves pulled out on both ends, the closed table had a double superstructure of steel. Because the tabletop was metal, my grandmother always insisted on a fresh tablecloth to be spread over it for every meal. Because there were six people in the house, you had to know your place at the table.

Papanonni always occupied one end, his place being at the head of the table. He kept Mamanonna seated on his right hand. If there were visitors or guests, or aunts, uncles and cousins, they sat on the other side opposite Mamanonna, on Papanonni's left.

Opposite Pa, as he was called by my mother, father and uncle, at the other end of the table was my mother, nearest the stove and the sink. Mamanonna was too old these days to be doing all the serving as she used to.

Next to Gerry, my mother, were her husband, Andy, and her brother, Augie.

Nobody stood on ceremony in our house. It was pull out your chair, sit down, reach and grab before it was all gone. Nobody asked you to pass anything, they just reached over you. Nobody said please and thank-you, because they had all gone through the Depression and the war and they were still worried that tomorrow morning all this would disappear again. Still it was not quite like a boarding-house full of strangers. My mother was always bustling to fill your plate, fill your glass, fetch something from the stove, they were always begging her to sit down and eat herself. I was in my high-chair at her elbow, so, before she fed herself, she had to feed me.

It was at this kitchen table that I first heard about the war. War and politics were the constant topic being aired out. Papanonni gave most of his time and opinions to my father, Andy Petrovich, as he liked Andy, and my father, as the only real outsider among them, did not have to repeat all the rituals and routines of the past growing up in this family. For Papanonni, he was a wind from the west. And—my father came from the mountains, just as my grandfather had. Besides, both of them read the newspaper, and nobody else in the family did. That was another habit they had in common. Altogether, my grandfather felt fortunate to have, not lost a daughter, but, in my father, gained another son.

Uncle Augie never had an opinion about any of this back-and-forth between those two opinionated experts. He never opened his mouth unless somebody gave him an opening by raising the subject of the Red Sox, which Augie considered safe to talk about. He had landed at Omaha Beach on D-Day, so at this point in his life, he was not looking for any more wars to fight. He was happy to be at home and have his mother take care of him and he would withdraw to his own room in order to stay out of everybody's way.

But my mother adored him, even at the expense of her husband.

To her, as to all of Augie's four sisters, he was their kid brother who had grown up to tower over them all. At six-foot-two, he was a high-school sports star, in football, basketball, and, his favorite, baseball.

My mother and my Mamanonna looked on at Augie with concern and consideration, making always sure that, in his presence, they did not overtly give away their fears by word or gesture. They did not know what happened that day at Omaha Beach but they knew something happened. They would never have asked him and had long ago given up waiting for him to say anything but they could not help but be solicitous of his every wish and always rushed to fulfill his slightest needs.

I too watched and waited. I knew that, as surely as if they had forgotten to turn down the gas under the water roiling on the stove for the macaroni, something was going to boil over.

"Fee-fi-fo-fum, I smell the blood of an Englishmun!"

It was my Uncle Augie, stooping down to put his nose next to mine.

From time to time, he would erupt in a private hilarity, and then walk away to leave me puzzled.

You could see the thought cross his face, tickling his funny bone, but you could not make head or tail of what he meant.

Another time, he was walking away down the driveway, and toddler-me, tugging at his pants, implored, "Where ya going, Unk? Can I come?"

"I'm going to Chicago to see a man about a horse."

Chicago again! The mysterious, far-off place where they had life-saving baby formulas and you could see a man about a horse. But what about the horse? And how could you smell the blood of an Englishmun? And shouldn't it be man, not 'mun'?

I was disconcerted by pronunciation, since I had yet to disentangle Italian from English and I had to go by the sound of every word to figure out what they were trying to say, and to reply, I had to imitate them, sound for sound.

The world of the grownups was not one I was able to penetrate, and it frustrated me.

For instance, where was No. 10? They were always talking about "the shop" and "No. 10."

I knew that every day, Papanonni opened the doors of the garage, climbed in his big black Buick, with the shiny chrome trim, put it in reverse, and backed down the driveway, climbing out to open the gates at the bottom near the street, then leaving the car running, out there in the middle of the road, while he climbed out again to go close the gates.

Anyone coming down the street would have to wait for him to perform this ritual, and I knew that the gate was closed for one reason: to keep me in so that I couldn't get out. Every day that I was allowed to go out and play, Mamanonna, from her seat in the kitchen window, would yell at me. *"Tu tenga d'occhio!"* She did not want me to go too far down the driveway where she couldn't see me because she had to keep an eye on me.

I was her prisoner.

In the mornings, if I scratched my arms during the night when I was sleeping, I was still to blame for it, according to my mother. She would lecture and scold me while she applied the 'cream' all up and down my arms. "How many times have I told you? Don't scratch! Look at you. Inside your elbows, your skin is weeping!"

This while she was twisting me by the wrist with my arm pulled out full length to show me the crime I had committed. Oh, how that soothing 'cream' could sting!

My Mamma, like Papanonni, when in front of her mother, only used English with me. It made me think sometimes, when I got old enough to realize the difference between the languages, that she was trying to keep her mother from knowing what she was saying to me. They were both in the same kitchen all day, and when my mother was not cleaning or cooking, they sat at the table drinking coffee, conversing in Napoletano.

On the other hand, which was a phrase I picked up, without any idea of what it meant, when my Auntie Peggy was in the house, with her two sons, Henry and Ronnie, sometimes Mamma and her sister talked in yet another language, Pig Latin. I was baffled. So were my cousins Henry and Ronnie, or Uncle Tommy DiPrima, the truck-driver, Mamma's brother-in-law, if he happened to be dropping by while he was in the neighborhood making his deliveries. All I could decipher of that tongue was that if they told me to *imshay amscray,* it meant I had to leave. This Pig Latin was designed to be a secret language for the sisters to say anything they wanted about the men in the room without the men understanding.

Of course, Italian served the same purpose when it came to my father, the ex-coal miner, who was in the Navy during the war. He came home for lunch everyday because he worked down at Page's Lumberyard, on Foster Street, just off Broadway, where the Shawmut Bank stood on the opposite corner. In those days he was making 40 bucks a week on an apprentice carpenter program through the GI Bill and the carpenters' union so he could not afford to own a car, nor did he need one, since he could walk to work, an easy stroll down Central Ave. My father had been walking to work for a long time, ever since he left school in the sixth grade to go to work in the coal mine. He was 500 miles away from his home in the mountains of western Pennsylvania. That was another land I heard of back then, which, along with Chicago, stood for something impossibly far away, utterly unimaginable, but which the grownups seemed to know all about, just as they knew all about all the king's horses and all the king's men and the big bad wolf, red riding hood, and Mary who had a little lamb.

Papanonni would come by and squeeze my nose, then stick his thumb through his first two fingers and wiggle it, and say, "See? I got your nose!"

And every time I would feel my face to make sure my nose was still there.

Uncle Augie would come by and say "Hey, kid, I hit at the track today, so here, here's a nickel—where's your piggy bank?"

The 'track' went into my piggy bank alongside 'Pennsylvania' and 'the wall' Humpty Dumpty sat on; the piggy bank was where all the nickels of my collected mysteries rattled around. Though the sounded like they amounted to reality, actually, they added up only to a child's-worth of questions, conundrums and confabulations.

Every Saturday, or *Sabato,* as Mamanonna would say, Pappanonni did not need to go to the shop. Instead, he would take me for a ride in his big black shiny new '47 Buick with the chrome trim and the ivory shift-knob on the steering column which operated the Dynaflow transmission. We would go down Route 1 past the track and the airport and pass into the Underworld when we dove nose-first into the Sumner Tunnel. Fascinated, I would watch through the windshield, watching and waiting, hoping and praying, until, at the end of the long tunnel-hill under the harbor, we burst out into blinding sunlight, emerging into the North End of Boston, where we would park the car and stroll together through the Haymarket. Papanonni would squeeze, test, handle and select all the good things to eat for the week, starting with the butcher shop that used to belong to Mamanonna's Papa and not ending till we visited the pastry shop on Hanover Street and the wineshop next door where he would purchase a bottle each of Muscatel and Zinfandel, to be blended together into his favorite glass of Sunday dinner beverage.

On Sunday, or *Domenica*, he would take me again in the Buick, this time, to Mass with him at St Anthony of Padua's magnificent church on Revere Street. Here the open air plaza with the low steps leading up to the tall oak doors was flanked by Christopher Columbus, holding in his hand a cracked globe on one side, and St Anthony cradling the baby Jesus on the other. Despite the heat of the day, in August or July, inside it was dim and cool as my eyes adjusted. The rays of light coming through the rose window would fan out to merge with the gold and saffron colors of the interior columns while the red, blues and greens of the stained glass windows and the ruby-red candle-glasses soothed and seduced. Papanonni always held my hand as we marched up the steps to the imposing, tall oaken doors, and once inside, the deep and profound hush would settle itself on your hearing, erasing the noise of the traffic of the world, to merge and blend with the soft beating of your heart.

One day Mamanonna disappeared, and I could never find her again.

I looked everywhere to find out where they were hiding her.

I knew she had been in poor health because I often heard my mother sighing sadly.

I knew she was very sick because Mamanonna had taken to her bed and Mamma used to go in there and close the door and not come out for a long time. And eventually Mamanonna did not come out of the bedroom at the back of the kitchen on that side of the house that she shared with Papanonni. She did not come out anymore to sit in her chair by the window and watch me play.

They told me she had gone to heaven. Yet another place like Pennsylvania, the track, No. 10, and Humpty Dumpty's wall.

Time moved so slowly that it all seemed to be one long endless day. I knew that I remembered her but I knew that I was forgetting her, too. There was no one to speak Italian with anymore. I was forgetting how.

At last all I had left was the image in my mind of her sitting in her chair by the window with her large body overflowing the boundaries of her purple dress, the dress with the big white flowering polka dots; and her ankles bulging out over her high-top brown shoes so that she had to roll down her nylon-stocking tops to get some tenderness and relief.

I went to bed with my teddy-bears, Rabbit-boy and Brownie-boy, and I talked to them and told them how sad it was, and they comforted me, and so with their help, because they were so understanding, I could go to sleep.

Then Uncle Augie, the veteran of the D-Day landings, came along and told my mother, "You better take those teddy-bears away from him. If you don't watch out, you're gonna turn him into a girl. I dunno. Maybe you wanna put a dress on him."

My father, who had sailed to Murmansk during the war on board the *USS Ruby*, a destroyer escorting the merchant ships on the convoy to Russia, did not disagree.

My mother, who loved them both, and who looked up to her little brother, and not just because he was so much taller, but because she had glimpsed his warrior heart on the playing fields of Stoughton High School, and had seen him struggle every day since his return from Europe to regain that stout and impregnable pride of the winner he used to be— my mother thought she should do as they advised, as they were men, and knew better than she what it took.

I was furious, as I knew what they were up to, ganging up on me.

But I was no Achilles. I could not fight them.

The real Achilles in our house was a man who was six-foot-two and had found out from his own experience of war and peace that every man, whether in his head or his heart or his heel, has a vulnerability which he may not be able to overcome.

Chapter 4

The Angel of Mercy

Though one of us was gone now, I remained.

I remained but I was not the same. I was diminished by the change in the family. I did not like change, I wanted everything to stay the same, forever and ever.

Who was going to watch me now from the window? Who was going to make sure I didn't stray too far? Who was going to tell me to come here by saying *"Ven acca!"* in a voice that could not be disobeyed, and then wrap me in a hot, smothering embrace?

This fervent desire that nothing should ever change was all I remembered now of the eternity I came from.

But seasons come and seasons go. Although my life often seemed like one endless day, I sometimes forgot the morning by the time afternoon arrived. Nor could I recall yesterday, sometimes. And last week, or next month, were erased as soon as they happened, or beyond my grasp, as meaningless as 'the day after tomorrow,' which other people always seemed to be talking about. Yet I could always tell by Papanonni's garden that time was passing.

THE EDUCATION OF NICHOLAS PETROVICH

First the grapes in the arbor were ripening, then I was lying on my back in the shade on the arbor-bench on a warm September day reaching up to pluck the sweetness and pop it into my mouth. Then it was turning cold, and the garden was bereft of flowering green and plump red, and reduced to bare sticks and yellowing chaff and powdery, dust-blowing dirt instead of the rich, dark loam of spring.

Christmas was approaching, and my birthday, and I was stirred with anticipation. The tree in the parlor with the bright ornaments, the glittering tinsel, the shining star on top and, most of all, the gift-boxes gathered underneath in glowing packages of red and green wrapping paper, tempting me to rip them open, seemed to me a wondrous world of fairies and elves meant especially for me. My mother took me on a long trip on the lumbering wooden streetcar that passed along Beach Street at the foot of Payson Street and then went down Central Ave to turn onto Broadway in front of the fire station. When we got to Maverick Square I was frightened by the terrible noise of the streetcar descending into the tunnel, but when we got off the train and went upstairs onto Washington Street, I marveled at the displays of electric trains and erector sets in the windows of Jordan Marsh. For my birthday, Papanonni gave me a Hopalong Cassidy two-gun holster set. He showed me how to make a big noise firing the cap-gun, and told me to shoot him, like the cowboys did in the movies. Then he would fall back in his big armchair in the parlor. "Oh, I'm dead. You killed me."

But even though he was dead, he rose up again from the cushions, laughing.

I knew all about about Hopalong Cassidy from the television set Uncle Augie brought home one day.

It was a Zenith, they said, with a 9-inch screen. Zenith was a good model. They made good radios.

I knew all about radios because we had one in practically every room.

One thing I remembered from the radio was *The Tennesee Waltz*. I promised myself never to forget that song because of the lines where Patti Page sang,

> *I remember the night and the Tennessee Waltz,*
> *now I know just how much I have lost . . .*

I was lying on my back in my baby crib, I think, looking up at the ceiling, the first time I ever heard her singing that song.

Remembering meant that you lost something, and you wanted to get it back.

So why did I remember lying in my crib when I heard those words, that soaring melody? Did I want to go back to infancy?

My father played his radio down in the cellar when he was making things at his workbench. He used to take me down there with him to keep an eye on me for a while. He had a Philco. He used to whistle along and kick up his heels a little every time Hank Williams came on singing,

> *Hey, good-lookin,' whatcha got cookin?*
> *How's about cookin' somethin' up with me?*

The cellar was a mysterious place because you had to go down the back steps to reach the dark underground underneath the house. It smelled of cold stone and earthen floors and the old, disused coal bin, now that we had oil delivered. My father pulled the string on a single bare bulb over his workbench to shed some light on the darkness. Of course, he no longer had his miner's hardhat with its lamp to shine a beam. And he did not have to take a pick and shovel to these walls. But he often retreated to the cellar. He was happy working there making things with wood and with his hands and his tools. Down there he could work alone, beyond the overlooking gaze of the family upstairs. He felt comfortable down there, in the semi-dark of one dangling light-bulb, where you could smell the earth beneath your feet. Perhaps it was because he had spent his youth, and part of his childhood, underground. Perhaps it was the leftover smell of the old coal-bin. Or even the new oil-tank and oil-burner, which reminded him of the engine-room on board the *USS Ruby*.

Down at the far end of the basement gloomy shadows gathered in the recesses. Papanonni had his shelves of gallon wine-jugs down there. He made his own wine every year from the grapes he grew in the arbor out behind the garage. But Mamanonna's rows of mason jars were empty now. My mother no longer stacked them on the kitchen table to fill them with strawberries from the garden to make preserves the way her mother did. She said she was too tired and anyway she was never going to do that again when she could buy them already jarred at the A&P or the Gloria Chain. I thought she was sick because she was mad at me all the time and she was getting fat, like Mamanonna was. I worried that Mamma was going to go up to heaven the way her mother did.

I asked Papanonni, "Is Mamanonna dead, like when I shoot you?"

He said God had taken her up to heaven because he needed an angel of mercy.

"Will I die?"

"Not if you're a good boy."

"I am a good boy."

"You better be, cause you're gonna get a surprise pretty soon. How would you like somebody to play with?"

"You mean like Billy and Paul, next door?"

"Even better. A little brother of your very own."

Though the inhabitants of our house were fewer by one with my grandmother's passing, the population of ghosts, angels and creatures of the dark seemed to multiply accordingly to fill up the space left empty in my life.

There was the Boogey-man, who scared me with night-terrors.

Mamma would say, in the morning, "Oh, you were just having a bad dream."

There was Mr Sandman, who helped you get to sleep at night by throwing sand in your eyes. "So you better close them, right now!"

Mr Sandman even had his own song on the radio, so I knew he was real.

There were the Witches and Goblins of Halloween.

But they were evened out by the good little elves and dwarves of Santa's Helpers, who were named Grumpy, Happy, Sleepy, Sneezy and Doc. I could never remember them all, there were too many of them.

But who could forget Rudolph? Or Frosty the Snowman?

Or even Br'er Rabbit and Little Black Sambo. My dad took me to see them in the movie of Uncle Remus at the Revere Theater down on Broadway.

Uncle Augie used to delight in teasing me. "Better watch out, or the Boogey-man'll getcha!"

Of course, I need never be frightened to be alone or feel sorry for myself if I thought they were ignoring me because there was my Guardian Angel watching over me all the time, all through the year, not just at Christmas Time.

Then there was Snow White and—or were they the ones who were Santa's Helpers?

And what about the Wicked Witch of the West?

Uncle Augie used to delight in The Three Little Pigs, especially when he got to the part where the Big Bad Wolf, "he huffed, and he puffed, and he blew your house in!" There he would rise up like a vulture to expand his chest and flap his wings, and blow my house in. Then he walked away, laughing, shivering with cackles.

Mamma loved to read to me out of the set of Little Golden Books she got for me, saving up to buy them one by one. There was in her collection the Little Red Hen, the Three Little Pigs (which Uncle Augie expropriated for his own mischievous purposes) and Peter Rabbit (where I got the name for my lost teddy-bear) as well as one outlier, *The Little Engine That Could*, by Watty Piper. I loved that name. Watty Piper. I loved the sound.

And I especially loved to have Mamma read to me because that was when I got to sit on her lap. I would turn the pages while she held the book open. That was how I learned that a story had a beginning, a middle and an end. Perhaps the first thing I learned to read was *The End*. But also, being read-to this way made me feel that Mamma loved me, truly, and that being this close to her made me feel close to Mamanonna again. And being read to in this fashion was the beginning of something I could not have foreseen—the love of my mother, and her mother, transferred to the hard covers of a book fingered in my chubby little hands.

But one night after supper, in the parlor, as we watched Uncle Miltie on our little 9-inch television, as Mamma tried to adjust herself in an armchair to some level of comfort for her aching back, she told me I could not sit on her lap to be read to anymore.

She acted as if she were annoyed with me. An edge of exasperation was in her voice.

I could not understand what I had done wrong.

I walked off with my Little Golden Book clutched open in both hands, I strode off to pout.

I was mad at my mother. I hated her.

I was not listening when she said to my father, who was sitting on the sofa over by the windows, "I keep telling that Doctor Graham that it's twins. I know when there's two of them kicking me."

My father was tired after a hard day at work. He was not listening either. He was getting ready to laugh when Uncle Miltie got to the punch line. But slowly he turned his head and looked at Mamma, when it sank in what she had just said. "Oh, my Lord Judas Priest—Gerry!"

"Turn those rabbit-ears, willya?" she said to him. "Try to get that picture to come in."

Papanonni looked over the top of his newspaper at the screen.

Uncle Augie rose, saying "I'll get it." He thought of himself as the only one that could make that Zenith work. After all, he had bought and paid for it, and brought it to the house, thinking it was about time they had one, everybody else seemed to, and besides, it was something he could do for the family when no one else had expressed any great interest in it; you'd think they'd be grateful, they watched it all right, it was practically their religion. What the hell—at least he got to stretch out on the sofa on a Saturday afternoon and watch his baseball game.

THE EDUCATION OF NICHOLAS PETROVICH

The one household resident who never went away, and whom my mother never knew about, because I was afraid to tell her, was the Nothing Monster. This dread apparition of totally transparent blackness lurked in the corner of my bedroom at night. Beginning when I could not go to sleep despite trying with all my might, starting as a hole in the dark the size of a pin-point or the sharp end of one of Mamma's sewing needles, this scourge of my sanity would bubble and fester till he puffed up and expanded to a size threatening to engulf me. He would grow and grow and grow and swell and swell and swell until I was more and more and more certain and afraid and convinced and terrified as he loomed over me, as he hovered over my face, as he stared into the back of my head through the red rims of the cavities of my eye-sockets. The larger the dimensions of his ballooning sphere, the more he turned into a yawning, cavernous mouth, and the more I shrank back, horrified to realize that this hideous black emptiness was about to swallow me, that I was about to disappear into a vast unoccupied universe of space, not outer space, beyond the earth, but space inside me, *inner* space, a void so stutteringly s-s-s-serpentine, so h-h-h-hideously hollow, that it was y-y-yawning reality, turned inside out! The other side of the coin of me. Pressed like a subway token into the turnstile leading to the not-me. Slipped like a key through the door into non-existence.

The twins turned out to be an unmatched set, boy and girl. Again, my mother had to go through a cesarean section to give birth, this time at the Winthrop Hospital. It happened to be late February, and the Revere Children's, for some reason, couldn't take her. "No room at the inn," Uncle Gene commented. When it was time to go, on a cold and blustery, nor'easter night, Papanonni drove his daughter in his big black Buick through the blowing snow out to the windy peninsula of Winthrop, surrounded by howling ocean.

Again, it was cause for family gatherings. Group by group they trooped into the hospital room. Uncle Patsy and his wife, Auntie Mary, and their two kids, my cousins Anthony and Linda, lived in Revere, up on Reservoir Ave, the steepest hill in the city; Auntie Peggy, with Henry and Ronnie, who lived down by Revere Beach, at the corner of Rte. C1 and Revere Street. Uncle Gene LaStoria, Auntie Mary Laverna and Auntie Anna DiPrima, with kids, husbands and wife, all came over from Watertown. Again, my father bestowed cigars, and acted as if it had been a great accomplishment on his part, to Mamma's extreme annoyance, as she lay thunderstruck in her bed. Uncle Augie was the one who came up with the teasing line about the unmatched set of cuff-links. This time Mamma was annoyed with him, too, brother or no brother.

Again, the rest of the family gave way and waited for Mamma to announce the names she had chosen to bestow upon the new arrivals.

Nobody was very surprised or taken aback when she announced she was going to call them *Jack and Jill*.

I, however, was 'fit to be tied,' another expression I had picked up from them.

By this time, I was five years old, and quite convinced that I knew all about everything and was, probably, smarter than any of them would have given me credit for. I didn't let on to them, but I knew how to read, and in the fall, I was all set to start school in the first grade. There was going to be no kindergarten for me. Mamma wouldn't hear of it, and Mamma was the boss, when it came to such things. When she took me on the subway train from Maverick Square into Boston, and then out to Harvard Square, to catch the trackless trolley for Watertown, to go visiting, I could read all the signs in the stations, and I would boastfully turn to Mamma and make announcements, such as "Next stop, Central Square." The trick was to memorize them all. Same with the Little Golden Books. I could tell you what was coming on the next page before you turned it. Besides, those things were only for little kids. I was already onto *Treasure Island* and *Strive and Succeed,* which Uncle Augie got me for Christmas for my birthday, in paperbacks from Foyle's drugstore. I was old enough now to be sent to Rupp Brothers by Mamma when she needed milk or bread, and she even sent me down to the Shawmut Bank on Broadway to pay the mortgage for her. She trusted me with money and knew that I could count change. She thought I was smart. She was always bragging to her sisters when we went visiting.

Therefore, I was quite perturbed to hear her come out with *Jack and Jill,* in the crowded hospital room.

Her sister Anna had a new daughter, Lenore, named after a poem by Edgar Allan Poe. I knew all about him from Uncle Augie. He would draw himself up and spread his vulture wings, take a deep breath, swell his chest and intone, "Quoth the Raven—Nevermore!" Uncle Patsy's daughter was named after Linda Darnell in the movies. *I was named after St Nick!* I suppose I was lucky she didn't call me Rudolph, or Blitzen!

The general assessment seemed to be along the lines of "Oh, isn't that cute!" or "That's so adorable!"

I wanted to be sick.

Bad enough to be stuck in the corner and ignored while they brought in the two little bundles of joy—but to be saddled forever with *Jack and Jill went up the hill–!*

I knew well enough the pangs of teasing from playing with Billy and Paul, my friends from next door at the Merritts' house. Billy was the older brother, my age, and he was merciless towards his younger brother Paul.

Besides, all of a sudden, I was outnumbered. *There were two of them!*

Auntie Mary LaStoria from Reservoir Ave moved in promptly as soon as Mamma was home with the twins, staying all day long till suppertime was over to help with Jill, while Mamma took care of her favorite, Jackie-boy.

On the weekends, Papanonni valiantly took over the job of distracting me from all my newfound woes by getting me out of the house and into the garden, the kennel, the garage, the big black Buick.

He taught me weeding, he taught me dog-grooming, he taught me washing the car, he taught me watering Mamanonna's flowers, which he was determined would be looked after as if she were still here.

On Saturday, as usual, he would take me on his grocery-shopping expedition into the Italian markets in Boston, and fortunately for me, I was still thrilled to ride in the front seat of the big black Buick, and I always got a treat of Italian ice once we got to the North End.

Papanonni would stop outside St Leonard's to chat in Italian with the old guys sitting on the park benches by the church-gates. He seemed to know everybody. I hadn't heard so much of the rhythm and sway of the old language since Mamanonna disappeared from my life.

He never tired of showing me around. He would make sure I knew the brick building in Prince Street with the walk-down bakery next door, the building where he first met Mamanonna as a girl living with her parents, the Fabrizios. "That's the house where your mother was born, you know." He would show me the warehouse further down Prince Street where the infamous Brink's Robbery took place, just the year before. He would take me round the corner to North Square to show me the house where he and Uncle Patsy and Auntie Mary and Mamanonna and the others were living at the time of the Molasses Flood. Then he would tell me all about the anarchist bombing at the police station, and the time they all had to hide in the house for weeks on end from the Spanish Flu Epidemic.

On Sunday Papanonni would take me to Sunday Mass at St Anthony's in Revere, and he never failed to show me the Confessional on the left when you entered and the statues of St Peter and St Paul, standing on separate lintels above the Confessional, flanking either side, which he said, with a good deal of satisfaction, wrapped in pride, he and Mammanonna had donated to the church. And there indeed I would look up to the inscriptions beneath the Saints' feet reading their names,

Gioconda and Antonio LaStoria

And after Mass, on the way home to Payson Street, he would stop at the Tastee-Freeze on Broadway and we would sit there together in the sun on the picnic bench and lick our melting cones of softee ice cream.

Uncle Augie took turns getting me out to the driveway to play catch. Suddenly, I was the owner of a brand new baseball glove too big for my left hand.

Dad took turns, taking his 'buddy,' me, down the cellar, to "putter around."

But nothing helped with the long, boring days during the rest of the week, being exiled from the kitchen, sent to the Siberia of the parlor. There, if I were tired of playing with my soldiers and my castle, or reading my books for the seventeenth time, I had to watch the test pattern on television. I had to be quiet or else. I might wake up the twins when Mamma was trying to get them to sleep. One day when I was bored I decided to get Papanonni's old-fashioned upright player piano going in the hallway. That brought Mamma running and I got a licking on my bottom, which I did not like, no, not one bit. Mamma and Auntie Mary LaStoria would be spending the whole day with bottles and diapers out in the kitchen with *those two*. "Go in the parlor, Nicky—don't be always underfoot!" I was forbidden to touch anything in the dining room. Mamma had her mother's sideboard draped with her mother's crocheted doilies, under the windows overlooking the driveway. The windows had heavy green-baize drapes which could be closed with ropes but which never were, because Mamanonna's delicate translucent-white lace curtains were treasured by my mother, and she didn't want them covered over, hidden from view. On the other side of the dining-room table, against the wall enclosing Uncle Augie's bedroom on that side of the house, Mamanonna's tall-boy with the glass doors held all the family dishes and wineglasses, and in the drawers under the glass cabinets, the family silverware. So, I couldn't touch a thing in the dining-room, nor was I allowed to go outside to play—"How we gonna watch you? We're busy, you know."

What to do? *Wait for Howdy Doody to come on at 5 o'clock?*

THE EDUCATION OF NICHOLAS PETROVICH

But I managed to make two discoveries during all those months that never left my life afterwards.

The first was Mamma's family bible.

Mamma did not read the Bible but she did buy an expensive, leather-bound Roman Catholic family bible, with gold-gilt-edged pages when I was born, because it had several blank, lined pages at the beginning in which to inscribe family events, like births—and deaths.

In that Bible, which I found in the parlor wedged into a side-table next to Papanonni's armchair, sitting on top of copies of Readers Digest and dog-eared Saturday Evening Post magazines, I found that my grandmother was listed as a death in the family, on a certain date in 1951, about a year previously.

I was stunned, and closed the book immediately.

I was old enough now to know what dying was.

Of course, I would look into that book time and again, but I avoided that page, and concentrated on the page of my birth and the births of my brother and sister, Jack and Jill. And of course, I would be sitting in my grandfather's armchair, balancing that heavy Bible on my lap, and leafing through page after page, not reading the text, but gazing, for hours, at the beautiful illustrations of stories from the Bible such as *Joseph and His Brothers* and *Noah and the Flood* and *Jesus in the Temple*, reading the captions as best I could. That was my first introduction to the legends and myths of the greatest stories ever told.

When I tired of reading I would wander slowly around the room examining Papanonni's pictures, in minute detail, gazing intently for long periods of minutes and quarter-hours at a time at one or another inexpensive reproduction of great art—or flea-market prints.

You could read the mind of my grandfather in those pictures. There were bird-dogs in wooden frames. A pointer, a setter, a spaniel. The pictures were glass-covered. There were horses, in full flight through the tall grass of the prairies, or else, turning to stand still and peer directly at the artist. There were proud Indians standing tall astride barely-tamed mustangs in full war regalia and paint with eagle-feather head-dresses. There were cowboys roping steer, cavalry men charging through stampeding dust-clouds. There was the Sacred Heart of Jesus in a glass frame. There was a slender crucifix of a writhing marble Jesus with his head down, chin on his chest, the wood chestnut-colored, the marble arms, twisted and pinned on the cross, shining with the sweat of suffering. There was a magnificent full-color reproduction, enclosed deep in a three-dimensional oaken box, of DaVinci's *Last Supper*. I would gaze at that for minutes at a time trying to divine which one was Peter, who denied Christ, which one was Judas, who betrayed him, stories I had learned from breathless Sunday morning television shows such as *You Are There*.

Then there were two pictures which mesmerized me. They were silhouettes in metal-rimmed bubble-glass frames, about four-by-six inches. The first showed an Indian Chief holding a tall lance with drooping feathers, wearing a feathered head-dress which cascaded all down his back to his ankles. The Chief, in opaque black silhouette, stood tall in profile, upright, straight-backed; he sat proudly astride his alert black silhouette horse, whose knee was raised to stamp, whose ears pricked. Together they stood gazing down on a road below them where a wagon train was raising the dust. In the back-ground, the tall cliffs of Yellowstone ranged in full-color earth-tones of yellow ochre and crimson red, surmounted by puffy white clouds, counterpoint to the white covered-wagons. To my child's-eyes, the black silhouette traced on the bubbled glass gave a depth of perception to the flat-landscape of the background which I found utterly three-dimensional, and endlessly fascinating. The other four-by-six framed bubbled-glass silhouette gave the same exact impression on my mind, but it showed instead a thundering black stagecoach about to crest on the downhill pulled, by four black horses, with the backdrop successive waves of the peaks of the Rockies. These pictures pulled me into them and thrilled me with intense movement, though they were as absolutely stationary as a still-life.

There was one more book I found which disturbed me profoundly.

It was my Uncle Augie's photo-album sized Life Magazine pictorial history of WWII, so big and, for me, unwieldy, that I had to lie on the rug in the parlor to open it up.

It started with the decades leading up to the conflict, and showed many portraits of world leaders which were meaningless to me whether their names were Mussolini or Churchill or Stalin. But the action photos of soldiers in battle, the picture of men scrambling down the netting when the *USS Yorktown* went down, and many other such pictures, I liked, and was entertained by, without knowing why, or being able to really understand their meaning or significance, or true import, beyond what I could make out from the captions or comprehend with my five-year-old mind.

But there was one picture, as I flipped through page after page, which stopped me dead.

It was a photo taken from a very high, steep angle, looking down on the mounting steps of a colonnaded public building, in Nanking, China.

It showed prone bodies strewn face-down with all their clothing pulled up around their necks to expose their pale buttocks to the pitiless black-and-white gaze of the camera.

It was the first time in my young life that I saw, and understood at a glance, and was forced to visualize, the nakedness of the dead.

One Sunday Papanonni did not pull the big black Buick out of the garage to have me climb in and ride with him to Sunday Mass at St Anthony's.

Just the day before, on Saturday, we had gone together, as usual, to do the shopping in Boston.

When he didn't come home that night, I asked Mamma where he was.

I knew something was wrong, because I could see that she had been crying, but I didn't dare think what I was thinking. With all my might I pushed the thought away.

But when I went to comfort my mother by putting my arms around her middle, she pushed me away, and complained that "the kids" were crying, "What's the matter with you? Can't you hear them?"

The last thing I wanted to be reminded of just at that moment was that the twins came first.

From then on I began to watch their every move. The grownups, that is.

I asked my father where Papanonni was.

"Oh, he's just gone visiting over to Watertown."

I knew that wasn't true. He didn't go to visit them—they came to him.

Besides, his big black Buick was parked in the driveway.

Besides, my father was looking sheepish with guilt, so I could tell he was lying.

When I went to Uncle Augie, he just said, "Don't look at me." So, I knew he had been given his orders by my mother.

In the morning, I went out to check the garage. The Buick was there, but my grandfather was not.

They were all acting grief-stricken, except for my father, who was tip-toeing around trying to be careful not to utter a word except, "Yes, Gerry. All right, hon."

It was still early and I was trying to muster up the nerve to confront Mamma, but my Dad, with a loud sigh of relief, met me at the back door to propose, "Hey, buddy! It's a beautiful summer day. How's about you and me go down the beach, huh?"

We never went to the beach without Mamma. In fact, even though they were only five months old, we never went to the beach without the two butterball babies in their oversized double-baby carriage nudging each other to one side with the hood awning pulled up to keep the hot sun off their puffy little pink cheeks.

But here we were with a blanket rolled up under Dad's arms marching off down Payson Street.

We walked the whole two miles to the beach with the sidewalks getting more and more crowded till they were packed and you had to be careful not to step on the heels of the person in front of you. It was a warm July morning and old ladies were waddling down the middle of the road straight into traffic on Shirley Ave. with beach-chairs folded under their puffy, sweaty arms.

When we got to the last little rise before the ocean, neither one of us had yet said a word.

I knew it was no use going against what they told me to do. All I would get was another lecture about how *children are to be seen and not heard* or *spare the rod and spoil the child*. I actually felt sorry for my little brother and sister as they had no way of knowing what lay in store for them.

But as long as my Dad had a pocket full of noisy nickels, for once, and no objections to spending them all on me, and given all the other stuff going on, I'd be more stupid than I actually was not to take advantage.

It's amazing how sly and cunning you get to be in only five years.

We actually had a good time together that sunny July Sunday on Revere Beach.

To say the beach was over-crowded does not describe how we had to pick our way through the strewn bodies. If you wanted to be polite and not step on other people's blankets, purses, baskets or heads, you had to weave your way while doing a balancing act, with your arms out.

They came from everywhere on buses, trains and streetcars to Revere Beach at this time of year. Eventually we found a scrap of sand up against the beach wall, way past the bandstand, to spread out only half of our blanket. Dad took me in the water, weaving again, and held me up with his hands under my stomach while I thrashed arms and legs and splashes and he tried to teach me to swim. It was one of the few times I had ever spent time with him without Mamma hovering over the both of us.

The next day he was actually excited to announce he was going to take me out for breakfast, then down to the playground behind the ballfield on Beach Street, then to lunch, and, finally, to the show, in the afternoon. A Roy Rogers movie matinee was playing at the Revere Theater on Broadway. On a Monday, of all things. I didn't even know the show was open on a Monday.

To this point we hadn't left the house yet. It was early, yet uncles and aunts, older cousins, were arriving. Nobody had a car in those days, except Uncle Gene, but they got going early to counteract the vagaries of the MTA. Uncle Augie was already here, of course, and I had found his old Army things in his closet when he was out to work, so I had examined all his medals, and compared them to the medal and insignia pages in the big photo book of the war, but it was the first time I had ever seen him in a suit and tie. All my aunts trooping in were dressed in black. Everyone was whispering. All eyes were downcast to the floor. My older cousins wouldn't look at me and sat quietly with folded hands which told me they were trying to behave. I was actually happy to get out the back door with my Dad.

The movie we saw that day was called *Son of Paleface,* and it was starring Bob Hope as Peter Potter, the son of the frontier dentist, Painless Potter. Opposite him his love interest was none other than Jane Russell—"*va va va voom*" said my Dad, when we saw the poster in the lobby. We had the whole place to ourselves, and when we went out to the candy counter, we had to look around for somebody to wait on us.

I settled into the humid darkness of the show, shared the popcorn with Dad, and the two of us escaped into the fantasy life of Roy Rogers and his wonder horse Trigger. Jane Russell played Mike Delroy, the leader of the outlaw gang that stole the treasure out of Painless Potter's gold mine, while his son, Bob Hope, chased her around the saloon trying to get it back, and Sheriff Roy Barton, who was actually Roy Rogers (even I knew that from the television at home) tried to rope her into his romantic arms by playing his guitar and serenading her with a ballad.

It was a pleasant way to spend the afternoon. In those days the movies were the only place where you could get air-conditioning. But then it only delayed the inevitable moment when we'd have to shield our eyes against the hard light of a hot July afternoon.

Back on Payson Street, we found Mamma sitting in the kitchen alone while Auntie Mary LaStoria had taken both the babies in the big twin baby carriage on foot back to her house on Reservoir Ave, to give my mother some relief after the strain of a hectic weekend.

When I walked in the back door, I could see she had been crying again, and she sat there with her hands cupped in her lap as if holding onto nothing.

Having been held in so long, all my anger, fury and tears burst out of me.

"He's dead, isn't he?" I said to my mother. "Why can't I see him? He's *my* Papanonni! Where did you put him? Leave me alone! I hate you."

Chapter 5

The Spartan Mothers

These events marked the beginnings of my mother's unhappiness.

Like me, she did not want anything to change. Like mine, her existence in the house on Payson Street in Revere had the quality of an idyll in a pastoral paradise. In all her life, with the exception of her honeymoon trip to California, she had spent not one night that was not under her father's roof. Nor had she ever been desirous of flying off from the orbit of her mother's kitchen. She was twenty-two years old when she married, and twenty-four when she had me, and in both those acts, she was seeking the approval of her parents, and especially with my advent, she was winning her father's love. Her father's garden with its measured rows of good things to eat meant just as much to her as to me. Her mother's flowers filled her life with the sunshine of beauty just as much for her as for me. Now she had to pass through what seemed to her to be the end of everything.

My histrionic reactions to her father's death did not help.

Yet the morning following the funeral brought with it the return of her five-month-old twins from her sister-in-law's house, so there was no relief from pressing duties, no time to grieve, no moment to herself—no respite from herself.

In September, I started the first grade at the Shurtleff School across the street from our house.

I had been watching the children of six grades at their games during recess in the blacktop-paved schoolyard for years, and I was delighted to be permitted to join their ranks at last. I knew all about recess and summer vacations. No longer was I to miss out on all the fun. The picture I had in mind of school made me eager to go. My sole disappointment was that my friends Billy and Paul, from the Merritts' house next door at No. 49, were not going to join me. Billy was being sent to Immaculate Conception, and Paul was too young for school till next year.

My first day in first grade, my teacher, Miss Margolis, scrounched down on her haunches with her arms encircling her knees and peered, smiling, directly into my face and asked with a kind and friendly exuberance, "And what's your name?"

"Nicky," I said bashfully.

Miss Margolis was young and pretty in a tweed skirt and a pink blouse with a big flowery bow, and nothing like my mother.

No grownup I had ever known stooped to put himself or herself on my level before.

She sent me home that day with a gold star on my forehead.

I fell in love with Miss Margolis instantly.

I used to ride with my grandfather to Sunday Mass at St Anthony's in his big black shiny '47 Buick with the chrome trim and the three portholes on the fenders and the sun-visor over the windshield.

Now it stood idle and unused inside the garage and was never taken out.

Uncle Augie may have landed at Omaha Beach during the war, but, before and after, he had no interest in driving, and he had never gotten a driver's license. Everywhere he wanted to go on his own he went on foot, or by bus or streetcar, subway or train, nor did he ever call for a taxi. Every day when he went to work, he used to ride to the shop in the Buick driven by his father. Now, he was picked up in the morning by his brother Gene, who drove over from Watertown. Gene had taken over his father's job as plant manager at No. 10, but he had not yet moved up to driving a Buick, although he was getting there: he was driving a new '52 DeSoto. My Dad was still at Page's Woodworking, still on the Apprentice program at 40 bucks a week, still walking to work, and Uncle Patsy over on Reservoir Street had a used '46 Hudson. Nobody had any use for Papanonni's Buick, and nobody wanted to spend any money on it, least of all Ma.

I had taken to calling her 'Ma,' the same name by which she used to refer to her own mother, when talking to her brothers and sisters. I was still punishing her and 'Mamma' would have sounded, to me, stickily affectionate, and implying some degree of forgiveness on my part.

Ma coldly calculated that she had lost her father's income, and therefore she couldn't afford to keep that car, so she told my Dad to sell it. What he was bringing in and what her brother Augie was contributing did not amount to enough to keep the house on the same standard of living that Ma was accustomed to. Dad put the Buick down at the front of the driveway inside the gates where it could be seen with a For Sale sign from the hardware store pinned under the wipers on the windshield. In no time the Buick was gone.

Ma started taking me to Immaculate Conception for Sunday Mass.

Unlike St Anthony's on Revere Street, it was close enough to walk there.

First we walked down to the foot of Payson Street, then crossed over in front of the Knights of Columbus. Next to them, where Beach Street curved downhill, was Dr Graham's house, where the twins and I went for our checkups. In those days, Dr Graham would make a house call if you had a sick kid, but he also had an office in his house. Downhill from him, at the corner of Library Street, was the ballfield where Little League teams used to play. Next to their chain-link fence came the Revere Public Library, one of the Carnegie endowments, a brownstone building with steep front steps. You could see the racks of books through the front windows as you passed. Then came the imposing, long charcoal-brick edifice of the Revere High School, which extended all the way to the stoplights at the four-way intersection of Beach Street and Winthrop Ave.

Diagonally opposite the High School, the wooden church of the Immaculate Conception stood at the corner of Winthrop Ave.

This was the Irish parish where the priest had agreed to marry my mother and father during the war when the Italian pastor of St Anthony's refused them because my dad was Eastern Orthodox. The Irish priest had made Ma swear to bring up any kids produced in this union in the Roman Catholic religion. Even at my age, it was a story I had heard a hundred times.

Unlike Papanonni, who used to hold my hand to walk up the steps into St Anthony's, Ma would send me into the Immaculate Conception alone, to attend Mass by myself.

Meanwhile, she would wait across the street at Foyle's Rexall drugstore and treat herself to a sundae or a frappe at the soda fountain, browsing through copies of *Modern Screen* and *Photoplay,* while I was attending Mass.

Diagonally opposite the drugstore, and across Beach Street from the church, was the redbrick Immaculate Conception parochial school, where Billy Merritt went.

After Mass, I would have to go to Sunday School there.

Ma was still mad at St Anthony's over her wedding, but she was also determined to save my soul by bringing me up Roman Catholic, as she had sworn to do.

I did not remember being baptized at the Immaculate Conception, but now I was five years old and I was making my First Communion, the third of the Seven Sacraments.

My Ma always had me dressed up as a little gentleman with my collar buttoned up at my throat and a neat cardigan. If she put a necktie on me, it had to have a tie-pin to hold it in the middle so it didn't flap around. The sleeves of the cardigan had to be rolled up in tidy cuffs at the bottom. No lint was allowed to cling to me. I was the grandson of a tailor, a man who, to my mother's family, was prominent in the Boston garment industry, and the sense of being well-dressed was a family trait my mother was fastidiously determined to instill in me, five years old or not.

But I was an instinctive little rebel. As soon as she turned her head, I would loosen that pinching collar. As a protest against her making me "do your duties," as she would say, I would vote with my feet, and cross the street on the long walk to church, demonstrating my independence, asserting a mind of my own, determined to resist her every effort to make me behave, which often had an air of desperation.

"Why do you have to spit on the sidewalk like that? That's so disgusting. Where did you get such a habit? Must've been your father."

Across the street I would go.

The Catholic Church is nothing if not seductive. Their avowed objective is to capture hearts and minds when they are young. Yet the Irish parish of the Immaculate Conception in Revere left me cold.

The humble wooden church at the corner of Winthrop Ave and Beach Street had been built in 1888 by the descendants of the Irish Famine exiles who survived the coffin ships. It had none of the granite magnificence and gold-tinged allure of St Anthony's. Its clapboard exterior could not compare to the rose-window translucence of the Italian parish's monument to the Renaissance.

In Revere, in those days, these were the things that counted. The city was divided into ethnic enclaves between the Irish, the Italians and the Jews. You could not get to the beach from our house without passing through the Jewish section on Shirley Ave. The poor Irish were congregated around the hastily-thrown-up projects in the neighborhood of Coolidge Ave. Their lace-curtain cousins were everywhere. So were the Italians. Our street, Payson Street, was prosperous and tidy with houses packed in, all two-families, with tiny lawns behind chain-link fences, and all three groups interspersed. Restaurants in town were either Roma Villas or Cafe Lucias. The barrooms with the neon shamrocks were Matt Reilly's or Bucky's Taverns or the Hibernian Hall. Out by

Wonderland Park, the dog track behind the beach, where they had greyhound racing, you could find your Luau Polynesian Palaces or your Peking Gardens. The police were Irish and the building contractors Italian. The politicians were both, vying for the same offices. Around the corner from our house, on Tree Valley Road, began the single homes belonging to insurance salesmen and automobile-showroom owners, so the better-off lived right next door to those struggling from paycheck to paycheck.

Within this small seacoast city full of inhabitants, striving and conniving on the northern fringe of Boston, at age five, I lived a life of Platonic idealism.

The God I knew was a personal acquaintance, a man of flesh and blood, my own grandfather. I could sit and talk to him. I could hold his hand. Although he had died, he had not left the hollows of my heart. He was a spirit living inside of me.

I had a lot to learn at parochial school.

My first day in catechism class at Immaculate Conception was the closest I had ever been to a priest of the Church.

To me, they were remote figures dressed in beautiful robes making motions in the air on a distant altar.

The Reverend Father Francis T. Gallagher, however, the pastor of the parish who came to welcome us to the opening of our First Communion classes, was a man dressed in a black suit wearing a white collar.

"Good morning, children!"

We sat with our hands folded on the desktop in front of us, as we had been instructed. Father Gallagher was soft-spoken and kindly-looking. He smiled upon us and blessed us and wished us good wishes.

However, he devoted no more than thirty seconds to us, and then turned to leave, as if he had to catch a streetcar.

He was replaced by the Mother Superior of the school, Sister Mary Regina, of the order of the Sisters of St Joseph.

She, too, had to flee, perhaps to go to the hospital to nurse and comfort the sick and dying.

We were left with Sister Dymphna Bridget, who closed the classroom door on the other two with the thud of doom.

"Now, children," said Sister Dymphna Bridget. "Open your Catechism to Lesson First on Page 1."

As she spoke, she passed among us, passing out not loaves and fishes, but dog-eared copies of the Baltimore Catechism, left and right, with its well-worn plain purple cover, in a modest paperback edition suitable to be pored over by generations of communicants, puzzled and fearful.

I don't know why, but I took an instant dislike to Sister Dymphna Bridget, perhaps because I sensed, or knew, a bully when I saw one. It might have been the stiffness and rigidity of her posture, with her nose in the air, looking down on us trembling mortals the length of that red-frosted nose. It might have been the forbidding air of her flowing black nun's veil, which cascaded down around the massively stiff white headboard of her coif. It might have been the severity of the wimple tucked tightly under her chin, which reminded me of the collar constricting my own throat when Ma dressed me for Sunday Mass. In any case, I revolted immediately, in revulsion to her authoritarian manner.

Sister Dymphna Bridget commanded us to follow along and recite, in unison, after her.

"One," she said. "Question. Who made the world?"

"One, question, who made the world?"

"No, no, children. Only respond 'Who made the world.'"

"Who made the world?"

"Answer. God made the world."

"God made the world."

"Two. Question. Who is God?"

"Who is God?"

"Answer. God is the Creator of heaven and earth, and of all things."

"God is the Creator of heaven and earth, and of all things."

"What is man?"

"What is man?"

"Man is a creature composed of body and soul, and made to the image and likeness of God."

"Man is a creature composed of body and soul, and made to the image and likeness of God."

"Why did God make you?"

"Why did God make you?"

"No, children, you must respond 'Why did God make me.'"

I raised my hand. "But that's not what it says."

"Nevertheless, you respond, 'Why did God make me.'"

"But that's not what it says."

"Are you defying me?"

I shrank back in my seat.

"What's your name, young man?"

"Nicky."

"You mean 'Nicholas?'"

"I guess so."

"Well, Nicholas, stand up. Did God make you?"

"I guess if He made all things, he musta made me."

"Why did God make you. Read. Read the answer to the class. Follow along with your finger, if you have to."

"I don't have to. I know how to read. 'God made me to know him, to love Him, and to serve Him in this world, and to be happy with Him forever in heaven.'"

"Do you want to be happy with God in heaven for ever after, Nicholas?"

"Yes."

"Then you'll have to be obedient, won't you?"

"I guess so."

"Do you know where little children go who are disobedient?"

"No."

"They go to hell. And in hell they burn for ever after, for all eternity. Do you know how hot the fires of hell are? Do you know how long eternity is, Nicholas? That's right. For ever and ever. And you can never escape the flames in all that time. Think about *that*, Nicholas."

I thought about it until I crossed the street after Sunday school to rejoin my mother at the drugstore soda fountain.

"Ma–."

"Don't whine, Nicky. God, I hate that when you do that. You want a sundae? How about a lime rickey?"

"Ma! Am I gonna burn in hell for ever and ever?"

"Who told you that?"

"The sister said if I disobeyed–"

"Oh, I don't know why they have to scare you little kids half to death with that kind of stuff. Here. Have a stick of *Juicy Fruit*."

There were days of pure blue, rolling high with the sunshine over the black and white hills of the Cyclone and the merry-go-round of rainbow-colored umbrellas of Revere Beach.

There was the pure sugar of blushing pink cotton candy sticking all over your face, and the eyes-screwed-closed ordeal of Ma dosing you with your daily spoonful of cod-liver oil. How I hated the sight of that brown bottle of *Squibb's*. But also I loved the freedom of taking a ride on the swings in the schoolyard, leaning back pulling hard and kicking your feet way up, legs straight, toes pointed at the sky, and then the back-swing when you coasted up up up to the moment of high suspense and then swoosh! down into the trough with all your might. And all I had to do was cross the street. I was a big boy now and could let myself out of the gate at the foot of the driveway. No more Mamanonna to call after me, *come here where I can see you!* In the winter it seemed we never got enough snow. Why were the grownups always complaining about the snow? I wanted to go out in the backyard to build a snowman and a snow-fort. Then Billy and Paul could come over and play in my yard. On television I saw that they had plenty of snow in Korea. Uncle Patsy said we should just drop the bomb on them, why were we fooling around like this? I was going to turn six years old at Christmastime and Sister Dymphna Bridget said that when we all reached seven years of age we would attain the Age of Reason. So one more year, and I would be all grown up. Ma couldn't tell on me anymore to her Pa to try to scare me into behaving and anyway I never got any lickin's from him. Nowadays she would say, Wait'll your father gets home, but usually by that time she forgot. Ma had a snowsuit for me that was an agony of zippers and fur. And when I got back in the house after she yelled at me for an hour and a half to come in, she wouldn't let me in the kitchen till she pulled everything from boots to hood off me in the back hall and I was left shivering and sweating standing in a pool of melting snow. *Get in the house now and change those wet socks!* That Christmas I got a brand-new American Flyer sled, the kind you could steer, and again, our sliding hill for all the kids in the neighborhood was right across the street. The paved-over schoolyard in back of the Shurtleff had an embankment that descended from the level of Payson Street, which was higher than School Street, which ran parallel, and which was where the front door of the Shurtleff was located. I also got a brand-new, used, American-made Schwinn bicycle, the kind with the wide tires, from Uncle Augie. He told me it was a boys' bike and explained the difference between that and a girl's bike. I was terribly proud to have a real boys' bike because it meant that I was officially beyond the tricycle stage. When springtime came my Dad took me out to the driveway, closed the front gates, and started teaching me how to ride. It was getting closer to summer vacation and Miss Margolis was still sending me home with red and green and blue stars on my forehead. She told me I could already read on a third-grade level and I worked hard on my penmanship. We were learning to sculpt cursive style lettering onto yellow paper. I loved to lean my head over on my desk until my cheek rested on the scarred wood while I reached up to dip my pen in the inkwell, then I would stick my tongue out and with my face level to the paper, begin carving the flowing lines of my lettering. I got high marks for penmanship. All my grades were excellent. Ma would sit herself down and open up my report card in her lap, and go, *hmm*. All she would say was, *see that you keep it up*. But I knew she was pleased because she never missed a chance to tell her sisters when they came over that I got straight-A's. Then I would have to listen to my cousin Anthony from Reservoir Ave. telling me that I was a smarty-pants. Ma always had visitors in the house all day long. If it wasn't the insurance man it was the Fuller Brush man, or Uncle Tommy DiPrima dropping in for a cup of coffee when he and his delivery truck happened to be in Revere, or Auntie Peggy Fabiano who came by to listen to Babe Rubenstein calling the races at Suffolk Downs on the radio, and to use the telephone, and she always had my cousins Henry and Ronnie with her, unless they were spending the month at their father's, way out in Wilmington, wherever that was. Auntie Peggy was the hostess down at The Frolics on Revere Beach Boulevard. In the wintertime she would go down to Florida with a man Ma said was her boyfriend, Rings Romano. He was the owner of The Frolics. The Frolics was a place the grownups called a nightclub, but it was a restaurant, too, so in the spring or summer, when we took the kids down to Revere Beach in the twin-stroller, we always would drop by the front door of the Frolics. I would paste my face to the glass and try to peer inside the opaque interior. Auntie Peggy would leave her lectern by the door and come to stoop down and wave to me through the glass with a long wine-colored gilt-edged menu in her hand. Soon it was going to be time for me to make my First Confession. I tried with all my might to think up a good list of sins that I had committed, but in my heart I knew that my only really and truly black spot on my soul was that I loved my little brother Jackie-boy, but I hated my little sister Jilly-girl. The thing I really, really resented was everytime Ma would start fussing over them or feeding them bottles or changing them or warming their bottles on the stove or stuffing big spoonfuls of farina down their gullets for breakfast, she would start cooing these pet-names she had for them, Jackie-boy and Jilly-girl. I felt like swearing like a grownup, *Jesus, Mary and Joseph*. I knew I loved my little brother and sister, but I didn't like them. It seemed that when they were born Doctor Graham, our pediatrician down at the end of the street, told Ma they were underweight, because, well, they were twins, and to be sure that she watched the twins' weight carefully. So Ma took it personally, like he was accusing her, and blaming her, saying that it was all her fault. She was afraid he would find fault with her being a bad mother again at their next checkup. *So she showed him.* Sometimes at the table I had to wince because she would keep forcing the spoon into their mouths till they were turning their heads and scrunching up their eyes and starting to squeeze out a crybaby. I felt sorry for my brother Jackie, but that Jill, she was a real actress. How she did carry on. Now that Papanonni was no longer in the house Ma couldn't depend on my Dad to make me behave, and Uncle Augie refused the job because, after all, he wasn't my father, and he didn't want to make things awkward between him and his brother-in-law living in the same house. Pa would've made me behave with just one look because I was terrified of losing his love and approval. Ma tried to get my Dad to be the disciplinarian who gave out the lickin's but I could tell his heart wasn't in it. If Ma got me I would really catch it, but she wasn't fast enough, and she had the kids on her hands. That's how I thought of my brother and sister, as 'the kids.' The trouble was that I loved them, like I was supposed to, but I didn't like them. They were five years younger than me, absolutely useless as playmates. I didn't have anybody to play with but Billy and Paul next door. Ma wouldn't let me have friends I made at school come over the house. And she wouldn't let me go down the street. And she wouldn't even let Billy and Paul come over. She told me I couldn't watch TV except for Howdy Doody or when Roy Rogers or the Lone Ranger came on or on Saturday mornings when there was no school, and I had to be in bed by seven on a school night. Everybody else got to stay up and watch. I could hear them laughing at *I Love Lucy* in the other room while I had to stew in bed. It wasn't fair. I would get awful mad at Ma. One time she asked me how come there was a pile of dead ants at the bottom of the back steps. I wouldn't admit to it, but she just looked at me with a sneer and said, "Savage amusement." *What did that mean?* All I know is I never could take pleasure in stepping on ants to kill them after that. Then one time Ma cooked a beautiful steak for my Dad because he happened to mention he was tired of pork and beans, which is what he called *pastavazoole*, every night. But I wouldn't touch the plain fried steak, dripping with red juice—instead, I ate up a second helping of Ma's fried potatoes, which were always delicious. So Ma decided to invite Dr Graham to the house one night for supper. She told him I wouldn't eat my meat. He leaned over to me and kindly said, a growing boy like you needs his protein. That carried a lot of weight with me, Dr Graham showing that he cared enough about me to explain, instead of Ma telling me all the time, *Do what you're told, and no backtalk, either.* I suppose, that thing with stepping on ants, I thought I wanted to know how God felt when he killed my grandfather—to see what it felt like to have that power over another living being. *There—that's the end of you.* But how could I explain all this to the priest in the Confessional? I hardly understood or believed it myself. It sounded to me like I was making up stories. So I settled for telling him I disobeyed my mother three times this week and my father twice and my Uncle Augie, well, four times, that sounded pretty good. I got three Hail Mary's and four Our Fathers for my penance, and went home scarred for life. I was so relieved. Having to stand in line on a Saturday afternoon at three o'clock in the dank recesses of that wooden ark of a church, Immaculate Conception, with your hands folded, waiting with all the other kids, under the scrutiny of all the adults also waiting to confess, and wishing these kids would just hurry up and get out of the way, *of all the luck;* and standing there thinking, all these people can see right through me, and they know I have sinned. *Bless me father, for I have sinned.* When it was over I was so relieved I ran all the way home, drinking in big bowl-fulls of fresh air, so thrilled to have escaped. I was so happy, knowing the next day I would be so sanctified that I would be able to dress up in my white communion suit and feel completely pure and free of that awful, awful guilty feeling, I just had to find something to do to let off thunder-claps of joy. Billy and Paul were out in their backyard, playing. Round that side of the house there was a white picket fence. My dad had told me it was our fence. He said you could tell who a fence belonged to by the way the pickets were facing. So, since the top rail of the picket fence was on our side of the property, that meant the picket fence belonged to us. So, that meant that it was okay for me to walk along the top of the picket fence, because, after just confessing and having just been absolved and cleansed of all guilt, I wasn't about to add a sin to my ledger by walking on top of somebody else's fence. So, to show off to my pals, Billy and Paul, I cried "Watch this! See what I can do?" and I climbed up onto the top rail of the fence and began to tiptoe along, pretending I was the high-wire act on TV. But then I caught the bottom cuff of my pant-leg on a picket sticking up and when I went to take the next step, my leg wouldn't move. I realized I was caught when I turned by head to look down. I felt myself twisting and suddenly I was losing my balance, there was a rip, of cloth sawing apart, I was falling head-first, and I knew it, so I put out my right arm to break my fall, and instead, I broke my arm.

I ran into the house through the back door, crying and howling with unbearable pain, and Ma ran to call Dr Graham on the phone, and the next day I made my First Communion dressed in my white suit with my arm in a sling.

THE EDUCATION OF NICHOLAS PETROVICH

The ghosts in our house now numbered three. There was my grandfather, Antonio LaStoria, whose spirit permeated the walls, and whose gentle brown eyes looked out at me from the portraits of the bird-dogs adorning the parlor. There was my grandmother, Gigi LaStoria, whose empty chair by the kitchen window was nevertheless filled with the enormous bulk of her love, the love which had brought my mother and her six sisters and brothers into this world, and eventually dawned on me with the radiance of a sunflower. And then there was the Holy Ghost.

His name had not yet been changed to Holy Spirit, nor was English ever heard from the altar of our Latin Mass. So many things then were a mystery. So many things were immutable and were meant to last forever and never to change.

So to my young mind, forming out of inchoate formlessness, to approach the threshold of the Age of Reason, there was God the Father, God the Mother, and then, the Holy Ghost.

This was the Trinity who had their abode in our house.

When you are a child who is given gifts by the Wise People, for no other reason than the idea that you are a child born in their midst, and something in them brings them from far off through the arid desert of winter to bow down to you, to worship you, they may not know why, except that you constitute, and you represent, *the thing that they have lost.* It is easy then to begin to think that this is your due, that life owes this reverence to you, and you alone. Angels flock to your side, along with lambs and oxen, and a star stands watch over you, and this star guides others from afar, also bringing gifts to kneel at your feet.

So was I, in that house, surrounded by love and adoration, but desiring only more gifts.

My mother expressed her love to me through her love of cooking good things for me to eat, traditional Napoletano peasant fare, and she poured her love onto the plate she placed before me, but I wanted other, impossible things from her, things that she could not give.

I wanted to hear her tell me that she loved me.

My father expressed his love for me by trudging to work each day and bringing his pay packet home to hand over to my mother at the end of each week, but I wanted other, impossible things.

I wanted him to play with me.

My Uncle expressed his love for me by holding to the small space of his corner in the house, his place among the three of them, and not intruding his tall stature or his athletic magnetism or dominating size and powerful strength on those he loved, the five of us.

I wanted him to be my father.

At night, in my dreams, where I was haunted by the Holy Trinity, God the Father, God the Mother, and the Holy Ghost, the family figures, the Wise People of my dreams, gathered around me to urge me to understand, to learn to understand.

They told me I had to learn to share.

They told me big boys don't cry.

They told me I had to look after the little ones, to look out for those who were smaller, weaker, less able than me to look out for themselves.

All the things I was told in the daylight of wakefulness, in haste, or impatience, or irritation or kindness, repeated themselves in my dreams at night.

So the mystery multiplied and I was left to founder for myself through the muddle of many voices.

There was a boy who went to my school, Chuckie Stuart, and he was in the third grade. Chuckie lived further down Payson Street, towards Beach Street, in a tiny single-story home wedged between all the other two-families lining our street.

That house of his was different. I knew Chuckie from school as a well-known bully who picked on other kids, as long as they were smaller and weaker and dumber than he was. I knew because all the kids talked about him. They said he lived with his grandmother because his mother had died. What about his father? Oh, that was his dad's mother, and they both lived with him now, because his dad had lost his wife and needed somebody to watch Chuckie after school while he was at work. I realized then that Chuckie's dad was the insurance agent who came, usually around once a month or so, to sit down with Ma at our kitchen table over coffee, and collect. He was a very friendly, nice man, who loved to chat. I began to feel sorry for poor Chuckie in the third-grade once I realized all this.

One day after school I was playing by myself outside our front gate, riding circles on Payson Street on my new bike that I got for Christmas. I could ride now, but I was being a good boy that day, and not straying too far, so my mother wouldn't have to worry, or start yelling at me when I went in.

Chuckie Stuart came by. He wanted to know if I wanted to come down to his house and play.

Sounded dubious to me. I was a little afraid of Chuckie because he was bigger than me, and he was in the third grade, and I knew his reputation. As soon as I thought of that I was afraid of him, period. Besides, I knew his front yard with the chain-link fence and the flowers and vines clinging to it from passing it on foot so many times. It was a tiny front yard, and those bushes had pickers. So where were we going to play? The more I thought of that tiny little wooden house with the low-slung porch-roof and the flower-pots hanging from the pillars holding up the sagging roof the more I began to picture his grandmother as a wizened old witch of short stature, too short to stir the big wooden paddle in her boiling pot. But now I was too afraid to say no.

So I got off my bike and walked it down the street beside Chuckie on the sidewalk, nervously trying to befriend him as we went.

"What do you want to play, Chuckie?"

"Oh, we'll think of something."

"Isn't your yard too small?"

"Oh, well, we can always go inside."

That shut me up.

When we got there, Chuckie smoothly took the bike-handles right out of my hands, and placed the bike leaning up against the picker-bushes inside his fence.

Then he closed his front gate in my face and turned to me, saying, "Game's over!"

He laughed and crossed his arms on his chest as if to say *Dare ya to get your bike back!*

Still laughing, he open the gate, to invite me in to get my bike back, but I didn't dare, I thought he was big enough to kill me, so he closed the gate in my face again, and went into the house, laughing at me.

I was so mad! It wasn't fair! He'd fooled me! He was bigger than me!

I burst into tears of frustration and ran straight home and sped into the kitchen, crying the way I had when I'd broken my arm.

"Ma!–Chuckie Stuart stole my bike!"

"What!"

"You gotta go down there and tell his grandmother to tell him to give it back to me!"

"I will not."

"But, Ma–!"

"Nicky!—how could you let him do that! Now you go march right down there to his house and get that bike back!"

"But, Ma—he's bigger than me!"

"I don't care. You don't let anybody do that to you. It's time you learned to stand up for yourself! I'm not gonna spend good money like that and have you just throw it away! Now, march!"

I turned on my heel to hide my fury and tears and sped out the back door and down the steps. I told myself I hated my mother, and that I'd show her.

No tears scald your eyes and burn your cheeks like tears of shame.

As I ran down the driveway, she shouted at me through the open kitchen window.

"And don't come back here without that bike!"

Chapter 6

Death of a Piano

The dogs began to howl early in the morning, in the weeks after Papanonni died. They wanted to be fed and they missed the hand of their master ruffling their heads. Their agitation was contagious and in the end they were baying like a pack of wolves.

Ma was overwhelmed by the early morning cries of the twins while getting me ready for school and Dad out the door for work. It fell to Uncle Augie to look after the kennel.

But he had no heart for the chore. He performed the duty but without even the amount of enthusiasm he had once mustered up for KP in the Service. His interest in going hunting for quail and pheasant in the Lynn marshes, as Papanonni used to do, was nil. Uncle Augie no longer desired to rise early to spend the day in the woods of Ponkapoag hunting deer, as he had before the war, in his youth in Stoughton; nor would he even open the door of the closet where his father's shotgun and rifle stood on their butts leaning against the wall, unused. Since the war ended, he wanted to smell no more gun-oil.

The dogs, evincing their bereavement, were waking the whole neighborhood. The Sullivans, next door, across the vacant lot from Mamanonna's flower-garden, threatened Ma with the police. The dogs had lost their will to behave. With their instinctive needs choked off, they felt abandoned. Mrs. Sullivan informed Ma that there were laws against a public nuisance such as those dogs. Mrs. Sullivan knew very well who ran our house, now that the Old Man was gone.

It was a terrible day for me when I had to go with Ma to take my dog Daisy to the pound.

Ma knew I was upset. Daisy knew I was upset. Papanonni had given that dog to me, to be my dog. So Ma left Daisy behind alone in the kennel when she brought all the other dogs to the Revere Police Station.

But Mrs Sullivan was relentless. She wanted Daisy gone, too.

On the fateful day, Ma and I walked down Beach Street with Daisy on a leash. We turned at the corner where Immaculate Conception and Foyle's Rexall Drugstore were and proceeded down Winthrop Ave.

I think Daisy knew she was going to her final destination.

She was walking with her head down, plodding. She was not romping and playful. She was morose with the thought of the empty kennel where she had spent the last three weeks alone without her friends. She was worried that she would never see them again.

The Police Station was at the back of the Revere City Hall. There was a parking lot, but it was unpaved and on a spring day after rain it was rutted and muddy. The back of the City Hall was lower than the front doors on Broadway, so the entrance to the rear door of the basement, where the dog pound was located, was narrow and tomb-like, with high, sloping sides, a veritable primitive burial mound.

We opened the glass-paned green door and the click of the brass-handled door-knob echoed in my ears with a hollow doom.

Inside, the cement of the basement floor was all wet with the tramp of policemen's muddy shoes.

On the left was the stairway with the brass handrail and the metal runners lipping each separate cement step up to the Station-house on the floor above our heads.

Ahead, in the dimness, after the greyness outside, I could make out a long corridor with office doors staggered on either side.

At the end of the long corridor I could see the bars of the dog-pound.

Ma went up the stairs to fetch an officer.

I knelt down and put my arms around Daisy's neck while she nuzzled my cheek and licked my ear.

They came down and we walked down the long corridor and I could hear the keys jingling in the policeman's hand.

At the end of the hall in front of the barred door the entire floor was a standing pool of dog urine.

I was looking directly into the eyes of indifference and cruelty.

The door of the cell swung open and the other dogs with their chins on the cement floor did not even bother to look up when a new inmate was introduced into their midst.

The grind of the key turning in the lock scraped on my soul.

It was cold, dank and and dark in there, with the upturned brown eyes of dogs lit by a single bulb dangling from a chain.

All the grief bottled up inside me since the day I was prevented from attending Papanonni's wake came pounding through my heaving chest, bursting out of my eyes in hot tears that would not stop.

That was the first day in my life my heart was broken.

Why I could not cry at my grandfather's death, but I cried Mississippi's at the demise of a dog, I will never know.

But worse, for me, than a heart breaking in half was the gall rising in my throat at the sight and smell of those prisoners lying on the cold floor of a dungeon in puddles of their own urine. Ever since that day I have held it against the police of the world, no matter where or in what country, for the neglect of the poor creatures in the dog-pound in the basement of the Revere Police Station.

Across the street at the Shurtleff I no longer got to enjoy the presence and the aura, the enchantress vision, the delicious scent, of my beloved Miss Margolis, every day. Instead, in second grade, I got starchy old Miss Clark, who was the principal of the school, and who, in her blue serge suit, and white hair, and frilly white blouse, and buttoned-up suit-jacket, and battleship stern, seemed to be as old as George Washington, whose portrait in the faded, bleached frame of Gilbert Stuart hung above the blackboard behind Miss Clark's desk.

I was pleased to have been promoted, but I missed Miss Margolis. At home Ma told me that my cousin Anthony from Reservoir Ave. had to stay behind in fifth grade at the McKinley. I never wanted to stay behind, I would much rather get promotions, but still, it did not make up for the loss of Miss Margolis.

In second grade, we had a cloak-room. Miss Clark made us remove our snow-capped galoshes out there, and hang up our winter coats before we were allowed to enter her classroom proper. Miss Clark was nothing if not proper. She would not allow me to put my head resting on the desk to carve out my letters in penmanship. She stressed posture. If anybody misbehaved, she did not threaten to send them to the principal's office. She *was* the principal. She thought it was not necessary for me to stick my tongue out when I was writing. She stressed developing good habits. Every day in Miss Clark's class you had to recite the Pledge of Allegiance to the Flag, which hung over the room from a stanchion next to George Washington. You had to put your hand over your heart when reciting the Pledge.

However, Miss Clark was not unkind. Perhaps it was not thrilling to be near her as it was with Miss Margolis, but she taught me one thing which was not on the curriculum, and that was the idea that old people can be nice, that you need not fear them, that, even if you encounter them outside your own house or your own family circle, even if you do not know them, even if they are strangers, if you are nice to them, they will be nice to you.

And Miss Clark played the piano. One of the features of her classroom was the fact that she had a big black upright piano placed diagonally across the left side of the front row, near the school-windows. When we had Music, she would play the accompaniment, as she taught us *My Country, 'Tis of Thee*. There was a lot of memorizing you had to do in second grade with Miss Clark, from the Pledge of Allegiance to *America the Beautiful* to *Old Susannah*. But it was worth it. You might not get stars on your forehead, like with Miss Margolis, but you might get a big round of applause from all the parents for singing *God Bless America* in the Glee Club at the school concert at the end of the year, and that felt just as good, even better.

I also met Mary in the second grade.

She was new to the school. She had blonde hair which she wore in pigtails. Not the kind of blond hair that was white but the kind that was golden-wheat-toned, and her hair shone, glowing, braided like that, with red-velvet bows. She came from Minnesota. She moved to our city because her father got a new position. She did not say he got a new job, which made me think, somehow, that her father was very lofty, far above the station of my father, who went to work in heavy-duty white house-painter overalls.

One day in the cloakroom Mary said to me, as we were hanging up our coats, "Wanna smooch?"

I knew she liked me because she was smart and I was one of the smart kids in class, and us smart kids did not like to hang out with the dummies, but I did not know she liked me that much.

"I don't know how to smooch," I said.

"It's easy," said Mary. "You just pucker up, like this."

"Like this?"

"Right. Only you gotta close your eyes."

I did as I was told. I always did as I was told.

She planted a big smoocher right on my lips.

"There. Now you'll be my boyfriend, and I'll be your girlfriend."

We started smooching in the cloak-room on a regular schedule. One day Miss Clark caught us and intervened with a hand on each shoulder to gently separate us.

"Now, children, you don't want to be passing germs."

And she walked away with the tiny hint of a smile escaping over her shoulder as she shook her head.

One Sunday as Ma was walking me to Mass at Immaculate Conception, I told her, "I got a girlfriend now, you know."

"Oh, you do?"

"Yes, Ma. Her name is Mary Nordstrom."

"Sounds Swedish."

"Or maybe Norwegian?" I was so fond of *I Remember Mama* on television every week, I wanted Mary to be Norwegian.

"There's no Norwegians around here."

I knew Ma was thinking of old Mrs Nelson, who lived upstairs on the second floor of our house, and rented from us. She was Swedish. That week Ma was having a big argument with her sister Peggy about whether she should go up on the rent on old Mrs Nelson, who never went out. Auntie Peggy took the position that now that Pa was gone, it was stupid to keep charging old Mrs Nelson forty bucks a month. But Ma said she didn't want to go up on old Mrs Nelson because she was quiet as a mouse and you couldn't even hear her walking around up there over your head, and where was she gonna find a tenant quiet like that who never asked for nothing and always paid on time, and anyway, she had to defend Pa because, you know, he was the kind who would give you the shirt off his back. Whatever that meant. I tried to picture it, but I couldn't.

"That's where my girlfriend Mary lives, Ma, right over there."

We were just passing the curve of Beach Street approaching the corner of Library Street, where a tidy white clapboard building with a modest square peaked steeple, short and stubby, crowned the edifice on the corner opposite the Little League field.

"You mean she lives in the apartment at the back of that church?" said Ma.

"I guess so." I hadn't thought of that building as a church of any kind. It certainly didn't look anything like St Anthony's, or even Immaculate Conception. And there was no cross on the peak of the roof.

"So this Mary must be the minister's daughter," said Ma. "Well, then, she can't be your girlfriend."

"Why not, Ma?"

My mother pointed at the green sign with the gold lettering that stood just inside the black-iron railings surrounding the tiny white lawn of the church-building.

* * First Baptist Church of Revere * *

"She's a Protestant, Nicky! You're a Catholic!"

I had to tell Mary that week in the cloakroom.

"We can't be goin' steady anymore."

"Why not?"

"'Cause, Mary, I'm a Catholic, and you're a Protestant."

Mary didn't like that. "Oh, very well. If that's the way you feel about it. I'll just have to find another. And don't think I can't."

Ma was always inviting people into the house, whereas I wasn't allowed to have anybody over. The milkman, the mailman, the Fuller Brush man, the insurance man, Dr Graham, they all had to sit down at my mother's kitchen table for a cup of coffee. I was surprised she didn't have the ragman come in on the days when he'd come slowly sauntering down Payson Street with his wagon and horse, yelling "Rags!"

Dad was home everyday about five after twelve, for his lunch, and so was I, as I only had to cross the street from the schoolyard. Half the time I would find Uncle Tommy DiPrima sitting there with them, or more often Ma's sister Peggy, with or without Henry and Ronnie. Uncle Augie was never there for lunch because he rode to work each day in his brother Gene's DeSoto. The shop was in faraway Boston, but Uncle Patsy, Ma's other brother, used to pop in from time to time, because his wife, Mary LaStoria, was Ma's nanny, so to speak, for my sister Jill, while Ma, who preferred boys, it seemed to me, doted on my brother, fat little Jackie-boy.

The consequence was: we always had a houseful. Things had definitely changed from the days when my ailing grandmother took up all of Ma's time and the kitchen wasn't her own. Now with both her parents gone, Ma was not going to let anybody rule the roost but herself.

My Dad was a fast walker, so he always got up and left at 12.25 on the dot, as he had only a half-hour for lunch break at Page's Woodworking, which was all the way to Broadway. When Ma sent me to the Shawmut Bank down on Broadway to pay the mortgage for her it took me a lot longer to get there than that.

Ma trusted me for errands like that. She knew I was smart enough. I was smart all right, smart in school, but there was a lot I was learning around that kitchen table, too. Auntie Peggy sometimes brought a man with her, and she would describe him to me as a friend of hers, but I knew he was a racetrack regular, because the three of them would always spread out the daily green sheet on the table and delve into the mystifying calibrations of mudders and finishers and owners and trainers, and quarter-pole splits and five-furlong times, jocks and the silks they're wearing, the results from the nag's last five finishes, who's under Tony Despirito at Suffolk in the seventh today, the argument was on. Auntie Peggy taught me how to read the green sheet line on a horse, which she said was the pony's lifetime record, from left to right, the date, the racetrack abbreviation (AQU for Aqueduct, HP for Hollywood Park) the race number, whether the third or the fifth, the course conditions, muddy or dry, the handicap on the horse, the post position, the order of call, which meant how far behind the leader the horse was at the half-mile or at the wire, the jockey's name, the weight carried, the number of horses in the race, and, finally, the odds. All these things made a difference, she explained. Anything you wanted to know about horse racing all you had to do was ask my Auntie Peggy. If it wasn't for her I wouldn't have known the difference between 3 to 1 and even money, or between Win, Place and Show. Sometimes she just liked a horse's name, or the colors the jockey on board was wearing; sometimes, if she had a dream that morning, Ma would drag Mamanonna's Italian Dream Book down off the shelf and they would consult that to give them the winning numbers. Auntie Peggy always made sure her friend had a car with him. Then they would rush out because they had to make it in time for the Daily Double. That's when Ma would dip into her purse and my Dad would start making faces behind their backs. When we were alone, he'd complain to me, "It's just throwing your money right down the drain."

One day after school the front doorbell rang.

That never happened. Everybody who knew Ma just barged right in the back door. I wasn't even allowed to go through the front door, it was always kept locked. Ma said, "Must be a salesman, wanna bet? Jesus, Mary and Joseph, how many vacuums can I buy?"

It was a salesman, all right, but he wasn't selling encyclopedias.

Besides, we already had a set of *The Wonderland of Knowledge* in 12 volumes in the house, which Ma had bought from a guy who rang that front door-bell, when she found out how smart I was, back in the first grade. "I'm not gonna throw away money on you, so you better use them, but I guess with you, I don't have to worry, your nose is always in a book."

I promptly made a lifetime decision that I was going to read every single article in the *Wonderland of Knowledge,* starting with *A* for *Aardvark,* whatever that was.

This time it turned out the guy was selling music lessons.

I was lurking behind her trying to see when she unlocked the front door and opened it.

The front of our house at 45 Payson Street had a tiny lawn enclosed by the chain-link fence. There was a flight of red-brick steps leading up to our front door. Mrs Nelson's stairway-door at No. 47, leading up to her second-floor apartment, squeezed in our front hallway, because on the first floor, we had a sunporch, which we called the *piazza.* There was no access from the front hall to the piazza, you had to get in through the French doors from the parlor. But the front hall was also occupied by Papanonni's big upright player-piano.

Our front hall was as dark as a subway tunnel, but the door-to-door music-lesson salesman's eyes lit up when he spied the piano behind us. He must have said to himself, *I came to the right house this time.*

Naturally, my mother invited him to step into the parlor and have a seat and be comfortable.

No, she said, violin lessons would not do, as his cousin Henry is already taking, so we don't need another Stravinsky in the family.

That was my mother's little joke.

The salesman smiled weakly. What about the piano? With a nod in that direction.

That piano is not really meant to be played. It's a player-piano and it belonged to my father, who's no longer with us, may he rest in peace.

Well, there's the guitar, the trumpet, the saxophone–

We already have a mandolin in the house. My father played. By the way, could you take a look at it for me? It's a real antique and I'm sure it must be worth something.

The salesman took a wild guess and said, if it's the old-fashioned bow-backed kind they brought over from the old country, there's not much market for that kind of thing these days. Look. I think I have just the thing for you. How would you like a nice red 12-bass starter accordian, sonny? Mrs, you can start him out on a rental—you won't have to go to the expense of purchasing until after we see how he does with it the first few weeks.

Well, I think that sounds pretty good to me. His father is from that polka country, down there in Pennsylvania, you know. He loves to dance the polka. We met at a dance, during the war. You want me to sign something? Why don't you come out to the kitchen table and have a cup of coffee and we'll take care of all that?

We all stood up and headed to the kitchen, as the salesman ruffled my head, and avowed that the accordian is the easiest of all the instruments to learn how to play, and once you learn on that, you can go to any other instrument you like, with ease.

The accordian was not easy to play, not to me, not at all, at least, not in the beginning. But the world of music it introduced me to, and the world of special closeness between me and my mother that it opened up, I could not have imagined.

When Ma heard that the music store where I'd have to go for lessons was located on Washington Street in the heart of downtown Boston, and that evening hours were available, she must have leapt at the chance to get out of the house, with a good excuse that none could gainsay her.

Not only was she tired of being cooped up in the narrow confines of a housewife's house-bound existence, but she was feeling that she was not getting any younger, and she was missing the old days when she was single and she and Peggy used to occasionally go out on the town, even if just for a movie.

Besides, she reasoned, she had been through a lot, what with nursing her dying mother through her last days on earth, the terrible passage of her father's death, seeing that he was the one she doted on, and then her cesarean and the turmoil of bringing up underweight twin infants who couldn't be left to starve to death and required 24 hours a day of cooking, feeding, burping and cleaning before she herself could lay down her own head—goodness–she needed a break, a little diversion, some time to herself, just to be herself.

So she decided on a night out once a week, with a new boyfriend, and that turned out to be me.

I think she felt, too, that the time we spent going to Sunday mass at Immaculate Conception was just not enough time, or the right kind of time, being spent with just me and her. She was fulfilling her obligations to me and keeping her promise to bring me up the right way, but it was all so dutiful. There was no fun in it, and the way I was behaving, ever since the twins came along, told her something was amiss with me, too.

So Ma arranged for my lessons to be at seven pm, on Tuesday evenings, for the standard 30 minutes, which meant that there was plenty of time to fit in a movie for me and her afterwards.

For Ma, it was dress-up night. She would have gotten the butterball-twins ready early in the afternoon, and then spend a couple of hours on herself, bathing, dressing and making up in front of her mother's vanity, which she had moved into the bedroom she shared with Dad. After getting home from school,

I would spend hours quivering with anticipation. When I could stand it no longer I would sneak into her room to stand beside her and watch her in her mirror while she did lipstick and eyeshadow. She would still be in her girdle and bra and I would examine her reflection unabashed. It was exciting to be so near her, to be so intimate. She would be so self-absorbed she didn't notice I was there until I started to play with her lipstick on the vanity shelf at her elbow or lean my cheek on her shoulder. Then when I came out with something stupid, like "What does lipstick taste like? Can I try?" she would become suddenly impatient with me and shoo me away with, "No, you cannot. What's the matter with you! That's not for boys! Now get outta here and wait for me in the kitchen. And shut the door."

Then we would push the twins in their double carriage halfway up the steep incline of Reservoir Ave. to Auntie Mary LaStoria's house so she could watch them and we would double back to Broadway to catch the streetcar to Maverick Square.

I could tell she wasn't mad at me, even if I declared my independence by insisting I had to sit in a seat by myself, apart from her. I would peek back over my shoulder and catch her being proud of me. She would have me dressed up, too, the way I was for Sunday school, so when we got off at our stop I would rejoin her and slip a mittened hand into her suede-gloved hand. I was her little man.

Maestro Emilio's Music Shop was located near the corner of Boylston and Washington, downtown, opposite diagonally across the street from the Pilgrim Theater. It wasn't as pretentious as its name, but a humble storefront, with plate-glass windows on either side of the glass door that had No. 661 in gold-leaf numerals on it. They showcased instruments for sale in the window-bays either side, accordions on one side and clarinets and brass on the other.

The booths for giving lessons were on the second-floor walk-up above the store. You had to go up a narrow hallway with a steep flight of steps lined with bright green linoleum. If someone turned the corner at the top and wanted to come down, they had to wait for you.

My mother used to sit in a tiny waiting room lined with chairs with chrome arms and ripped red seat-covers, with other mothers and fathers, and she riffled through magazines, the kind they had in a barbershop, like *Ring Magazine,* the *Police Gazette* and *Charles Atlas.* The imaginations of Maestro Emilio and his teachers did not run as far as the *Ladies' Home Journal.*

But it was a social hour for my mother as she made friends with the other parents, no doubt to compare notes and commiserate over what it was costing them. My mother could be very competitive where I was concerned.

Meanwhile, in a lesson booth a little bit bigger than a phone booth, I would sit and study music with my teacher, Mr Tombarello. I was lucky. He taught children the right way. First he kept me six months playing only the right hand before he even let me touch the buttons on the left. He stressed correct fingering. He started me out on things like *Mary Had a Little Lamb* and *Three Blind Mice.* Of course, you had to learn how to read music.

From the very beginning, I found the world of the staff, the G-clef and the bass-clef, the treble keyboard and the bass-buttons, the whole notes, half-notes, quarter-notes and sixteenths a separate, fascinating universe, and I dove feet first into total immersion in this separate world that no one else knew about, unless they were specially initiated, like me and my teacher. I felt that even Miss Clark at school would be proud of me if she knew I, too, was studying music. And that's how Mr Tombarello approached it. "We are studying music, and we may never stop, because there is no end to it." And he would grant me a tender smile with a wistful look in his eyes.

After six weeks he told my mother. "He's a very conscientious boy. Does his homework, I can tell. He's improving every week. I think he's gonna make it. You may have a talented kid here, Mrs Petrovich, we'll see." And every six weeks he would have another sheet music book in the series to sell to my mother. I cherished these graduations. I loved to get promoted. Mr Tombarello would mark each lesson for me in the margin of the sheet music. He had only four grades: *Poor, Fair, Good,* and *Very Good*. He would write them in pencil at the bottom right of the page, and underline it twice. Sometimes, not often, he gave me a *Fair-Do Over*. That meant you had to stay on this same song for another whole week of practicing it. Mostly, I got *Goods* and *Very Goods*. Then you could get off that song and go to the next, and gradually they got harder. Which was how you learned.

As soon as the lesson was over, we would head up the street to theater row, where the neon glow of glamour and adventure beckoned. My mother took me to see pictures like *Peter Pan*, when that came out, or *The Robe*, or *Quo Vadis*, or *Shane*. You had your pick of the RKO Keith Memorial, the Loew's, the Paramount or the Orpheum. Those were the big theaters of Washington Street, the movie palaces showing the latest releases. We would sit there together in the dark devouring our popcorn before the Coming Attractions were finished. My mother knew all the stars. She would say, that's Jimmy Stewart or that's Lauren Bacall. The movies were so real to me I wondered how someone could be Alan Ladd and Shane at the same time.

When *Rear Window* came out, we went to see it at the Paramount, the grandest theater of them all. Everyone was dressed in their best overcoat or in matching heels and purse. The line to the ticket booth went snaking way down Washington Street. I clung to the back of the seat in front of me, knuckles white, my chin burrowing into the seat-back, while the killer slowly climbed the stairway on the left, with Grace Kelly, who you could see through the rear window of her apartment, and who you knew didn't know the murderer had his hand on her doorknob, was innocently combing her hair at the vanity, just the same way my mother did, and I wanted to scream, "Watch out!" I was never so terrified in all my life.

Afterwards, downstairs in Park Square, waiting for the trolley to take us back to Scollay Square, to change for the new line which had been opened to extend all the way out to Wonderland Park in Revere, my mother bought me a pack of *Juicy Fruit* for a nickel, my favorite, at the newsstand. "Were you scared?" she said. "Yeah," I gasped. "Me, too," she said.

Those days when I was first taking lessons were the days when I first discovered my mother loved me.

The end of our street dipped downhill, after you passed the foot of Tree Valley Road.

There was a time in my life when I did not pass that point in my wanderings, because I was being a good boy, doing what I was told.

But now that I was in the third grade and I was used to going downtown by myself to see my Dad at Page's shop or to go shopping at the A&P with Ma, now that I was accustomed to helping Auntie Mary LaStoria mind the twins, I was more grown-up, more responsible, and I felt more venturesome. I was ready to break the taboo, to set out exploring on my own.

When I crested that dip in Payson Street and saw for the first time what lay down there in the bottomland I became on the instant enthralled.

It was the far side of the moon. It was the towers of Timbuctoo. It was a ruin, like the mist-covered Scottish castle-ruins I had seen at the Orpheum in *The Master of Ballantrae*. It was a bombed-out lunar landscape that looked like the photos of Stuttgart or Mannheim I had perused so many times over and over in my Uncle's brown-covered Life magazine photo album of the war.

I had heard talk about the Brickyard from kids at school and now I was looking at it, from above, with a panoramic view, and it seemed an entire city unto itself, a legendary place, a citadel of the past, a lost civilization.

The Brickyard was an abandoned brick foundry which had gone over into disuse, nobody knew how many decades ago. The sweating men stripped to the waist who once had stoked the ovens there were now long dead.

But as you approached, past the last houses on Payson Street, you could not help but feel the haunting atmosphere which emanated from the Brickyard, like smoke still rising from the yawning arches. It was almost as if no one had dared build a house for people to live in any closer, down at the bottom. It was as if they were frightened to rouse the enmity of the ghosts who inhabited the Brickyard; they had not the temerity to approach any closer.

Payson Street itself was abandoned to weeds as you came nearer to the verge. The very asphalt of the paving crumbled into clops and crevasses, and then there was only dirt, and sand. And then you were entering the Brickyard.

I climbed over piles of bricks and brick-dust. I ran my hands along stuttering walls. I peeked round the edges of the arches of the old ovens to look into the interiors of what seemed to be the houses of Pompeii buried in the avalanches of smoke and soot and molten, pouring rivers.

There were two colors in the Brickyard, dun-colored red brick, and powdery grey concrete. Only weeds survived there, and they were not healthy and green, but wilted and brown and downtrodden with the effort to rise out of the ruined soil.

I adopted the Brickyard as my secret playground. I told my mother nothing about going there. It was my own personal Leptis Magna. I played the part of the Lone Ranger there, and Tonto, too. I was Sgt Rock from DC Comics and I re-fought the Second World War in the Brickyard at the end of my street. I rescued fair maidens and machine-gunned dirty Nazis. I was Lancelot, Gawain and Galahad all rolled into one. I was a Roman Centurion on guard at the gates. I was the last man standing at Stalingrad.

The greatest mystery I discovered from the Brickyard was the idea that it might have been at one time much more extensive than it was now, in 1953.

This discovery occurred when I let Billy Merritt next door in on my secret. He claimed to know all about the Brickyard before I ever told him.

"Did you ever see the Indian grave up on the hill?" said Billy.

"An Indian grave?"

"Yeah. It's right behind your house."

Billy took me round the corner of Tree Valley Road and we crossed through somebody's backyard till we got to the rear of the property from Cary Ave. that abutted Papanonni's cement wall at the back of his garden. Sure enough, there was a hole in the ground up there on that hillock, but it was man-made, not burrowed by some animal. You could tell because it was square and when you pushed back the margins of the overhanging grass you could see bricks embedded underneath.

"This is your Indian grave?" I said to Billy.

"How much you wanna bet there's arrowheads down there?"

"How would you know?"

"I been down there. Go see for yourself."

"Is it deep?"

"Oh, don't worry. I'll pull you back out. Whatsa matta?—you chicken?"

I lowered myself into the square hole with considerable trepidation. When I was dangling in there, with my elbows askew holding me halfway in, I still couldn't feel the ground beneath my feet. I let myself drop and I was squatting on dank wet black earth, with four walls of bricks surrounding me, at arm's length. It was so dark I could see nothing. I ran my hands along the soil like a blind man, and then I felt it. It was pointed and had sharp edges. I saw sky above my head in the square opening, but no Billy. I threw out the object.

"Hey!" I yelled. "Get me outta here!"

I saw Billy's grinning face peer down over the edge. He reached in and pulled me up.

We cleaned the packed dirt off the object, and it lay there on a bed of grass, unmistakably an arrowhead.

"Told ya," said Billy.

Yes, he did.

I never knew, then or later, how that square hole in the ground got up there on that hill, nor the nature of the brick-lined chamber beneath it. I suspected it was all a part of an extension of the Brickyard some quarter of a mile distant. But it remained a mystery. And of course I never told my mother about that day when I descended into the damp tomb-like darkness of the fabled Underground. But after that Billy and I often went up there to play and took turns lowering each other down. It was cold and clammy down there. Every time I came back up I had the feeling of being rescued from a grave.

I was playing down the street in the Brickyard by myself on a Saturday in late April when I realized the nice weather had me losing track of the time and I better get back home before I was late for supper. Saturday night was always Ma's night for hot dogs and beans and the very thought made me hungry, if I wasn't already. As I came up across the rise in Payson Street I was astounded to see Uncle Tommy DiPrima's two-ton truck parked outside our house and Uncle Tommy and Uncle Augie coming down the front steps vigorously balancing Ma's side table from the dining room. I knew that Uncle Tommy drove for a moving company and I started running as fast as I could. I ran past Uncle Patsy's Hudson parked at the curb outside the house on the corner of Tree Valley Road. Then came the Merritt 's house and Uncle Gene's DeSoto was parked outside Billy and Paul's. The whole family was there! I rounded the nose of Uncle Tommy's cab and that's when I saw my father on the tiny front lawn inside the chain-link fence chopping up Papanonni's player piano with an ax! Freshly bleeding splintered wood with its yellow insides torn like corn husks was lying askance every-which-way all over the lawn and my Dad was sweating and swearing in a sleeveless tee-shirt as he tried to pull piano wire out of the guts of the wood-pile.

"What is he doing to the piano?" I cried, beside myself.

My mother was there and her reply was, "Where have you been all this time? We were looking for you everywhere!"

I was jumping up and down. "What's going on? Tell him to stop!"

"We're moving, and it's too big to take with us. We could never fit it in the truck. It would've been impossible to lift. Your father had to take out all the windows on the *piazza* to push it out on the lawn and it still took him and three of your Uncles! What am I doing, explaining to you!"

"Ma–whaddya mean, we're moving!"

"I sold the house."

"You sold Papanonni's house!"

I saw Auntie Mary LaStoria pushing the twins in their stroller back and forth in front of the driveway gates, and she wrinkled her forehead in sympathy when she saw me so agitated.

"We can't leave here! That's my school over there, all my friends are here, this is *my* house!"

"Nicky, now, that's enough," said Ma. "You get over here and behave yourself—my house!"

"I won't, I won't." I looked beseechingly at Auntie Mary and she looked distraught. She was a gentle soul who hated to see anyone fighting.

"*Ah fa nabbala*," said Ma, and she slipped into torrential Italian, addressed to Auntie Mary, which amounted to, *I knew this was going to happen, and I couldn't find him the whole day long to get him out of here.*

I knew exactly what she was saying, but I had to jump out of the way because my two uncles were coming with the sideboard. I didn't know what to do but I found myself running circles around the truck with my chest heaving trying to contain my fury and keep myself from bursting into tears.

It was getting late in the day, the truck was packed to capacity, and they were revving up the motor, ready to leave, and my mother was yelling at me to jump into Uncle Patsy's car with the twins and Auntie Mary because we were going to stay in Watertown tonight.

"Watertown!" I knew my Uncle Gene and his family lived there, on Boylston Street, Uncle Tommy and Auntie Anna, too, on School Street, and also Auntie Mary Laverna and Uncle Charlie, on Dewey Street, with cousins Tony and Gerry—the whole family lived in Watertown! *Now us, too?*

"Ma—why can't I just stay with Auntie Mary and Uncle Patsy over on Reservoir Ave.—at least I could keep going to the Shurtleff!"

"Nicky, cut it out, I mean it. You're gonna get the biggest lickin' of your life if you don't stop this right now! You're embarrassing me!"

I saw my mother glance up at Mrs Merritt, who was watching out her front window at all the commotion.

I ran up the steps to the Merritts.'

The front of their house was not arranged in the same manner as ours. Mrs Merritt had a brown-shingled covered entryway with a peaked roof and side windows. I threw open the outer door with the glass panes and confronted the front door to her house, which was solid, with a fanlight high up. I was banging furiously on her door and I could see her on tiptoe looking down from the fanlight. The poor lady was quietly opening her door and I was gasping out, "Mrs Merritt, can I stay with you and Billy and Paul?" while my mother came crashing through the glass-door behind me, thoroughly humiliated by my behavior, and Mrs Merritt found herself suddenly embroiled in a domestic farce not of her own making. Both women rushed to apologize, as if each of them were at fault, and then to reassure one another that *everything will be all right, he'll settle down, just one of those things, I don't mind, not at all, I understand, I'm so sorry, don't apologize,* and so on and so on and–.

But I was hellbent in my own mind that I would never settle down and never would I forgive them, *ever,* and I was going to make them have to kidnap me, and as I was bundled into the back seat of Uncle Patsy's car, with Uncle Augie assigned to sit on me, if necessary, I twisted myself pretzel-wise to get one last-chance lingering look out the back window of the Hudson as we pulled away down Payson Street, the last glimpse I would ever have of the earthly paradise where I was born.

Part 2

SPICKET FALLS

Chapter 7

The Cat in the Hallway

My exile began in 1954 in a place called Watertown.

My very first night torn from my roots was spent on the second story of a rundown building on a side-street called Grove Street.

My first complaint was, "Ma, the back hall stinks."

"Well, get used to it. The landlady has a cat."

How we had come down in the world! Back in Revere my mother was the landlady and Mrs Nelson upstairs was our tenant. Now we had to live on the second floor and we were the tenants.

Grove Street branched off a main cross-street called Arlington Street, which intersected with another prominent artery called Mt Auburn Street. This crossroads, Coolidge Square, bled into a nondescript strip of neighborhood shops, the Town Diner, the Victoria Spa, Stella Pizza, a Mobil gas station with the flying red horse, and the Mt Auburn Grill. Anchoring Coolidge Square was the massive yellow-brick edifice of the Bell Telephone Building on the southeast corner. Across Mt Auburn

Street, the long east-west thoroughfare that led from Harvard Square in Cambridge all the way to Watertown Square, was the Coolidge School—where I had to go, starting Monday morning.

The expression 'going down the Square' back in Revere meant you were going down to Broadway, the biggest street in the city, where all the landmarks were located, from the fire-station to the Gloria Chain store to the Shawmut Bank, the A&P, Page's Woodworking, where my father worked, the Revere Theater, the City Hall, the Police Station and the high-school football stadium where my father had taken me to see the 4th of July fireworks.

Coolidge Square in Watertown was not even the center of the city.

But although I had no roots in Watertown, it was more than familiar to Ma, and I had first cousins who were born and raised there who called it their hometown.

Back before my time, at the beginning of the war, Papanonni had moved from Stoughton, on the South Shore, to Watertown, to be closer to his work in Boston. Wartime gas restrictions meant he would have to become a streetcar and subway commuter again. Ma was already a grown woman of 21 when that happened.

They lived on Kimball Road, which entered on Coolidge Square; Uncle Augie lived there, too, before he went away in the service. Their sister, Mary Laverna, was already living close by on Dewey Street, which ran behind the Coolidge School, ever since she got married to Serafino Laverna, back in '36. No doubt she was the main reason the rest of them ended up in Watertown when Papanonni was house-hunting.

Eventually, when the war ended, Uncle Gene LaStoria was re-settled on Boylston Street. Watertown was his wife Celia's hometown. Auntie Anna, when she married Tommy DiPrima, had traded up to a two-family on School Street, the next big cross street on Mt Auburn before Watertown Square: St Theresa's Church, with its beautiful bell-tower, was located at this intersection.

Meanwhile, Papanonni, who was only renting on Kimball Road, had found the house he wanted to buy, with land enough for his garden, grape-arbor and dog-kennel, in Revere, so he left Watertown, followed by his son Patsy, his wife, Mary, and son Anthony, called by that name so that the family could distinguish him from Mary Laverna's boy, Tony.

Now, in 1954, Papanonni was gone, Mamanonna, too, so were the dogs, the grape-arbor, the wine cellar, Mamanonna's mason-jars of homemade preserves, the big wash-tub that used to be in the back hall on Payson Street, the player-piano, the old way of life. Jettisoned to the junkpile. I never did find out whatever happened to my grandfather's old bowl-backed mandolin.

In 1954, in Watertown, I had cousins on Dewey Street, School Street and Boylston Street.

But it didn't matter to me.

My mother was circling back to another, earlier period in, not only her own life, but that of the family circle.

My father was just along for the ride.

There were plans afoot in my mother's family that I knew nothing about.

Uncle Patsy had sold his two-family on Reservoir Ave. in Revere and found a newly-built single-home, a nice Cape

Cod-style house, on Reynolds Road, in a new development in Peabody, north of Salem.

Auntie Peggy was left behind, alone, in Revere, in her little studio flat on the corner of Revere Street and North Shore Road. Even Henry and Ronnie had gone to stay in Wilmington with their father and his new wife for the interim.

My father was going to have to look for work. He had just turned journeyman carpenter and joined the Massachusetts Carpenter's Union.

That first weekend Ma was at her wit's end trying to move all our belongings into a cramped two-bedroom 2nd-floor renter's flat. She was going to have to pay 70 bucks a month for this dump, and it did not improve her mood. The twins, Jack and Jill, were two years old now and constantly underfoot just when she needed them to go take a nap. Everybody from Uncle Charlie Laverna to Uncle Tommy DiPrima was over to our place for the whole weekend to help Ma get settled: all of them talking, laughing and dispensing free advice.

Ma told them all, standing there with pizza slices and beer bottles, "If you're not gonna lend a hand, get outta my way!"

Uncle Gene was deep in consultation with Uncle Patsy, Uncle Augie and Uncle Tommy, and Auntie Mary Laverna, about their plans.

Only Uncle Tommy, the truck-driver, wasn't buying in. He needed his wife Anna staying put, right here in Watertown. All of his own family, the DiPrimas, his brothers Bruno and Freddy, and his sisters, Gloria and Estelle, were in Watertown, all his old friends from Watertown High, from before the war.

Uncle Gene also had his daughter, Joanne LaStoria, who was my cousin Gerry Laverna's age; as well as Leon, a toddler, and Marie, still an infant; he said, "Fine, I'm not moving from Watertown, either. My kid is in school."

How I wished my mother had thought of that when it came to me.

Uncle Gene was not as tall as his brother Augie, or his brother-in-law Tommy, or even his brother Patsy, but he was the handsomest of them all, the one with the most All-American looks, the one with the business-manager's sense inherited from his father; and like his father, his shirt was always pressed, clean, and one color, white. The collar might be open and the sleeves rolled up, but it was a white shirt.

I had no idea what was going on. Nor was my Dad being consulted. Although, as he confided in me, "I'm sure they'll find they need me, to fix this, and build that—for nothin', of course. What's a brother-in-law for?"

Dad said he was gonna get him a paying job on one of them new developments going up so fast these days out in the suburbs, like the one in Peabody that Uncle Patsy and Auntie Mary were moving to with my cousins Anthony and Linda. All he was waiting for was for a phone call from the union hall. 'Course he was gonna have to get him a car. He could just see what Ma would have to say about that. "We're in for it, buddy. We're in for it now."

We were taking a breather out on the back steps. I had never entered my own house through the front door in my life and I wasn't about to start now, cat's pee in the hallway or no. I was spending a miserable first weekend in Watertown, mad at the world, and when Monday morning came, I had to go to a new school where I knew no-one and no-one knew me.

Mercifully, the schoolyear ended and summer vacation came before I had to talk to anyone at the Coolidge.

I went there with my mind made up from the start that I didn't belong. I didn't want to make friends. I didn't want to wait in line at the stoplights in the morning for the crossing guard with the white garrison belt to lead us children in front of the growling cars he held up with the red-light button at Arlington and Mt Auburn. I had never walked to school before. In Revere, I had only to cross the street from my house. Here the other kids came trickling out of Grove Street and the side streets adjacent to Arlington Street, in twos and threes, and they were friends and neighbors, they knew each other since first grade. I didn't want to look at them and I didn't want them looking at me. I didn't want to hear *who are you?* and *where did you come from?* I was an intruder on my own life.

At recess, I didn't want to play. The recess area outside was flanking Arlington and Mt Auburn and was penned in with a high chain-link fence. It was a prison-yard. All that was missing was the barbed wire. The playground the fence enclosed was scrubby dirt and dying grass, nothing like the solid blacktop of the schoolyard at the Shurtleff, with its winter sledding slope and springtime jungle-gym. I missed the games we used to play at the Shurtleff. Tackle football there was banned, even for the sixth-graders, because the hard pavements would tear you up, but instead, everybody played stickball. Because it was the back of the school facing my house, and not the front, the janitor had put a white-painted circle on the back wall of the school, under the row of windows on the first floor, on the right-hand side of the playground. That was our strike zone. Our bats were made out of ordinary house-broom handles. The ball was a pinkish hollow rubber-ball so that, after every pitch, it would bounce back off the brick wall of the school to the pitcher's hand. Nobody played catcher. A catcher wasn't needed. The rest of us would spread out in the outfield. We had a diamond painted on the tar and the corners of the diamond were the bases. If somebody hit a home-run, it would go over our heads and bounce high off the sidewalk at the top of the sledding-slope and maybe go over the roof of a passing car. We'd have to chase the ball down up against the little white ankle-high railing in front of the Merritt's house. When I got to the third grade in Revere, I was big enough to get picked by the big kids when they were choosing up sides. At recess, we'd be having a stickball game on the right-hand side of the schoolyard while the girls played jump-rope on the other. In Watertown, nobody played stickball. I couldn't understand it. The girls at the Coolidge skipped rope, but the boys? How could they not play stickball?

That summer in Watertown, I was driven back on my books. I could not locate a library in the town. If there was one, it must be miles away. In Revere, I had the entire Carnegie Library conveniently two blocks from my house; here I had to depend on the library at the Coolidge School, which was barely one room. And you couldn't spend the afternoon there after the bell rang to send you home.

Then on the way home there was the temptation of the Golden Cookie Factory.

My first few days in school I noticed right away that all the kids walking home on Grove Street never failed to drop into the main door of the two-story yellow-brick building on the left. I broke my rule and asked someone what was going on, and was told, "You can get all the free cookies you want, only they're a day old."

I waited for a day when I thought I could slip in unnoticed.

There were double-glass doors in the entryway which admitted you to a factory outlet showcase room on your right.

Nobody was in attendance and all the cookies were inside a bakery case. You couldn't see into the factory; there was no office, like at school, and everything smelled like cookie crumbs.

Magically, a lady appeared through a door. I tried to glimpse inside but she was too quick for me. Evidently it was a national secret of some kind, how they made those cookies. She asked, nicely enough, if she could help me.

"Well, the kids told me you give away free cookies."

She was already opening a wax-paper bag.

"Not too many now, we don't wanna spoil your supper."

Grownups were always worried about spoiling your supper, or spoiling *you,* if they spared the rod.

I devoured my bagful before I got home.

Soon enough I was getting the third degree from Ma about my poor appetite.

I also discovered they made only one kind of cookie at the Golden Cookie Factory, vanilla cookies with vanilla-cream fillings. I guess that's where they got the Golden Cookie idea. But I didn't mind. I got to looking forward, actually, to walking home by myself, and keeping all those cookies to myself. Even a day old, they tasted better to me than Oreos bought from the store. Although that did not stop me from eating those when I got home and Ma wasn't looking. Glass of milk, too, while you're at it. I was allowed a snack after school, that wouldn't spoil my supper. However, I didn't escape censure from Ma, who thought it was her job to have a finger on the pulsation of everything that went on in her house.

"I dunno," she said one day. "I cook you everything good to eat, and you can't clean your plate? Don't you know a growing boy needs his nourishment?"

When she started taking it out on the supper dishes that she was theoretically washing in the sink, that was my cue to slip into the other room and watch 15 minutes of news on Uncle Augie's TV. That's how I knew that the Korean War was over and President Eisenhower had gone golfing. I still wasn't allowed to stay up and watch TV after seven on a school night. Ma herself never sat down till she had the whole house cleaned and the twins put to bed. I would hear gushers of laughter coming out of the other room at whatever they were watching on TV and feel left out and cheated. Dad was working now as a journeyman carpenter faraway in some town called Middleton in a big development where they were throwing up dozens of wood-frame houses. That was his job, doing the framing. Other carpenters came in after him and the crew he was in to hang the doors and windows and do the finish work. They were the master carpenters. Dad's crew went back in after that to do the roof shingles and the clapboarding. Dad had picked up a little used Studebaker and Ma was making him bring her his receipts from the gas station. This was not an expenditure she had ever had to budget for before. That was her father's province, but, now, he wasn't here, so it was up to her to step into his shoes. All this I was picking up at the supper table with my big ears. Uncle Augie was getting home later in the evening, too, because he was riding to work every day with Uncle Gene in Uncle Gene's DeSoto, to someplace even further away than Middleton, a city called Milltown. Later, lying in bed, trying my mightiest to eavesdrop on the TV show, without success, I would get my flashlight out and open a book. I was reading about Thor Heyderdahl on a raft in the South Pacific sailing out to the giant statues on Easter Island in *The Saturday Evening Post*. I was reading about Sir Gawain and the Green Knight, as well as The Race to the South Pole between Scott and Amundsen, way back in 1912, which was before the First World War, even, in my 10-volume set of *Collier's Junior Classics*, with *Stories That Never Grow Old, Hero Tales, and Sport and Adventure*. They were telling me before I left the Shurtleff that I was reading on an 8th grade level. *Treasure Island* was an old standby which I was reading over again that summer for perhaps the tenth time, and Uncle Augie was steering me onto the big rocks with his recommendations for must-reading for boys. He turned up one night with paperback copies of Horatio Alger from the drugstore, titles which I didn't already have, *Luck and Pluck, Fame and Fortune,* and *Sink or Swim,* and he also got me started on the *Illustrated Classics* comic books, with *Mutiny on the Bounty* and *The Virginian*.

"What's the matter with you," my mother said. "how come you never go out to play anymore?"

"Have you seen the yard out there, Ma?"

There was a bald, muddy path worn into the brown grass on one side of our dingy brown hovel of a house on Grove Street, a path I trudged with my head down on my way to the back door after school—the back door leading into the dim shadowy back hall that smelled like cat's pee.

"Besides, there's nobody to play with." I was being obsessive about every detail of life in Watertown that year because I felt so wronged about being torn way from Revere—*my* hometown.

"Well, I don't blame you if you don't know anybody in this neighborhood. But you know your cousin Tommy. Why don't you go over Auntie Anna's house on School Street and play with him. The two of you are the same age, for cryin' out loud."

"You'll let me?"

"As long as you behave yourself over there. If I get any bad reports from your Auntie Anna, that'll be the end of that. You know how she is. Not like me. Fussy about her furniture."

Thank God for my cousin, Tommy DiPrima. He saved my summer. The first time I went over there, he led me to his mother's back hall, where he had his ball, bat and glove stashed behind the sliding masonite door under the built-in coat-rack closet that my Dad had put in for Auntie Anna and Uncle Tom.

"Wanna go down the Hosmer and play some ball?" said Tommy.

"Is that where you go to school?"

"Yeah, of course, it's right around the corner."

I peered into the shadows as Tommy pulled out a scuffy brown baseball with a worn cover, torn where some red threads still stuck out, taped round and round with sticky, bulging black electrician's tape.

"Oh," I said. "My mother won't let me play hardball."

"Why not?"

"She's worried I'll get hit in the head, like Uncle Augie did one time."

My tall, skinny cousin, Tommy DiPrima, looked down at me, sadly shaking his head.

"You don't have to do what your mother tells you to do all the time, you know."

Nobody had ever told me that before. I must have looked dumbfounded, because Tommy turned to push open the screen-door to his back porch, still shaking his head.

"Come on. Let's go. You carry the bat. You're lucky I got an extra glove I'll let you use."

We played hardball down the Hosmer every day that summer, and I forgot all about the Golden Cookie Factory.

Chapter 8

The Bronte Sisters

Watertown was a small, tidy city of about 25,000 souls bordering on the northern bank of the Charles River, wedged between Newton and Waltham and Belmont, just to the west of Harvard Square and the city of Cambridge. It was a bedroom community, for all I could tell, full of neat and tidy two-families, dotted with a sprinkling of single-homes that looked more modern, to my eyes, although it was known for the massive Watertown Arsenal, which since the end of the war had gone into disuse. To my mind, the people who lived in Watertown, like my Uncle Gene and Uncle Augie, my Dad, too, worked elsewhere. Well, they weren't building any new homes in Watertown. The city was already built and had run out of room.

The only difference between Watertown and Revere was the difference between the Arsenal and The Beach. Otherwise they were identical, the same city, about 13 miles apart, if you went by the Revere Beach Parkway, which we always did, once my Dad got the Studebaker.

Every day that baseball summer of '54 with my cousin Tom at the Hosmer ballfield, I would beg my mother for the carfare to Revere. I knew how to get there on the subway because of all our trips into town for my music lessons. You picked up the new line to Revere at the Haymarket station after switching from Park Square through Scollay Square. The two occasions my mother had taken me on the subway out to Watertown to visit her sister Mary and my cousins Tony and Gerry on Dewey Street had enabled me to memorize the route from downtown Boston on the subway across the Charles out to Harvard Square, from which you then changed to the trackless trolley to Watertown.

I may as well have asked my mother's permission to run away from home.

Nor was I going to get an allowance, like my cousin Tom got from his mother. I complained that it was embarrassing to always be having Tommy buy me a popsicle all the time. I got the lecture about how kids today didn't know how lucky we were, we should try growing up in the Depression, like they had to when they were kids, and, furthermore, if cousin Tommy goes jumping off a bridge, does that mean you're going to follow him?

My Dad knew I missed Revere almost as much as he sometimes missed his old childhood home grounds in faroff Western Pennsylvania. We were buddies. So surreptitiously, on the weekend, a couple of times that summer, when my mother sent him grocery shopping, he would let me come along, and then drive me to Revere, where we would cruise up and down Payson Street a couple of times, so that I could sit there gazing out the window at our house, and try to picture who could possibly be living there now.

I quickly got to be at home on the route from Watertown to Revere by way of the Fresh Pond Parkway and the Revere Beach Parkway. That route avoided the traffic jams on Memorial

Drive, and also the toll-booths on the Mystic River Bridge to Chelsea. That route took you through Arlington and Somerville and Medford and Everett and Chelsea before you got to Revere. It was a winding route with lots of scenery, stoplights, the Somerville high-school football stadium, even a stream or two, a brook, a creek, or a tributary of the Mystic, and looking out the window with my Dad driving, I memorized every intersection, bridge, tree and bush.

Ma would be irate by the time we got home.

"What took you so long?"

"Gerry, we went to Revere, so we could find the things on your list from the A&P, and the Gloria Chain."

"And how much did that cost me in gas? For cryin' out loud, you could go to the Star Market, right down the street here in Watertown!"

"Judas Priest, you're never satisfied."

My mother was digging through the paper bags. "Look at this! SOS pads! I told you Brillo pads!"

My poor dad got yelled at on my account.

Cringing, I stole into the next room, to sit on the couch, where the twins were staring at Rex Trailer on the television.

No sooner had I found a best friend in my cousin Tommy than I was torn away again, to start all over again, in a new place, with new kids I had never met and, in any case, didn't want to know.

Despite my familiarity with the MTA, I had never been to Dorchester, or Mattapan, or Southie. Therefore, I had never seen a triple-decker in my life, and nothing had prepared me for Milltown.

I should have known something was up. In fact, I did know, ever since that day they were loading up Uncle Tommy's truck outside the house in Revere. I just tried to put it out of my mind because I got to thinking hateful thoughts about my mother. My Dad was exempted from blame, by me, because I could tell he was just along for the ride. None of this was his doing. It was all Ma's family, her and her brothers, especially Uncle Gene.

However, I didn't blame him. I liked Uncle Gene. He was as easy-going as his brothers Patsy and Augie. A kid couldn't ask for any better than those three. They were confident and self-assured in the manner of the war veterans who came home to claim their rightful place in society, and found everything changed for the better in the early fifties, now that the Depression and the war and the Forties were over. It was a new day, it was their day, and they had earned the right to relax. Nobody was more easy-going than Uncle Gene, except maybe my Dad, and yet Uncle Gene had taken all the burden of starting a new family-business venture on his own shoulders, for the benefit of everybody. I knew it was something sacred to him when I heard him proposing, that day in Revere, that they should call the new family business, *Gigi Sportswear*, in honor of their mother, Gigi, who had given them their start in life.

Now his plans were finally coming to fruition. That's why we were moving to Milltown. Uncle Gene had found cheap space to rent in nearby Spicket Falls. Dad was going to be closer to his job at the housing development in Middleton, and Ma was going to go to work for her brother Gene in Spicket Falls, as one of his stitchers.

Milltown was built on the banks of the Merrimack River in a bygone age, the 1840s, long before my grandfather ever came to America.

Eugene Christy

It was built as a designed city by a consortium of rich Yankee industrialists with names like Abbott and Bartlett and Saunders and Nesmith, who formed the Water Power Association to buy up the land on the north and south banks of the Merrimack. The Great Stone Dam was built starting in 1845 by Irish immigrants who hauled stout blocks of granite down from the mountains of New Hampshire by oxen-sled. These were the men who worked and died to build the great dam on the Merrimack and the canals on the north and south bank that would power the new mills. Milltown was designated by its owners for the manufacture of woolen textiles. Lowell, further upriver, was the cotton capital, and Haverhill, downriver, the shoe-city. The lowrise outline of massive redbrick mill buildings, hugging the riverbanks, once the fishing grounds of the Pentucket tribe, became the profile of Milltown.

I had never seen anything like it. For a boy going into the fourth grade who would be turning nine at the end of 1955, the mills of Milltown blotted out the sun and dwarfed humanity.

The Wood Mill, on the southern bank of the river on the east end of the city, was the largest woolen mill in the world. This mill alone was a mile long running down the straight-arrow length of Merrimack Street in South Milltown. On the opposite bank, on the same part of the river, where the green girders of the Duck Bridge carried you over from South Union Street to Union Street, was the enormous six-story monolith of the Everett Mills. If you stood at the end of Essex Street, the main shopping street of the city, in North Milltown, as I did when I first came to the city, the Everett Mills cast the entire Roman Catholic Church of the Sacred Heart, on the corner of Essex and Union, including its steeple, into shadow.

And the towering smokestacks of Milltown, which dotted the horizon, stately and tall, in the late afternoon sunset of early

September, were the tapering redbrick sentinels of a ghostly past, a past, for me, still waiting to be discovered.

I was not about to make the same mistake I made when I landed in Watertown, to retreat into a cocoon so smothering that only my cousin Tommy could pull me out of it. There wasn't going to be any Tommy this time. I was going to have to make friends of my own, or else withdraw completely—into what? Books? I had a whole city to explore. I could thank Tommy for my liberation from Ma's dictatorship, and it came just in time for Milltown. I simply omitted to tell my mother where I was going and what I was doing. It was easy. I just let myself out the back door and I was gone.

We were living in the upstairs flat on the corner of Winthrop Ave. and Boxford Street in South Milltown. Mr Torrini, the landlord, and his family lived downstairs. He owned the Italian supermarket over on South Union Street. Ma found the place one day when she spotted a *Flat to Let* sign in the window. Dad was driving us in the Studebaker from visiting Uncle Patsy's on Reynolds Road in Peabody. The highway from Peabody to Milltown was Route 114, which passed the foot of Reynolds Road and, at the other end, 15 miles away, became Winthrop Ave when it entered South Milltown. So Ma stopped right then and there because she felt she was going to be living on the same road as her brother.

What Ma did not know, or care to find out, was that Boxford Street, a very long east-west street cutting through the entire south side of the city, on this short section of it, after it crossed Winthrop Ave, came up short, abutting directly on the massive South Milltown railroad yards. The sign at the corner of the street warned: *Dead End.* We were now going to be living on the proverbial 'other side of the tracks.'

As I never went out the front door, when I came down the back hall from our upstairs flat, I emerged down the back steps and went through the gate in the chain fence, which let me out on the Boxford Street side of the house.

Behind our house was a duplex.

Then came a three-decker, the first I had ever seen; and then one more two-family, and then a board fence, with a hole in it, at the foot of the boardings, which dogs had burrowed out. It looked big enough for a boy my size to slip under. But I decided I better not. On the other side of that fence was the railroad yards.

I went out instead to the corner at the front of our house and turned left on Winthrop Ave, heading north towards where I suspected the river to be.

The first place I came across was the library I had failed to find in Watertown. To my disappointment, this yellow-brick oblong building on the corner of Parker and Bailey turned out to be only a branch library. But across Parker Street from the library was the school where I was going to start fourth grade on Monday morning. This was a public school called the Packard, which, like the Shurtleff in Revere, was red-brick and looked to be from the last century, and moreover, was surrounded on all four sides by a black-top schoolyard, just like the Shurtleff. But unlike my old school, this one was closed in with a chain-link fence which made the schoolyard look like a compound in a penitentiary.

Next to the library on Parker Street, at the intersection of Salem Street, there was a parochial school called St Patrick's. It was also solidly red-brick, but much tidier-looking, and bigger, in two segmented sections, than my school, the Packard. I knew my mother wasn't going to send me there because it cost money, and public school was free.

So far, I hadn't yet glimpsed sight of the river, but I decided to turn left on Salem Street and see what I found.

That led me across a green-girdered, hump-backed bridge over the railroad tracks to a long street heading north and south. South Broadway was the main street of South Milltown. At the stoplights, to my left stood the stout brick pile of St Patrick's Church. This church replicated the recurring redbrick theme of all the massive working-class mills of the city. Yet it did not veer too close to the holy or heavenly, but evoked instead a formidable Irish lace-curtain respectability.

Across from the church, further northward on South Broadway, a storefront caught my eye because of the rows of shiny new bicycles for sale behind plate-glass windows. It was called *Victor Hugo*, why, I didn't know. Maybe the owner of the store? But I didn't stop to look in the windows there because something told me the river was not far off.

This came to me as a whisper, subtle at first. I headed north toward the whispering. There was a lot of traffic heading in both directions out in the street. But everything looked so different than when you were riding in a car. You could stop and look, gaze, survey, turn around completely till you came back to where you started. Gradually the whisper turned into low throaty roar which actually hummed louder than the sound of the traffic.

I came to the corner of the thick concrete railing bordering the Broadway Bridge where the cornerstone said *1935*, and balancing my elbows on the top of the railings with my hands over my ears I gazed out on the magnificent outpouring of the Falls of the Merrimack.

Pencil-strokes of white water came endlessly over the top in a perfectly rounded and smooth stream. A white wall of water gave rise to clouds of mist from the collision with the dark rocks at the bottom of the stone dam. From there squiggles and curlicues of white foam snaked their way toward you and went draining and speeding under the bridge you were standing on, a bewitching dance of banners, pennants and folderols of foam, tempting you to peek over and follow them into the shadows under the bridge. But the thickness of the bridge railings cut off your line of sight.

I raced across the road between cars and caught myself on the railings of the other side, only to find all the white foam dissipating as it emerged from under the Broadway Bridge.

Disappointed, I suddenly caught sight of the black iron railroad bridge running parallel to the auto-bridge, standing on thin girder-legs spread spider-wide and planted in the slippery river bottom. I ran around the cornerstone of the Broadway Bridge, heading for the railroad bridge.

I didn't know what I thought I was doing. The wild impulse to cross the river on that flimsy-looking black iron railroad bridge took me by surprise.

I stood there debating with myself. Did I dare to double-dare? Or, at this exact moment of confronting all the brand-new temptations of my very first days in Milltown, was I going to back down? Would I disappoint myself and have to slink away defeated? Finally, I chose. Finally, I made up my mind. *I just had to try. I had to.*

My heart was high up in my chest at the root of my throat as I walked precariously across the railroad bridge, looking down between the railroad ties I was walking on, step by careful step, at black water, swirling sixty feet below.

Looking down was dizzying and desperately I did not wish to throw myself off balance. I better get hold of things and make sure I made it across.

Now and then I would look up from under my brows to scan the endless redbrick walls of mill-buildings in a solid rank on the northern bank of the Merrimack, a wall which headed downriver from the Falls as far as the eye could see.

The thrill of danger was intoxicating. The specter of what would happen to me should I slip and fall rose up each time I glimpsed the jagged rocks below angrily bubbling with dirty white foam.

Finally—finally!—I came to the end of the railroad bridge and verily *leapt* back onto the solidity of a sandy stretch of pebbly ground. I realized with horror that I had been holding my breath for what seemed like the whole way across.

In time, in time, I would come to see the legendary names of those mills, lined up on both banks of the Merrimack, names carved in granite lintels over dim-lit doorways—the Ayer Mills, the Everett Mills, the Arlington Mills, the Wood Mill, the Upper Pacific Mills, the Duck Mill, the Lower Pacific Mills, the Washington Mills—as blots upon the landscape, as curses cast against the high hopes of youth.

But not on that day.

Downstairs at the Torrini's apartment the landlord and landlady had two daughters with jet-black pigtails and charcoal-pencil eyebrows called Charlotte and Emily. They were not twins like my brother and sister, but they were close in age. Charlotte was going on 9, like me, and Emily was going on 7. Charlotte was in my class at the Packard. They used to camp out on the back steps of their house, and they were pretty bossy.

The first time I met them, they were sitting on the steps and they wouldn't let me pass.

I was coming downstairs from our flat with the plan of going to my new South Milltown Branch Library up the road on Parker Street to take out a card and borrow some books to read.

"Excuse me," I said.

"No," said Charlotte.

"No!" said Emily, with clenched jaw.

"If you just move over a squidge, I can get by."

"This is our house. You don't get by without paying a toll."

"I don't have any money. Besides, our rent is paid. Ask my mother. Or ask your father."

I knew that because Ma had been complaining that Mr Torrini wanted a whole extra month's rent for a security deposit just to let us into the flat upstairs before we even lived there, and she had to give it. She drew the line at signing a year's lease, though, telling him we were only gonna stay 6 months.

"Are you gonna pay the toll?" said Charlotte.

"What's the toll gonna be today?" said Emily.

"A pork-chop bone," said Charlotte, giggling.

"I don't have one of them either."

"Our Daddy's a butcher," said Emily, smugly. "We've got plenty of pork-chop bones."

"Are you girls gonna move over?" I was losing my patience.

"You'll just have to step over us," said one.

"Like to see you try," said the other.

I grabbed the wrought-iron railing next to Emily's shoulder, took a giant step backwards, launched myself, and easily cleared their heads with my feet as they ducked and I vaulted over the railing, making sure to hang on tight with my right hand so that I wouldn't crash-land on my rear.

"Boy," said Emily. "What a show-off you are!"

I was letting myself out the gate onto the sidewalk when Charlotte called, "Hey—where are you going?"

"I'm going to the library, if it's any of your business."

"Oh, that's right, Emily. He hasn't got any money, that's why the poor boy has to borrow books."

My mother often repeated to me, *Sticks and stones will break your bones, but names will never hurt you,* but these girls were evil and stuck-up, and as I marched off, I didn't really feel any better till I got to the library and was lost in the stacks, and when I had my books ready and went to the main desk at the front, I was comforted to find that the motherly librarian-lady treated me with the kindness and respect due to a little boy who only wanted to read.

When I got back to the house with an armful under my arm, they were still there, waiting for me. Again, they didn't want to let me pass without paying.

"Tell you what," said Charlotte. "I'll swap ya."

She ran into her house while Emily spread her arms out to guard the stairs.

Charlotte came back with a book called *Little Women*. "This is my favoritest book in the whole wide world, so you better not get macaroni sauce on it."

I gave her one of mine, and said, "Same to you. I gotta return that book in two weeks, you know."

With relief I passed up the stairs, but I paused at the doorway to my back hall steps.

"Were you two really named after the Bronte sisters?"

Charlotte said, "I don't know about that, but our parents made us watch the movie when it came on TV."

"Yeah," said Emily. "Boy, that poor kid had to stand on that stool for hours and hours, till she fell over."

"Glad we don't live in the olden days," said Charlotte.

I was nothing if not up on my children's literature approved as appropriate for borrowing by nine-year-olds by the nice lady at the library, so I was tickled to find out there was another Italian lady besides my mother who had given cutesy-pie names to her children, names taken from fairy-tales or nursery rhymes and such, and I mentioned this to Ma, who had been listening to everything on the back steps the whole time through the open kitchen window. "Guess what? There's two Italian sisters–."

"They're not Italians. They're Sicilians."

Curious, I asked, "How do you know that, Ma?"

My mother understood that I wanted to know how she could tell.

"I know by the way they talk. I know by the way they look. I know by the way they act."

She took her waving hands out of the air and placed them on her hips, looked at me and shook her head. "Ask a stupid question, get a stupid answer."

Chapter 9

The Railroad Yards of Milltown

I loved the dirt in Milltown. It was a different kind of dirt than the concrete dust I used to glory in back in the Brickyard in Revere, or the clumpy grey sand of Revere Beach, or even the flat dusty dirt of the infield at the Hosmer in Watertown, which puffed away on the slightest breeze. This was dirty dirt that you could really get under your fingernails. The red-brick buildings I had known were schools like the Shurtleff and the Hosmer. There they had janitors who at least attempted to keep the place clean. The mill-buildings of Milltown were nothing of the kind. They were mines of dirt, quarries of dirt, dirt at least a hundred years old, it seemed to me, greasy dirt full of machine-grime and cobwebs, and the people going in and out of the mills were not the kind who worked in banks in a set of clean clothes, they were people who got dirty on the job. I admired their ability to get dirty. My father came home in the evenings from his job on the construction site in Middleton and he used to try to clean his hands and nails in the bathroom sink before supper but he could never quite manage to get them pink and dirt-free. He could dig out the dirt under his nails mostly, but a stubborn rind of caked, embedded dirt would always cling to the circles of his cuticles. He tried everything, scrubbing-brushes, nail-clippers, even tar-soap. I couldn't wait till I grew up and I was allowed to get dirty like that. The best dirt in town was right at the dead end of our street in the railroad yards. There they had piles of black cinders for raking between ties on rail-beds and acres of spilled coal from gondolas and entire prairies of oil-streaked dirt. There was nothing in a railroad yard that had to be paved over. Everything you walked on could be left in its original state of naked, natural dirt. The rail-spurs themselves were built on a bed of dirt. The Boston & Maine Railroad ran the yards and they were the main-switching center in the Merrimack Valley for everything traveling north from Boston, whether heading inland to Manchester and Concord, or coastal to Portsmouth and Portland, or east and west to Lowell and Haverhill and Newburyport. The railroad yards of South Milltown were a separate world of dirt. It was so dirty in there that even grass wouldn't grow. There was no roundhouse or train-shed in the yards and everything was left out in the open air night and day, month after month, to get dirty: the boxcars, the tankers, the gondolas and flatbeds and gravel-hoppers. Even the big yellow snub-nosed yard-switcher looked like it was painted with oil-based diesel-dirt. I longed to get in there and play in the dirt. But I didn't know if I dared to sneak under the fence at the dead-end of our street. I was torn between my love of dirt and the need to be a good boy.

    I was never safe from the perils and temptations I faced in my life till I finally climbed into bed at seven at night. I was trying to get my mother to stretch that to seven-thirty or eight. After all, I was going on nine and in the fourth grade now.

Our flat upstairs at the Torrini's was always full of people coming and going. Uncle Gene was passing by every day to pick up his brother Augie and take him to work in Spicket Falls, building their new business. Uncle Patsy lived in Peabody on Rt 114, which passed right in front of our house, so he frequently stopped in on his way home from Spicket Falls for a bite to eat with the others. Ma was the cook and chief bottle-washer and she was both secretly delighted and outwardly put-upon to be the center of the family circle again. Just as she had stayed always at home with her parents, now she was the only of the four sisters who actually moved to the Valley to be near Gene's new sportswear company.

By this time I was figuring out my mother. This was the madness in her method. She was the one who appointed herself to look after the rest of them. We were not staying in Milltown anymore than we were staying in Watertown. She was looking for a new place next door in Spicket Falls, a place to buy, this time. These were exciting months to be staying up later, inch by inch. Sometimes I managed past eight o'clock because Ma was so busily distracted.

However, when I finally did get in bed, it would have been boring just lying there trying to sleep, so I had my library books. I had discovered a whole series of Hornblower sagas at the South Milltown branch library. But the book that surprised me was that one I had swapped for with Charlotte downstairs.

I would never have admitted to my uncles that I was reading *Little Women* under the covers with my flashlight. My uncles were my war-hero idols. I made a point of bragging to my Dad about the Hornblower books because he was Navy. I started drawing British Navy frigates with my colored pencils. And all the time, secretly, without knowing quite how, without wanting to, I had fallen in love with Meg and Jo and Amy and Beth.

I was glad I was alone and under the covers and no one could see me when I came across something I never-in-my-life expected, the death of my beloved Beth.

How could God have taken such a perfect creature, the one sister who was so unselfish she gave up even her life for others? I kept hoping and hoping till the last second, unable to conceive that all the signs and signals of the story could possibly lead to this. It wasn't fair, and I was burned down to my inner being by the fire of tears that gushed from my eyes when I read the fatal lines.

Uncle Mike Kowalcyzk was the Polish uncle I didn't know I had. He walked into my life one day when he arrived suddenly without any warning at our house on Winthrop Ave in Milltown.

He was married to my Dad's sister Stasija, and I had never met her, either. All I knew was my Dad had four sisters, the eldest Adrijana, called Adrienne, who lived in the Bronx, and then Anastasija, nicknamed Stasija, for short, and then Andjela, called Angie by everybody, and finally baby Ana, whose name needed no translation to American. I had no idea who these people were. I remembered Auntie Rose, on that side of the family, only because Uncle Alek Dad's brother, brought her on a visit to us back in Revere, when I first met my cousin Roseann, back in the summer of '47. But, of course, I didn't actually remember them, I was too young: what I remembered were their photos taken in our yard in Revere, in our family album, my Papanonni standing there with his arm circled around the waist of my strawberry-blonde Auntie Rose Petrovich, dressed in her flamboyant sun-dress, another Polish relative, whose maiden name was Novakowski. But my strawberry blonde Polish Auntie Rose was only my aunt by marriage. It was all just too confusing for someone my age.

I wasn't about to meet Auntie Stasija Kowalcyzk that day, either, since Uncle Mike had left her behind in Pennsylvania, along with his two daughters, my cousins, Patty and Michelle, whom I had never met, also. At least I thought I hadn't. I couldn't be real sure. I had only one vague lingering picture in my mind of Uncle Alek climbing out of a 2-door fastback Chevy in my grandfather's driveway, a car that looked nothing like Papanonni's big black Buick.

After that visit from the Pennsylvania branch of the Petrovich clan, my mother got bogged down with her mother dying, and her father, and having the twins, and so she didn't want any company from Pennsylvania for a while.

Then we were busy moving and she didn't have a proper place for them to visit in, not enough room for them to stay over, and so on.

Then all of a sudden Uncle Mike Kowalcyzk shows up on our doorstep in Milltown.

It seemed to be the season where everyone was moving, looking for one thing, or maybe two: a new job, and a new place to live.

Uncle Gene, Uncle Patsy and Uncle Augie were starting their new family business in Spicket Falls, where none of them had ever worked or lived before.

My dad, who used to walk to work every day in Revere, his new job was in Middleton, and he was living in Milltown, and there was no MTA in Milltown, so now he had a car.

Everybody was moving around and everything was changing.

It was no different with Uncle Mike Kowalcyzk. It turned out he was going to stay with us awhile, till he got settled, anyway. Now I was going to have two Uncles in the house.

What happened was that, as Uncle Mike said, "I got laid off for just about the umpteenth time."

I was standing there, staring, and I thought his accent was funny, strange and new and different, and undoubtedly, what they called a southern drawl.

My mother, of course, invited him to sit down and have a cup of coffee at her kitchen table.

From time to time, we had visitors at our kitchen table, people I hardly knew, and I always stood there and stared. For instance, there was my mother's childhood best friend, Hildie, from the days when Ma was growing up in Stoughton, way on the other side of Boston.

Come to think of it, she was another Polish lady. Her name before she got married was Hildie Radzilko, then she married a guy named Walter Baynis, and they had twins, like Ma did, and Hildie's twins were called Peter and Paul, and Ma's twins were called Jack and Jill.

That's what happened when you were best friends in childhood and ended up both having twins. You ended up with a Jack and Jill and a Peter and Paul Mounds Bars.

My mother had left Stoughton behind, long ago, but not Hildie, she stayed right there in the town she grew up in, all her entire life. On the other hand, unlike my mother, whose father always told her, *anywhere you wanna go, I'll drive you,* Hildie Radzilko learned how to drive a car, and then the next thing you know, she shows up at our kitchen table for a chit-chat and a remember-when and to catch up on the latest and show off their kids and have a cup of coffee.

No wonder I stood there and stared. How could you figure out these grownups? They never told you anything and you had to try to piece together everything from listening to them talk to each other over your head, completing ignoring you, thinking you wouldn't know half of what they were talking about, and you didn't. But you still learned a lot.

Now the story with my new Polish Uncle Mike Kowalcyzk was that he grew up in my Dad's hometown, Pershing, Penna., down near the West Virginia line, and he and my Dad and my uncle Alek, my dad's brother, all worked together in Germantown No. 1, in Shawnee, which was then, and now, and always would be, the biggest bituminous coal mine in the world. At least I knew that much, all right.

But now it was twenty years later, and a new decade. Times had changed. Coal-mining wasn't what it used to be. My Dad had got out, but not Uncle Alek, his brother, and not Uncle Mike, his brother-in-law.

Now Uncle Mike was saying he'd got laid off, yet again, and saying, "I'll tell you, I'm about sick of it, and I'm thinking of finding me another line of work altogether."

My Dad was trying to help out Uncle Mike and his sister Stasija and their kids.

What was happening in Milltown was that Mayor J.J. Murphy was sounding off every day in the local newspaper, the *Eagle-Tribune,* about Operation Bootstrap, his plan for urban redevelopment of the city of Milltown, with its 100,000 or so inhabitants, the newest of which was going to be my Polish Uncle Mike Kowalcyzk.

My Dad had called him up in Pennsylvania, long-distance, to tell him "Why don't you come on up here, Mike? They got a project on about to get started to tear down one half of the Wood Mill, which runs a country mile along the river. There gonna need a lotta men. It's so big the job is bound to last two or three years, maybe four or five. Mike, it's so goddam big they're only gonna be able to tear down half of it. They're hiring right now, buddy, for laborers, you know, pick and shovel men. Think you could handle that? Why don't you just get your lazy ass on up here?"

Uncle Mike was stirring his coffee and lamenting the loss of the old life, telling my mother, "I'll tell you, coal-mining hain't what it used to be. Hain't no President Truman gonna take over the steel mills for us now. Ike's out golfing. With his rich buddies. I'll tell you, hon, every time the Buckeye's got a surplus built up, they lay us off again. Then they bring you back and work you 3 shifts seven days till they've gone and built up their surplus again and turn around and tell you '*the market for coal is down*,' and it's another layoff. The working man can't win, hon."

Uncle Mike Kowalcyzk was the first guy I ever heard call my mother,'Hon.' But she didn't mind. He called me 'Laddie,' and I wondered where he could've gotten that from. Maybe *Lassie,* that show on TV?

I was staring at his open sunburned face, his twinkle-blue eyes, and the butch crew-cut that stood up in a straight row across his forehead, and he said to me, "You and me's gonna go fishin,' Laddie. You like to go fishin'?"

My mother said, "Oh, I wouldn't eat anything they dredge out of the Merrimack, Mike. It's filthy. Just go over in the pantry there and turn on the tap and you'll smell it, they have to put so much chlorine in it, or you couldn't drink it."

"It's the same with the Mon, hon. It's just turned brown. Well, there must be somewheres around here to go fishin.' Don't you worry, Laddie, we'll find out, and when we do, we're gonna get us a rowboat and go fishin.'"

And so we did. We found out the place to go was Lake Cochichiewick, out in North Andover. We even got the rowboat. But first I had to ask Uncle Mike one question. "Were you in the war, Uncle Mike?"

"Yes sir-ee-bob, you bet your bottom. I was in the motor pool, Company D."

"Wow. Just like Sgt Bilko on TV!"

That admitted Uncle Mike into the exclusive club of my uncles and my dad, who were all in the war. He was one of them. That meant it was okay to go fishing with Uncle Mike. He was a new war-hero to add to my pantheon.

I loved my Uncle Mike. He didn't care if we caught anything today, we could always go again tomorrow if we didn't. He couldn't see why a kid would want to stay home on a Saturday morning watching cartoons when he could go bowling at the Recreation Lanes on Canal Street in North Milltown. What he couldn't understand is why in the hell they had these candle-pins up north here, and those bowling balls that fit in the palm of your hand, instead of proper ten-pins like they had back home.

I loved my Polish Uncle Mike because he left the biggest bituminous coal-mine in the world on the banks of the Monongahela and boarded a bus for the long trip north to join the crew tearing down the biggest woolen mill in the world on the banks of the Merrimack.

He was one of the men of those days.

Now my mother had finally found the house of her dreams, and the only trouble was that it was going to take another six months to get it ready to move into.

That was why we ended up spending Christmastime of 1955 in the upstairs flat at the Torrini's house on Winthrop Ave in South Milltown.

I had been in the fourth grade at the Packard for three or four months, and here I was going to have to move again into yet another new school. But at least, the way it worked out, I would get to finish the school year at the Packard.

The new house was actually not going to be in Milltown at all. It was going to be on Elm Street in Spicket Falls, in a neighborhood known as Glen Forest, on the west side of Spicket Falls, exactly one street across the city line from North Milltown.

Haverhill Street was the big east-west street in North Milltown and it ran over the crest of Tower Hill. When you came down the hill, Plymouth Street was the last street before you crossed the city line. The typical Massachusetts Shield sign was posted there, reading

Entering Spicket Falls
Est. 1726

Elm Street ran parallel to Plymouth Street. It was the first street in Spicket Falls. Beginning at Haverhill Street, Elm Street was a long road that wound around till it joined Lowell Street and ran all the way into Spicket Falls Square.

Ma said she had taken out a mortgage with the Arlington Trust bank and that it was going to be better for me because I was going to be in a much better school, the Ebenezer Parker in Spicket Falls, instead of the Tarbox, in North Milltown. She said she was getting the new house for only $11,000, which was a steal because it needed so much fixing up. She said I ought to be grateful I would never have to go to Milltown High, which had three thousand students. Spicket Falls only had a population of about 12,000, so my classrooms would be much smaller than at the Packard, and that would be better for me.

Still, she wasn't happy with the transaction altogether. She would much rather have found something to move right into, because she hated paying rent to that goddam Sicilian Torrini, and she was worried she would never get her security deposit back because she had refused to sign his lease-for-a-year, and now, here she was going to stay nine months or more in his upstairs flat. But she fell in love with the new house and she just couldn't pass it up. She wasn't happy with the Arlington Trust Bank, either, because they wanted her to open a joint checking account with her husband's name on it, and she wasn't happy with the real estate agent because she wanted a six percent commission, which she would have to get from the seller, she wasn't going to get it out of my mother, and the seller had his own real estate agent, and these people, between the bank and the realtors, sure had some racket going for them, they all wanted a cut.

Still, it was Christmastime and she had a house full of people and the twins were growing up, and hadn't died of starvation yet, and soon she would be going to work at the new shop in Spicket Falls with her brothers and sisters, and, not this year, but next year, the whole family was going to be able to come over for Christmas dinner in Gerry's new house on Elm Street in Spicket Falls.

The first time I set eyes on it I thought I had never seen anything like it.

It was a stone house.

It was not a brick house and it was not a stucco house. I had seen those type of houses in Revere and Watertown, and the house we lived in now, in South Milltown, was a typical wood-frame two-family with rough-pebbled red-and-green-colored tar shingles.

This new place was a fieldstone house with the exterior composed of sizable grey boulders that looked like they had just been taken from a farmer's stone fence hundreds of years old.

The only wood on the outside of the first floor was the columns holding up the roof of the front porch and window-trim. These were painted a cream-color.

The second floor was wooden shingles painted a dark red, with cream-colored trim.

The combination was very handsome. Looking up and down the street, it was easily the most distinctive, impressive home on that section of Elm Street, from Haverhill Street all the way to the corner of Woodland.

Christmas or no Christmas, my mother and father had a big argument over Dad's car. He said he needed something he could haul lumber in for everything he would have to do to get the new house ready for her, the Studebaker just wasn't the right type of vehicle. My mother just didn't want to spend the money, what with everything it was costing her to close on the new house while still paying rent on the old place, and this being Christmas for the kids and everything, and all the extra groceries for his brother-in-law Mike, but Dad insisted. He wanted the new place to be just perfect for her, and he was going to do all the work himself, or else what was he a carpenter for? But he just had to have something with a tailgate that you could fit two-by-fours into, plus a rack on the roof. Ma insisted it better be a used car, she wasn't about to buy him a new car like his brother Alek, who had a new Chevy every two years, but that didn't cut any ice with Dad, and the argument was on, Christmas or no Christmas.

I don't think my Dad exactly won that argument, but he did end up with a new second-hand dark red Willys Jeep that sort of matched the color of the 2nd floor of the new house and fit perfectly into the long driveway and the garage at the back. And it had a radio.

Now that I knew I wasn't going to stay at the Packard, I was glad I hadn't formed any attachments to anyone I could call a buddy or a best friend among the classmates I had to put up with in that place. My teacher, Mrs LaFarge, was all right I suppose, but the kids gave me the impression all the smart ones must be across the street at St Patrick's. At least I could count on spending the afternoon at the Branch Library and not running into anyone from the Packard.

But evidently there was a boy who wanted to make friends with me, and of all things, his name was Tommy.

He came from Garfield Street, which came out on our little dead end street two houses closer to the railyard fence. You could see his house on the corner from my back porch upstairs.

And he happened to come along just when a new gap in my life had to be filled.

Uncle Mike Kowalcyzk had found a flat to rent, top floor of a triple-decker, way at the other end of Boxford Street, a mile off or more, and he was moving out, so that he could get things ready to bring Auntie Stasija and my cousins Patty and Michelle up from Pennsylvania.

I was left standing in the middle of the train station that our house had become. The trains were all leaving without me.

It must have been about this time when I first noticed this new Tommy when he began to show up whenever I happened to be outside sitting on the back steps with Charlotte and Emily.

"Who's that?" I asked finally.

"Tommy."

"He used to be a friend, but we don't like him anymore."

"Why not?"

"'Cause we just don't, that's all."

"He's a problem child."

"Yeah. He's a jerk."

That aroused my curiosity. Anybody Charlotte and Emily didn't like must have given them some reason, but they weren't telling.

This kid would come out of his house, walk past our back gate, disappear around the front of the house, and then, awhile later, come back and go back in his house. So the next time he came around the back gate pretending he wasn't watching us, I made sure I went over there and waited for him to come back to his house from wherever he went.

The first thing he said to me was, "You always play with girls?"

"Nope. But there aren't any boys around here my age to play with."

That was all. He was a boy of few words who had found out what he wanted to know and then went into his house.

I figured he would come back some other time.

When I got back to the steps, the girls told me, "He hasn't got any father, you know."

"That's why he's such a rotten egg."

"My mother says he's trouble and not to let him in the yard."

Nobody I had ever known didn't have a father. That made me feel sorry for him. And I ought to like him because his name was Tommy, and I loved my cousin Tommy, so maybe I should try to befriend him. He might need a friend. I knew I did.

The next time he came around I was waiting at the gate and I said to him, "What do you kids do for fun around here?"

"What do you mean, around here?"

"Well, I'm not from around here, so I don't know. I'll tell you what we used to do back in Revere, where I come from. We used to hop on the back of the streetcars and hold onto the trolley-cable housing and ride it all the way down Central Ave to Broadway. But you don't have any streetcars in this town."

"We have buses."

"Not the same thing. There's no trackless trolleys here, either, like we used to have in Watertown. That's because the MTA doesn't run up this far. It's like the middle of nowhere out here."

"Yeah, but there's stuff to do around here. Plenty of stuff."

"Like what?" So now we were talking and it wasn't long before we were leaving the girls to sit on their stoop and hitting the sidewalks instead.

Tommy took me all over that city, to places I wouldn't have even known to look. It was thanks to him that I got to know my way around before I had to move to Spicket Falls and get stuck among a whole bunch of kids in my new neighborhood up there who had never even been across the line into Milltown, only one street away, much less had they ever heard of places like Medford or Melrose or Malden.

Tommy was a kid with light-colored straight hair that was always falling in his eyes and he always seemed to be wiping his nose on the back of his hand and then wiping the back of his hand off on the backside of his dungarees.

It was because of him I got into an argument with my mother about how she wouldn't allow me to get a pair of dungarees like Tommy's when I had perfectly good dress pants to wear and everybody knew only hoodlums wore dungarees.

It was Tommy who took me to the swimming pool in O'Connell Park in South Milltown, over off of South Union Street, just after you passed Torrini's Italian Supermarket. It was Tommy who took me across the Merrimack on the Duck Bridge and up the steep hill behind the Everett Mills to where the Oxford Paper Mill was. Over there we could climb up on the mountain of wood pulp that was at the back of the mill by the banks of the Merrimack, and from way up there, we had a bird's eye view of the demolitions going on over across on the south bank where my Polish Uncle Mike was working tearing down one-half of the Wood Mill. We walked everywhere together. It was Tommy who showed me the monumental US Post Office on the corner of Essex and Broadway in North Milltown, and the row of movie-houses that started on the next corner, the *Modern*, the *Astor*, the *Broadway* and *The Palace*. Thanks to Tommy I found out about the downstairs department at W.T. Grant's on Essex Street, which was the only place in Milltown which made me feel like I used to feel going into the subway stations around Boston. We used to rattle the gum-ball machines outside the entrance down there trying to get some to fall out till they came and chased us away. Tommy went bowling with me and my Uncle Mike to the Recreation Lanes on Canal Street in North Milltown on a Saturday morning and Uncle Mike paid for our bowling shoes and we played three strings, and we got French Fries at the counter afterward. One day Tommy said to me, you ever been up to the Sandbanks? He took me over the top of Tower Hill and down the other side on Haverhill Street, across the line into Spicket Falls, right past the new neighborhood where we were going to move to, and then, across the road from the new school I was going to go to, the Ebenezer Parker, right across the road was the Sandbanks. It was a sand quarry with tall peaks that looked like pyramids and you could scramble up the sides on your hands and knees with sand sliding into your shoes and when you got to the top, slide all the way back down on your backside. Once in a while a gravel truck would pull in but mostly it was just deserted. And where could you find a playground slide that tall and exciting, on any playground, in back of any school you ever saw?

By this time Tommy was my best friend in Milltown, and finally I got around to asking him, you ever been in the railroad yards?

"Sure," said Tommy.

He led me to the fence at the dead end of Boxford Street and under it we went through the hole the dogs had dug.

Once we were in there we climbed all over the boxcars couplings and gondola-buckets. When we got tired of that we climbed up the ladders and walked on top of the boxcars and down the other side. Nobody was around and it was easy to imagine all sorts of romantic trips to faraway destinations that were hinted at by the names we could see painted on the sides of the freight-cars, names like *Erie Lackawanna, Chesapeake & Ohio, Great Northern, Union Pacific*. I was immensely satisfied to have gotten, finally, on the other side of that fence and into the railroad yards, so it didn't occur to me at all to be a bad idea or anything when Tommy proposed we should throw some rocks at the windows in the trainman's shack, so we picked up some cinders from the rail-spurs and selected some nice hefty ones and we started our target practice, and soon enough we had a symphony going, a concerto of shattering glass.

"Hey, you kids! Whaddya think you're doing?"

The trainman himself came running around the corner of the shack and we scattered like pigeons. Tommy got caught by the ankle as he was trying to squeeze under the fence but I ran the other way, all the way out to Andover Street and around the bank on the corner and then back down Winthrop Ave and this time, figuring I could be seen if I rounded the corner of the house, I did go in the front door, as fast as I could, and up the front hall steps and crashing into the parlor where I collapsed on the sofa just as my mother came in and said, "Oh, there you are. Get out in the kitchen, it's time for supper. What are you so out of breath for? Go wash your hands in the pantry. Look at you—you're covered in soot! I'm tired of patching holes in your knees. God Almighty—you act like a wild Indian!"

Chapter 10

The Fieldstone House

When my Dad and I first went into the new house, we found empty whisky bottles stacked from floor to ceiling in the closets.

My father laughed. "Crazy Canucks! Guess they were a little too happy livin' here!"

The Rancourts were the family my mother bought the house from. But actually when it was first built, back in the 1920s, it was constructed to be the rectory for the priests of the parish of Ste-Jeanne d'Arc, over on Plymouth Street.

That was why Ma wanted it. This house had been born with mystique. The legend of St Joan in my mother's mind cloaked this house with meaning. As a practical matter, it had been built to accommodate a mission in society. It had four bedrooms upstairs. Private quarters for each man of God in which to lay down his burdens at the end of a day of counsel and contemplation. Along with a spacious, full bathroom, these were ranged around a central stairwell. Downstairs, there was a den with French doors and a fireplace, where the priests could meet privately with a grieving family or petitioning parishioners.

On the other side of the central stairway was a full parlor, also with a door that closed. At the back of the house on that side was the formal dining room. A door opened from there onto the pantry, which led on the other side to the kitchen, the back hall, and the back porch.

It was a house with a certain formidable presence, which hinted at the possibility of magnificence, but it had been wrecked by the Rancourts, who bought it when the parish, during the war, was building the new church, with its pale peach-colored bricks, which replaced the original wooden church. On Plymouth Street, a new rectory was built of the same bricks right next door to the new church.

Thus the house we were going to now move into had two legacies, one sanctified, and one insouciant.

Dad brought me along with him at the beginning of the summer, once the school year was over at the Packard. It took that long to get the Rancourts out of the house. He said I could help him, because he had a lot to do. "Ma says you're underfoot all the time. Ask too many questions. Bet you'll be glad to get away, too, huh?"

Dad ripped the guts out of the place. He didn't take out any of the features which made the house specially interesting, such as the fireplace in the den, or the built-in bookcase next to it, the stately front door with its full-length oval window, or the built-in linen cabinet that stretched across the hallway between the bathroom and the right-rear bedroom at the top of the stairs, but he wanted the pantry torn out and he wanted the French doors opening from the hallway into the den gone, and because of the condition the house was in, he had to rebuild the whole staircase and bannister up to the second floor, plus the entire kitchen.

The house had holes in the wall where you could tell punches had missed and doorknobs which were wrenched half-off which made you think the inhabitants had been chasing each other around, trying to hide from pursuers.

On the other hand, there was a small room upstairs, at the opposite end of the hall from the linen cabinet which Ma thought would be a perfect sewing-room for her, and she wanted to put one of the Singer machines that Uncle Gene had picked up in his search for second-hand equipment for the new business into that room, which stood at the front of the second floor between two bedrooms.

So Dad had his work cut out for him. He subscribed to *Popular Mechanics,* so he had all the latest innovative do-it-yourself projects stuffed in his head, and he was full of plans to make the house an open-floor-plan space and take out walls and doors, beginning with the French doors, but he also had a lot of work to do outside. The Rancourts had neglected the ivy that once was so attractive when the house was a new parish rectory: it had by now gone yellow and dead, but also had sunk its teeth into the mortar that kept the fieldstones in place; so he had to re-point all the stonework of the exterior. The overhead garage door of the fieldstone garage didn't work. He wanted to tear out the decayed and decrepit screened-in lattice-work of the front porch so that it would make the verandah, which stretched the entire width of the front of the house, open to the air, and remove the dim and dingy look from the front of the house, so that you could see windows full of light in the evening, instead of glowering black screens. There was a big argument between him and Ma because he said he absolutely had to spend the money on an extension ladder in order to take care of this new place. "Gerry, you just can't own something like this, and not maintain it. How do you think it got into the shape it's in, in the first place? When things break, you gotta fix them!" Dad was going to replace and repaint the wooden shingles of the upper story so that they weren't dark red anymore, but the latest thing, charcoal-grey, which would go so handsomely with the fieldstone of the first floor. Dad knew all about the latest thing in colors for houses because of the construction site in Middleton where he worked, where they were throwing up dozens of new houses in hues of charcoal-grey and forest-green and seaside-blue. The old days of white and brown houses were over.

My job was to patch the plaster walls with spackle. I loved helping my Dad. Now I got to stay up late any time I wanted. It was summer and school was out. I could get dirty building stuff just like my Dad did. Every night that summer, after he worked all day in Middleton, we would drive over in the Willys Jeep to the new house, after supper, and work till ten or eleven with the electric lights on. On the weekends, it was all day out doors as long as the light lasted. Uncle Augie came along to help with the heavy lifting and he just did whatever Dad asked him to do. Uncle Augie was going to get the bedroom upstairs at the right-rear of the house, the northwest corner, which would be the coldest in winter, Dad said I was going to get a bedroom of my own, in between the bathroom and the twin's bedroom, on the southeast corner: the warmest room in winter because it was sandwiched between other rooms. Ma and Dad got the other bedroom opposite the twins, which was what Dad thought of as the most likely to be dubbed the master bedroom. These were the bedrooms where the priests had prayed on their knees at night and the Rancourts had fought on their feet.

It took us all summer and we had to be supervised and inspected on the weekends by Ma. She wanted to know what was taking so damn long because she wanted badly to get out of the Torrini's house. Not only was she spending her last dime on the renovations of the new house, but she was paying rent and a mortgage at the same time. She just couldn't go on like this. Why was Dad still tearing out walls and why wouldn't he let her move in? He was building all new cabinets in the kitchen where the pantry used to be, with formica counter-tops, and a built-in bench-seat, curving round from the back-window of the kitchen overlooking the clothes-lines to the side-window looking out on the lawn, for booth-seating, like they had in restaurants. Ma just wanted to know why she couldn't move in now, while he was still working on it. He told her she'd be in his way, but she didn't want to hear that. School would be starting soon, and Nicky had to be in class at the Ebenezer Parker, which she had enrolled him in back in May, already. Here it was August now, and she wasn't gonna be caught living in Milltown and sending her kid to school in Spicket Falls, that was ridiculous.

Uncle Augie and I were rushing to finish the wall-papering. I was getting colonial mansions, covered bridges and Revolutionary War frigates, and the twins were getting lambs and teddy-bears.

Dad was trying to retain his sanity while installing his masterpiece, a bent-wood bannister on the stairway to the second floor, which he had re-built entirely.

He was outside on the lawn where he had built a four-foot-long steam-box which he had balanced on two sawhorses. He had a fire of scrap-wood going inside a galvanized washtub sitting on the ground. Over it he balanced a three-legged charcoal-grill frame with the pot removed and a large metal gas-can sitting on top of it with a car-heater hose leading from the gas-can nozzle to a pipe in the side of the wooden steam-box. Inside the gas can over the fire, boiling water was making steam.

Three holes he drilled in the top of the far end of the steam box let the steam escape and the draft from the air-holes pulled the steam down the length of the box. He opened the door on the other end and one by one, inserted the ¾-inch dowel-rods into the steam-box and shut the door, to bend them. After 5 minutes he put on a thick canvas glove and pulled out the hot dowel and bent it to spec on a form lying on the ground before the hot wood set. He did this for twenty-six dowel-rods because the stair had thirteen steps. The round wooden dowels cooled and dried quickly and kept their shape. There was only one simple bend in the wood to make, and then two dowel-rods pinned together in the middle, turned upside down, made an inverted-Y. The top of the Y went into a hole in the handrail and the two legs of the Y sat in double-holes drilled in the step below. It was ingenious, and it made an elegant finished bannister.

I was watching this whole lengthy procedure, fascinated, *thinking how does he know how to do stuff like this?*

Ma was objecting that everything was taking too long and those blond-waxed kitchen cabinets of his that he said were the latest in the natural wood-grain look?–she didn't like them.

Dad just put down his thick glove. "Judas Priest, woman, I can't win. You're never satisfied."

My introduction to the house where I would spend the next eight years consisted of removing her bathrobe to reveal her skeleton. In after years I don't think I ever quite let go of the image in my head of vast crags of plaster ripped out to unveil the moldy slats that lay behind, or the holes in ceilings with thick black curled and bunched tangles of wires dangling a single naked light-bulb.

Yet the fieldstone house became my house and my attachment, my bonding to it was just as permanent as the cement we mixed in buckets in the yard to point the stonework. In my own mind, my own heart and soul, I called it my house, just as much as my mother, who bought and paid for it, did.

My teacher at the Ebenezer Parker in the fifth grade was a novelty to me because he was a man, Mr Wendling, who told us to call him Jack, which I never did because, to me, that was beneath the dignity of one of my teachers. The other kids in my new neighborhood had no problem with that, but then, I expected things to be new and different.

I also expected to be here in my new house and never to leave. I think I had planned the future of Uncle Gene's new family business in Spicket Falls, *Gigi Sportswear*, to be an unqualified, guaranteed success, which would also last forever. It all added up to the idea that I was now free to make new friends and keep them.

The first was Billy McQuaid, who lived in a grey colonial with a circular drive at the corner of Woodland and Elm, in the direction of the town Square.

I met Billy in class and he invited me over to his house after school to play with toy soldiers. I had a castle made of tin which I could assemble and we sprawled out on the floor of his living room so that my knights and chargers could attack his army of GIs.

Spicket Falls in those days still retained the feel of a New England country town from the nineteenth century. Behind Billy McQuaid's house there was nothing but a mile or so of empty land sloping down to the Milltown line in the vicinity of Railroad Hill and the Arlington Mills. The empty land was waiting for people to die, because it was owned by the Bellevue Cemetery, which was populated with headstones on the opposite shore of Woodland Street, on the lower slopes of the northwest side of Milltown's Tower Hill.

Billy McQuaid was the first boy to take me to explore Tower Hill.

This hill was one of two prominent, steep elevations which flanked Milltown, east and west. On the east side of the city lay Prospect Hill, crowned by a modern steel water-tower whose bulbous tank was painted a sky-blue. You could see it sticking up over house-tops from the pulp-stacks at the Oxford Paper Mill.

Tower Hill was similar in its vast size and steep streets, with clapboard triple-deckers tilting crazily, from North Broadway up the slopes to the top, but it differed distinctly because it hosted not only the enormous city cemetery covering acres of hill and dale, but it also was the site of what Billy McQuaid and all the other kids called *The Rez*.

There were almost as many dead people in Milltown as living, maybe more, I thought, from trying to gauge the rambling groves and pockets of the Bellevue Cemetery.

Surmounting this vale of silence was the plateau of the city Reservoir, *the Rez*.

But the *pièce de résistance* of Tower Hill, like the happy couple atop a wedding cake, was the ornate, five-story tall, red-brick water tower rising next to the placid mirror of the black-gated reservoir. This tower of Victorian fancy, topped with its grey-green conical hat of a roof, looked like nothing less than Rapunzel's fantastic abode in the fairy tale. It was the crowning glory of some long-dead gilded-age architect's dream of the decorative summit which should dominate the skyline of the subservient city of workers below it. Such classes of people would thus be signaled to gaze adoringly upon the magnificent mountain of the gingerbread mansions of their wealthy masters.

This then was the magical kingdom of the living and the dead in which, at the age of nine, I landed. The crest of Tower Hill was composed of a body of water, with a view of limitless horizons, surrounded by rolling glades and dells, hidden with carved concrete mausoleums, surrounded by the decaying manses of nineteenth-century millionaires. It was truly a city within the city; a soaring destination, where the hovels of the living, marching uphill, in ranks of assembled acolytes, mounted up to the celestial abodes of the dead.

I turned ten on Christmas Day of 1956 and everything changed.

People sometimes do not realize what is happening to them at the time it is happening. But a boy newly turned ten is aware of a mighty milestone passing.

For me, it did not happen in just one day, but took a year to unfold.

And the year did not begin with my birthday in December, but with the start of school the previous September. Momentous undercurrents invaded my soul and swept me away. In so many ways I was no longer a child in a child's realm but a sentient being caught in the turmoils of a wider world. These came not from the classroom but from the den of our new house on Elm Street, where my Uncle Augie had set up, in the diagonal front corner between the verandah windows and the windows looking out on the side lawn, a new, 21-inch black and white Zenith console which he bought for the family as his house-warming gift.

Even though it was still warm out, Dad started a fire in the fireplace at the back of the den. He couldn't wait for winter. He had to christen the new house now. But the real heat came from the television screen, where on a Sunday night Ma and Dad and Uncle and I and even the four-year-old twins, Jack and Jill, all gathered to watch the Ed Sullivan show.

Anticipation had been building all summer long. In May, on his last appearance on the Milton Berle show, a new singing sensation had managed to outrage all the newspaper editors and parents in the country by wiggling his hips. The controversy escaped my attention because I had been too tired all the time from helping Dad get the house ready to be staying up past my bedtime. But now for the past week everyone in the house had been talking about this new phenomenon. Ed Sullivan had announced publicly that he would never, *never* have this 'boy' on his show. But then he suddenly reversed course and told the New York papers that he was going to pay the boy $50,000 for three appearances. Tonight, September 9th, was the first one. *Elvis Presley, on the Ed Sullivan show.*

I had never heard of anyone with a name as outlandish as Elvis Presley.

"Well," said Dad, "here's our chance to see what all the fuss is about."

"Not even Mickey Mantle gets that kind of money," said Uncle Augie, "not in New York, not for playing just three games, nor Ted Williams for that matter. They might be getting that much for the whole season, but I doubt it."

"Frank Sinatra must be turning green with envy," said Ma.

Charles Laughton came out in front of the curtains and introduced the boy wonder, and when Elvis launched into *Don't Be Cruel,* one of his biggest hits, he started throwing his head and shoulders all around and you could see the neck of his guitar waving, but you couldn't see anything else but his back-up band in the background.

Dad started yelling, "What a put-up job! Can't see a thing!"

"You think he's doing it, Gerry?" said Uncle Augie, with palm-smacking delight.

"Shut up! I can't hear a thing!"

"It looks like it to me," said my uncle.

"Well, they're just not gonna show it," said Dad, as Elvis took a bow and started on a ballad called "Love Me Tender."

"Listen, now, let's see if he can sing," said Ma.

"This is disgusting," said Dad.

"Shush!"

When Elvis took a bow for that one, Ma admitted he had a good voice. "But I don't know why they can't just stand at the mike and sing, like Rosemary Clooney does. What do they have to jump all around for? Why can't they just be nice? What do they call this stuff anyway, Andy?"

"Rock and roll, babe," said my Dad.

Ma looked at him from under her eyelids, and said, "You would know."

"Shush yourself now. He's gonna sing, 'You ain't nuthin' but a hound dog!'"

"Mamma-mia," said Ma. "If Pa could see this now! You know he used to collect Caruso's records. We had one of those hand-cranked victrolas back when they first came out, in the twenties, yeah, I'm telling you, Nicky, when I was your age. They didn't have records back then—they had cylinders. You never saw one of them old-time phonographs, did you?"

I was not so impressed with Elvis Presley. I could see the grown-ups were all excited but the big noise fell flat on my ears. I was a student of music myself, and I knew more about it, I was quite sure, than my mother, or any of them. I could read music, and I could play, and I was not yet ready to rock and roll. But I might as well try to explain that to my little brother Jack as to the grownups in our den on that curious landmark Sunday.

Nobody played stickball in Spicket Falls, it was unheard of, but that fall, in the fifth grade, I was introduced to something the kids at school called *Relievio.*

Unlike the redbrick Shurtleff in Revere, with its paved-tar playground, the Ebenezer Parker had brick walls of butter-yellow, and an enormous grass-covered playground in the back, big enough to accommodate two entire baseball fields, complete with dirt infields. At the west end, the diamond had a wooden backstop, at the east end, the backstop was taller and chain-link. In between, where the two grassy outfields kissed, was where they played Relievio, every day at recess, between two stout trees bordering the swamp behind our school. The trees marked the end-lines of our game.

I spent so much time at this school every day for three seasons of the year that it appeared in my dreams. When my friend Tommy from South Milltown had first brought me to the Sandbanks, that was when I first saw the Ebenezer Parker. The school was built in the shape of a letter T: the upright leg of the T was facing the apex of the junction of Woodland Street and Haverhill Street, and it was occupied by the school gymnasium, which also served as the auditorium. None of my of my previous schools had come equipped with their own basketball court. Tall and wide windows allowed you to see into the gym from outside. Two front doors to the 2-story classroom section of the school, the crossbar on top of the T, flanked either side of the auditorium. School assemblies could be conducted from up on the raised stage at the rear of the gym, and our principal, a fat middle-aged Scotswoman with a double-chin called Miss Corbie, presided over the opening of the school year in September from up on that stage. In her curious accent, she addressed all six grades, seated on folding chairs for the occasion. When assembly was over, we had to fold up the chairs and stack them under the windows on both sides, revealing the markings of the basketball court on the polished floor. Grades 4, 5 and 6 were eligible to try out for the team, and we played against the other elementary schools in town, the Corliss, the Oakland and the Ashford.

Relievio was a free-for-all game that kids of all grades joined into, although the first-and-second graders tended to stick to the hopscotch squares painted in white on the small, oblong paved area behind the school where the two black-iron fire-escapes came down from the second floor hallway doors. Almost all the girls played jump-rope on the tarred area, but the bolder ones, the ones everybody called tom-boys, played *Relievio* with the boys.

The idea was to relieve the prisoners in the goal at each end of the field. Each side passed a red-rubber ball the size of a soccer-ball back and forth between their own members while the other side tried to intercept it. When you got intercepted you had to put a prisoner in the opponents' goal. If you could weave your way through the whole opposition down the field and hit one of your own side's prisoners with the ball, the prisoner got released and rejoined their side. The more prisoners you got released the easier it was to out-pass and out-run the other side, but usually we all were exhausted with running and soaked in sweat by the time the 15-minute recess was up and we had to troop back into class. It was a stupid game, I thought, and I was sure it was something made up by the teachers just because they couldn't leave us alone at recess, they had to organize it for us.

Because I was new to the school and I was trying to fit in among strangers, I tried out for the school team in fifth grade even though I had never dribbled a basketball in my life.

I was hopeless at dribbling and unable to shoot a basket, even especially awkward with the jump shot that all the other boys seemed to accomplish with verve, so the coach in the grey tee-shirt and blue sweatpants with the whistle around his neck, my 5th-grade teacher, Mr Wendling, tried to teach me the set shot. I ended up sitting on the bench a lot but I got to wear the blue-and-gold school colors like all the others. I even got my mother to buy me the sneakers I needed, a new pair of black Converse high-tops, with white laces, because Coach said you couldn't go out on that basketball floor with regular shoes. Ma hated spending that money, but she had to. All the other boys were way ahead of me, I thought, and I set my mind to accepting that I had a lot of catching-up to do in Spicket Falls.

In the autumn, when school was starting, all the boys in my new neighborhood used to rush home right after school to watch the Yankees in the World Series. I decided that if I wanted to be like them I should do like them, and so, that fall, I was rooting for the Dodgers, because, as I explained to the boys, unlike them, I was from Boston, (assuming they'd heard of Boston) and the Red Sox were my team, so I hated the Yankees because they were from New York. All the boys said they were Red Sox fans, too, only New York was in the World Series every year, right? It seemed as natural as leaves falling in autumn. And at least the Yankees were the American League, so you root for your league. I said I was also a Boston Braves fan, but they moved away on us, so therefore, it was all right to root for the other league if you wanted to.

But that fall, as the shadows crept across the infield in Yankee Stadium on the black-and-white Zenith in our den, and the crab-apple-tree in our yard was nodding shadowy limbs in the window-glass above my mother's new colonial-themed Republican-cloth half-curtains, Don Larsen was twirling a perfect game; I was becoming a baseball-historian tutored by Mel Allen, and my life, sometimes to my dismay, was curving just beyond the flying bat of Pee-Wee, Jackie and the Duke, turning the Dodgers, World Champions just the year before, into this year's also-rans, and the dreaded Yankees into winners once again.

Early in December, we were just beginning to get comfortable, as a family, in our new house. The chill in the air was beginning to make Dad's new woodpile, stacked against the wall of the garage under the crab-apple-tree, and growing daily higher with scrap-wood he would bring home from the building sites where he worked, a welcome harbinger of a cozy fire in the den. That was when a new drama insinuated itself into the family circle through the seeing-eye of the television screen.

It seemed the last time I was allowed to be gripped by anything on TV was back in Revere in the days of *Howdy Doody* and *The Lone Ranger* and Saturday morning *Goofy* cartoons. In Watertown and South Milltown, it seemed that there was too much upset going on in my heart, too much consternation in my head, for television to get through the static to me. But now, since the advent of Elvis, since the new house, suddenly, we were not eating supper in the kitchen anymore, as used to be the iron-clad rule back in Mamanonna's day. Suddenly, we were carrying our plates into the den, and arranging ourselves in a circle of TV-tables, to eat there, because it was the hour when the nightly news was on, and the nightly news was not coming from Korea now, it was coming from Alabama.

Just as the year before we had never heard of Elvis Presley, just as the year before Don Larsen was a second-stringer, now, for the first time in our lives, a Negro was playing a starring role on the news, a Negro who, even a year before, was unknown to the world, and a Negro, moreover, who was referred to, with respect, by John Cameron Swayze, by Walter Winchell, as Dr Martin Luther King, Jr.

Moreover, we were now being exposed nightly to news footage of Bull Connor, the police chief down in Alabama, turning his firehoses on the Negroes. Or the kids in Little Rock trying to integrate the high school. President Eisenhower had to send federal troops to protect them. Why were the white people down there so hateful, I wanted to know, and of course, at ten years of age, I had no answer to that, just a sense of vague unease, a suspicion that something was wrong, maybe even very, very wrong about the world. It was great for Jackie Robinson to integrate baseball, or the Boston Celtics to bring in Negro stars and suddenly start winning the championship (as my uncle's nephew, I copied his devotion to the sports pages in the papers) but nowadays, in this new world being born, right here, right now, on the TV in our den, it was still a world divided between right and wrong, good and evil: right here, right now, integration was good, and segregation was evil.

Uncle Augie was a curious onlooker. He recalled the Army, during the war, at home, Stateside, and in the camps in England, and then, afterwards, on the rapidly advancing frontline in France, as a strictly segregated Army. Negroes in the Army had been typically separated from the all-white combat units. He remembered them in uniform, but they were stevedores on the docks in Cherbourg, and freight-handlers loading trucks in ammo-dumps behind the lines. On the other hand, there was Joe Louis, and he was Champion of the World, so you had to respect that, but lately, Rocky Marciano had proven that the Great White Hope was no myth. So, to Augie, this entire question still hung in the balance. Where would the scales of justice come down in the end?

Ma was sympathetic because she remembered how much she liked Hattie McDaniels, the actress who played the mammy in *Gone With The Wind*. So much of Ma's life and her lost youth, now disappearing so rapidly, used to be all tied up in her love of the movies and worship of the movie-stars. The mammy in that picture stood out in her mind as a representative of the loving-kindness and matronly-wisdom of her race. There was something universal in that poor slave-woman's sheer humanity that pulled at my mother. It was heartbreaking. That alone, for my mother, erased all racial barriers, and proved, that deep down, we were all one human race.

Of the three adults in the house, my Dad was easily the one most certain that things would never be the same again. He had spent his formative years growing up ten miles from the Mason-Dixon line. He knew Jim Crow. He went to six grades of a segregated school in Pershing, his hometown. He knew the colored folks in his community all lived down by the riverbank in a hollow called Gray's Landing. He worked in the coal industry, where there was a stout color line, enforced by an unspoken code, behind which fellow miners, fellow *union members*, lived by the creed of hate and the gospel of racial separation, black vs white, us vs them, superior vs inferior. It was a living memory to him, as clear as a telephone ringing. You picked up the receiver and the voice said, *You can't fight city hall.*

And yet, even then, all the way back in the Thirties, Dad knew, things were changing, and it was clear as soap-bubbles to him, that it was the government that was going to have to lay down the law to the recalcitrant whites. Now, in this new day, twenty years on, it was the same damn thing, and Dad had a rooting interest in seeing which way the worm would turn, after all this time had gone by—*or, did some things never change?*

That December, there was day-to-day suspense on the nightly news, on the television in our cozy den, with our comforting fireplace warming our backsides, and creeping up our backs to our pale white necks. There was day-to-day uncertainty surrounding the final outcome of the Montgomery Bus Boycott, down in Alabama. And we were just beginning to feel the flames.

I knew where I stood, though. I was deep into the series of hardback biographies in the pale blue covers that I had found in the school library at the Ebenezer Parker, George Washington Carver and Sojourner Truth and Harriet Tubman, plus *Uncle Tom's Cabin*. Abraham Lincoln was my hero, so there was no question which side to be on. Just like Superman said, *Truth, Justice and the American Way.*

As I explored my new neighborhood, I laid out strict boundaries to it in my mind, to try to get my bearings. The boys in our group were the ones who attended the Ebenezer Parker and lived on just a few streets clustered together. My classmates who lived on the other side of Haverhill Street, on Cypress Ave, and Wellington Street, did not belong to my neighborhood. Nor did those who lived down past the school on the streets opposite the Sandbanks, or the kids who came everyday in yellow school-buses, from places like Lowell Street, Forest Street, and even Rte 113, which led to Dracut.

My neighborhood was bounded by Billy McQuaid's house on the corner of Woodland and Elm. From Billy's house it came back toward my house, at Elm and Glenwood Ave. Glenwood led in the direction of the Ebenezer Parker. It dipped downhill at the corner of Durrell Street. At the bottom of the hill, Hazel Street branched off. That's where the path through the woods started, the dirt path leading across the brook in the swamp to the back of the school playing fields. This unmarked path was never used by adults. But it was trodden dutifully by our generation of schoolkids. It was our shortcut. When you're a kid you need to scout out shortcuts because your life is lived on foot. If you were a kid and you went to the Ebenezer Parker, all roads led not to Rome, but to the path through the woods.

Jimmy Dillard lived at the corner of Glenwood and Durrell. Frankie Fidelio lived at the other end of Durrell, at the corner of Woodland, on the second floor, above Jerry Ellsworth. Frankie's dad rented from Jerry's dad. Across from them, in the tidy sky-blue single-family with the welcoming porch where we all used to gather, lived the princess of our neighborhood, the beautiful Corinne Beauschene, and her brother Brian. In the middle of Durrell Street, on opposite sides of a wide parking lot, Sharon McCoy and Steven Morelli lived. Steven's dad, Mario Morelli, rented out a row of four garages at the back of his paved parking lot. Sharon didn't have a father at home, but she had a little sister. Steven Morelli was the only kid in our neighborhood who went to sister school, which was across Haverhill Street from the Parker, up the long driveway at St. Anne's Orphanage. Next to Steven, at the corner of Glenwood and Durrell, on that side of Durrell, across from Dillard's, was Bobby Dolan.

Behind our house, on Glenwood, there was a vacant lot, stretching two house-lots, down to the corner of Durrell Street, opposite the Dolans' one-story white house. From my back-window, you could see only the black roof of the pale blue house sitting on the hillside across the road from Mrs Dillard's two-family. In the blue house lived Carol Clapp. She was in my class. Paul Lamond was too, in the single-family at the corner of Glenwood and Hazel Street.

The vacant lot behind our house was owned by the Perrault family. They had five boys, who formed a basketball team of their own. They had built a dirt court on the vacant lot by putting up a regulation ten-foot steel-pole outdoor basketball backboard and hoop, complete with net. The five Perrault boys ranged in age from Guy, the oldest, who played on the high-school team at Central Catholic, the other big high school in Milltown, down to Roland, the youngest, who was my sister's age. There was Guy, Paul, Jean, Raymond, and Roland, all blond, all, except for Roland, of course, broad-shouldered French-Canadians. Their house was a single home painted baby-blue which had a front door on Hudson Street, but whose back yard ended at a retaining wall overlooking the vacant lot with the basketball court. Their mother was as big as her middle boy, Paul, and she had never had a daughter, only five boys. There were two other kids that had the same last name who played on that court, and they were good ball-handlers and shooters, rangy and tall, the brothers Ronnie and Ray Robillard, who lived on Elm Street, between me and Billy McQuaid's. They had a hoop and backboard on the front of the attached garage of their white ranch-style single home, and sometimes I used to go up there to play in their driveway, but more often, they came down to the Perrault's court, when they wanted to play four-on-four or five-on-five.

In that new neighborhood of mine, you had plenty of chances to practice basketball. The kids were crazy for shooting hoops. When the World Series ended, I was out there every day on the Perrault's court, which was right on the other side of our driveway. I begged my Uncle Augie till he bought me my own basketball, because I explained I was trying to make the team at school, and I needed to practice after school, when the gym at the Parker was locked. I wasn't big enough in fifth grade, and I didn't know enough, to get picked when the other boys were choosing up sides, but it was on their court where I taught myself to shoot a jumper, after I found out the rudiments from Coach Wendling at school. It was a question of trying until you got over being clumsy with it. Then it was easy, the more you got your body into the flow of it, but to get good you had to shoot a lot of them. I always asked permission to use their court whenever I stepped over my driveway, if the Perraults were out there. If not, I just went ahead. They never said no. If you belonged to that neighborhood, you were welcome. There was no pavement or markings, just the grass worn away to dirt from so many years of kids shooting hoops there. If I didn't get chosen, I just stood to one side and tried to pick it up from watching their moves. Guy Perrault was over six feet and he was really good. He was a starter on the Central Catholic five, the big parochial high school down in Milltown, which served five or more communities, Milltown, Spicket Falls, Andover and North Andover, even Boxford and Tewksbury.

The only bad thing about shooting hoops every day after school was when my mother would stick her head out the back door at precisely 4 o'clock and yell, "Nicky!—get in the house now! It's time to practice your accordian!"

I would turn four or five shades of shame-faced red while the boys were hooting at me, "Nicky! Nicky! Be a good boy now and listen to your mother!"

It never occurred to Ma that she was making me a laughing-stock in front of the whole neighborhood.

Chapter 11

The Shop

In the summer of '57, when the school year ended, and my ten-year old self got promoted again, as usual, this time to the top of the school, the 6th grade, I started working at 'the shop,' Uncle Gene's garment factory down in the Square. I could consider myself a child no longer. As far as I was concerned, doing a job and getting paid for it meant you were all grown up.

Never mind that the pay consisted of nickels and dimes and spare pocket change from trips down into the bowels of the mill-buildings to fetch coffee and English-muffins wrapped in wax-paper from Jack Lane at his lunch counter.

The fact that I was a bundle-boy, doing the same job that my grandfather had performed at the same age, in the year 1898, in New York City, meant to me that I was duplicating his feats. Carrying on in his footsteps. Joining the family trade. Fulfilling my destiny.

Being a bundle-boy involved simply carrying work-bundles from station to station, upstairs on the second floor where the stitchers dwelt with their gasping and groaning, stuttering and chattering electric sewing-machines. Your job was to save the stitchers, all of them ladies, from having to constantly all day get up and down to go fetch these bundles themselves. The bundles were prepared by Uncle Augie, the cloth-cutter, downstairs: they were parts, tied together in a strangle of twine: sleeves, fronts, linings, pockets. They were stacked at the back wall of the manufacturing floor, over by the chute and Uncle Augie's major-league scoreboard. You picked up the bundle that was wanted (they were marked in white cutter's chalk), threw it on your shoulder and carried it to the stitcher's station, where you threw it down next to her machine, where she could untie it and reach for the parts. There was a lot of standing around to this job, but it kept you fairly busy. They would call you with a wave of the hand. You got to know which ladies did which parts of the raincoat. My Auntie Mary specialized in pockets. My mother did buttons and zippers. This was the kind of work a kid could do. It wouldn't pay my Uncle Gene to hire a grown-up to do this, and in fact, during the school-year, Uncle Augie himself had to do it. But summertime was when the meet was on at Rockingham Park, just three or four miles away over the line in New Hampshire, so this freed him up to go to the track in the afternoons.

I was ten years old. The year before, when I was nine, I would not have deemed it possible. Now I was doing it.

Now, as opposed to when I was five or six years old, I need not daze my mind trying to figure out what they were talking about when they went on and on about the 'shop,' nor try to imagine where it was located, where they were hiding it, somewhere in a far-off, mythical Boston.

Now I knew exactly where the shop was and what it looked like, smelled like, and felt like.

And it wasn't long before I found out, in July and August, why they were called sweatshops. The windows were thrown wide open, in hopes of a breeze, but they only admitted more heat into a stuffy, windless workplace of ancient rounded floorboards, moldy rafters, paint-chipped metal posts and exposed walls of roughened red brick; and lint, everywhere; and the cloth-dust, hanging suspended in the slanted beams of sunlight flooding in from the tall, west-facing mill-windows in the late afternoon, when the mind was weary and the back sore from bending over eye-straining, jammering needlework for the last four hours since lunchtime.

Uncle Gene could not have found a location to start up *Gigi Sportswear* more fixed to the heart of Spicket Falls than the Oxford Mills.

These mills ran flush alongside the Falls on the Spicket, and staggered down the jagged course of white-water jammed in between the foundation walls of the mills and the high natural rock wall on the other side.

In this narrowed nature-made ravine a black stone dam no more than fifty feet wide had been levered in between the natural rock shoulders of the riverbanks to ram the river into a speeding funnel, which ran straight between the walls to the end of the mill-buildings before twisting southward to pass under the green-railed Oxford Street bridge a few feet from Broadway.

Originally, in the 1850s, water-wheels buried in the sidewalls of the mills' foundation, produced the electricity to power the mills. Nowadays, in modern times, they had fallen into disuse, and the power came in from the electric company. Also gone were the old coal-fired furnaces, replaced with oil, which heated all parts of the mill in the winter with steam-heat running through bulging, asbestos-jacketed steam pipes all through the bowels of the buildings. Whether coal or oil, the winter landscape of the town Square in all times, in all decades, for a hundred years past, showed the flag of white smoke pouring from the tall brick cylindrical smokestack of the Oxford Mills.

Uncle Gene rented his space in the two-story extension of the mills that directly overlooked the Falls.

If you were upstairs in the second-floor stitching-room looking out the windows on the north wall, you were looking directly down on top of the Falls. Yet the thunder of the sewing machines at your back would overrule the crash of the Falls.

But if you went outside and stood next to the first floor of that very set of windows, the thunderous trumpet of water tumbling 25 feet straight down, only to dash up a spewing tower of foam on the mountain of boulders below, drowned out everything, man-made, avian-made, or heaven-made.

As often as I could I went out, just to stand there and gaze at the Falls, for the sheer pleasure of it, to watch the black water as it timidly approached the lip of the dam in sheets, to see it helplessly pour over the edge and turn into solid white tubes endlessly falling; to hear the mighty music coming from the throat of the river, to feel the spray rising in wind-borne waves against my cheeks; to lose my mind, imagination and logical thought in the endlessly swirling, bisecting, coagulating, crisscrossing tangles of whitewater tumbling over the rocks, pouring downstream.

To me, these mills, this river, pre-dated any of the mills lining the canals on the Merrimack in Milltown; they were older than history, they came before the world came. They throbbed with the solidity of eternity itself.

I may have supposedly been working, but I had plenty of time apart. I may have been feeling all grown up, but there was inside of me nevertheless a child astounded by the wonder of all things incredibly magical or intensely real.

Uncle Gene had his office at the front side of the mill-extension, facing the unpaved dirt parking lot full of rocks. Everyone who worked at *Gigi Sportswear* entered through a door leading from the loading dock of the mills into the first floor; Uncle Gene's office door was left, everyone else turned right and went up the stairs at the back wall overlooking the river.

Next to the stairway a green chute came down from a rectangular hole cut in the second floor, and from this chute finished coats would slide down to land in a train of canvas-lined wagons which would then, when loaded, be wheeled away. After Uncle Patsy pressed them, and all wrinkles were smoothed over, the coats were hung on hangers and plastic protective film was rolled down over their shoulders. The racks were wheeled out through the double-doors onto the loading dock to go on delivery vans. These were things a boy my age could easily lend a hand to. We were making raincoats for London Fog, on sub-contract, because frequently they could not meet the demand from their own factories in Maryland, and they were shipped direct from our plant to retail destinations. For local deliveries, and to convey to the Milltown railroad station, we had our own tall but low-slung, wobbly black van with the white lettering spelling out *Gigi Sportswear*. Our coats would travel by rail to stores in places like Vermont and Connecticut, New York and New Jersey.

In the office there was a nice lady named Sally, very large and pleasant, with dark hair, who was Uncle Gene's secretary. She had a big black manual typewriter and was always typing out invoices and running an adding machine.

My mother was finally back to work at her trade of stitching, now that the twins were five years old. What with the new house, she was trying to make a few bucks to supplement her income, on top of what Dad made framing houses. She therefore wasn't about to spend hard-earned money on a baby-sitter to come into her house. She used me, and brought me and the twins to work with her.

Uncle Gene would pick us up at our house in the morning, or maybe Uncle Patsy, either one, on the way to work. I had to mind the twins in the office sometimes during the course of the work-day, and for that alone, I was earning the money I was making. It was an all-day affair trying to keep the restless Jackie-boy amused and at the same time placating the little-girl whims of my sister Jill. Fortunately, for me, having had a lifetime dose of Ma's scary domineering thrust down their throats along with the cod-liver oil, they had been taught to behave. I suppose they were actually very nice little children, but I was ten, and they were five. I'm afraid minding the kids and making sure they stuck to their coloring books and paper-dolls and did not fuss was not my favorite thing in the whole world. Again, I was lucky, as I had Sally there to help out, and Uncle Gene, too.

About ten in the morning it became my job to go around and collect all the orders for coffee break and go downstairs to the bottom of the mill-complex to Jack Lane's luncheonette.

Connected by brick and mortar to our 2-story extension, the rest of the Oxford Mills was five stories tall, but Jack Lane's was buried in what must have been the third sub-basement down, with all the asbestos-wrapped steam-pipes.

Jack was a middle-aged guy with freckles and red hair who wore a white uniform and a paper-hat like a hot-dog vendor at Revere Beach, a guy who never had time to talk or fool because he was too busy flipping sausage patties on the grill with his back turned to the customers while he took the orders they were calling out over his shoulder.

He had one straight counter with only four stools and the entire luncheonette couldn't have been more than twenty feet long. But everyone who worked in all the businesses in the mills must have had coffee break at ten in the morning because it was always three-deep in Jack Lane's. He had a girl who helped out, and between the two of them, they couldn't squeeze past each other behind the counter most times. Either one or the other was always at the manual cash register pushing the levers with the big circular pedals with the numbers inscribed.

I loved it in Jack Lane's. It always smelled of steam and frying bacon and cinnamon. I thought Jack would bite his own lips off he was thinking so hard as he rang up a sale, with the cigarette clenched between his teeth. I would hear the cash register ring-a-ding and look up to spot the white flags with the prices jumping up and down in the register-window.

I would stack all the orders on a chrome lunch-cart. They were parked in the steam-pipe hallway outside Jack's door. I would push the wagon down to the freight-elevator and take it up to the second floor, then cross on the bridge over the loading dock to our factory. I would deliver all my orders and that's how I collected all the tips that made up my week's pay. In the afternoon I would go back down to Jack Lane's, when it wasn't busy, and buy my brother and sister a tonic or a cinnamon bun. I counted my pennies because I was saving up to get *Classics Illustrated* Comic Books down at the Woolworth's or the Kresge's on Essex Street, and *Revell* models, a plastic *Flying Tigers P-40* or a twin-boomed *P-38 Fighter Plane*, to glue together. The ship models could run as much as a dollar-ninety-eight for *The Battleship Missouri*.

THE EDUCATION OF NICHOLAS PETROVICH

Sometimes I would wander out of the office and stand and watch Uncle Augie rolling out the big rolls of beige and ivory cloth that arrived at the loading dock. Although he was enormously strong, nobody could have lifted those rolls. You needed a fork-lift and cranes to handle those things. My Dad was the one who installed the crane-runners along the underside of the rafters. My uncles would stand around and watch. They would assist, but they waited on Dad's instructions. They knew he was the expert on building anything.

Uncle Augie's specialty was cloth-cutting. He would stack the cloth five layers high and use a powered band-saw to cut out all the parts which were to be assembled by the stitchers upstairs. The big black cord for the band saw descended from the rafter above and followed the band-saw wherever you pushed it. It was fascinating to watch Uncle Augie stand there, eyes darting, trying to figure out how to assemble all the patterns in such a way as to minimize the wasted material after making all the cuts. It was like a giant jig-saw puzzle. He would set the pattern-segments this way and that and then re-set them all and look and consider. He told me that sometimes their whole profit margin lay in the extra cloth that ended up on the floor. Or, maybe he would find a way to save enough material for Uncle Gene to use in the *Gigi Sportswear* coats he made to sell from the factory outlet showroom next to the office. It all depended on how good of a cloth-cutter you were.

Sometimes they would call me to rush upstairs and carry bundles, when they stacked up. At those times, Sally in the office would relieve me of minding the kids. I would rush through that chore and then stand and catch up on the latest standings in the American League.

Uncle Augie had created a board on the wall, painted green with white outlines, that was his own makeshift replica of the scoreboard on the left-field wall at Fenway Park. On this board he updated the standings every day, using the white cloth-chalk he used for tracing patterns downstairs. The scoreboard was hung on the wall over the hole in the floor where the chute went downstairs to land coats in the canvas wagons. I would study the board and then throw down a few coats to make a cushion for myself to land on, and, instead of taking the stairs, I would slide back down to the first floor.

I loved working at the family business.

Uncle Patsy was our presser. He had his steam-press over in the corner of the first floor, at the end overlooking the Falls. He would stand there wiping the sweat off his forehead while clouds of steam were rising. All day long he opened and shut the press on coat-lining after coat-lining. Summer or winter, he always stripped down to his tank-top when he was working. In summer he wore bermuda shorts. These shorts were extra large: ever since his underfed days in the war, he had been making up for lost dinners. Once in a while he would have to go and slake his steam-parched throat at the water-fountain over next to the double-doors.

One of those times when he wasn't there I came running, looking for him.

Wreathed in lingering wisps of vapor, there was Marilyn Monroe, on her red calendar, on the wall behind Uncle Patsy's steam-press, posing for all the world to see.

I was struck dumb to see an undressed woman. I was wondering what those rosy-tipped mounds on her chest were.

I must have been staring, because when Uncle Patsy came back, he started howling with laughter.

"Hey, Augie," he called, "willya look at this kid over here! Hypnotized!"

It was just my luck that Uncle Augie was there that day. A lot of times he would disappear in a taxi headed for Rockingham for the whole afternoon.

Uncle Augie yelled over, "Nicky! What's the matta? You never seen a naked woman before?"

The two of them were about to bust a gut, they were laughing so hard.

But Uncle Augie, he lived with me, in my house. Now I would never hear the end of it.

In spite of all that, I was having the time of my life working at the shop that summer. Too bad it all had to come to a crashing halt.

Uncle Gene came out of his office one day looking for me. He found me and put a hand on my shoulder. "Nicky, come here a minute, I gotta talk to you."

He took me outside to the front steps next to the loading dock and sat down with me on the steps. "Look, kid, it's nothing you did wrong or anything. But a State Inspector from the Labor Board came to visit me today, and he saw you carryin' bundles upstairs. He came back to my office and sat me down and said I can't have you workin' here anymore."

"But, Unk, I'm only doin' what Papanonni did when he was my age."

"I know, I know, Nicky. We've all heard that story, time and again. But that was in the old days. Times have changed.

Nowadays they got child labor laws. I know you're disappointed. Somebody musta made a phone call. I wonder who it was? It coulda been anybody. Not necessarily one of our girls. Coulda been somebody from any one of these businesses in the mills here that seen you one too many times down in Jack Lane's."

Uncle Gene's head was bowed over his elbows balanced on his knees when he noticed I had turned my head, to hide tears.

"Nicky, I'm sorry. Nothing I can do. Do you forgive me?"

"Uncle Gene, it's not your fault."

I ran off as quick as I could and left poor Uncle Gene sitting there by himself. I ran around the back of the building and didn't stop till I had my fingers locked in the chain link fence that kept you from falling into the Spicket, and as I leaned my forehead on the cool metal, I watched, through my tears, the white-water roiling, hoping that the roar of the Falls would drown out the sound of my sobs.

Chapter 12

Roseann

That was the summer, the summer of '57, when I hit my little brother, five-year-old Jackie, in the side of the head with a baseball bat, on the lawn just outside our kitchen window. I thought I killed him but he got up laughing before he fell down again. I got a good lickin' for that one from Ma, even though it wasn't my fault. I told the kid to watch out, I'm gonna swing, and he wouldn't listen, and I hit him on the back-swing.

That was also the summer Ma was showing off her new house to the whole family. The big date was set for a Fourth of July picnic in our backyard. Dad built a brand-new picnic bench out under the crab-apple tree, and my cousins were all there. I hadn't seen cousin Tommy since the day we left Watertown, cousin Linda and her big brother Anthony came from Peabody, and Tommy's little brother and sister, Lenore and Timmy. Auntie Peggy arrived without Henry and Ronnie, who were in Wilmington for the summer with their father and his new wife. Auntie Mary Laverna and her husband Charlie drove up from Watertown in the DeSoto with Uncle Gene and his family—Auntie Celia sat next to Uncle Gene in the front and their daughter Joanne squeezed in by the window so that her little brother and sister Leon and Marie could fit in the back with Uncle Charlie and Auntie Mary. Cousin Gerry, who was Auntie Mary's daughter, and who was named after my mother, wouldn't have fit in, and my cousin Tony, who had just graduated the year before from Watertown High, was still laid up with a broken leg. Everybody said he was the cousin who took after Uncle Augie—over six feet and a helluva football player. He was the starting quarterback on the 1956 Watertown High team that won the state Class A Championship, against none other than Milltown High. He was recruited by Boston College and played on the freshman team the fall before, but when spring football drills came, that's when he broke his leg. My cousin Henry was two years older than his brother Ronnie, who went to Wilmington High, but Henry graduated from Revere High School, and had already joined the Marines, at 17.

What a fight *that* was around the picnic table. Ma and the two Auntie Mary's were parading out of the kitchen with a steaming pan of lasagna, with *insalata*, roast beef, potato salad, and God knows what else. Uncle Patsy, who loved to cook out, was grilling hot dogs and hamburgers on the new three-legged charcoal grill Dad had got from Sears and Roebuck's down on Essex Street, and Auntie Peggy was arguing with her brothers, the three veterans, that she should never have signed for her son Henry to go in at seventeen.

They were all saying *best thing for him, make a man out of him*. The memory, to them, was fresh, of Henry's father, Henry Fabiano, during the war enlisting in the Marines and getting the worst of it on Guadalcanal.

But Auntie Peggy was distraught because Henry had told her he was studying Russian and expected to be posted to an air base in Japan soon, and she said she hoped to hell he wasn't gonna try to bring home one of those slant-eyed little geisha-girls to his mother, and she was being polite because the kids were around. "I can't understand how come we have to rebuild their country for them after those little yellow bastards knifed us in the back."

Uncle Gene said, "Well, for that matter, if it wasn't for the Marshall Plan, where would Europe be today?—down and out, that's where."

Uncle Patsy joined in from the grill. "I keep telling you people, we shoulda dropped The Bomb on the Chinese when we had the chance. Instead, we send our boys in with two hands tied behind their back. And then look what happens!"

Ma noticed her brother Augie fuming at their sister Peggy while clamping his lips shut.

"Sit down! Sit down!" Ma yelled. "We'll fight the war some other time, now it's time to eat!"

Ma loved to cook, everybody said it was her passion and she should open her own restaurant, she'd make a million. Auntie Mary LaStoria raved about her sauce, claiming she tried Ma's recipe at home, just the way Ma told her, but somehow it never came out the same, nobody could make it like Gerry. Auntie Anna and Uncle Tommy, who came up from Watertown in their Oldsmobile 88, tended to agree, or at least abstain, but Auntie Mary Laverna sniffed that it wasn't thick enough, like her own, she liked to make it nice and thick so you had to peel it off the ladle with a spoon. Auntie Peggy, whose idea of cooking was to open a carton of take-out Chinese, said she'd never stick to her diet if she ever moved in with us.

After the grown-ups had spent three or four hours gabbing and eating and were feeling too lethargic to push back from the table, and Tommy and I were exhausted from chasing the younger kids around the yard, that's when, well before mosquito-hour, Ma called me over to say, "Nicky, go get your accordian and play us a tune."

Reluctantly, hanging my head, shoulders sloping as if resigned to the gallows, I trooped inside to drag out the big case along with my music-stand and my sheet music.

Her new house was not the only thing Ma had to show off that day. For my last birthday, when I turned ten, she had bought me a new accordion. It was a brand-new 120-bass black Excelsior piano-accordian, with a chrome grill and white shift-buttons and a full-size two-and-a-half-octave keyboard, made in Italy. It cost her a thousand dollars, on time-payments, five bucks a week. Balanced on my lap, when I was seated to play it, you could not see me behind it. In snapshots they took that day, I looked like two hands playing buttons and keys, and a forehead visible over the top.

I had been taking lessons, ever since we first got to the city, at Milltown Music on Common Street. It was the big music store in the city and there were at least a dozen studio-rooms for lessons at the back. Roland Moore taught guitar and Chaz Parmenides taught woodwinds and brass, but my teacher was Jerry Bellanti, a Milltown High kid only two or three years older than me, who was a prodigy accordianist. The owner of Milltown Music was Mario Morelli, Steven Morelli's dad; their family lived on Durrell Street, right around the corner of Glenwood from us, Ma boasted.

It was Mr. Morelli who came to sit with my mother in her new kitchen to explain that she would not be wasting her money to invest in a beautiful musical instrument made in Italy such as this for me. Mario Morelli was a local Merrimack Valley legend, a big-band leader from my mother's day, and all the guys from his generation, my uncles' age, who were teachers in his shop used to be members of his band. He was Italian and that was good enough for Ma. After all, a thousand bucks was a lot of money. But Mario Morelli made the payments easy for her and guaranteed that when I was old enough, he'd find a place for me, just like he had for Jerry Bellanti—who, after all, wasn't gonna be there forever, who is?

Thus was I anointed to the succession.

However, at this moment in the July sunshine of 1957, I did not feel anything but the spotlight of the sun burning my neck as I trudged out there to play for my family.

Dimly, I was aware that I was going to be judged by the grownups, who remembered their father playing the mandolin for them at many an outdoor picnic in the backyard in Stoughton, or even in Hingham, thirty, thirty-five, maybe forty years earlier. I was carrying on a family tradition and I would be examined to see if I measured up.

How could I ever measure up to my grandfather?

I felt as scrutinized as if I had forgotten to put clothes on.

Nevertheless, I turned over the sheets on the music stand. There it was, *Arr. By Charles Magnante,* staring me in the face. I wanted to start with something slow, to get my nerve up, so I played *Come Back to Sorrento.* Then I did *Carnival of Venice,* a waltz, and then *Santa Lucia,* a song which would make stones cry. Now I was going pretty good, and I wanted to play one of my great favorites, a song which I loved to practice, never mind play, the gorgeous and tender *La Paloma—The Dove.* But my Auntie Mary Laverna asked for her number-one all-time favorite, *Ave Maria.* I played it, but I made mistakes on the arpeggios, which did not escape Auntie Mary's notice. Finally, satisfied that I passed their stringent audition, the grownups relaxed and, in one voice, called for *Lady of Spain,* a song made famous by Dick Contino. Inwardly, I groaned as I turned over the sheet music. I hated "Lady of Spain," especially the bellows-shake on the repeat. I wasn't very good at the bellows-shake.

Nevertheless, I got the big round of applause, Uncle Patsy joking "Watch out, Myron Floren!" Of course, the applause did nothing but embarrass me, as I shrugged off the straps from my shoulders and gently lowered the thousand-dollar accordian back into the open case on the ground. I did not give myself high marks: too many mistakes. *Well,* I said to myself, *they make me nervous.*

Afterwards, my cousin Tommy thought he would do the noble thing and help me carry my gear back in the house. Meanwhile, he sniggered under his breath, "Show-off!" He pushed me on the shoulder. "I thought I told you once you don't always have to do what your mother tells you to do, didn't I?"

"Yeah. But you didn't tell me how to get out of accordian lessons."

That night, the Fourth of July, 1957, was the night my mother and Dad took us kids and all the aunts and uncles, for the first time, in our new town, to the fireworks at the O'Neill Playstead.

All the playgrounds in Spicket Falls, even the one behind my school, the Ebenezer Parker, were called *'Playsteads,'* a novel term to me. I remembered vividly, when I was little, being scared out of my wits by the fireworks, the first time my Dad ever took me to see them at the DelloRusso Stadium in Revere. The O'Neill Playstead was nothing like Revere's high-school football stadium.

But it was a spectacular night of deep indigo, with a tropical breeze. On its journey to empty into the Merrimack, the Spicket River, after it came down from The Falls and passed under Broadway by St Monica's Church, snaked behind the O'Neill. Swarms of local families crowded the grounds. They drove in the gate and parked their cars on the outfield grass at the backstop end of the baseball field. All my mother's family surrounded me. We spread out blankets and baskets of good things to eat and reclined on the grass to look up at the stars and wait for bursts of light and showers of thunder. Over our shoulders the shadows of the Searles Castle loomed from across the road. This odd, out-of-place stage-set was actually an extensive ring of stout 12-foot-high grey granite castle-walls, built in a miles-long oval surrounding the estate of Old Man Searles, who was a nineteenth century industrialist, long dead. Nobody knew what possessed him to create such a curious monstrosity in the center of Spicket Falls. But it lent the evening a spooky sense of 'royal madness' peeking down on you from the formidable black-iron castle-gate and the baffling battlements: crenellated, as if for war by bow and arrow, garishly lit up by the intermittent lightning flashes from the inky night sky full of blossoming fireworks.

The week after the Fourth, another branch of the family, this time Dad's side, did move in with us, although it was only for two weeks.

Uncle Alek Petrovich was on two weeks summer vacation from the coal-mine and he drove up from Pennsylvania in his latest brand-new '56 Chevy with Auntie Rose and my cousin Roseann.

It was a big reunion of sorts for Uncle Mike Kowalcyzk, and my Dad, too. Uncle Mike was now ensconced with his family in that third-floor flat he'd found on the far end of Boxford Street about the time when we were getting ready to leave South Milltown. All my Pennsylvania relatives, or at least some of them, were now converging on our new fieldstone house, and I was about to meet girl cousins I didn't even know.

Uncle Mike and Auntie Stasija, my Dad's sister, had two girls, Patty and Michelle. Patty was eleven, and I was going on eleven, and her sister Michelle was two years younger but I had never met them.

It was looking like I was going to have to be on my best behavior, meeting girls who were strangers, yet related to me. My little brother and sister, the twins, Jackie and Jill, didn't really count in this picture as anything but nuisances, they were too young. But I was on the spot.

Roseann was my other girl cousin on that side. I did not really recall her, although when she was little, she came to Revere. I remembered her from pictures in the family photo album, more than any recollection I could call my own.

So? Well? I don't know. But I was not prepared for the moment when my cousin Roseann emerged, with her head bowed, from the backseat of her dad's two-door Chevy convertible with the red-and-white two-tone paint job standing on the black tar of the lengthy driveway in back of the fieldstone house.

She looked up and tossed her tawny dark blond head of wavy hair back over her shoulders, and it was like seeing a glamorous Shirley Temple, on the verge of adolescence, stepping out of a regal carriage in a Hollywood extravaganza of the antebellum South.

She looked up from under the lids of warm brown mysterious Serbian eyes, eyes with angular, oval corners that spoke of a long Polish descent from the steppes of inner Asia.

She did not need a cape of soft fur caressing her cheeks for me to know immediately that she was a princess from a storybook.

My mother was rushing over to embrace Uncle Alek's wife Rose. She loved Auntie Rose, with whom she had formed a strong, girlish attachment when she had briefly stayed in Pershing, Penna., in my Dad's childhood home, when they were on the way back to Massachusetts from their honeymoon in San Diego, in the late fall and Christmastime and New Year's after the war ended. So it was a reunion for Ma, too, with someone she was fond of whom she hadn't seen for years now.

The first thing Uncle Alek did when he got to our driveway was hop out of the Chevy to grab Dad's push-mower out of the garage and start mowing the lawn for my Dad. Our lawn went around all four sides of the fieldstone house, and was big enough, on the kitchen and den side, to fit another whole house. Then he hooked up the hose on the outdoor spigot under the two windows to the den and started to 'worsh' his car. Uncle Alek arrived on a Monday while Dad was at work. He had been driving the weekend 500 miles straight through from the Pennsylvania Turnpike and the New Jersey Turnpike and then all the way up to Hartford and Boston, and after all that long ride sitting, went straight to work, to loosen up his limbs. He wanted to surprise his big brother when Dad got home.

Just then, Uncle Mike was arriving in his new second-hand Plymouth with Auntie Stasija sitting practically in his lap in the front and the two girls Michelle and Patty stuffed in the back.

There was a lot of excited talk, the twins, Jack and Jill, underfoot, the relatives trooping up the back-porch steps into the house, exclamations of wonder at the cabinets my Dad had built in the kitchen, my mother eagerly inviting her sister-in-law Rosie upstairs to see the rest of the house.

I could see nothing but my cousin Roseann.

Not only was Roseann pretty to the point of painfulness, she was pleasingly bashful, not at all aware of her beauty, and friendly, too, in an open, unguarded way that I was not used to. She came from a rural place where you knew all your neighbors and left your doors unlocked. I came from an urbanized, East Coast world of caution and coolness and native New England reserve. But what I did not know was that Roseann was taking accordian lessons, too.

Uncle Alek popped open the trunk of the Chevy and got out suitcases and—an accordian case.

My mother put us in the dining room and closed the door.
"She always does that," I said.
"Doesn't she like to hear you play?"
"She hears every mistake I make, right through that door."
"What do you want to play?"
"I don't know. You go first."
"I brought you a present." She pulled out a music book from under the red accordian in her case. She handed it across to me. I had my accordian in my lap. I was reaching over the top to unfold my music stand. I saw the book was *Slovenian Polkas,* arr. by Frankie Yankovic.
"Is that what you take lessons on?"
"We play polkas for the dancers every Sunday after church."
I loved her accent. She laughed at the way I said the word *'cah'* instead of car. I teased her about how her Dad had said

'*worsh*' instead of wash. We had so much in common. My accordian was black and hers was red. She got straight A's and I got straight A's. She was the first person other than myself and the twins to come into my life who shared the same name as mine, the name of Petrovich. Our fathers were brothers. We were first cousins. We swore we'd stay in touch. We were going to become pen-pals when this vacation was over and she had to go back home. We were the exact same age. I was a boy and she was a girl. She was the first person in my life of my own age of the opposite sex to actually talk to me, to take an interest in what I said, to believe in me, even just a little. She said she was going to miss me when she had to go. I was in love, in the way that only a boy going on eleven can be: in pure romantic adoration.

Chapter 13

The Wonder Bar

Our next invasion of relatives came when the summer meet opened later in July at Rockingham Park, just over the border from Spicket Falls in southern New Hampshire.

Auntie Peggy pulled into the driveway one day, chauffered by what she called her "friend" Jerry.

This "friend" Jerry was an older man, obviously too old to be a boyfriend.

That made everything morally satisfactory in front of us impressionable kids.

Jerry drove a modified 9-passenger station wagon with jump seats in the rear, a vehicle he dubbed the Rockingham Limo.

He would charge several dollars each to ferry horse-players from Revere or Everett or Medford and Melrose up to the pari-mutuel windows at *'The Rock,'* as he called it. My Auntie Peggy was along to chat up Jerry's customers, make them feel at home, and provide a party atmosphere, especially to buck up the losers on the long ride home.

Auntie Peggy knew from the 4th of July gathering that Ma was feeling a generosity of spirit that summer, and she waited till she knew that Uncle Alek and Auntie Rose and cousin Roseann were gone back home to Pennsylvania before she descended upon us.

Auntie Peggy was always a welcome guest with us kids. When she came to visit, she came to stay, and all the rules of the house, so steadfastly enforced by Ma, went out the window.

We could eat all the ice cream and potato chips we wanted.

We could run crazy through the house and make a lot of shrieking noise. She would chase us.

We could make fudge in the oven and forget to turn it off till the fudge came out glazed and brittle as obsidian and we had to break it with one of Dad's hammers from the cellar and suck on it like triangular popsicles. Only Auntie Peggy could make frozen fudge in a 350 degree oven!

For amusement outdoors, Auntie Peggy explored the neighborhood with us, not forgetting to include the twins in the game. She hit the jackpot when she found blueberries growing along the fence of the Immaculate Conception graveyard up on top of Railroad Hill. This hump-backed peak just north of Tower Hill afforded a panoramic vista of the Arlington Mills, which ran along Broadway on the Milltown side of the Spicket Falls line. The Spicket River, at this point, had doubled back on itself, re-crossing under Broadway below St Monica's, only to re-settle, to wiggle and waver, in a wide stagnant pool behind the Arlington Mills. I would be picking blueberries and lose myself in gazing at this still-life lake from a dizzying height above it, higher than the tallest smokestack in the mills.

Railroad Hill was a haunted place. The cars would whizz by while you were picking berries, which grew along the disheveled chain-link fence bordering the decrepit graveyard, whose tottering monuments were much more ancient than those opposite, on the slopes of the pedicured Tower Hill. An automobile would have to accelerate to get up the steep hill of Railroad Street from the Gill Avenue Playstead on the Spicket Falls end of the Hill. They would then come zooming over the crest into a steep gully and a set of S-curves, up and down, up and down, before they ever saw you picking berries by the side of the road.

But Auntie Peggy was not afraid of the cars, or the gravestones, or the ghosts. Nor was she afraid of the woods.

In our neighborhood the woods ran behind the Clapp's house and the dead end of Hudson Street, between there and the playstead of the Ebenezer Parker, complete with a brook that ran through a pipe under the path we took every day to school with the patrol line. Auntie Peggy took us there to hunt for mushrooms. She affected surprise that we did not know how. You had to know which side of the tree to look on. Answer: the dark side, away from the sun. And you had to be able to tell the good ones from the poisonous ones. She said every kid back in her day had to know that or they might starve in the Depression. She found black trumpets hiding in mounds of leaf litter. Pear-shaped puffballs on rotting logs. Oyster mushrooms climbing tree-trunks. Puffballs are safe, but you gotta cook 'em, but those little brown mushrooms? They can kill you, they're poisonous.

Auntie Peggy also cast a spell on us by playing children's games indoors on rainy days. Right alongside of us she would play as we whiled away the summer with Chinese checkers and Monopoly and the Ouija board and a game of world conquest called Risk, which was good for geography. How to play solitaire and Old Maid and poker and the Italian card game called *scopa* were highlights on her agenda. When the call for the seventh race came on the radio on the kitchen windowsill, Auntie Peggy had me and Jack and Jill sit in three chairs in a circle in front of the radio and she would hand out three dimes to us, one each. We had to study the green sheet and pick a horse, for win, place or show. Of course, we bragged about who won to Ma, who scolded her sister for teaching us bad habits.

By the fall, when the meet at Rockingham was over, and there was no more friend Jerry coming around with the Rockingham limo, Auntie Peggy suddenly recalled that she had forgotten to tell Ma that her lease ran out in Revere, and she had no place to go back to.

That's when I remembered her little studio apartment in the house on stilts with the Cape Cod shingles at the corner of C-1 and Revere Street. The picture of her bead curtain leading from the sleeping room into her kitchenettte with the hot plate jumped into my head, and I suddenly remembered how awful I felt, running all the way home to our house on Payson Street, the day when I was 8 years old and I stumbled in on her while she was cannonading her poor son Henry with a fifty-gun barrage of verbal tirade so violent it made the bead curtain dance. I wished I hadn't remembered because it forced me to admit how sometimes Auntie Peggy could be as hateful as she was, other times, mischievously impish.

In the end Auntie Peggy was living behind the closed door of our parlor, sleeping on the couch under the front porch windows, drying her stockings on a clotheslines she ran between the pillars of the alcoves flanking the opening between the parlor and the dining room. Dad had taken out the folding doors that used to be hung there, to open up the space. She had moved her tiny studio life from Revere into our house. Instead of working as the hostess of the Frolics on Revere Beach Boulevard, she was bartending at *The Wonder Bar*, a German tavern at the corner of Lowell and Broadway, the next block up from Movie-house Row, down in Milltown.

That place, *The Wonder Bar,* was nothing but a dive. Even I could tell that. When they unlocked their doors in the morning, they never even bothered to keep them swinging, they just hooked them on the latch, so that the doors stayed open all day, and every drunk and wino in town who found change lying on the sidewalk could stroll in for a nickel beer.

I used to go see Auntie Peggy at work. I would cross over Tower Hill up to the top on Haverhill Street to where Lowell Street came off of it, then take Lowell all the way to the end where it joined Broadway. When I got to *The Wonder Bar,* I would stand on the sidewalk outside the wide open back door and try to peer into the gloomy darkness inside. The wash of stale beer and disinfectant would come rushing up in my face. When I couldn't spy Auntie Peggy in the dim interior, I would go in and pull out a barstool, to sit and wait for her. I'd watch her laughing and joking with the men, pushing a rag, pulling a tap-handle. She would come round eventually and tell me I couldn't stay. She'd pour me a sasparilla, and say, "Now drink that, and then, get outta here before you get me in trouble."

I would leave feeling sad, because I remembered Auntie Peggy when she was hostess of *The Frolics* . . .

Chapter 14

Jimmy Dillard

My puritan ardor for my cousin Roseann was tested in a way I could not have imagined when Thanksgiving came around that extraordinary year.

My mother's family had adopted the custom of rotating holidays, and the big traditional gathering for Thanksgiving this year was held at Uncle Patsy and Auntie Mary's in Peabody.

My girl cousin on that side, Linda LaStoria, like Roseann Petrovich, was exactly my age.

Linda was also altogether gorgeous but in a very different, Italian way. She used makeup and teased her hair, even though she was only eleven. She painted her nails and wore bracelets. She wore lipstick and had smoldering Mediterranean eyes. She was very fair-skinned and had the allure of a Lollabrigida, quite unlike the olive passion of a Sophia Loren. And after the big dinner in her house, when her father had gone for a nap on the living room sofa, and all the aunts were washing the dishes in the kitchen, Linda wanted to play *Spin the Bottle*.

So she got her cousins Tina and Lorraine from her mother's side and me and cousin Tommy DiPrima and her brother Anthony and dragged us into her bedroom and shut the door.

Because she shut the door, I knew that Linda knew what she was doing was wrong, or least naughty, or, at least, she didn't want to get caught.

Amazingly, there was so much gaiety and uproar going on in the kitchen, and snoring coming from the sofa, that nobody gave a thought to us, locked in Linda's bedroom.

I ended up having to kiss Linda's cousin Lorraine. I played the game. I puckered up and closed my eyes. But I felt no thrill. It was pale and antiseptic. I had given my heart to my cousin Roseann.

The next years of my life passed in a dream. Roseann and I corresponded faithfully, pledging our undying devotion, sparing no everyday occurrence, leaving no passing schoolyard drama to go un-memorialized, making immortal our innermost 'going-on 12-year-old' passionate musings; I passed from the fifth to the sixth grade as if by magical forgetfulness; I began to become a big brother at last when little Jack and Jill had to start the first grade and I had to hold their hands, one on each side of me, as we traipsed daily through the woods at the bottom of Glenwood Avenue with the patrol line from our neighborhood, crossing the brook on the path over the pipe in the swamp, only to emerge into the Parker Playstead; where I cautioned the kids to come straight to me if anyone tried to bother them, in class or in the hallways or at recess, especially if they tried to make anything out of that Jack and Jill thing: as, a sixth-grader now, I knew how cruel kids in school could be.

As I daydreamed my way through sixth grade, something I was barely conscious of was bothering me. All the other boys in our few closely-knit streets seemed to be paired off with a best friend: Jerry Ellsworth with Frankie Fidelio, because they were up-and-down neighbors in the same house; Jimmy Morelli with Bobby Dolan, because he lived next door; Sharon McCoy with Carol Clapp, because they were girls, of course. The Perrault boys with themselves, because naturally they were five brothers, it was hard to dent their solidity; the same with the brothers Robillard, Ronnie and Ray, who were close together in age: they didn't need outsiders. In the end I was left to flounder and feel left out because I was the latest to enter the field, the newcomer, and the MacDougals, Freddie and Steven, across Glenwood from us at 36 Elm, they were not to my taste: their parents were country-club members, and they went to private school, and they had a tall hedge to hide their house from everyone, the only such hedge in the neighborhood.

I fumbled and faltered through these pre-teen agonies until one day when Jimmy Dillard invited me to supper over at his house.

I accepted with gladness and relief. I found, from his invitation to come over his house, that maybe Jimmy Dillard was also feeling left out, that maybe he was looking for that elusive best friend, too.

I hadn't seen hide nor hair of old Tommy since the day I left South Milltown, nor had I given hardly a thought to Billy McQuaid, who no longer had me over to his house, the charcoal grey Colonial at the corner of Woodland; perhaps Billy had grown out of the toy soldiers phase?

But Jimmy Dillard lived only a few steps away, in the grey two-family at the corner of Durrell Street, just at the end of the Perrault's vacant lots, right across from the Clapps' blue house, where Glenwood Ave went abruptly downhill to the corner where Hazel Street and the path through the woods to school began.

And after I went to supper at Jimmy's house, my mother interrogated me as to what Mrs Dillard was like, and what kind of food she cooked, and I explained she served us meat and white potatoes, with brown gravy, and Ma said how other people wished they got as good at home as we did, I didn't know how lucky I was, they had to go to a restaurant to get a taste of Italian cooking. Ma always made it sound like I was anointed by God to be so lucky as to be born Italian, while other nationalities had to be cast into the outer gloom of non-Italian-hood.

But she wouldn't let me have Jimmy over for dinner, to return the favor, which I didn't understand, and I held it against Ma that she didn't want to know the people in the neighborhood. She didn't want to have anything to do with them, and she didn't want them knowing her business, either, which made it hard on me to have a best friend.

But Jimmy Dillard didn't make an issue out of it, maybe because he was an only child and didn't have a father at home, which I remembered was the same case with Tommy in South Milltown.

And maybe that's why I liked Jimmy, because I felt sorry for him, not having a father, and his mother having to work to support the family, and him being home alone all by himself all the time every afternoon after school. But in Jimmy's case, it was double feeling sorry for him, because as soon as we became friends, he told me right away that he had lost his Dad in the Korean War, and that his dad was a war-hero, and he missed him a lot, and so did his mother, and so I felt extra-double-sorry for Jimmy Dillard, to have to go through something like that. I didn't have to in my family, so I should maybe try to be a good friend to Jimmy.

So now I went out of my way to see him every day, and sit with him on the fire-escapes after school, and to have him come over to play baseball cards at my house, which he liked to do, because we had a back stoop where we could fling the cards and see if we got leaners or topsies, which was a game we liked to play together, at his house or mine. My Dad had built the new back-porch steps when we bought the house, and so we had a nice smooth cement walk intersecting with the brick walk with the rose-bush that led to the driveway.

Jimmy took me down to *Rosie's*, which was a tiny variety store set in the front of a white house across from the Sandbanks, just past the Parker school on Haverhill Street, and Rosie was this old, old, wrinkle-puss lady who used to come down the steps from inside her house, whenever the bell that rang when you opened the front door of her shop sounded, and she would stand there with folded arms on the other side of the candy counter while you thumbed through the revolving rack with the Topps baseball-card bubble-gum packages. Rosie suspected all the kids who came into her little house-front shop of stealing her blind.

Jimmy was really great at blowing bubbles, while I couldn't manage it at all. I admired him for that. He knew it, too, because he used to blow big bubbles just to show off and pop'em. We used to laugh like heck at the tangles of soupy-stringy bubble gum that ensued all over his hands. It was a whole new sit-com watching Jimmy try to extricate himself from the gooey mess and stuff it back into his mouth.

I spent some of the money I made at the shop on starting a collection of baseball-cards so that I could trade and swap with Jimmy. We could try and win them off of each other with our back-stoop baseball-card game. If you flung a card against the step, from five feet away, and you got a leaner, you could top the other guys' leaner by knocking it down with your next fling; or topping it without knocking it over; or if your fling lay flat on the ground, you could get topsies on that one, and that's how you won the other guy's cards.

So we would play this game all the time, that school-year of the sixth grade, until February came that year, and it so happened that we were having a mild winter, or a thaw or something that week, and all the kids in the neighborhood got their snow-shovels out and we went down the Parker to shovel off the basepaths so we could start playing real baseball in February, how about that?

Now that I was a sixth-grader, I was experiencing what it felt like to be at the top of the school and be looked at by all the other grades as one of the big kids, especially since my brother and sister were now in first grade. So I would have Jimmy come over to my house to play baseball cards every day, because my mother was at work at the shop and I had to mind the kids after school till she got home at five to cook the supper, and I told all this to Roseann in my letters, because now I was thinking about Jimmy and how we were best friends. Every night when I was going to sleep in my bed, he would be the last thing I was thinking of, and so I told Roseann in my letters how I really, really liked him, and what a great kid he was.

But I didn't know then how much Jimmy meant to me.

Back at the beginning of the school year in sixth grade, the Little Rock school-desegregation saga was playing on television in our den.

Auntie Peggy was sitting there watching with the rest of us. She came out with the comment, "Look at those little monkeys."

I swiveled my head at this, in time to see my aunt overtaken with an involuntary shudder that gripped her shoulders, shook her, and traveled down her arms, a shudder that was like a wet dog trying to shake off water-beads.

Auntie Peggy looked straight at me. "Ooh, those niggers, they make my skin crawl."

My mother flew off the handle at this and started a big war with her sister. "What's the matter with you? Don't you know big-ears repeats everything he hears from you?"

"Well, maybe this is something he needs to hear."

My mother was enraged, but she was not about to win an argument with her older sister Peggy.

It was shortly after that when Auntie Peggy moved back to Revere and we didn't see her anymore.

I wasn't too upset at that. I knew she'd be back. In fact, I found out from Uncle Patsy that she had moved in with them, in Peabody. Until she had enough money to get a place of her own in Revere. Or so she said. She just didn't want Ma to know what she was up to or where she was.

My mother stopped me in the hallway one morning before school, a few days later.

"Now listen to me," she said. "I don't want you using that word 'nigger' that you heard from your aunt."

I began to protest, as she was acting like she was mad at me, and I hadn't done anything.

"I don't care! There's bad words for every nationality! French are frogs and Germans are Krauts and Spanish are Spics! They're all bad words! How would you like it if someone called you a Guinea or a Dago or a Wop? And believe me, they will! And as to Petrovich—do you know what they'd call you down in your father's neck of the woods? A Hunky, that's what!"

I took my little brother and sister by the hand to school that day wondering at the vehemence of my mother. I didn't hate anybody. If anything, I was on the side of those poor school-kids in Little Rock, and I believed everything the TV reporters said on TV, and they all seemed to think Ike was doing the right thing to send in the troops. What did it have to do with us, anyway? We were northerners, we weren't like those people down south.

So that February, when we were shoveling off the base-paths at the Parker, I wanted to go down and play baseball after school that week, at least while the thaw lasted. I was in sixth grade now and I had gotten plenty of practice at recess. I was getting good enough so even Jack Fallon and Dick Nickerson, who were the leaders in our grade of the bunch that came from the other side of Haverhill Street, would choose me, even if Frankie and Jerry, from our neighborhood, left me off their team. I figured I could bring along little Jack and Jill and have them sit on the bench and wait for me while I played after school. I just wouldn't tell my mother, and swear them to keep the secret, and we'd be home in time for supper, or at least before Ma got home.

But Jimmy Dillard was jealous. He didn't want me playing with other kids. Jimmy was tall and kind of awkward, bigger than me, but as thin as the fire-escape railings. He wasn't getting picked by the teams when the guys chose up. He didn't own a glove and he didn't want to play. He wanted me to go over Rosie's and get some new baseball-cards.

I went because he asked me to. But when we got there, he wanted to get a pack of Lucky Strikes off of Rosie. He told the old woman they were for his mother.

She was so old all the kids used to say she'd be dying any day now. But she was the kind who grasped after pennies that little kids have, and so she wasn't going to pass up the chance to sell a pack of cigarettes for 35 cents, even if the kid was only 11 years old.

I had my little brother and sister with me, so when we got outside and Jimmy offered me one, I said, "No—I don't want to stunt my growth."

Which was the honest truth. My Uncle Augie was the greatest athlete I personally knew and he never smoked a cigarette in his life, because, he told me, it took away your wind, so, of course, I wasn't about to start on them when I wanted to be a ballplayer just like him.

Something was going on with Jimmy.

One day after school he came over and we were playing baseball-cards up against the stoop on my back porch. It was springtime, and he was openly smoking now. He was wearing a white tee-shirt with short sleeves, and he had his pack of Lucky Strikes stuck on his shoulder up under the rolled-up sleeve, which he had seen some older kids do. He had a lit cigarette clamped in his mouth and the smoke was biting my eyes.

"That's a leaner," he said, after his throw.

"Is not," I said.

"Is so," he said.

"I'm not gonna play if you're gonna cheat." I went up the steps and started pulling open my screen door. I heard him start chanting in a sing-song.

On top of spaghetti,
All covered with cheese,

I turned around and he was walking in a tight little circle on my dad's cement walk.

I lost my poor meatball
When somebody sneezed.

"Stop it, Jimmy."
He stopped and ground out his cigarette on my walk.
"You better get outta my yard."
"Who's gonna make me?"
"I don't wanna have a fight with you, Jimmy."
"Why? You chicken?"

I flew off my top step and into his arms. We fell down in a heap and started rolling over and over on top of each other down the brick walk. He was trying to get me in a headlock when I rolled over on top of him and he was underneath me and— and his head fell under the rosebush into the dirt.

The rosebush was bordered with some bricks from the old sidewalk which my father had torn up. He planted these bricks in the dirt diagonally, in a circle around the rosebush, as a kind of decoration, to make it look fancy, and set it off.

My head was in the thorns so I suddenly didn't care if I was going to fight dirty or fight fair, so I grabbed Jimmy by the hair and pushed his face into the bricks with my other hand.

The bricks were embedded slantwise in the dirt, so the top corner of each one was like a knife-edge pointing in the air.

As long as I was on top, I was afraid to let Jimmy up. But he started howling when the bricks cut into his cheekbone. Kicking his legs, with a rush of tremendous energy, propelled by pain, he jerked himself out from under me.

I stood up and he stood up. He started backing away, holding his hand up to his face, looking at me, wordlessly, accusingly, and there was an awful hurt look in his eyes as he backed out of my yard, with blood trickling between the fingers of the hand he held up to his face.

That night in bed I couldn't sleep as I twisted this way and that, thinking. Thinking. Unable to get out of the vise grip of my thoughts. *He was just trying to see if he could take me. I shouldn't have let him get my goat like that. I shouldn't have let him. I lost my temper. I shouldn't have done that to him. He's gonna hate me now. I wish I could call him and tell him I'm sorry.*

The next day when he saw me coming down Glenwood towards his house, he crossed the road.

I didn't tell Roseann about any of this in my letters. I didn't know what to say. I didn't know how I felt, or why I felt the things I was afraid to be feeling. I didn't know what was happening to me. It was better by far to keep my thoughts to myself.

Chapter 15

Guilt and Innocence

The dream went on, wending its way in eddies and swirls, as swift and turgid as the whitewater of the Spicket, passing and pausing, hissing and spitting, caught in the backwash, urged on ahead by the falling forces of time, spent time, time endlessly rushing onward behind the passing moment, pushing it out of the way, turning this moment into the past almost before it has a chance to be the present . . .

Opposed to this onrushing torrent, as solidly as the hard granite walls which hemmed in the river, adamantine reality threatened to dam the flood.

The previous Christmas, when I turned eleven, my mother gave me the gift of a handsome, leather-bound Sunday missal, with gilt-edged pages. This enabled me to follow along as the priest at Ste-Jeanne d'Arc said the Mass. As if to spite the Irish priest who had married her in Revere, my mother was stubbornly fulfilling to the letter his command to bring up her children in the Catholic faith. Still stung by the dictates of the male hierarchy of the Church, after all these years, she somehow imagined she was using me to revenge herself. Though she no longer paid even lip service herself, she made sure I knelt and was bowed down.

The Perrault boys next door were altar boys at 'Saint John Dark,' as I called it, to myself, and Raymond attended parochial school at St Anne's Orphanage, across the road from the Parker; though Guy, Paul and Jean, the older ones, went to Central Catholic High School in Milltown. I wanted to emulate their pious enthusiasm but my mother refused absolutely to let me go in for an altar boy, just as she refused to sign the permission slip for Little League.

Nevertheless, I was growing older, and now it was time for me to take my little brother and sister by the hand down the street to Sunday mass with me, and pick up the Sunday newspapers and bring them home while I was at it. My mother either had forgotten or was pointedly ignoring the pastor at St Jeanne d'Arc who told her she couldn't be officially admitted to the parish rolls because she wasn't French; and when I followed her instructions to bring home the envelope from church, each week she made sure she filled out her name and address and had me slip the envelope into the collection box on the following Sunday. Soon the parish was mailing us the envelopes. The next thing you know I had to start going to Confirmation classes at St Anne's on Thursday afternoons after school.

I made my Confirmation when I was in the sixth grade, the ceremony conducted by the auxiliary archbishop from Springfield, Mass. Why we had to have an auxiliary guy come in all the way from Springfield when we had our own Cardinal Cushing, archbishop of Boston, so much closer to home, I would never know. But they say the ways of the Lord are mysterious.

Afterwards, I posed for pictures, on the sidewalk outside St Jeanne d'Arc, on Plymouth Street. My mother took the photo with a little Kodak strapped around her neck, held at her midsection, the kind with the flip-top viewer, so that her usually tidy hair-sprayed curls hung down in her eyes as she snapped the shutter.

After the pictures came back from the drugstore, there I was, dressed in ankle-length red robes, holding my palms flat together before my heart, as I had been taught, with the fingers pointing straight upward, mimicking the shape of a gothic window. I was the epitome of virtue. The paragon of innocence. For as long as it took for the shutter to snap.

The dream went on, wending its way in eddies and swirls, and in after-time, I don't think I ever again spent a moment of my life when I was so innocent, so pure and unblemished, as that instant when I posed for the camera, dressed in a red robe, with my hands pressed devoutly together, pointing heavenward . . .

They told us that our Confirmation marked our passage from childhood into manhood and that we would henceforward and forever be full members of the Body of Christ.

I felt sanctified for approximately one day.

Then I went back to floundering in the doubts and misgivings, the pains and perturbations, of eleven going-on-twelve.

Uncle Augie caught me one day in the midst of the typical morning rush yelling up the stairs to my mother, who was desperately trying to get the twins ready for school so that she and her brother could catch their ride to work. "Ma, come down and make me some pancakes for breakfast! I'm hungry!"

Uncle Augie told me I could make my own. I protested that Ma wouldn't let me touch her stove and, besides, I didn't know how to make pancakes, so right away, he said, "I'll show you, it's easy, how do you think we got through camp in England if we couldn't cook our own flapjacks, and over an open fire in bivouac, too."

Somehow, I felt a lot more grown up and fully a member of the Body of Christ after Uncle Augie taught me how to make pancakes. He taught me to watch for the bubbles to burst before flipping my flapjack. One by one I watched them break open and cave in, mouth watering with anticipation. When I sat down to eat, I felt more sanctified than I did after receiving the auxiliary archbishop's thumb, dipped in the holy oil of chrism, on my forehead.

Soon I was noticing hair growing on my upper lip.

My father told me not to start shaving, or else it would only start growing in blacker and bristlier.

'Bristlier' was one of those words my father made up on the spot, like 'hummid,' (rhyming with 'hum a song,') when it felt like a muggy day.

These days it seemed I got annoyed with the most trifling things, and I was being very critical of both my mother and father. Was he trying to be funny, or did he simply not know how to pronounce these words?

My sister Jill was giving my mother a hard time over going to school. At least according to my mother. It seemed that Jill was getting sick on a regular basis, throwing up in the morning whenever she didn't want to go to school. My mother claimed she was doing it on purpose, and she wasn't going to let her get away with it.

But I had to take the both of them, Jack and Jill, by the hand, one on each side, and walk them through the woods to school each day in the column of the patrol line led by Fat Alice Dankworth from Odile Street with her white garrison belt and badge, and I felt awfully sorry for Jill. Here I was, telling the kids to come to me if anyone tried to bully them at school, when I couldn't do or say anything about the way their mother was treating them. It didn't seem right.

One morning we were all in a rush, and Jill and I were in the bathroom upstairs, brushing our teeth together at the sink. Ma was yelling up the stairs to make sure Jill washed her face. The kid took the bar of soap on the sink and I told her not to get it in her eyes, to make sure she kept her eyes shut tight till she had a chance to rinse her face off, and the next thing you know, sure enough, she's howling at the top of her lungs because she got soap in her eyes.

Ma came rushing up the stairs and into the bathroom. She had told us always to make sure not to close the door when we were in there together, so she could keep an eye on us. Thus there was nothing to slow her down in her headlong rage and she came at me with both her hands flying like oven-mittens, trying to hit me in the head. I started yelling that I didn't do nuthin,' and trying to explain that what really happened was just like that other time when Jackie-boy got hit in the head with the baseball bat, the kids wouldn't listen to me, they wouldn't mind me, but—my mother wasn't listening and so furious was she that I was back-pedaling and soon ended up in a heap on my haunches in the corner with my elbows over my head.

The blows didn't hurt, not at all. But the shame I felt at the tears of frustration I was having to bite back, that scorched. And the anger at my mother I felt, which I had to swallow, that nauseated. I wanted to cry not because my head hurt physically but because the injustice of it all gave me an Excedrin headache.

I truly hadn't done anything wrong. In fact, I was trying to make sure my sister didn't cause herself any pain or discomfort. I was being responsible, I was being a big brother, but here I was in a maelstrom of Ma yelling and me yelling and Jill crying like she was on fire, and I'm collapsed in the corner.

I filed that one away for future reference.

Chapter 16

Pershing, Pennsylvania

Soon Dad and I were getting away from them all and taking a two-week vacation down to Fayette County, Pennsylvania.

What an uproar that caused.

Uncle Mike Kowalcyzk and Auntie Stasija had moved into a new place in Spicket Falls. Auntie Stasija wanted out of the third floor in South Milltown. Firetraps like that did not exist in her prior life in rural Fayette County, and she hated it. They found a small apartment with two bedrooms and a balcony squeezed into the attic of a single-family home. Downstairs the landlords were the Dumonts, a sprawling French family with six or seven daughters, all named with the letter D, Denise, and Darla, and Debbie and Doreen and so on. It was close to our house, but further up Elm Street, past the McQuaids' and around the bend before you hit Lowell Street.

I met my cousins Patty and Michelle for the first time, and I didn't like them. They seemed like a whiny bunch to me, when you put them together with their mother, my Aunt Stasija. My Dad's behavior changed before my very eyes when we went up Elm Street to visit with Uncle Mike and my Aunt. He became a mush-mouthed complainer, like them. His sister kept asking him how he was getting along with my mother. I took note of that, and it bothered me.

My new cousins, Patty and Michelle, were as dumb as treestumps. I couldn't believe it. The difference between them and cousin Roseann was the difference between a National Honor Society student and pupils two grades behind in reading. Patty was my age, and Michelle two years younger. That Michelle was a trouble-maker, that I could tell. I could not get over the way they talked. I said 'Aunt' and they said 'Ant.' I said 'ours' and they said 'ou-wers.' They laughed at me when I called it 'tonic' while they called it 'pop.' They teased me about my accent, and I insisted I didn't have one. They were the interlopers, not me. Why couldn't they be nice and pretty and intelligent and accomplished like my wonderful cousin Roseann, instead of frumpy and rough-house and girly-girly. Roseann wrote me nice long, thoughtful, chatty, frequent letters, you could tell she cared. Patty and Michelle didn't care about anything but themselves. Patty at least was merely self-centered, but Michelle was an awful, selfish brat. Between the two of them, I didn't think they knew a book from a doorstopper. As ridiculous as the idea of all the D-girls downstairs at the Dumonts sounded, I preferred them to my own cousins upstairs.

Obviously, it meant a great amount to my Dad to have his sister living up the street. But it was very uncomfortable for my mother. She had no problem at all with Uncle Mike Kowalcyzk, and even enjoyed having him live with us in South Milltown when he first came up to New England. He was just the kind of guy everybody liked at first glance. But Ma could not tolerate her sister-in-law Stasija. Long ago, my mother had picked out Uncle Alek's wife Rose as the woman amongst her in-laws that she could call a girlfriend. Auntie Stasija and her mealy-mouthed, simpering, oh-pity-me manner just didn't sit well at my mother's kitchen table. Ma thought Uncle Mike ought to get nominated for sainthood for putting up with her.

But to me, strangely, I could tell that Uncle Mike really cared for her, and his daughters, too. Maybe that was the whole problem, he indulged them. Not for the first time I was finding that one of my uncles behaved entirely differently when he was around his womenfolk than when he was on his own.

The crisis came to a head when Dad announced that he felt like it was his turn to pay a visit back home on summer vacation, instead of his brother Alek coming up here all the time. Ma refused to go, she said it would be too long a trip for my sister Jill, who got carsick. She said she couldn't take the time off, they were just starting to get the *Gigi Sportswear* business going. Dad said, well, in that case, he was going to take me whether she liked it or not. Ma didn't want me going, either, but I wanted to go. It was the chance of a lifetime and I couldn't pass it up. I had never been anywhere. I had the chance to see New York. It would be just me and my Dad together, and how often was it like that?

We took Dad's Jeep, and he said I could be the co-pilot and keeper of the road-maps in the co-pilots seat, just give him enough warning when he had to turn, and keep an eye out for the road-signs. We took a route that Dad developed which he thought was shorter, after consulting with Uncle Mike. We took Route 15 through Connecticut, and in Hartford, Dad said, "Let's stop here, I've heard about it, the hamburgers are only 15 cents, let's try it." It was the first time I ever saw the golden arches, way down the road at the bottom of a wicked long hill. We didn't have any McDonald's in our area.

We got to the Bronx and stayed overnight with my Aunt Adrienne. That was the first time I ever met her, and she was nothing like her sister Stasija. She was not small and overly delicate, like Stasija, she was built like a longshoreman whose muscles had gone soft, she had black hair, and didn't wear any lipstick; there was a man living with her, but she didn't introduce him as her husband, she just told him to fetch her a beer out of the fridge. I could not believe she was my Dad's sister. She was all New York, and talked about the muggers on the subway and how these days, going to the grocery store, she had to watch out for the Spics who tried to snatch her purse. She was loud and abusive and kept saying, you want another one? My dad hardly drank at all, so he kept saying, I'm fine and nursing the one he had. Aunt Adrienne could drink six to his one without interrupting the constant stream of vituperation coming out of her mouth. She walked around her apartment in bare feet and kept checking the door down the long hallway to make sure the chain-lock was engaged. She sent us out to get White Castle hamburgers for our supper, and when we got back, she was peeking through the eye-hole and my Dad was positioning his head so she could see him, and she wouldn't let us in till he said something so she could identify his voice.

On the Pennsylvania Turnpike, Dad kept saying "Wait till we get to the tunnels." It seemed to take forever to get there. We kept going up and up, and on the downhill, we had to outrace the big trucks barreling down on our heels. The tunnels did indeed turn out to be thrilling. As we finally approached the point on the map where we had to turn off, the mists kept gathering about us. Finally I was going to see for myself the hidden valley where my father came from.

Pershing, PA, was my dad's hometown. Everybody there seemed to know him as *'Good Ole Andy, you're back, it's been a coon's age.'* Dad's cousin Joe Petrovich was the police chief over to Latrobe. People admired Dad's Jeep. Women stopped him in the street to give him a hug and a peck on the cheek. They all wanted to know what he'd been doing with himself and where he'd been keeping himself all these years. The town was full of people I didn't know who seemed to have long histories with him. I came from an urban, metropolitan place, this was the first time I had ever been exposed to truly backcountry people. They seemed warmer and friendlier and more neighborly that my own people.

I wanted my Dad to take me to the Germantown No. 1 mineshaft but he wouldn't do it. He said it was nuthin' to show off to a kid. I saw my Uncle Alek come home from that mine after work and take a shower in the basement, in a shower stall he and my Dad, in their long-lost youth, had rigged up down there. Uncle Alek went in by a side door in the basement, and after work, he wouldn't come up the back stairs into the kitchen at all till he had washed. Even then you could see him rubbing the back of his neck as he came in the door from the stairs. He said you could never get the feel of that damn grit off your neck.

I saw my Uncle Alex give himself his shot of insulin in the arm at the kitchen table before he ate. I knew he was a life-long diabetic from the stories my Dad had told me. The trip down from Massachusetts was the longest time we had ever spent together alone and I found out my Dad was so different when my mother was not around and not likely to pop around the corner anytime soon. He actually talked to me and I actually listened. I asked questions and he told me stories of real people and things from a real past that seemed half-legendary to me.

My cousin Roseann and I also had a chance to spend a lot of time together. We could take a walk uptown to Kitka's store where my Auntie Rose worked behind the counter. We went for a root-beer float at the counter in the Ben Franklin's five-and-dime. We went to the Esson gas station on South Main and got a sody-pop out of the machine, for 10 cents. Instead of Coca-Cola, like up my way, they had Dr. Pepper's.

On Sunday we went to church at the St Sava's Serbian Orthodox Church and afterward Roseann played her accordian with the rest of the band. Young and old, they were parishioners who played for the polka dancers who trooped up the steps to the dance-floor of the concrete bandstand under the canopy in back of the church. There was an outdoor barbecue going and people had blankets spread for a picnic on the grass: so different from St Jeanne d'Arc, back home, where in back of the church was a tarred parking lot full of shined-up cars. Here the cars pulled up a dirt road beside the church and parked beyond the trees behind the grandstand. Kids were running around and everybody was happy to stay long after Mass, not rush home as soon as they could escape, with the Sunday funnies tucked under their arm.

At home at my Uncle Alek's on Maple Avenue I met my *Jedo*, my grandfather on my Dad's side, for the first time. My grandmother had passed away several years earlier, the only other time I ever knew my Dad to go home to Pennsylvania. My grandfather was in his upper 80s, and he spoke only Serbian, so my Dad said just to call him *'Jedo'* and if he said anything to me I didn't understand, just to shake my head up and down and say *'dobra,'* which meant 'good.' My Uncle Alek would talk to his dad in Serbian, which was the first time I ever head that language. Auntie Rose was Polish, like Uncle Mike Kowalcyzk, so she managed to get along with her father-in-law in Serbian, a little, but she let Uncle Alex do most of the talking. Auntie Rose was a kind soul, and she didn't mind feeding her father-in-law Gerber's baby-food with a spoon at the supper table.

After supper Roseann and I would retreat to the bed in her bedroom and spend the whole night sharing our secrets. We renewed our vows of eternal devotion but our love for each other was pure and stainless, the way we imagined the love between a priestly advocate and a novice nun must be, if we even questioned it that way, which we did not. We were just a boy and a girl who were cousins who loved each other. Even though Roseann was developing, and I had hair on my upper lip I hadn't shaved yet, the love between us passed from our eyes looking into each other's eyes and seeing each other's souls. Roseann to me was like my long lost twin-sister whom I remembered from before we were born.

The only time Roseann and I ever touched during my visit to Pennsylvania was the day my Dad took us in the Jeep over to Carmichaels to visit his sister Angie and her husband John Pacinda, on Uncle John's farm, and we were climbing this steep hill to a fence above, and we didn't know what was waiting for us.

When we had scrambled to the top, and were out of breath, suddenly we came face to face with Uncle John's bull, who was poking his nostrils through the fence rails. We shrieked and slid heel-first downhill, grabbing onto one another to keep from falling on our faces, thanking our stars for our last-second escape. At the bottom we walked away looking at each other and bursting with relief into paroxysms of helpless laughter.

THE EDUCATION OF NICHOLAS PETROVICH

I saw things in Pennsylvania I did not know how to grasp. But they left a permanent impression on me which I carried forward into my life, not knowing then how, or why, they would come back to haunt me.

I saw poverty, the kind that only Appalachia wears on its face, without any hypocrisy, without trying to shovel it under any rugs.

I saw mist in the hot August mornings rising like steam from the pockets of lowland heat trapped between the crooked knobs of the piney hills.

I saw the coke-ovens in red glowing rows ringing distant hills in the dark night.

I saw the statue of the Christ figure standing tall on the steep hill overlooking Uniontown, with his arms open wide, so that his figure formed a *Sign of the Cross* in the sky, with the drapes of his robe flowing from his hands and elbows in the floodlit night from the top of a ridge; Jesus Himself, looking down on his flock below, giving benediction to the darkness.

And I saw the Pittsburgh Pirates, in Forbes Field, one Saturday when Uncle Alek said, "Come on. Forget your Dad. We're going to the ballgame. No, Roseann can't come. Just you and me."

And we drove north-northwest fifty miles on country roads, up and down, skee-daddling round corners, freewheelin' on the long down-slopes, in Uncle Alek's brand-new 3-speed standard-transmission 283-cu.in. 230-hp V-8 Turbo-Fire '58 Chevy, with Overdrive.

It made me think that maybe somewhere inside, deep down in his own soul, my Uncle Alek maybe had a secret wish, that he wouldn't admit to himself every day, to have had a son like me; that he envied his big brother Andy, just that one thing, that he had never had a son, like his brother, who had been lucky, maybe more than he knew . . .

And, you know, I could tell, from seeing them when they were together, nobody ever loved his daughter like my Uncle Alek loved his daughter Roseann. Still . . .

Chapter 17

Central Junior

Things did not stay the same, as the dream wore on, weaving its inscrutable patterns into the dust of yesterday, as if that dust were meant to obscure the vision of tomorrow, and bury us in the tomb of the present moment, from which we could see neither backwards nor forwards . . .

My voice was changing and I did not know what was happening to me. I was starting the seventh grade and I was riding the yellow school-bus now. Central Junior High was my school now, and it was in the middle of Spicket Falls.

On the other side of Broadway from the Oxford Mills, Oxford Street continued just a short spell. Where it merged, Milltown Street began. Central Junior sat there on the right. Just before St Monica's parochial school, underneath the steep hill from the Square where the Red Tavern dwelt, catty-corner from the Searles castle walls, and prior to the O'Neill Playstead. Actually, the front doors of the school were on Poplar Place, but nobody ever went in the front. The back of the school was on Milltown Street, flanked by a wide, dirty grass area which substituted for a schoolyard, bordered with a stone wall topped with a black-iron fence. Yet another dull brick school that gave the impression of a prison compound.

I was wearing glasses now because I caught the measles in sixth grade and when the doctor said I had to stay in a darkened room with the shades drawn, my mother was bringing meals up to me in my bedroom, where she closed the door on me; but she didn't know I was reading *The Rock of Chickamauga* and *The Guns of Shiloh* and the other Civil War novels in the series by Joseph A. Altsheler, with a flashlight, under the bedcovers pulled up over my head so that she wouldn't see the strip of light shining under my door as she came up the stairs.

I had discovered the magnificence of the Nevins Library, beyond the Square, on top of the steep hill leading north to New Hampshire, where Broadway ascended to head past the MSPCA farm into the wilds of the Granite State. This was the very same Rte 28 which started on Cape Cod, went through Boston, and eventually, I later learned, north of the state line, passed directly by the front door of Robert Frost's farm in Derry.

The Spicket Falls library was an imposing brownstone edifice with stately arches at the top of a circular drive, a gift to the town from one of its benefactors, a nineteenth century industrialist, Nevins, this time, instead of Searles. It was old and ivy-covered and had massive doors so heavy parents had to open them for small children. Inside, it was everything I remembered from the days of the Carnegie Library in Revere, and the landscaped grounds in the rear of the library were made not for automobile, but for horse and carriage. The head librarian would not let me take out books like *A Tale of Two Cities* or *For Whom the Bell Tolls*, but she guided me instead to

Washington Irving and James Fenimore Cooper. Uncle Augie told me I definitely had to read *The Last of the Mohicans,* and I did, but then I discovered Altsheler's series on my own, and I dropped Cooper. I also kept dropping my new eyeglasses, and breaking the lenses, which made Ma mad at me because I was costing her money, and it was my own fault for making my eyes go bad.

At Central Jr., I was thrown in with kids from all over the town. I came from the Glen Forest section in the West End, and now we had strangers in our classes from the East End. Spicket Falls was shaped more or less like a cloak draped over the shoulders of North Milltown. The East End, where farms were strung out along the low flatlands of the Merrimack, was called Pleasant Valley, and the Ashford was the school out there. The Corliss was in the middle of the town, around Broadway, where the slums of North Milltown crept over the line and tiptoed up Camden Street and Phillips Street. My end of town contributed kids from the Oakland and the Parker to the jumble thrown all together at the Central Jr. I didn't know anybody from the Ashford, the Oakland or the Corliss. I had to start all over again, after trying so hard to fit in for the last two years at the Parker. But so did everyone else, and nobody seemed to know which end was up, there was a lot of sorting-out going on, and kids started complaining about cliques.

One day I saw the most vicious schoolyard fight I'd ever seen when a red-headed kid pulled the coat over the head of his opponent and was just whaling on him. You could see the blood-spatters jumping through the air like the 'Pow-ee' bursts in the Saturday morning cartoons of 'The Road-Runner.' The kids from our end of town were saying watch out for the hoods from Pleasant Valley because they were bringing knives to school in their engineer-boots, but they were probably saying the same thing about us. The schoolyard was like a vacant lot, surrounded by a low concrete wall topped with black wrought-iron railings. Across the street you could see the grade-schoolers at St Monica's parochial school playing the games we used to play at the Parker, but nobody played at recess at the Central, they just milled around in groups, trying to stick to their own for protection, expecting to be attacked any second.

The Yakabonis Twins came from way out in the countryside on Forest Street, and they knew me from the Parker, where one of the twins had a nasty reputation as someone to stay away from because he used to gross out the girls by picking his nose and then eating the boogers off the tip of his finger with his licking tongue. I don't know if it was Ronald or Bruce, they looked exactly alike, they were identical twins, and the third guy they hung out with was Hollis Hershey, who was just as big and looming as the Yakabonis brothers.

These three were having a hard time living up to their reputations at the Central because in Junior High you couldn't just play the class clown and make kids laugh by being a dunce all the time. If you got into a fight here, blood was going to flow. I arrived in school wearing glasses, which I wasn't wearing the year before, and the Yakabonis twins decided I was an easy target and started calling me 'Four-Eyes.' I tried to ignore them, but every day when we had to line up on the walk leading to the back doors waiting for the bell to ring to enter school, they were maneuvering themselves into position at my back so they could pretend to stumble and shove me into some poor girl in front of me in line. This started to be their entertainment every day, until finally one day I got fed up with the insults and shoving and I turned around suddenly when Bruce Yakabonis wasn't looking, slugged him in the side of the head, right on his left ear, which must've stung. After that, they never bothered me again.

The eyeglasses made me a target of another kind, too. Either it meant you were hopelessly near-sighted and therefore totally stupid, or you were some kind of intellectual. If you dared to raise your hand in class and answer a teacher's question, you know, help them out as they tried their mightiest to engage a lot of bored, inattentive kids, you got pegged instantly as one of the smart kids. As soon as that happened, they all wanted to cheat off of you on quizzes and tests.

Two kids who sat next to me in Mrs Dalton's homeroom, only because she arranged the seating alphabetically, were Dennis Rousseau and Benny Nader. It was Nader, Petrovich and Rousseau at the back of the room.

One day in Miss Rushton's English class, the other two concocted a scheme to amuse themselves at Miss Rushton's expense.

Miss Rushton was the most ancient creature anyone had ever seen, but far from giving her the respect due to her age, the kids ridiculed her for her purple hair. The poor old lady was in her sixties and should have retired long before this, but she didn't seem to realize that when she was trying to dying her hair silver, it was coming out wrong. Miss Rushton was teaching us Coleridge's poem, "The Ancient Mariner," and she proceeded to beat out the rhythm with a ruler on her desk, to demonstrate. She was trying to teach us the idea behind poetic meter, but it came out,

There   was   an   An-   -cient   Mar-   -i   -ner
     (slap!)   (slap!)   (slap!)   (slap!)
And he   stop- -peth   one of   three . . .
     (slap!)   (slap!)   (slap!)

When the bell rang and we spilled out into the hallway to go to the next class, Denny and Benny were doubled over punching each other with laughter, reciting "Now wherefore stopst thou me?" to which the other would respond, "By thy long grey beard and thy glittering eye!"

These were the two who were constantly trying to lean over and look at my paper and copy down what I wrote, or the box I filled in, till finally I gave up and just let them.

Denny came from the Ashford, but he didn't live that far out in Pleasant Valley, he came from Milk Street. Benny was from the slums, near the Central itself, he had gone to the Corliss; he lived on Phillips Street, which everybody said was the worst street in town.

This particular day, the scheme they devised to torment poor Miss Rushton was positively diabolical.

The old lady used to come into the classroom every day, and the first thing she would do is lift up her skirt so that she could lift up her leg and tamp down the wadded paper in the top of the waste-paper basket next to her desk. She had a tiny foot shod in a low heel, so she was in no danger of getting her foot stuck, and she really pressed down on the mountain of paper. So one day, before she came in, Denny and Benny grab the basket and take it out in the hall to the janitor's closet, to fill it with water. Then they bring it back in to its usual place and arrange the crumpled papers floating on top of the water so it looks no different than it always did.

Of course Miss Rushton came in and of course she stuck her foot in the basket and of course the water went everywhere and of course I get sent to the office for it.

Afterwards, Benny said to me, "I guess you're all right. You didn't squeal on us."

Denny said, "How do you get all that grammar?"

Miss Rushton was using *The Harbrace Handbook of English Grammar* on us. I loved the feel of it, the 5-inch by 7-inch size, the stiff covers, the heft. "I like diagramming sentences."

"You *like* diagramming sentences? You need help, Nicky. Seriously," said Benny.

Chapter 18

The Facts of Life

The dream went underground into caves and caverns and swirling pools of eruptions bubbling up to the surface to perturb and perplex, dredging up monsters of the deep, thought to have been conquered long ago, throwing me back into the night terrors of not-knowing, at the mercy of volcanic forces, unable to stem the flow or to steer it into pathways of peace and quiet, so that at last I was convinced I was disturbed and evil and hopelessly lost . . .

One day in math class, Betty McGarrity was sitting next to me. Betty had boobs and they were bubbling out of the halter-top of her dress. When the bell rang, I had to sit down again. A steel girder was poking a hole in the front of my pants and it was painful. I was positively sure that my face had gone fire-engine red, right to the tips of my ears, which must have turned pointed by now, like a leering wolf's. I was so embarrassed I was immobilized. I was going to force myself to sit there until I *thought it* into quiescence. I didn't know what was happening to me. Was I losing my mind? The next class was filtering in and taking their seats. I had to get up and move. Benny and Denny were calling me from the door. I had to pick up all my books and hold them in front of my crotch. I could barely walk. *The Harbrace Handbook* slipped off the pile and fell with a thud to the floor.

All the kids were talking about the Facts of Life. All I knew was the Mysteries of Life. I listened in every chance I got but I was afraid to betray my ignorance by asking a question. I thought maybe I could go to the library and look them up, you know, the Facts of life, why not? Turns out you couldn't. The head librarian at the Nevins had taught me how to use the Dewey Decimal system card catalog, but the Facts of Life weren't even listed. Kids were using four- letter words and making jokes about parts of the human anatomy that I never heard of. I knew how to swear. I learned how by imitating Jack Fallon and Dick Nickerson in the infield at the Parker in fifth and sixth grade. But I had no idea that all these words had something to do with *s-e-x* sex. What the hell was a jerk-off? What in the world was cunnilingus? Well, that one you could look up in a dictionary, and I did. Turned out to be Latin. Who knew you could talk dirty in Latin? Why didn't somebody take you to one side and fill you in? How come you had to learn all this stuff in the street from ignorant kids who didn't know any better than you did?

All I knew was that I was looking at the girls just as much as Denny and Benny and all the other boys were. Suddenly I had this great interest in girls. When did that happen?

All of a sudden I wanted to go to the Central Jr. dances. They were having record hops on Saturday nights. All of a sudden I was conscious of my looks, combing my hair, disgusted with those dumb glasses I had to wear.

Eugene Christy

I put on my best cardigan my mother bought me and combed my hair and walked all the way from Elm Street to the Central Junior High, three miles, by myself, on a crisp Saturday night in the fall.

The dance was being held in the school basketball gym and you had to go in the front doors on Poplar Place and buy a ticket, whereas everyday when we arrived at school, the busses pulled up in a row at the back of the school, on Milltown Street.

Everything I had ever known about school felt different. It was starting to get dark out and the dance hadn't begun yet. Some of our teachers were standing around as chaperones. There was a refreshment table, and the Dee Jay was up on the stage with the curtains, behind the refreshment table. All the girls were standing on one side of the basketball court, under the balconies, and all the boys on the other. I took my glasses off so I wouldn't spoil my looks. I had my hair combed in a DA like Ricky Nelson on TV, and I used some Brylcreem to try to make it go straight, like his, but it wouldn't, it kept curling up in bunches. I worried about the way I looked. I was sure no girl would like me, and I was afraid to ask somebody to dance and get refused. They dimmed the lights and the music started. *Dion and the Belmonts. Why must I be a teenager in love?* I patted my back pocket to make sure my glasses were there. I had put them in the soft case my mother got me, with the pocket-clasp so you could slip them in your shirt pocket, and they wouldn't fall out, but I put them in the back pocket of my pants. I didn't want to dance with some girl and have my glasses stick her in the chest. Nor did I want to drop them and break them again, or my mother would kill me for sure this time. Good thing Denny and Benny weren't there at my first dance. They would've hooted me out of the hall, laughing at me. They were both going steady with somebody already, so they didn't need to come to any old dance, looking for a girl to say *hello, what's your name?* I stood there in the shadows under the balcony on the boys side and I couldn't even see far enough without my glasses to make out the girls on the other side.

But it was even worse to stand there and be a wallflower, so I ventured out there to take my chances.

I asked a girl wearing glasses to dance, figuring she wouldn't refuse me as she probably felt as bad about wearing glasses as I did. She turned out to be a nice girl. I picked a slow dance, as I didn't know how to jitterbug any more than most of the boys, although the girls all seemed like they ought to be fast-dancing on *American Bandstand*. I held this nice girl tentatively at a polite distance away as we danced a slow dance, my hand resting lightly on her waist and the other hand holding hers high. She was a good follower, she didn't try to lead. Her name was Merrilee Krupp, and she was in some of my classes, it turned out.

"Say that again?"

"Merrilee. I know, I know. *Row, row, row your boat, gently down the stream, Merrily, merrily, merrily*—my mother was stuck on that nursery rhyme."

Merrilee knew me but I hadn't noticed her before. She said I was one of the smart kids and so was she. I liked her right away and thanked her for the dance and went back to the boys side to wait for another slow one.

The next girl I asked to dance was not a nice girl. She got me out on the floor and pulled me in right tight to her body. She was as slender as one of the cast-iron railings in the schoolyard, and she stuck her leg between mine as we danced a slow one. She put her hand up on the back of my neck and was rubbing it where the hair touched the skin and I got that steel beam again.

She spun me and snuggled in closer and I could feel her breath in my ear as we slowly, softly twirled, barely moving. I couldn't breathe, I couldn't talk.

But afterwards I knew I wanted to dance with her again.

I was glad they had dimmed all the lights so nobody could see the condition I was in. We danced every slow dance that came up the rest of the night, or, at least, halfway through it. Then she grabbed me by the hand and pulled me outside through the front doors. It was dark out now and she found an alcove in the wall by the side of the front steps where the streetlight peeking through a tree threw everything in deep shadow. She seemed to know exactly where to go. She threw her back up against the wall and invited me in. Then we were kissing. I didn't even know her name. She seemed to want to kiss me so hard that she would rub the lips off my face. She scared me to death, but I couldn't, I couldn't stop myself, I wanted to kiss her back just as hard.

I wasn't the same for weeks after that. At least I could tell Benny and Denny I made out with a girl. But I didn't really want to kiss and tell. They kept asking, who is she, who is she, do I know her? But I didn't know her myself, I had never seen her around the school, I didn't know how I felt, I thought it was my own business, I'd like to keep it to myself, what are we keeping score here, what is this game? Whether I got to first base or second base, who cares, none of your damn business.

I had an incident in the shower at home. I didn't know what was coming out of my penis but I thought I was going to die. I was afraid to ask anybody, especially my father or my uncle. All I knew was I wouldn't be able to wash myself with soap in the shower like that anymore. What was happening to me?

Then I had another incident, in bed, at night. I woke up in the morning and the bed was wet. I could see discolored stains on the white sheets. I figured my mother would find out for sure and want to kill me. I had to talk to somebody. I decided it was better to talk to my uncle because, after all, he wasn't my father. If I wouldn't talk to my mother about this, out of shame, how could I talk to my father?

"Don't worry," said Uncle Augie, "you just had a wet dream, that's all. We all get them at your age. It's natural. You're growing up. You're going through a phase. You're not gonna die! Come on, let's go out in the driveway and I'll teach you how to throw my twelve-to-six curveball, okay?"

Chapter 19

Gently Down the Stream

Part of the past came floating back to me on the swirling river: the watery image of that snapshot of myself dressed in red robes outside the church, with my palms pressed together in holiness; but as I reached out to retrieve it, the water slid between my fingers, the image floated away, out of the reach of my grasp; it dissipated and dissolved as it sped on down the stream, around the corner of the mill, out of sight. I knew it was going to be disappearing under the little green bridge a few feet from Broadway, and soon, would be gone forever . . .

Just so did I glide elusively from day to day without direction or drive and, seemingly without effort, pass from the preliminaries of junior high to the main event of high school. Although the days of straight As on my report card were behind me, I was not discouraged. I loved school, I wouldn't miss a day, I loved my books, and visiting the library. Every day in my life turned a page and started a new chapter.

But my mother wanted to know what I thought I was doing. How could I explain to her that it was more interesting to end up in detention with Benny and Denny than to try to get Mr Daignault to admit me to the Honor Society, where my little friend with the pointy eyeglasses, Merrilee Krupp, presided? My mother and my dad thought that junior high was where things got tough and you had to start to buckle down—but what did they know? My dad had gone as far as the sixth grade, my mother only to the seventh. I was bored in school. I already knew everything in the text book by the end of the first week and I could pass any multiple choice test without half-trying. I didn't need to study because I read, I read avariciously, I read all the time, even while I was eating my supper at home, I had a book propped up in front of me. My mother knew that. She could see. She was the one who said to me one time that I always had my nose stuck in a book, I better be careful in case somebody came by and snapped it shut on me.

But when I begged her to send me to Central Catholic in Milltown, so that I could get what I heard, from the brothers Perrault, all the time, was a superior education that would get me into a better college, my mother refused steadfastly.

She wasn't thinking about me going to college. I was, but she couldn't see it. I felt hopeless, convinced that since such things were beyond Ma's experience of life, she couldn't picture them. She would say things like, "Public school was good enough for me, it's good enough for you." I quit trying in school, and started to look for diversion from the deadly routine.

Jenney High was the first modern school I'd ever been inside of, opened in 1953. It was named after the third of the town's benefactors. The Jenney family had a string of gas stations around Spicket Falls and Milltown, with white neon signs showing a bright red mule throwing his hind heels in the air, setting off sparks, surmounted by the slogan 'It Kicks!'

But before I started there I had to get through the summer after 8th grade. I found myself gravitating towards St Monica's Fair, which was held in the schoolyard across Park Street from the Central Jr. each July. It was close to Benny's neighborhood on Phillips Street and Denny would come over from his house and the three of us could hang out. They were looking for some girl, or girls, who were 'hot to trot,' so they could 'get laid.' I thought they were out of their minds talking like that. Benny claimed it was no big deal, just make sure you wear a rubber so you don't get her pregnant or catch some wicked bad disease, like the clap, so your pecker rotted off and you had to walk around bandaged, with a crutch.

Those two knew how to make me laugh, but I wasn't about to follow their lead. After my experience with the girl at the seventh-grade dance, I was afraid to go there again. I wasn't ready for those things, and I wasn't going to be pushed. Boys were so competitive, always trying to outdo you, always pretending. You couldn't believe half the things they claimed they were aces with. I made sure I never told them about that girl. She may have got my blood up, and stirred me up with fantasies, but that was like, just another problem to add to my pile. Where was she, by the way? I never saw her again, although I looked. I never even knew her name. Maybe she came from out of town. Somebody's cousin. Just visiting. *Maybe I just dreamed the whole thing.* She certainly had disappeared off the face of the earth.

As time went by, it didn't seem real to me anymore. When I got tired of the Denny and Benny act, I would go find Merrilee Krupp. She was coming out to the St Monica's Fair every night that summer. I would stroll around with her and her girlfriend, Peggy Whalen. They were friends for life, they had gone to grade school together at the Oakland. Peggy's family had a summer camp up on Forest Lake and she invited me to go swimming any day I wanted. I thought she liked me, but I wasn't about to get involved because I knew her father was on the Spicket Falls police force. I thought that as soon as I showed up at her front door I'd have to pass his inspection.

In the end we decided the three of us would take a bike-hike one nice August day and go up to Tower Hill and have a picnic. Except Peggy didn't show up that day. So it was just Merrilee and me, in the shadow of Rapunzel's Tower, by the shores of The Rez. It was a very nice day, just boy and girl talk, no flirting, no hint of anything remotely suggesting anything romantic, almost as if we were kids seven years old, instead of 13 going on 14. It was pure, it was innocent, it was fun; we had a picnic. Afterwards, we stood there, side by side, holding on to our bikes, looking out over the vistas below from the height of Tower Hill, and we didn't want to leave. It was as if the day were ending, but we didn't want it to end, because that would mean we were leaving the day behind us, and we'd never get it back.

Try telling that to Benny and Denny.

"So did you get in her pants or what?" said Benny.

"Who?"

"Merrilee, jerk-off."

"No!"

"You must be the only one who didn't," said Denny.

"What are you talking about?"

We were standing in the parking lot behind Jenney High, a couple of weeks after we started freshman year.

"Haven't you noticed she ain't in school?" said Benny.

"Come to think of it–"

"She got expelled," said Denny.

I whirled on him. "Why!"

"She got pregnant, you asshole," said Benny.

I was in utter shock. I just could not believe it. I was in such shock that I vowed never to go near Peggy Whalen again because she had been as close as a sister to the smartest girl in junior high, who went and got herself pregnant—at, what, 14? I was dead certain sure that anybody who showed up on the doorstep of Merrilee Krupp's best friend Peggy Whalen would be met by Sgt Whalen in full uniform with regulation sidearm in hand. Worse than that—it could've been me! Just then it was dawning on me that it might have been no accident that Peggy didn't show up that day. Now, never mind Sgt Whalen, with his pistol drawn—*what would my mother have said if I got a girl pregnant when I was 13 and she was just turned 14?*

Chapter 20

Lindy Bergan

It was September of 1960. Much better to turn your attention away from teenage tragedy to the exciting race on the national stage between Richard Nixon and the favorite son of Massachusetts, John F. Kennedy.

Thank goodness there was some good news that year when Kennedy won. We all knew it was going to happen as soon as we saw the first debate on television. Still, it was close. I lived in a house with a veteran who served under Eisenhower's command, and Nixon was his lieutenant. From the Sputnik to the civil rights campaign to the missile gap the issues were life and death to me, and I assumed, the nation.

To say that an atmosphere of goodwill and almost holiday-happiness spread through the town of Spicket Falls, the city of Milltown, the Commonwealth of Massachusetts, would be a mild approximation of the excitement we felt. One of our own had made it to the top and we were all going to be so much the more better-off for it.

And while the glow from that gift from heaven was still percolating, and hadn't yet worn off, or, maybe, because of it, since all things new and possible seemed suddenly to be opening up, my scrape with the unknown nymphomaniac, and my near-escape from a life of perdition with Merrilee Krupp, were sent into eclipse, like last week's feature at the Riverside Drive-in, down on the Lowell Boulevard.

I had met the love of my life, the one and only true love, the absolutely forever meant-to-be only-one-for-me, and within two weeks of the opening of school, amid the escalating excitement of the Presidential campaigning, and then, the head-swooning, pennant-winning fever of final victory, while I was still a freshman wet behind the auditory appendages, I had fallen victim to a lovesick derangement at the unintended and yet absolutely merciless whim of an unattainable Nordic goddess, who forced me to fall into hopeless, senseless, impossible love with her, simply by taking the seat next to me in Biology.

Her name was Lindy Bergan and she was a Norwegian blonde with pure platinum hair, which shone like an arctic sun-blast, and which she wore Kim Novak-length, caressing the back of her statuesque neck, and she had blue eyes with a bright, shimmering, icy dazzle, like a pair of blue mirrors buried in snow, reflecting the sun.

She was the head-cheerleader of the Jenney High squad and she was dating the captain of the football team, Greg Gilbert, the quarterback.

She was lithe and bouncy and tanned.

She was a California girl, caught on the wrong coast.

She was a senior and I was a freshman, yet Lindy was nice to me. Lindy talked to me. She was an older woman, but she was not supercilious, she did not talk down to me simply because I was a lowly freshman.

I think she sensed how she made me feel, she knew how I felt about her. I was a melting popsicle whenever I looked at her. She treated me like a friend, as if she genuinely liked me. She talked to me as if I were important to her. She saw the real person inside me and conversed with that hidden boy. I was in a puddle at her feet.

Lindy Bergan was as beautiful as any Hollywood starlet. And yet she was gracious and kind. She had every quality that a boy like me adored in the pages of Arthurian romance. She was a queen who deigned to take up the mantle of a princess.

It was crazy, maddening, thrilling.

I could not believe I got to see her every day.

I spent the weekends in desperation, wishing for Monday to arrive.

At night I could not stop thinking about her. I tried to sleep. I tried turning on Johnny Most, calling the Celtics game from Boston Garden, on the radio on my nightstand. I would get lost in the dribbles of the Cooz and the dirty fouling of arch-rival Dolph Schayes of the Syracuse Nats, but it would only last a minute compared to the all-night torment of longing that ensued at the final whistle.

"What's wrong with you these days?" Uncle Augie asked me. "You're mooning around like a calf that lost his mother."

I couldn't help it. I confessed my adoration for the magnificent, the incredible, the unattainable, Lindy Bergan.

"Oh. So you've got a crush on her."

A crush? *This was madness!*

"Don't worry, it will pass. You're just having a good old-fashioned case of puppy love. Look at it this way. She's a senior, right? That means she'll be graduating?"

No, no, no, Lindy, don't leave me!

Chapter 21

Victor Hugo

By the next summer, Kennedy was in the Oval Office, and I was too old to go back to the St Monica's Fair. That was kids' stuff. I needed something substantial. Besides, Merrilee Krupp was not about to show up to go strolling with me, and that meant Peggy Whalen was sure not to show up, and moreover, Lindy Bergan had graduated, and I no longer saw her every minute of my every day and all night long, too. I had fallen into the void. I was a crack in the sidewalk. Life had skipped over me. I needed something big, something vast, something overpowering and overwhelming, to fill in this newly-discovered black hole in the universe.

    I found it at the Nevins Library. It was *Les Misérables*.

    In the beginning I was simply looking for something to read that was long enough to last the whole summer. I had learned to avoid the old-lady librarian at the front desk. I would feel sorry for her whenever I made her have to rise creakily from her desk to check out a book for me. And she was the one who wouldn't let me take out a book if the title was *The Scarlet Letter*.

In school, on our summer reading list, they were assigning us *The Catcher in the Rye,* which the old lady certainly would have considered immoral.

There was a newly-hired, young librarian, who wasn't from the last century. I had learned to time it so that she was the one who checked out my books, and so I had been reading things like Hemingway's short stories and Thomas Hardy's *Tess of the d'Urbervilles.*

These were things I had found on the shelf at Lauriat's new bookstore down on Essex Street in Milltown. I would stop there on my way home after my music lesson on Common Street. Signet Books and American Library were putting out the classics with new, updated, attractive covers, with artistic renderings of lonely houses and predestined lovers, at 98 cents a throw. Still, I couldn't afford them, but the classics shelf at Lauriat's gave me my summer reading list. At the library I could borrow them for free. I wasn't going to waste my time reading anything that wasn't a classic.

From the opening pages, with the story of the bishop's silver candlesticks, Victor Hugo seduced me into an uncertain world of the rich and the poor in a time and a place which I could not identify in the template of history in my mind. I had no concept of where and when poor fathers who stole a loaf of bread could be condemned to pull oars as a galley slave, but it made no difference. The mystery and the misery of being Jean Valjean was so powerful it penetrated to the depths of my soul. His rise to wealth was no mere tale of Horatio Alger striving to success, because you knew he was being hunted and haunted by the boot-heels of Javert, clicking on the cobblestones. His love of Fantine and Cosette was predestined to be doomed because you knew it was not possible on this benighted earth of ours for Jean Valjean to ever repay his debt to the bishop.

Such redemption, such balancing of the scales, would have to wait for a place like heaven. Our world was a world of injustice. To know that, all you had to do was to glance at the front page of the daily *Eagle-Trib*.

I was determined to read this book slowly, to read every word, to turn even the pages with tenderness and reverence. I knew in my heart that next year might be too late. I would turn 15 and at 15-1/2 I would be eligible to get my working papers and I was planning already to get a real, paying job, even if it had to be bagging groceries, at the new Grand Union that was going up at the site of the old Sandbanks across from the Ebenezer Parker. By then the shopping center they were putting up would be open. Even now they were paving the parking lot. The world was changing, the town of Spicket Falls was growing, by next year, even I would not be the same.

So I set aside my 14th summer, and devoted it to reading *Les Misérables*. I would take my hardcover library copy with the blue covers in hand and walk all the way to the Nevins grounds in order to spend the afternoon reclining on the grass beneath a tree in back of the library, with the gentle shadows of the tree-filled nineteenth century carriage-park to comfort and caress me. I had a spot under a tree where the lawn rose on a gentle incline and I could recline, lying on my back with the book propped open on my chest.

I was used to walking all the way to the Square in Spicket Falls.

Long ago, it seemed, the state had sent someone by the factory to tell my uncles they could not have me on the floor at the shop because of child-labor laws. That freed me from a destiny like that of my grandfather, Antonio LaStoria, who was fated to spend his days as a child inside the walls of the back rooms of Manhattan clothing emporiums and midtown garment district sweatshops.

Instead, with the help and encouragement of my uncle Augie, the one adult in our house who had actually been to high school, and who, moreover, was a three-sport star athlete at Stoughton High in the thirties, I joined the Spicket Falls Police League to play baseball.

That summer when I was fourteen was my second year in the league. The next summer would be my third, and last. I played for a team sponsored by the Ingalls family, one of the prominent, old-school Yankee business families of the town of Spicket Falls, who provided the members of the school-board and the selectmen. My coach was Sgt. O'Rourke of the Spicket Falls police force. Uncle Augie had simply brushed aside my mother's objections and told her she had to let me grow up. Playing hardball wasn't going to kill me.

So, that summer, when I was fourteen, I spent my days either walking to the Pelham Street baseball diamond with my Ingalls uniform on and my cleats slung over my shoulder, or walking to the library with *Les Misérables* in my hand.

I had no idea, then, that this book, this masterpiece by Victor Hugo (until then nothing more than the name of a bicycle shop on South Broadway)—I had no idea then that this novel, this story of the bishop's silver candlesticks, this epic of love, loss, pursuit, and redemption, would seep into my being to the bottom of my soul, *that the barricades of Paris would one day rise up in my mind like the reminders of ghostly promises and send me to my own fated destiny.*

I should have known. I should have realized that the bicycle shop on South Broadway, which I first noticed when I was only 9 years old, and brand-new to the Merrimack Valley, was meant to be there, was meant to be there *for me to notice*. A signpost. A symbol. A clue. To what? *To the deeper meaning. To the true significance.*

After all, what did Victor Hugo have to do with bicycles?

No, that shop must have been named by its owner for some other reason. That owner must have known the French author of *Les Misérables*. His life must have been affected as deeply and profoundly by the writings of that author as mine was, as I was.

Milltown and Spicket Falls were populated by a large proportion of French-Canadian immigrants, because of the mills. In my neighborhood alone, there were the Perrault family, the Lamonds, the Beauschene family, and the Robillards. The nuns at St Anne's Orphanage and the nuns at Mt Carmel's School, down by the Square, they were all from French-speaking Canada. This element had been missing in Revere, absent from Watertown. Something had drawn my lifeline to Milltown, something magnetic.

Perhaps this was it, the encounter with a book, with an unforgettable character; with a writer, with a towering figure. Could it be? I would never know. Not for certain. But the suspicion would never leave me. There was nothing that was not encompassed in *Les Misérables*: hell, heaven, love, hate, revenge, redemption. As Victor Hugo himself once said, *"wherever children lack a book to learn from . . . Les Misérables knocks at the door and says: 'open up, I am here for you.'"*

Chapter 22

The Stardust Lounge

The dream recurred, flowing, swirling, eddying and coalescing within the fluid reflections in the long mirror behind the bar of the dimly-lit interior of The Stardust Lounge on Route 28 in Reading, Massachusetts . . .

The year was 1961 and I had just turned 15 and it was New Year's Eve and the boys in the band were stuck for an accordian-player.

My teacher at Milltown Music on Common Street, Jerry Bellanti, was only two or three years older than me, but he had enlisted in the Service, to get his draft obligation out of the way.

Mario Morelli, the owner of Milltown Music, the piano-teacher who lived around the corner from me on Durrell Street, was the one who set me up with the gig.

I was the next in line to take Jerry's place at the store. It was going to be up to me to fill in for him while he was away. Any gigs, any groups, calling for an accordianist, were going to fall to me.

I was going to make some real money, at last, decent money, playing music, 25 bucks for my first gig. Mario Morelli was going to take out my musicians' union entry-dues out of my take. He vouched for me with the other two guys in the band, whom I had never met, older guys in their thirties. Acting as an entertainment agent for the Valley was one of Morelli's side-hustles: weddings, bar-mitzvahs, company Christmas bashes, you dialed up Mario's number at *MM Talent Agency*, which was nothing more than his office phone at Milltown Music. I was taking Jerry B's place in the lineup.

It was a trio. That was the way things were being done these days. The era of the Big Band was dead and gone. Mario Morelli and his Orchestra, once upon a time, headlined at Canobie Lake in New Hampshire, the boardwalk at Salisbury Beach, and at the Hampton Casino and the Lowell Auditorium. Now he was more or less semi-retired. He just rested on his laurels, ran the store, and distributed bookings between rounds of golf. His kids were growing up and the band-members who were his lifelong friends were scattering to the four winds. Nowadays he was a member of the Merrimack Valley Country Club in Spicket Falls. The two guys in the trio who wanted to hire me were guys Morelli knew from the business.

They both lived way up on Forest Street in Spicket Falls, way out of town, at least one of them did, Neal, the guitar-player, and vocalist, the one who had the pick-up truck. His partner was Scotty, on drums. They would pick me up in the pick-up truck and take me all the way out to Forest Street in the woods. I would throw my Excelsior in the back and squeeze into the cab with the two of them. It was winter, no snow yet, the back yard at Neal's place was a gravel driveway and trees, with a kid's tricycle dangling off the back porch of the ranch house. We practiced in Neal's basement. He was the singer, so naturally, he was the leader. The repertoire was things like Errol Garner's *'Misty'* and Sinatra's *'Fly Me to the Moon.'* I could play off the sheet-music, all I had to do was follow along, play sustained chords, take a melody lead on the bridge, and then Neal would come back in with the lyrics. Scottie was playing brushes behind me. It was lounge-music. The practices came in handy because the night of the gig, I just told my mother I was going to another practice at Neal's house. She would've killed me had she known I was going to a paying gig at *The Stardust Lounge* in Reading when I was underage and all that.

You went down Broadway through North Milltown, crossed the river by the dam, continued down South Broadway, which turned into Route 28, and that took you to Andover Square, where it became Main Street; then you passed Phillips Academy's campus on the left, went under the overpass carrying Route 125, where the road became Route 28 again, passed through North Reading in an eye-blink, and then you came to Reading itself. If you continued, Route 28 would take you all the way into Boston, and then some. But north of Reading Square, we pulled over into the dirt parking lot of *The Stardust Lounge*.

Neal and Scottie didn't talk much to me, all the way down, not really. They really didn't know me or have much in common with a 15-year-old. They were two guys in their thirties, late thirties, with families, wives, and kids my age. We didn't have that much to say to each other. I was a high school kid who played. They were grown men with problems. I wasn't in the band, not really. I certainly wasn't Jerry Bellanti.

We were taking a break after the second set. I was sitting at the bar drinking a ginger-ale. They were shoulders-together on stools next to me, grousing about their wives.

I was sitting there thinking, *is this my future? Is this what I'm going to turn into? Am I gonna end up like them, nursing a drink and stuck in a lousy marriage?*

I thought of standing on the stage, glancing from the sheet music over the heads of the dancers, just a little bit ago, while we serenaded the dancers with *I'm in the Mood for Love*. The dance-floor was a scrap of parquet flooring in front of a low, carpeted stage. It was only one half-step below where I was standing, playing back-up four-fingered chords, trying to sway with the brushes, the revolving lights sweeping over couples who were slow-dancing, imperceptibly swirling to the music, slowly turning, dance-step by dance-step, clinging to each other, waiting for midnight, *in the mood for love* and a midnight kiss on New Year's Eve. The lights were turned way down low in *The Stardust Lounge*, so that a few inches away, you could see, not faces, only shadows.

As I sat there on a bar-stool nursing my ginger-ale, sip by sip, wondering why I hadn't spoken up for myself and ordered a sasparilla, like the one my Auntie Peggy would've served me, if this was *The Wonder Bar* on Broadway in Milltown, the next block up from Movie-house Row—my thoughts were racing, chasing one another, like the liquid lights skating across the bar-length mirror in front of me—I felt somebody touch me.

It was just a tap on the shoulder. A light touch. One finger. *From behind me.*

I swerved to look and see who it was, but there was nobody there.

I felt a sudden chill between the shoulder-blades.

I had the profound sensation that I had just been tabbed by an invisible hand.

With a shiver, I looked up into the liquid lake of the long bar-mirror, where I saw the blood-red reflection of a guitar hanging on a guitar-stand on the stage behind me.

The shape of the upright-standing guitar was the shape of a woman's head, with fiery-red tresses falling down over her shoulders.

She was the damsel in peril waiting expectantly, holding her breath for me to rescue her.

Or was that me, holding my breath?

Why was I holding my breath? I should breathe.

The revolving lights of the Stardust Lounge were playing back and forth across the lake of the mirror, shifting and melding, liquid and blending, glinting with highlights, dazzling into shadow, swirling downstream, flowing around the corner of the mill, disappearing under the little green bridge . . .

What was happening?

The scene in front of me was the scene behind me.

The scene behind me was the scene in front of me.

I grabbed a bar-napkin. There was the bartender's pen lying in the recessed groove that ran along the interior edge of the polished bar.

I wrote, without thinking, without missing a heartbeat, the words just came into my head from nowhere and flowed down my arm into the sword of my pen:

> *In the mirror, on a guitar stand,*
> *Hangs the head of a maiden,*
> *Who found herself lost in a land*
> *Called Aden . . .*

Chapter 23

A Death in the Family

That winter, after I turned 16 on Christmas Day, when February came, we had a storm that dumped two feet of snow in the driveway behind the fieldstone house.

My Dad had been working in Boston since they started the Prudential Center project in the Back Bay. The union hall sent him there. He was finally bringing home 500 bucks a week. It wasn't interesting work, just hammering together the wooden forms for pouring the concrete foundations, but he was trying to hang on to get into the crew that would eventually be doing the inside finish work if they ever got the whole 52 stories up there. He couldn't be late for work and he knew the storm was arriving, so he was up by 5 am. He had to be on Boylston Street in Boston by 6.30 in the morning. Fortunately, they had just opened the newly constructed Route 93 Interstate bridge over the Merrimack, at the rotary on Haverhill Street, Rte. 110, about a mile and a half from our house—but who knew in these conditions if the Interstate would be plowed? It was still so new that only a few straggling cars could be seen crossing the bridge on the morning commute.

Uncle Augie got up to help Dad shovel.

The driveway at the back of our corner lot was at least seventy-five feet long, running along the edge of the Perrault's basketball court.

I got up, too, to help them, the house was in such a commotion.

But they told me just to stay out of their way.

Something possessed them, that early, cold morning, God knows what, two grown men, to act like boys again. They had decided to make it a race. Each of them would take one side of the driveway and shovel all the way down to the garage doors. Uncle Augie was on the right, my Dad on the left half. Dad had the advantage because he could throw the snow in a natural direction off to his left. My Uncle had to twist and throw right with every shovel-full. It was a whole extra motion, pulling back, then throwing, on his half, on every shovel-full. But Uncle Augie, at six-foot-two, was a lot bigger than my Dad, who was only five-foot-eight, and skinny. But in his youth, my father had shoveled coal in a coal-mine. He was strong, a lot stronger than anyone would have thought to look at him. I knew because when we were fixing up the new house, I'd seen him handle an extension-ladder like it was a toothpick.

I stood there watching, half-heartedly shoveling the brick walk by the rosebush, but actually mesmerized, with mounting excitement, as they moved down the seventy-five feet, heads down, backs bent, in a shower of flying snow.

Neither one of them wanted to let the other one win.

But when they ended up at the garage door in a dead heat photo-finish, they stood up straight and looked at each other, with puffed-up red faces, and burst into laughter.

I stood there, saying to myself, *I will never in all my days be able to measure up to men like that.*

One night in 1962 we were all in bed at three o'clock on a Sunday morning, when the phone started ringing downstairs.

It started ringing and it would not stop.

In my bedroom, behind my closed door, I raised myself up on one elbow. I didn't like the sound of this. With an unaccountable sense of sudden foreboding, I leaned my head over to listen.

I saw pale electric light come on in a sliver under my door. I heard my mother shuffling down the hall past my door in her slippers. When she reached the head of the stairs, she flipped on the light switch and under my door, a golden band appeared.

I strained to listen to try to catch what she was saying into the phone downstairs.

There was a chance I could make it out. The phone was on top of the phone-book at the very last scrap of room at the end of the curving formica counter-top my Dad had built in the narrow section of the kitchen that used to be the old pantry. The phone sat across the hallway from the cellar-door leading down. There used to be a closed pantry-door there that my father took out. It was directly below the head of the stairway upstairs. If I listened enough, I might be able to hear.

No good. I would have to get up and go down there. It was easy to see I wasn't going to be able to get back to sleep now anyway. But more than that, worse than that, I just had to know.

I crept down the stairs, trying not to wake the twins, still, fortunately, at ten years of age, covered in the blissful blankets of slumber.

Let them stay that way. Let them not feel the trepidation I felt with every downward placement of my bare foot on another step.

At the bottom of the stair, I turned and saw my mother silhouetted in the white flourescent light of the kitchen, her head hanging down, hair hanging over her eyes, slouched over in her padded housecoat, supporting herself with one hand on the counter by the phone, which now was silent, the receiver replaced on the hook again.

She looked up at me when she heard me, and said, from five feet away, "Go back to bed."

"What is it, Ma? What happened?"

"It's your Uncle Augie." There were no tears in her voice, only resignation.

Uncle Augie had left home that morning. Or was that yesterday, Saturday? Yes, Uncle Gene had come to fetch him in his new Buick Roadmaster. Uncle Augie was moving out, going to Providence, down in Rhode Island, to start a new life, I didn't know why.

Ma hadn't mentioned Uncle Gene.

"Was there an accident? Is Uncle Augie all right?"

"He's gone, Nicky."

"Gone? How could he be gone?"

"Cerebral hemorrhage, that's how." She waved her hand in front of her face. "Go back to bed. There's nothing we can do now. It will all have to wait till the morning. Your Uncle Gene is already calling up everybody."

I went back upstairs. I didn't want to intrude upon my mother's grief. I closed my own door and climbed back in bed. I wanted now to be alone, to wait for the tears to come. But they wouldn't. I lay there in the darkness, sixteen years old, thinking *after this, nothing will ever be the same again.*

In a while, I heard my mother coming back up the stairs. She went into the bathroom and shut the door. I heard her lower the seat. The house was still. Neither the twins nor my father had gotten up. The bathroom was just on the other side of the wall from the foot of my bed. She sat down and she put her head in her hands. In my mind's eye, I could see it, because I could hear her start crying muffled tears while she sobbed uncontrollably into her hands. The house was still. She had closed the bathroom door so that she could grieve in private. At that moment, I was the only one in the family who could have shared her grief. But I lay there on my back in darkness, bedcovers pulled up to my chin, frozen, staring at the black ceiling above my head.

. . . nothing will ever be the same again.

Chapter 24

Time is a River

The river passed on downstream, leaving behind eddies and pools, and these were the memories which the river had no time left to recapture. The river could not return. The past would have to be left to those who remembered it . . .

I walked outside and I looked up at the sky. I wanted to know how I could go on.

I wanted to know from somebody, God, my guardian angel, anybody— the elemental forces?

I did not receive an answer. And that made me angry. It infuriated me.

But go on, I did. I didn't think I could. But it turned out—that I had no choice.

One day follows the next and inevitably, step by step, heartbeat by heartbeat, time trudges on, and you and you find out that you have to go—there.

I began to send away for college catalogs. I tried out for the JV football team at Jenney High. My friends, Benny Nader and Dennis Rousseau, thought I was nuts. I was too small. But I had it in mind to try to emulate the beloved uncle I had lost. My father told me I'd be sorry, don't come crying to him when I got hurt.

I did not appreciate that. My uncle was the one who sat me down in front of the TV in the den to watch the greatest game ever played, the 1958 NFL championship between the Baltimore Colts and the New York Giants. I picked the Colts, because my idol, Johnny Unitas, was the quarterback. It was the first overtime, ever, in the history of the game, and the Colts won.

I treasured that memory, now that Uncle Augie was gone. My father would never have thought of doing that with me. His brother Alek might have, but not him. He was outside in the yard building a fireplace for next summer's cookouts. While we watched that game. He would have turned his nose up at us for wasting our time. He probably did.

Besides, he was sure his brother-in-law had a betting interest in that game. Such issues, held under check in the fieldstone house while Uncle Augie was with us, seemed to be rising to the surface, now that he was no longer there. My mother didn't have her father around to tell her to show her husband a little respect. And now she didn't have her brother around to make her feel like she ought to spare him the fallout from openly fighting with her husband right in front of him.

Neither did my Dad have his father-in-law around any longer to make him feel as wanted as an extra son. My dad was fed up, as he would have said, with years of nagging. Now he no longer had to hold his tongue in front of his brother-in-law. He was tired of begging my mother for gas money or cash to get an oil change. He wasn't going to just hand over his whole paycheck every week any more. He was going to hold back a little for the things he needed. He wasn't going to humble himself anymore because he was allowed to live with his wife's family, *in her father's house*. He was making a little money for the first time in his life and he deserved better. Things had changed.

Yes, things had changed, and they weren't going back to the way they used to be.

Somehow, some way, in some subterranean fashion, it was turning out that Tech.Sgt.Augie LaStoria of the US Army Signal Corps, Omaha Beach, D-Day, 1944, may he rest in peace, was the substance that held that house together. It sure wasn't the mortar that pointed the fieldstone exterior or the spackle that filled in the holes punched in the bedroom walls.

I found my mother sitting on the foot of my uncle's bed one day, holding his shoes in her lap.

She said she was going to give me his bedroom, on the northwest corner of the house. She wanted to move ten-year-old Jackie into my bedroom in the middle. She would keep Jill with her. She was no longer sharing a bedroom with my Dad.

My Dad got into Uncle Augie's bedroom and installed a built-in wrap-around desk in one corner. He had some formica countertop material left over from the kitchen. He was trying to make it up to me. Somehow he had divined the way I was feeling, I don't know how. I put my growing collection of college catalogs arranged flush up against the wall on my new desk, bracketed by bookends so that they would stand up and I could read their spines: *William and Mary, Wake Forest, Syracuse.* I sat there and surveyed my future. The future that was coming, like it or not, step by step, heartbeat by heartbeat. I opened the catalogs one by one and read the course descriptions and I began to dream of *getting out of here*.

It was easy to tell when Ma was mad. She would start banging the kitchen cabinet doors downstairs. When those two were fighting the upset would drift up the stairs and steal under my closed door, the door I shut to keep it all out. It was my room now, it was my life now. I would got out and cross the hall and get my sister and brother into my old room together with me and we'd shut the door and play board games or maybe just sit there on Jack's bed and hold onto each other. I was trying to protect them, to save them from all this. Who else did they have?

The Cuban Missile Crisis came along in October. We huddled in the den, in front of the TV that Uncle Augie had bought for the family, for the new house: a family that no longer talked to one another. We were left with no defenses against the world coming to an end in one super-massive mushroom cloud.

One day my sister Jill fell down the stairs. She didn't fall down all thirteen, just the last four. She slipped and more or less slid down. She ended up in a heap in the corner by the parlor door. My mother came rushing out of the kitchen at the noise and the sound of Jill crying. "What did you do?" she demanded. "What's wrong with you? Are you all right?"

My sister was sobbing, "I'm all right." She was more afraid of what my mother was going to do than she was of whatever pain she was in or what parts of her body hurt from the fall.

My mother was raising her voice. "I'll give you something to cry about then." She began slapping my sister around the head so that my sister's arms went up.

I was standing in the den, frozen. It was so unexpected, I couldn't move, I couldn't save my sister.

I was livid. When they had finished and moved out of the way, I went up the stairs and slammed my bedroom door. My mother wasn't the only one who could slam things to let their feelings be known. The linoleum in my room had a pattern like a throw-rug that ringed the bed. I began pacing round and round my bed for about an hour trying to calm myself. No child deserved this kind of treatment. What was I going to do? There was nothing I could do.

What? Call the cops? *I couldn't even tell anyone about this.* I was the one who was going to have to keep this shameful secret. I was furious at my mother. It was plain to me that she lost her temper and took it out on Jill. When she calmed down, she was sorry. What was *I* going to do? Honestly?—*nothing*.

Sometimes, when I was alone, when nobody was there to observe and criticize I would go stand and look at the bookshelf built into the alcove next to the fireplace. I would run my gaze over my mother's handsome set of John Steinbeck, which she had owned since the Thirties. All the titles. Next to novels by Lloyd Douglas. And the 12-volume set of *The Wonderland of Knowledge,* in blue covers, with inlaid pictures on the spine of *The Lighthouse of Alexandria* and *The Wheels of Industrial Progress* that she bought from some long-forgotten encyclopedia salesman who came to the door in Revere when I was seven years old. *What did it all mean?* My mother had been so proud of this house when she first bought it, she stood back and regarded those books after putting them on the shelves, just so. Her eyes would run up and down over the grooves of the carved woodwork of the alcove, thinking of the priests who once sat in this room with the French doors closed, by this bookcase, in front of this fire, with grieving parents, trying to console them for their loss, trying to get them not to abandon the idea of God or of filling their weekly parish envelope with folding money for the Sunday collection box.

Why did everything have to change the way it did? Why did Uncle leave? Why, if we were happy here once, why couldn't we be happy again? Was there something about this house?

I remembered then that I had overheard Ma's sister Peggy having a fight with her about this house, some complicated fight about Peggy being cheated by my mother out of a share of the money when Ma sold Papanonni's house in Revere. I remembered vaguely something about Peggy trying to claim there was something wrong with this house, something that lingered in the corners. I couldn't put my finger on what exactly Peggy had said, but I had the distinct feeling that she was cursing the house and prophesying that her sister Gerry, my mother, would never be happy here.

Chapter 25

Playing Ball

. . . I wanted to dive into the river, I wanted to make a big splash, so big the world could not ignore it, I wanted to immerse myself in the flow of time and emerge under the little green bridge and shake my head free of the clinging droplets, and refreshed, open my eyes wide, and see . . .

If only I could have gone back again to the summer before all this happened. I would have been happy to stay there and never return. It was the last time everything was simple and uncomplicated and I was free to be myself and be happy.

The summer when I was 15 years old, I played ball in the Police League for the last time. The league was for 13-15 year-olds. After that, you had to move on to Babe Ruth ball. But I knew that I wasn't going to. I was going to start bagging groceries at the Grand Union in the fall. This was my final season.

I dedicated that season to my uncle Augie. I did it in memory of all his legendary successes as a ballplayer in the training camps of England. When genuine major leaguers told him he really had what it took.

I took out all my aggressions on that white ball heading for my strike zone. Whatever I thought back in 1958 when my uncle and I were watching that memorable championship game on TV, whenever I fantasized growing up to be a football hero, I knew now it was not going to happen. I had been on the JV squad at school the previous fall, and much to my chagrin, my father's prediction that I'd get hurt came out. I messed up my knee. These days I hated for my father to be right about anything. If he told me to do anything, such as cut the grass, I wouldn't. If my uncle had told me, I would have. My father knew this. It didn't help anything.

Sgt O'Rourke of the Spicket Falls Police, the coach of our team, the Ingalls, got my grudging respect, but even he was a pale substitute for my uncle. Neither my father nor my mother ever came to see me play in a game. I didn't want them to anyway. I wanted to be left alone. I wanted my uncle to come to my games, but that wasn't going to happen. Even were he still alive, perhaps he would not have wanted to stir up memories of his own past glories that were gone forever.

But that was not true. That was my own pain and loss and hurt talking. I knew he was watching. I knew from little things around the house that he was proud of me. I knew from the dog-eared paperback novels with the torn covers he'd left behind, the ones I found in the top drawer of my bedroom bureau, his old bedroom: Kyle Onstott's *Mandingo,* and the sequel called *Drum.* I knew from the shined black dress shoes with the soft-pointed toes that were sitting empty on the floor of the closet in that room: dead man's shoes. I knew from the night when Ma and I were sitting at the kitchen table and we heard his footsteps in ponderous stocking feet crossing the hallway upstairs from his bedroom to the bathroom, making the floorboards creak: he was a big man. We looked at each other and held our breath waiting for the sound of the door closing behind him. He would have given me a pat on the ass if he could have strapped on a glove and played the game beside me. It was Uncle Augie who saved clippings for me of game reports that got printed in the *Eagle-Trib* if my name got mentioned, even though I held the scissors: he guided my hand. He knew I hit .300 that year. He saw me catch that ball in centerfield that was hit over my head that clinched the playoffs for us. When the season was over, I carried home my trophy *for him*, I placed it on my bureau in my bedroom, *for him to admire.* He knew how proud I was to wear the championship patch on the baseball jacket we were awarded after the season was over and we had the break-up dinner at the Arlington Club.

I dedicated that season to my uncle, in my own mind. I myself was getting to run around the bases re-living his past triumphs. I played the game for him. Life was simple between the white lines. Everything else was put aside while the game was on. It was life and death until the last out. I was happy just throwing myself with my whole body and soul into the game.

Now I was 16. This summer I was pulling down 20, 25 hours a week bagging groceries at the Grand Union, where the Sandbanks used to be.

My mother was working at Papagallo's down in the Everett Mills now. The family business was over. The days when the three sons of Tony LaStoria, Patsy, Gene and Augie, were carrying on their own business, in the name of their mother, were gone.

It wasn't just our house where Tech. Sgt. Augie LaStoria, survivor of Omaha Beach, was the mysterious figure who moved out of the shadows and gave light to the room. Although Patsy was the oldest, and his mother's first-born, he knew that both his parents preferred to adore Augie, their youngest son, and Patsy gave his whole-hearted worship to his kid brother, who was something he could never be, the idol of Dame Fortune, the tall, athletic one, the pick of the litter.

Although Gene wished for nothing more than to model himself on his father, to follow in Tony's footsteps, to manage the factory floor himself, to exceed his father, the General Manager, by becoming himself the Owner, still he bestowed precedence on his younger brother Augie, to whom he could never measure up because Augie had something, that something that was out of the ordinary, that something rare and priceless which could not be obtained by following in the footsteps of another, but which was given, without asking, without seeking, only to the chosen few, the ones who felt the tap on the shoulder.

Augie's older sister Peggy started a lifelong war of attrition with her own father simply because she blamed him for making her brother quit school and go to work in the CCC instead of following his star and making something out of himself. For that family, in that generation, Augie was the lodestar, Augie was the flag-bearer.

When he died, the stream of sub-contracts from London Fog died, too. His brother Gene found his office empty and his dream hollow. He took an offer from London Fog and went to work for them in one of their plants down in Tennessee. He closed his own business, the LaStorias' family business, and became what his father had been, a middle manager for a corporate owner, a subsidiary arm of a conglomerate-octopus, a functionary who functioned to make another man rich, a cog in the wheel.

The death of my uncle was the reason my mother was working at Papagallo's down in the Everett Mills instead of her own *Gigi Sportswear* in the Oxford Mills.

The death of my uncle was the reason I was not going to be working at the family business, now that I was old enough, learning my trade from the ground up, as my uncles had, beginning at the bottom, the scion of a dynasty; but instead, was going to bag groceries. For strangers.

Chapter 26

Molly Jones

One day early in September when I was a senior at Jenney High, I had gone over to Phillips Street to see Benny Nader, but he wasn't in. He was working that afternoon at the First National grocery store a couple of streets over.

I went to see him there. I cut across an alley that led from the middle of Phillips Street to the middle of Camden Street. These two streets were known as the slums of Spicket Falls. They were two long, parallel streets that ran south from Milltown Street in Spicket Falls down to the Milltown city line. From Camden Street, a driveway cut-out led into the back of the parking lot of the First National on Milltown Street.

I wanted to see Benny's new car. He had picked up a used '56 Chevy convertible. He told me he couldn't get out of work, come by his house later. We were going to go riding up to Salisbury Beach with Denny to see if they could scoop some girls. They were always out to scoop some girls. Sometimes Benny would disappear under the boardwalk with some girl he just met that night. I just went along for the ride. I wasn't about to try to compete with those two. Benny had a convertible, Denny had a wicked roving eye. They thought they were babe-magnets, but I just laughed at them. Still, it got me out of the house. It was better than staying home. One time Benny came back from the boardwalk, leaned over the back seat of the convertible where I was sitting, and passed his finger under my nose. "Smell that? That's pussy." It just grossed me out. He could be wicked crude at times. Other times, he was polite, courteous, a charmer. He turned it on and off. He was Lebanese and he tanned very well in the summer sun. Denny was French and his tan came from the Riviera, he said. I laughed at them, I laughed with them, I envied them. But their girl-chasing sport was not my speed. One time they got me in the back seat with a couple of girls who came at me from either side, trying to make out with me. I couldn't wait to get out of there. Later I looked back on it like a bad dream. Maybe it never really happened. If I was lucky. I wasn't looking for a one-night stand, like those two. I was looking for a nice girl, someone I could talk to, if I was looking at all, which I wasn't. I still believed the only reason those two hung out with me was so that they could cheat off me in school.

That particular afternoon Benny said he was getting out of work when the store closed at nine. I was off that night, I could only get 20 or so hours a week out of the Grand Union. Benny said to meet him at his house, but be sure to bring money to fill his gas tank, he wasn't riding me up to the beach for nothing.

Typical Benny. I left the store, thinking *what the hell, I got nothing better to do. So it's gonna cost me a buck, maybe two. I'll try and chisel him. I'm saving my money for college. He's welcome to spend his on cars and girls. He has to work for it just like I do.*

I was passing back the same way I came, through the parking lot, but there was a girl sitting on the rickety, tilted picnic table outside the store. This table was balancing on the crags of some broken tar-paving next to the bushes where the employees parked their vehicles on that side of the First National. It was probably the table where they sat to grab a bite on break or have a smoke. I knew I would have to pass her, but I didn't know her, so I didn't know what to do or how to act, exactly. So I just sort of nodded hello, so as not to be totally stuck up about it, trying, you know, not to really make eye-contact either, so she wouldn't think I was trying to get fresh with her. I was already past her, when I heard her say to my back, "Hey."

I turned, and looked at her quizzically, my head on one side.

"I know you," she said. "I'm in one of your classes, and I'll bet you never even noticed."

She was dressed in short shorts and a blouse. A pink blouse, I think it was. Pale apple-green shorts. Somehow she made them go together. I thought she was cute, now that I was looking right at her.

"Your name is Nick Petrovich," she said, to prove she knew who I was.

I had come to a dead stop, at this point, and I stuck my hands in my pockets. I wasn't accustomed to girls stopping me in the streets. "And what's your name?"

"Molly Jones."

"Well—Molly Jones." I felt suddenly awkward and stupid, standing there with my hands stuck in my jeans, eyeglasses and all that. "So, what are you doing, sitting out here? You work at the store?"

"No, I'm just waiting for my girlfriend."

"Oh."

When I didn't say anything else, and didn't move, she said, "So—see you around, huh?"

"Okay. Guess so."

I turned and left, my hands still in my pockets, thinking I had seen the flicker of an amused smile on her face as I turned, but, why would she want to be teasing me? Then it occurred to me, she hadn't said *waiting for my boyfriend.*

And I went over to Benny's house on Phillips Street, to wait for him on his front steps till he got out of work, and later, we went up to the beach, and then, by the time I got home again, and was in my bed, trying to sleep, and couldn't get to sleep, I realized I was thinking about Molly Jones. I was trying to picture her in my mind and decided she had a kind of, I would call it, light brown hair done up in a flip, more or less neck-length—I think—if I wanted to be unkind, I would've called it mousey-brown. But why would I? What did I care about Molly Jones? She was kinda cute, though. Hey. Again, she stopped me dead in my tracks. Hey, I know you. Dead in my tracks, lying there, trying to get to sleep, Molly Jones wouldn't leave me alone. But what class of mine was she in? For the life of me, I didn't know, or why I had never noticed her. I'll bet you never even noticed. She was right, I didn't. Maybe I should have. Maybe I should check her out. Oh, my God. Molly Jones just isn't gonna leave me alone . . . and she hadn't said *waiting for my boyfriend . . .*

The next day it turned out to be Mr Frechette's Trig class. I was over by the windows, up front, and she was over by the wall, several rows back. No wonder I never noticed. But if she was in Trig, she must be in College Course, like me. Maybe I should have noticed. Trig was hard enough for me—now I had to sit there being conscious of wanting to turn around to look at her and having to force myself not to. Math was not my strong suit. My junior year college boards I was in the 700s on English and only the 500s on math. What was I thinking? All I wanted to know was the color of her hair . . . and her eyes . . . and . . .

When the bell rang, I made sure I was there, waiting for her. "Well, Molly Jones."

She picked up her books, like girls do, holding them up to her bosom. "Where are you going next, Nick?"

"Um, study hall." Turns out her hair was not mousey-brown: depending on the light, there were golden sunflower highlights.

"Can you walk me to your locker?"

"Why?"

"Cause I wanna find out where your locker is."

On the way, she said, "You can help me in Trig, you know. I know you're smart. I'm lost."

"Oh, I don't know if I'd be of any help—I'm lost, too."

"No, suh. Hmm. I don't believe that, okay? So I'll meet you right here tomorrow morning before first period."

"What color are your eyes?"

"Why?"

"Because I wanna know."

"Well, they're not blue, and they're not grey. They're somewhere between. Depends."

"Yeah, I know. Depends on the light, huh."

The next morning Molly Jones was at my locker bright and early. It was September of my senior year. She was only a sophomore, but she was fifteen. I was still only sixteen. I wouldn't turn seventeen till Christmas. It was me and Lindy Bergan all over again, only this time I was the senior and she was the underclassman.

"Listen—if you really want me to help you with your trig, why don't you meet me at the Nevins after school—and we can study there, where it's quiet."

If I could get a girl to go to the library with me, then she must like me. So it was a test question.

Molly Jones passed the test.

The library didn't really work. The big study-tables were over past the stacks. It was an open area. There was too much whispering going on between us. It's hard to do trig problems whispering all the time. We were annoying people sitting in chairs trying to read.

"What are we gonna do?" I said. I was leaning my head over looking past the fringe of her flip into those grey-blue eyes. Her hair wasn't really light-brown. I was wrong about that. It could be lustrous and auburn. The library had flourescent light overhead, so her hair shone, fine and silky. What was I thinking of? She had me saying "we" already.

"We could go over my house," said Molly.

That worked much better, for several reasons. We could study at her kitchen table. Her Dad worked at Oxford Paper and he wouldn't be home till suppertime. Her older brother was an order-picker at Yankee Warehouse, the wholesale auto-supply in the Lower Pacific Mills; her mother waited on tables at the Bluebonnet on Essex Street. We were alone in the afternoons till suppertime. We could talk as loud as we wanted. We didn't have to whisper. It was easier to communicate. It was easier for Molly to pull me by the hand into her bedroom at the rear corner of the kitchen.

"Molly, we can't."

"Why not? Don't you like me, Nicky?"

"I like you way more than you think. I like you way more than what's good for me. If you only knew. Listen—what if your father came home—your mother? They could walk in any second."

"They won't, they won't."

"Mol-ly! Let's just go in the parlor and sit on the couch. If you're tired of studying, we can turn on the TV."

We didn't get too much television-watching done on the living room couch. At least we were there, with enough time to straighten our clothing when we saw Molly's older brother, Daniel, pull into the driveway. He made a point of coming in the front door, straight into the parlor. I couldn't blame him. I would've done the same if it was my sister. Thank God my sister was only eleven.

Daniel didn't like me, I could tell. He was being protective of his little sister Molly. He loved his little sister. He made a point of being unfriendly towards me. I think he wanted me to go away. But Molly didn't. In that case, he was gonna watch my every move.

Molly's mother was a different story. She was a short, rounded woman, pleasant enough, but not very talkative. Mr Jones was putty in Molly's hands. She just threw her arms around his neck and it was *whatever Molly wants*. She did the same thing to me.

"I liked you for a long time, you know, before you liked me."

"Really? How did you even know me?"

"I was watching you in the hallways last year. I figured I was just a freshman so what was the use? But now I'm a sophomore, and—you don't think I was sitting on the picnic table waiting for my girlfriend, do you?"

"You weren't? I don't believe that. Not for one minute."

"Yes, suh. I saw you out my window, right over there, crossing the street and go up the driveway, and I took a chance and went out there and waited, only I didn't know if you'd be coming out or not, or if you'd go out the other door. Lucky for you, you came back my way."

"Yes, it was lucky for me."

"Now, be careful, be gentle. If I get a hickey, my mother's bound to notice. My brother wouldn't, but she would."

"I don't like those girls who go around showing off their hickeys like some merit badge from the Girl Scouts."

"Disgusting, isn't it?" Molly made a face, but she was laughing.

We did have to be careful, though. I had to be careful to keep her far, far away from Benny and Denny at school. There was no way I was gonna let those two anywhere near my Molly Jones. But I was getting grilled on a daily basis.

"So, what's up, Tiger, we never see you no more," says Benny.

"His time's booked up," says Denny.

"Tell us—you get to second base yet?"

"Naw—he's going for the home cooking."

"Listen—you can always dry-hump her!"

"Right—can't get pregnant that way!"

"You two just stay away!"

"Okay, okay, but it's hard, man. You two are everywhere together, holding hands all the time between classes."

"They've got the whole school talking."

"So, you going steady, or what?"

That was the critical question. Liking was just the first step. That was easy. Then you proceeded to making out. That was dangerous because girls have hormones. So already you're tip-toeing on a knife edge. I wasn't about to say anything more than 'I like you' to Molly, not yet. I was madly in love with her but I wasn't going to let that particular four-letter word out just yet. I was already faced with the issue of getting serious. Getting serious meant to Molly a declaration to everybody, the whole school, and yes, extending to her parents, and her brother, that we were going steady. I was already at this crisis point by Halloween. God only knew where I'd be by Thanksgiving. Thank God I didn't have a car. I knew for shit-sure that I wouldn't have been able to stay out of the back seat, in a car, with Molly. Bad enough steering her away from her bedroom in her own house. I knew that Benny Nader was having sex with girls in the back-seat of his car, when it was too cold to go under the boardwalk at the beach. Dennis Rousseau, too, for that matter. He had a car, too, a Dodge. Everybody was doing it. That, and drinking Bud, or chug-a-lugging six Colt-45's in a row. According to those two, I was the only one at Jenney High who wasn't. But I couldn't help it. I was more interested in reading a book than I was in driving a car, owning a car, fixing a car, having sex in a car—in other words, getting pushed into sex before I was ready, willing and able. The old admonition of my mother rang true in my ears: if Tommy jumps off a bridge, you gonna jump off one, too?

Still, I had to devise a strategy to hold off Molly. I told her that she was driving me crazy with ardent desire, you know what I mean, do I have to spell it out? but we were just going to have to wait, that's all.

"Wait for what?"

"You know."

"No, I don't."

"Molly, I can't get you pregnant. Do you know a girl who used to be in school, but isn't anymore, a girl named Merrilee Krupp?"

"Come on, Nicky. Who doesn't. She lives right on the next street over, on Phillips Street. Her and her husband got an apartment up on the third floor."

"You mean she married that guy?"

"The one with the Harley-Davidson? Yeah. He's in Walpole now."

"What!"

"He robbed a bank over in Amesbury. You didn't know, Nicky?"

"I don't believe it. Do you know I took a bike-hike with her and her girlfriend up to Tower Hill one time, what's her name, oh, yeah, Peggy Whalen, the cop's daughter, over on Oakland Ave. Only thing was, Peggy didn't show up."

"Oh, so you liked this Merrilee before you liked me."

"Come on, Molly, that was years ago. We were kids. But the point is I am not gonna get you pregnant the way what's-his-name–."

"Michael Butterfield."

"God. What a name. The way Butterfield did to Merrilee Krupp. So, we're just gonna have to wait."

"For what?"

"Molly, I don't believe in pre-marital sex. I'm a Catholic, you know."

I was desperate at this point to climb out of the hole I had dug myself into. But it was the wrong thing to say to Molly Jones. Because the next words out of her mouth were–.

"So we're going steady, and I'm gonna wear your ring around my neck, and we're gonna get married, and then we're gonna do it!"

Everybody was happy after that. Molly was happy, her mother was happy, everybody but her brother Daniel, who would not let me call him Danny.

Molly saw the wisdom of my way because she thought it was really mature and responsible of me and that it showed that I really cared. About her.

But what about me? I wasn't even seventeen yet. I wanted to be a nice boy, I wanted a nice girl, I wanted to go to college and have a nice life. I never thought about Revere anymore, I never thought about Jimmy Dillard, who was once so important to me, and who had now started running with the greaser crowd at school. I hardly even thought about my uncle anymore. I only thought about Molly Jones. All day and all night every day all week.

It was lucky for me that Molly was a nice girl at heart, and that she really loved me, and that I really loved her, and she was willing to wait, for that reason, because of love.

That was all that Molly Jones really wanted, someone to love her.

Chapter 27

The Sixties Begin

We didn't get a chance to make it unscathed past Thanksgiving. On November 22nd, President Kennedy was assassinated in Dallas. I first heard whispers in the hallway getting out of fifth period. Kids came running in from the parking lot at Penney High, kids who had radios turned on in their cars while they were skipping class or going to 2nd lunch. I rushed to find Molly and we just held each other as tight as we could. Principal Larchmont came on the intercom and told us to go to the school-buses, we were being sent home. Molly and I walked home to her house with our heads down, holding on to each other.

The Sixties had begun.

Molly Jones and I were thrown back onto each other by the events of the day. Life was too important an enterprise to be taken less than seriously.

We began talking on the telephone constantly, every minute that we were not together. At some point each day, which we dreaded, we would have to part. As soon as I got home to my house, I would call her up to let her know I got home safely. I would take the telephone from its corner, stretch the wire across the hallway, and sit down with the phone in my lap on the top step of the cellar stairs, shutting the door. We had no secrets from each other. The smallest daily happening was subject to voluminous examination.

My mother wasn't talking to the rest of us. We didn't know why. It was almost a year now since she had uttered a word. She went to work at Papagallo's, she came home, she cooked, she cleaned, she served food to us, she washed the dishes, and went to bed, all without acknowledging us.

As a consequence, I fell back on Molly's support more and more. My father was no longer working at the Pru in Boston. He had taken a job in North Adams, in the mountains of the Berkshires. He said the union hall sent him out there. He stayed in a motel all week and came home on weekends. But then he would spend a half a day or more of that weekend at his sister Stasija's up the street. The travel-time amounted to three or four hours one way. His job was 150 miles away. While he stopped in to see his children, Ma didn't speak to him. He told Jack and Jill and me that North Adams, the mountains, reminded him of home. My heart hurt and I loved Molly for being there to listen to me, to sympathize with me, to buck me up. I leaned on her heavily.

It was as if the dam on the Spicket had held back the river, and held it back, and held it back, until it burst forth and sent the blockage careening downriver with the immense force of a terrible outrage.

In the dead of winter, in the February snow, I gave no thought to shoveling off base-paths this year. How could I help my poor brother and sister when I needed to lean on Molly myself?

Blessedly, from another world, the Beatles came through to relieve our country from the frozen state of mourning which winter had sunk to in the aftermath of JFK. They brought laughter, they brought spring, most of all, they brought change.

Molly had a hopeless crush on Paul. I found them resistable because my state of mind held me in close check and refused to give way to any hint of light-heartedness. At school I joined the cast of the Senior Class Play. Mrs Melansky was our director. She gave me a character part, a minor role, as a housepainter in a play called *Paint the Town Pink*. I went to her and told her I could make my role much bigger, and funnier, by doing an accent, which I modeled on my Uncle Charlie Laverna from Watertown, and re-naming the character *Mario Bacigalupo*, the Italian House-Painter.

My parents didn't come, but Molly and her family did. She even dragged brother Dan along. After my performance, the Senior Class voted me Class Clown.

The clown had tears of vinegar. My every day was an act. My heart hurt and my head was no help. I was practically living at Molly's house now. Her mother wanted me to come to have supper with them. She wanted me to go to church with them, to their church, on Sunday morning. Their house was a well-kept but old-fashioned single-family, with oversized grey shingles and white trim, a small, glass-enclosed front porch, and a tiny back porch on the side with their driveway, where Daniel's car and his father's could park. Molly's mother liked the idea that I always called her Mrs Jones. I think she wanted to make sure I was the right choice for her Molly, as she knew how Molly felt. Mrs Jones had no objections to her girl marrying young, or even leaving school, she just wanted Molly to be happy.

There was peace and quiet at their house. There was kindness. They said please and thank-you, pass the potatoes. People spoke to one another. I made Molly swear not to tell her mother what I was telling her on the phone about my situation at home. Their house was in the middle of Camden Street, sandwiched in between three-deckers, on the poorest street in town. They were not rich people, but they did not wear poverty written in their eyes. They were a loving family.

At just about this time, the Four Seasons had a hit record on the radio, *Rag Doll*. I learned to play it on my accordian, at home, when I was alone, practicing, with the door to the dining room closed. I didn't need any sheet music. I played it the way I heard it. I told Molly it was our song. It told about a poor girl who wore hand-me-downs when she came to town. They laughed at her and called her *Rag Doll*. The chorus went way up, high as a church steeple,

Rag Doll . . . . Rag Doll . . .

Then Frankie Valli came swooping in down low,

Though I love her so,
I can't let her know . . .

I went with Mrs Jones and Molly and her father, her brother, too, on a Sunday morning, to their church. It was called the New Hope Methodist Church, and it was at the bottom of Phillips Street.

I felt very strange sitting there with them. The church had none of the fabric-of-gold-cloth and red-wine-glass-candle-glow of a Catholic church. The interior was imposing, but arches of undecorated plain brick. There was no altar, only a round circular pulpit with a hidden stairway: it looked like the prow of an old wooden ice-breaking vessel. They said The Lord's Prayer, all together.

This had never happened in any Catholic mass I'd ever been to. They sang hymns, all together. The only thing the minister did was mount the pulpit to give his sermon. There was no casting of spells, no Latin, no back-to-the-audience mystery play, no magical transubstantiation of the host.

I wondered if I belonged there. I wondered if I fit in with the Jones family. I remembered my mother telling me, long ago, when I was little, that I couldn't have Mary, the minister's daughter, for my second-grade girlfriend, because she was a Protestant.

Until this very moment, I hadn't realized how deeply that was true of my Molly. I had kept this to myself, hidden in my heart. None of them knew, not even Molly, and I told her everything. I didn't want to offend her. The last thing I wanted to do was to hurt Molly Jones.

But I had gotten my acceptance letter from Boston College. I wanted to go. I had spent ten dollars on an application fee for Harvard, but they didn't take me.

Harvard wanted me to bring my father to an interview. This was to take place in a dean's office lounge at Phillips Academy in Andover. My father came all the way home from North Adams on a Friday to do this interview with me. I had no idea why it was deemed by them necessary for them to see my father, but it was their rule.

The alumnus who performed the ritual was a lawyer who was a graduate of both Phillips and Harvard. This man asked my father what he did for a living. *Carpenter.* He asked my Dad where he went to school. *Oh, I only went to the sixth grade, then I dropped out to work in the mine.* This man could tell from my father's accent that he wasn't from around here. As we were being ushered out, I could literally hear the man scratching out with his fountain pen the line *not our kind of people*. I was seething.

But Boston College was every bit as good as Harvard, in my mind, and my third choice, which accepted me, was Umass, and BC was definitely superior to them. My cousin Tony had gone to BC, he broke his leg playing football for them. I was going to be proud to be going to BC.

But it was a Catholic university. For the first time in my life I was going to go to school with Catholic churchmen, and not just the Brothers who ran Central Catholic in Milltown, but priests who were members of the Jesuit Order, priests who had been required to go to 12 years of seminary before they could be ordained, priests who were the elite of the Catholic Church world-wide. It was exciting, and more than a little intimidating.

Chapter 28

Molly, I Have to Go

My mother wasn't talking to me, so I placed the acceptance letter in front of her. After a moment's glance, she looked up at me with a look that said, *And you expect me to pay for this?*

Molly was excited for me, because she knew this thing had made me happier and more relaxed than anything in months, including rehearsals for the single-night performance of the smash comedy *Paint the Town Pink*. She put on her 45 of *I Wanna Hold Your Hand* and danced around her parlor.

But right now she was getting ready for the biggest event of her life, so far, my Senior Prom.

It was going to be held at *The Rendezvous,* out on Rte 110 in Pleasant Valley. She had selected a pretty, fluffy, flouncy apple-green gown with a strapless bodice and wide hoop-skirts, like Scarlet O'Hara in *Gone with the Wind.* Molly Jones was going to be belle of the ball. She had just turned sweet sixteen, and she was going to go straight from the Senior Prom to the Engagement party to the Bridal Shower to the August wedding at New Hope Methodist Church, and she might never have to go to school again, because she was going to do it, and then have babies, and I—I was going to go to Boston College. She had it all planned. Molly Jones was going to be married to a college man and never have to worry again.

We took our prom photos in Molly's parlor, Mrs Jones officiating with the Kodak flash-camera. 110-film immortalized us, Molly in her gown, wearing my corsage of pink carnations, me in my white tux with the black trousers with the black satin stripe and the red-tartan cummerbund. I had gotten my license that spring through Driver's School at Jenney High so we borrowed brother Daniel's car.

We danced at *The Rendezvous*. We danced and danced to the DeeJay's platters. We were the perfect couple. We were crazy about each other. We sat at a big round table with a white tablecloth with my pals Benny and Denny and their dates and we could see nobody but one another. When the hired quartet came on, we danced cheek to cheek on the slow numbers, with Molly resting her head on my chest, her arms thrown up around my neck.

I would have defied any red-blooded American male who had Molly Jones in his arms that night to resist her, but I had to. This was too perfect. I couldn't spoil it now, not on this night of nights.

And we stayed up all night, till dawn. It was expected. The prom organizers were throwing a movie to try to ensure that all the senior class would have someplace to go, together, after the prom was over, and not to have to go on alcoholic binges at somebody's summer cottage up at Forest Lake to continue the party and blow off those well-known youthful high spirits. So we went in Daniel's car on a perfect June night down to the brand-new Showcase Cinema, down on Rte 114 in South Milltown, across the highway from Memorial Stadium, the

Milltown High football field. We sat back and watched the all-night double feature, Doris Day in *Midnight Lace,* and Shirley MacLaine, in *Irma La Douce.*

Dawn streaking the sky with saffron over the football stadium, we drove home to Camden Street with Molly Jones playing sleepy-head on my shoulder. I had kept my promise to myself and to her to be a perfect gentleman, to care for her, to make sure I didn't get her, or me, in trouble. I looked down at the top of her head as I steered through the dawn. She was just a child.

I needed money. I wanted to save up at least a thousand dollars to put in the bank before I had to start school at BC in September. I got a summer job in the Dryer Room up on the fifth floor at Malden Mills, on Broadway, on the Milltown line, where the Spicket paused in a wide pool before running down narrow, twisting channels through the dense streets of three-deckers that blotted the north side of the city.

Once I had picked blueberries on top of Railroad Hill and looked down at this stagnant lake and the smokestacks of the Arlington Mills next door. But that was in another lifetime.

Now I sweltered in 100 degree heat up on the fifth floor, where endless rolls of dyed beige, brown and grey, green and blue and red synthetic shag carpeting slowly crept through ceiling-high dryers that ran the entire length of the mill floor. All day long for eight hours I tended to the machines with sweat beaded on my forehead, dripping down my temples. This was what a high-school diploma got you in Milltown. This, and drafted by the Army when you turned 18. *This was what your life was going to be if you didn't get out.*

High school was over. The daily dramas, the trips on the school-buses, the intrigues of the cliques, the games on the playing fields, where had they gone? Was it just yesterday that it all seemed to be so important, when it all seemed to be leading somewhere? Where? *To the fifth floor in the Malden Mills complex?*

Why had I gone to the trouble of dragging my father into a hopeless interview at a well-endowed academy with landscaped grounds, circular drives, and polished brass, where the sons of doctors and lawyers parked their BMWs in back of the ivy-covered dorms— where neither one of us belonged?

This was where I belonged. On the fifth floor of the Malden Mills. *Unless I got out.*

And what was going to happen to Molly and me? Was I going to travel daily to a campus in a major city 28 miles away and come home each evening to a third-floor flat with a wife who was still a junior in high school? Or was she going to drop out so she could go to work waiting tables like her mother to try to help me get through school? What kind of a life was that for her? How far was my thousand bucks saved up during the summer going to stretch then? How could I even think of getting married? I couldn't support myself, let alone a wife.

And if I didn't marry her, what then? Was she going to wait for me? *So that we could get married, what, in four years time?*

These are the kind of thoughts that kept circling round and round through my bedeviled mind as I sweated my way through that summer in the Dryer Room at the top of the Malden Mills.

I was accepted into a highly-regarded four-year college, a university most people would consider an accomplishment, for a nobody from nowhere—the chance of a lifetime.

Was Molly going to finish two more years of high-school surrounded by all the temptations of junior and senior year and stay faithful to a guy who couldn't talk to her because he had to hit the books? And, by the way, what if I encountered some nice-looking girl in class in my new school?

And the thing was, I loved Molly terribly, awfully. I didn't believe all those who said it was only a passing phase, it was only teenage lust, it was only a high-school soap opera. It was a deep insult to my feelings to think my dead uncle might have said *oh, don't worry, it's only puppy love, you'll get over it.* I knew in my heart I was never going to get over Molly Jones. I may not have said the words to her, just as I never ripped her blouse off, but I knew deep down that I did neither one for motives that were pure, and honest, and true, and nobody could ever tell me otherwise. I wouldn't sully my love for Molly that way. I never loved my mother the way I loved Molly Jones. I never loved my own sister the way I loved Molly Jones. I took from my mother, my whole life long, with never a thought of paying her back, I even took from my sister Jill, not to mention my poor, neglected kid brother Jack. Molly Jones was the only person in my whole life I had ever had the chance to give to, and I gave her myself, which was the greatest gift I had to give.

But love doesn't pay the tuition bills. And now I was finding out what did. Sweating in Malden Mills.

As the rest of my life fell apart, as I waited for my mother to stop banging cabinet doors and start to speak to the rest of us again, as I wished against hoping that my father would come home again, so that I could go to college and feel that my brother and sister, my little sister and my little brother could have some chance at normalcy, left behind, in that fieldstone house my mother once treasured so much—was I going to give up the one chance I might ever have to get out of Milltown? Or was Malden Mills going to suck me down?

These thoughts kept circling, in circle after circle, chasing after one another like snakes in a hoop-race, revolving in my head, as the sweat poured down my face.

When my shift got over at three in the afternoon, I left Malden Mills and crossed Broadway to the lights at Arlington Street, turned right, two streets, and left, up Molly's street, Camden Street. I got to Molly's house and I hadn't lifted my eyes off the sidewalk in front of me yet.

I took one last look around as I mounted the steps of that tiny back porch. The empty parking spaces where the two family cars squeezed in beside the 3-decker next door. The small patch of grass that was Molly's back yard, the chain link fence. After this, probably, most likely, maybe, I wouldn't be welcome to come to this house ever again.

Molly met me at the back door to the kitchen and pulled me in by the hand. She had me heading for her bedroom at the back before I could say a word.

"Molly—." She had her arms around my neck and she was kissing me on the mouth. "Molly—we have to talk."

Her reaction was swift. She threw herself on the bed and grabbed Fluffy, the teddy bear I won for her when we went up to Canobie Lake for the senior class outing. He was big enough for her to sit up against the headboard with her arms around him. She tucked one leg under herself, and wouldn't look at me. I glanced to the right, and saw her eyes, full of nervous trembling, looking up at me from the mirror over her dresser, two dots of tears quivering in the corners of those grey-blue eyes with the soft lashes. Her mother said she was too young to use make-up, and she was, except for that one night of the Senior Prom. Now she was flushed, the color rising to her ear-lobes, and I could see her chest heaving, rising and falling with the thumping of her heart.

"Oh, baby, please don't cry," I said. I sat down on the bed in a lump next to her.

"Please don't do this to me, Nicky."

My elbows were on my knees, my head was in my hands. "Baby, the last thing I wanted to do was to make you cry."

"Then why are you doing this to me? You're breaking up with me, aren't you."

"I just think it's the best thing for you–."

"I won't let you do this to me, Nick. I love you."

"It's not fair to you, Molly, it's not fair to be just tied to me when you've got your whole life ahead of you—."

"Say you love me too, Nick. Say it."

"Molly, can't we just talk about this—."

"Why can't you say it? All right, then. *Tell me you don't love me.*"

My head was in my hands and I couldn't, I wouldn't look at her, but I could hear her breath coming in gulps and feel her on the verge of bawling. Her question repeated in my head, with silent thunder, *tell me you don't love me,* and I said, out loud, "I can't."

"Then why are you doing this to me?" She practically screamed the question, but so choked was she, that she cut off her own voice.

"Molly, I have to go." I stood up and she grabbed after me, clutching my back pocket, but I was moving toward the bedroom door. I turned at the door and she was scrambling out of the bed losing her grip on Fluffy, tripping over him on the floor, trying to reach me. "I have to go if we can't talk about this sensibly."

'Sensibly' was mashed in my mouth by desperate kisses as Molly, passionately gripping me around the neck, tried to pull me back to the bed, but I was bigger than her, and I kept moving backwards, and her vise-grip on my neck tightened, and now, I was growing more desperate as I back-pedalled and she wouldn't let go, and I was trying to pry her arms apart behind my neck, and we were at the back door, and she was trying to drag me back into the kitchen now, and I was in a panic as to how I was going to get through the two doors outside to the back porch, the back door and the screen door, and I could feel the wet tears soaking my cheeks from her wet cheeks, the cheekbones of our faces grinding, but she wouldn't let go, and now I was dragging her through the screen door, and her grip slipped, like a necktie loosening, and her hands went sliding down my chest and as I was backing off the porch, trying to feel for the first step, she slid all the way down until she realized she was going to lose me unless she grabbed me by one leg. And she did. She put a headlock on my left leg and I had to drag her down the steps that way, holding on, as if holding on to her own life slipping away.

At the bottom I had to reach down and pry her arms apart because I was afraid I would tear all the skin off her legs dragging her down the paved driveway in her shorts.

The vehemence I needed to get her off me shook me as I backed away slowly. Then I turned, incapable of seeing her like that— Molly Jones, in a heap on her driveway, with all her hair hanging down, disheveled over her bowed head, touching prayerfully the back of one hand, prostrated on the pavement.

I had just dragged Molly Jones down her back steps. What kind of cruel, heartless monster was I?

I walked back down Camden Street the way I came with my head down, my eyes not seeing the sidewalk I tripped over, and I was shaking.

The following weekend, I went up to Canobie Lake, and as I was walking slowly, thoughtfully, along the promenade in front of the bumper-cars and the Funhouse, here comes Molly Jones, swinging along, holding hands with a sailor in his summer whites.

I knew that sailor. He was a friend of Daniel Jones who had enlisted earlier that spring.

The girl, I didn't know.

Part 3

BOSTON

Chapter 29

College on a Hill

When I stepped, for the first time, through the gates of the campus on Chestnut Hill, and was enveloped by the Towers on The Heights, I stepped into a world apart, separate from any into which I had ever ventured in the life I was leaving behind me.

As I proceeded down the sidewalk flanking the imperial drive, with St Mary's Hall, where the Jesuits resided, on my left, and Bapst Library on my right, I approached the purple-hued marble obelisk where the golden wings of the eagle unfurled and his eye looked down upon each intruding acolyte. Even the swish of traffic behind me on Commonwealth Avenue receded to a whisper. No cars ever came down this drive. This enclave was not to be sullied by beer-trucks. As I made my way around Gasson Hall, the administration building, I came upon the still and profound quiet enclosed by the four edifices around the intimate Old Quadrangle. Gasson Hall, Lyons, Devlin and Fulton were stout structures of old stone dressed in grey where gothic relics of medieval majesty seemed perfectly apropos, whenever the bells of the spires of Gasson behind you tolled the hour, reverberating, as if from eternity, far away.

I had come home again. I was back in Boston.

From my beginnings in the tawdry resort of Revere Beach, the network of the Metropolitan Transit Authority led directly to this spot, via the Green Line. I could trace the way-stations of my pilgrimage in my mind. Why had I ever been forced by my mother to take a detour through the outlands of the Merrimack Valley, the streets of Milltown, the playsteads of Spicket Falls?

This, here and now, was where I belonged, this was where I never should have departed. This was destiny. My destiny. The sign on the front of the Dallas-car which carried me here did not read Boston University. It read Boston College. I had been reading that sign in the Park Street Station since I first knew how to read. Down the hill, the MTA station across the street from the church of St Ignatius of Loyola, the founding father of the Jesuits, stood on one side of the road: the end of the line. On the other shore stood St Ignatius: the final destination? Or just the beginning?

I was taking the streetcar to school because of my mother. It was all at her insistence.

My father was back in the employ of Lou Perini, this time as a finish carpenter, hanging doors and office moldings as they struggled to complete the long-running Prudential project on Boylston Street. It was September of 1964 when I started school, and from the Heights of Boston College, on a clear day, you could easily see the Pru downtown, now standing tall in the Back Bay.

From Boston College station, when I stepped off the trolley, I walked uphill, along Commonwealth Avenue, to the front gates of the university, and each step I took elevated me to a new and further height.

Each day my father would drop me off in Kendall Square in Cambridge by no later than six-ten or six-fifteen in the morning. He had to drive from Spicket Falls to work at the Pru in any case, so why not take me?

This was my mother's way of keeping me at home.

Her scheme had been fomented during the summer while I was working at Malden Mills.

With a little more education, I might have recognized that she was having trouble cutting the cord. But starting over again as a freshman, I hadn't taken *Intro to Psych* as yet, that wasn't permissible until at least my sophomore year. So I was perplexed by, but not quite seeing into, her maneuvering during the summer.

For one thing, in my self-absorption, and my complete enthrallment with Molly Jones, I had failed to detect signs of my mother's distress and jealousy. Every time I pulled the telephone across the hall into my private office on the top step of the cellar stairs, it never occurred to me that she could listen in to everything I said to Molly, on my end, through the closed door. When my mother complained that I was tying up the phone for hours, what if someone was trying to get through, it never occurred to me that there was anything else behind that comment or under the surface of it.

When I broke up with Molly, I said nothing whatsoever about it to my mother.

Obviously, I was no longer calling Molly on the phone, every day, every night, every minute. Obviously, my woe-begone state was written all over my face, my averted eyes, my slouching posture. I thought my fatigue and despondence was only visible to others as the ordinary consequence of working an 8-hour shift in the 5th-floor swelter of Malden Mills in July.

I was a raw, untutored youth. What did I know of a mother's love?

She sat me down one night at the kitchen table. "All right," she said. "I'll pay for the tuition for you to go to BC."

"Thanks, I don't need you to." The tuition for my first year was only going to be 900 dollars. "I'm saving up at least a thousand bucks this summer, no problem."

"And what are you going to do for room and board?"

"I'll figure something out."

"You stay here. Your father will drive you to school every day. He's going there anyway, and I can't afford to pay for you to live in dorms down there."

She wasn't asking me, she was telling me.

Actually, I was thinking of living off-campus. Actually, I wasn't thinking. Back in the spring, when I got my acceptance letter, I placed it in front of my mother, sitting at this same table. No reaction. No word of congratulations. No *I'm proud of you, son*. If anything, she looked put upon, not proud. I expected her to come out with *you better get in there and practice that accordian, this is costing me two bucks a lesson, you know. You better not break those glasses again, do you know how much they cost?*

I assumed my mother didn't care, not about me. I assumed she cared about money, instead of me.

It hadn't dawned on me that my leaving home might remind her of her dead brother, Augie, leaving home, so long ago, for boot-camp.

When she said, to my complete surprise, *I'll pay for your tuition,* my first thought was *hey, maybe I can hold onto my thousand bucks.*

When she added, matter-of-factly, "You keep your money. You're gonna need to buy books."

Books? I never thought of that.

Neither did I see the sleight-of-hand, out of sight, underneath, with which she was dealing out the cards. *I pay the tuition, I keep you here.*

I was thinking I'd be a fool to refuse this deal.

She had me, right there.

At least I had a boon companion to travel with me to school every day in my dad's latest Jeep.

This was Slaney. He was my old bodyguard from the JV football squad at Jenney High School. I called him my bodyguard because he told me I needed protection.

"You're too small for football," he used to say.

"I'm not small," I would say. "I'm five-eight-and-three-quarters."

He would look dubious.

"Five-seven-and-three-quarters." I would be looking up at him as I said this. Slaney played left tackle. I played left end. He was my bodyguard on the JV squad.

But at Jenney High, we didn't hang together. He went on to play varsity, and he hung out with Jack Fallon and Dick Nickerson and Phil Goterch and Billy Michaud and the other jocks. But everybody went away in the summertime. Either they had cottages up at Salisbury, or a summer camp at Forest Lake. So, the summer after our senior year, in the neighborhood in Glen Forest, on the other side of Haverhill Street, where he lived, Slaney was left behind and alone. He lived on Wellington Street, two houses in, on the left, and he used to sit by himself in the long summer evenings on the steps of a neighbor's house on Haverhill Street to watch the girls go by.

"Hello, Slaney, what's going on? Long time, no see." His first name was Al, but we didn't use first names. I called him Slaney, and he called me Petrovich. "You still going with Denise Michaud?"

"Yeah. We're gonna get married."

"No shit."

"Well, maybe not this year. I gotta find me a decent job first. You still going with that chick from school?"

"Nah. I broke up with her."

"How come?"

"Cause she busted my balls, Slaney. I break up with her and the very next week I see her with some sailor up at Canobie Lake."

"Oh, yeah. I get that. You break up with her and she busted your balls. I get that. How you gettin' along with your old man?"

"I'm not."

"Ah, he's all right. In fact, I think he's a nice guy. What's wrong with you, Petrovich?"

"The Red Sox are ruinin' my summer."

Slaney started laughing. He was a tall, muscular, handsome dark-haired Irish boy, and as I stood there, leaning on the wall, when he started laughing, it struck me how much he resembled the new Sox rookie sensation who was getting his picture in the papers. "How about that Tony C, huh, Slaney? You know he's from my hometown, Revere?"

After that, we started hanging out, the rest of the summer, on the steps on Haverhill Street every afternoon, after I got out of work at Malden Mills. I didn't have anything better to do and it kept my mind off of Molly Jones. We'd just sit there shootin' the shit and checkin' out the girls going by in their short-shorts. Once in a while we'd cross the street to the Hillside Market at the corner of Elm Street and get a fudgicle or a Coke. Usually we hung out till it was time for supper. Then Slaney would say, "I gotta get home and have a beer with my Dad. Family that drinks together, stays together, or something like that."

Eventually, we got around to the point where I got Slaney convinced to at least consider going to college. I kept telling him and telling him that he could hitch a ride to Boston with me and my Dad once school started in September. I thought that since I was going to college, everybody should be. I told him I heard that even those two lunk-heads, Nader and Rousseau, my so-called best friends from Jenney High days, were going to college, which astounded me, since, "How they gonna make out when they don't got me to cheat off of?"

"Right. Well, I get that. As for me, I might take you up on that offer. Denise says I gotta do somethin,' man."

He started taking about a program he found out about at Boston State that would train you to be a surveyor. "You gotta study surveying, mapping, geomatics and a little trig and calculus and cartography, and then you take your state license exam, and you're in."

"What do you want to do that for, Slaney?"

"I like to be outdoors, Petrovich. Why? What are you gonna take?"

"I am going to college in the pure pursuit of knowledge."

"Oh. That'll get you far."

It worked out well, riding to school together every day. Slaney could sit in the front with my Dad because he needed the leg-room. That left the back to me, where I could crack a book. And Slaney could talk to my Dad, so I didn't need to.

I studied hard that first semester. Truth be told, I was more than a little intimidated to be actually going to BC. *What if I don't make it? What if I'm not good enough? What if it turns out I'm not as smart as I think I am. What if it's too hard for me?*

It took me only from September to about Christmas till I was saying to myself *this is easy.*

The clincher came when Father Macananny, SJ, called on me in Freshman Composition.

Father Macananny was my introduction to the Jesuitical mind. All the priests on campus who lived in St Mary's Hall had teaching assignments, ranging from theology to philosophy to English to calculus. They all wore black, as if to remind us young fools that death was inevitable. However, the most famous Jesuit of all, on campus, Fr. Drinan, was a lawyer, a member of the Massachusetts bar, and dean of the Boston College Law School; he wore a very business-like black suit, with clerical collar, of course, but he was indistinguishable, in that black suit-jacket, black trousers and black shoes, from an Episcopalian bishop. The same could be said of Fr. Joyce, SJ, the President of the University, and the other Jesuits on administrative assignment in Gasson Hall.

Father Macananny, on the other hand, appeared in class daily in full soutane. For shock value, he made sure we knew he had red tights on underneath. His entrances were calculated for dramatic effect. He would charge through the door in a cloud of swirling skirts and present to us his back, holding out his cape, waiting for one of several front-row bum-kissers to spring from his seat, seize the cape, and hang it up for him on the coat-rack in the corner. Then he would mount the dais and situate himself at his table. Not a desk, a table. This is where the red tights would come on display when he crossed his legs and hiked his skirts, modestly, of course. Just a splash of ankle. He would survey his seating plan and let us wilt in apprehension while he selected his victim. His classroom manner was that of a sadistic lepidopterist who clearly enjoyed the part where he pinned the butterfly.

As our instructor in Freshman Composition, Father Macananny was not interested in teaching us how to produce a clear and concise expository essay. He believed we should have been prepared by underlings before we got to his classroom. Instead, he began the semester by assigning what he considered a masterpiece of the form, E.B. White's essay *"Here Is New York."* He spent the first week of classes, his section being Mon-Wed-Friday, on the first sentence, which read,

"On any person who desires such queer prizes, New York will bestow the gift of loneliness and privacy."

The essay went on for 56 pages and 7500 more words after that, but we stayed on that one sentence for a whole week before we passed on to the second sentence.

We, the student body, took the word "queer" as a hand-picked message selected by our professor, (when considered in the light of the red tights, and in combination with 'loneliness' and 'privacy.') At least, that was the consensus of the sniggers out in the hallway after class. I had to bow to the superior experience of my classmates, most of whom were local boys who had been through twelve years of parochial school. I was a mere outsider, once again: at BC, the majority, by far, were of Irish extraction, and went home at night to the enclaves of Southie and Charlestown and West Roxbury. They were graduates of BC High and Catholic Memorial and St. John's Academy and Xaverian and St. Columcille's in Brighton. I was not quite sure exactly what a queer might be, but then I was from the wilds of

Spicket Falls, a place these boys had never heard of, and I was, no doubt, still picking the hayseeds from my teeth. I resolved to mention in future only that I came from Revere. They all knew where the Beach was.

I noticed at first for some reason, which strangely enough I could not fathom, that Fr Macananny never called on me. Gradually I resigned myself to the idea that he never would. From there, I passed into the happy valley of blissful unawareness and passed my time in his class paying not a bit of attention whatsoever. That's when he pounced.

The assignment that week, on the day before Thanksgiving break was to start, was Hemingway's short story, "The Killers." Naturally, I had already read the whole thing. I liked it. It was moody and atmospheric with menace. I was in my usual state of relaxed slouching when I heard Fr. Macanany say, "Mr. Petrovich."

He never called us by our first names. That would have been altogether too 'secondary-school.' We were in college now and were to consider ourselves young men. However, when Fr. Macananny called you 'mister,' you somehow were made to feel that you were flotsam of jetsom of a sub-species of unwashed, unlettered, and uncultured barbarian sent purposely by the Almighty to punish this particular Jesuit for never having risen in the eyes of the world, or The Order, above the standing of a minor poetic dilettante.

"Mr. Petrovich, what is the name of the lunch-room in Hemingway's short story, "The Killers?"

I answered, casually, quickly, without effort or hesitation, lifting one eyebrow, with one word: "Henry's."

I had read the story the night before. There is no mention in the story of the name of the lunch-room, except in the very first sentence, where Hemingway writes,

THE EDUCATION OF NICHOLAS PETROVICH

The door of Henry's Lunchroom opened.

Fr. Macananny never let me forget it. He called on me every single day from then to the end of the semester. He expended every effort, fair and foul, on nailing me for my effrontery. He would say things like, "We are fortunate to have Mr. Petrovich with us today." "What say you, Mr. Petrovich? I'm sure you have *something* to say." Arched eyebrow. "Class, we now turn to Mr. Petrovich to enlighten us."

That's when I knew I belonged at BC.

Chapter 30

Good Catholic Boys

It was inconceivable to me that I would not join Army ROTC as soon as I arrived on campus. Boston College was no more than about three or four miles from my cousin Tommy DiPrima's house, across the Charles in Watertown, and he had already joined the Navy and was gone, at 17, to boot camp. We were exactly the same age, born in the same month, three weeks apart. Our cousin Henry Fabiano, Auntie Peggy's son, had done a four-year stint in the Marine Corps, his father's branch of the service, and nowadays worked in Washington. Everyone said he was in the CIA. He had served in Japan, at Atsugi Air Force Base, where he learned Russian, and his hero was Winston Churchill. One of his classmates in Russian language had been a certain Lee Harvey Oswald, now dead. Oswald went to Russia and Henry Fabiano went to Washington.

I had never forgotten the time Henry came home on leave and came to visit us in the fieldstone house in Spicket Falls in his dress-blues with the red stripe down the trouser-leg. When he had gone upstairs to use the bathroom, he took the steps two at a time. When I saw that, I never walked up the stairs again; it was two-at-a-time for me, or nothing.

How did fate account for the fact that one Marine classmate killed a beloved President and the other went to work in the world's top intelligence organization, a patriot, serving to protect his country beyond even his military duty? But would one of our family such as Henry have done anything else?

Henry's younger brother Ronnie, not considered as brilliant as Henry, was now in the Air Force, where he had become a photographer. All of us cousins shared the same three uncles who had been in the European theater during the war. Tommy DiPrima had two more, Uncle Bruno and Uncle Freddy, on his father's side, plus his own dad. I had Uncle Alek on my Dad's side. Uncle Alek had been a navigator aboard C-47s that flew over the hump from Burma to ferry guns, ammo, rice and shoes to the Chinese. My Dad had been in the Navy and crossed the Atlantic on board the *USS Ruby* on escort duty in the U-boat winter of 1943 on the convoy run to Murmansk in Russia. Myself and all my male cousins who were eligible for the draft, my generation of a family of Servicemen, all had shared the same role models, men who asked not what the country could do for them. How could I not follow in the family footsteps?

It was 1964, President Kennedy had been gone for only a year. We had all seen Cliff Robertson at the movies playing in *PT-109*. Lyndon Johnson was the President now, and the Vietnam situation was on page 7 of *The Boston Globe*. I would have to sign up for the draft as soon as I turned 18, in December, and here was my chance, staring me in the face, to become an officer and a gentleman, a chance my uncles had never had. To me, it was a foregone conclusion that I would simply do my duty.

So I went over to see Sgt Ryan in the ROTC offices in the basement of Roberts Center, the basketball gymnasium, and signed up for two years of basic ROTC, during which I would attend military science classes, close-order drill, and two weeks of bivouac in the summer. When I finished sophomore year, I would then take a physical and be enrolled in the Regular Army under Advanced ROTC, to get my commission as a second lieutenant upon graduation, four years away.

Next door to ROTC in the Roberts Center basement were the offices and practice rooms of the Boston College Marching Band. I had no intention of playing my accordian at school. Nor would it have been welcomed in a marching band. After ten years, from the age of seven to seventeen, I had given up my lessons back home at Milltown Music. I was in college now, and that was my future. I need not stake my fortune on playing gigs here and there at *The Stardust Lounge* in Reading or *The Riverview* on the Lowell Boulevard. I was not Jerry Bellanti, my former teacher, getting out of the Army after two years as an enlisted man, and coming home to start playing with the local pick-up groups again. It was 1964, the British Invasion was on, and *'Satisfaction'* was playing endlessly on the radio: not on Boston's most prominent radio station, WBZ, where rock and roll was banned, but on WMEX, 1510 on your radio dial, on Arnie 'the Woo-woo' Ginsburg's show. I did not play guitar, and the accordian was a distinctly uncool instrument for a rock and roller like me.

However, I could read music, and if I could join the band, I could get into all the varsity sports-team events on campus, from football to hockey, for free.

Moreover, as a die-hard hoops player, a product of the Perrault's backyard basketball school back in Spicket Falls, I was a lifelong member of the Boston Celtics NBA Championship-dynasty fan club, a dedicated follower of Johnny Most on the radio, and, that spring, the Celts had won their sixth title in seven years. Legendary point guard Bob Cousy, known to legions of idolizing wanna-be's like me as *'The Cooz,'* had retired in 1963, and now was the coach of the Boston College men's basketball team. His office was upstairs from the ROTC in Roberts Center. You could see him sometimes strolling across the lobby.

I would be crazy to miss my chance to see him and the team play every single game for the next four years while never having to pay for a ticket.

So I dropped in on Dr. Firenzi, the conductor of the BC Marching Band and school orchestra, explained my situation, and talked him into it. He needed a glockenspiel player, and they were hard to find. As long as I knew my way around a keyboard, it would be a cinch for me to learn how to play 'the bells,' as they were known in the band. The glock was more or less a mini-xylophone, played with a mallet, and strapped onto you with a harness that passed around your neck and your waist, like the ones the flag-bearers wore. Held by a holster at the mid-section, and tilting forward, you could march around in half-time shows with the rest of the band doing fancy formations and spelling out *Win BC!* at the football games.

Studying anything my heart desired, in the pure pursuit of knowledge. Joining the ROTC, which set my course towards a future as a man with experience, know-how and responsibility. Joining the band, which got me into all of the fall football games as well as 'the Cooz's' hoops magic at Roberts Center, not to mention the BC-BU hockey rivalry at McHugh Forum—I loved Boston College!

I was getting my schedule in order. Three afternoons a week I had band practice, I had to take all the required courses, as a freshman, Theology with Fr. Shaughnessy, Logic, with Fr. O'Donoghue, English Composition, with 'Tights' Macananny, Geology, to fulfill my science requirement, with Mr Leopold, who was a lay teacher, and calculus, to fulfill my math prerequisite, with Mr Morton, another lay teacher. Fortunately, for me, I had planned ahead, back in Penney High, in spite of what the guidance counselor said, and as a member of the college course, taken all the math I could, from algebra to plane geometry to trig, but I was still hopeless at calculus. I expected as much, since I very well realized that although I had scored 750 in reading comprehension on the college boards, my math score was only about 525. What saved me was a kid in my calculus class named Dan Viola.

Dan Viola was going to major in math. He was an Italian kid from Watertown. I explained to him how I was Italian too, nevermind the Petrovich part, all my cousins were Di Primas, Lavernas, Fabianos and LaStorias, and some of them came from Watertown, like him.

Dan Viola was my first friend at BC. Between the two of us, we knew only one other Italian kid at school, and that was Dan's friend Peter Zammucci, from Waltham. Everybody else in the student body was Irish.

Because I always got to campus early in the morning after riding in from the Merrimack Valley with Slaney and my father, I arranged with Dan to meet up for breakfast in Lyons Hall, in the cafeteria in the basement, so that he could help get me over the hurdle in calculus.

This was the old cafeteria in the upper campus. We were avoiding the Irish and starting our own little clique. The Irish all hung out at McElroy Commons, which had the new caf, in the lower campus, or new quad. Lyons Hall dated all the way back to the original opening of the Chestnut Hill campus back in 1907. The lower campus had all the newer buildings at BC, and the style was much more modern, with light-colored orange-and-rust granite facades, not the gloomy, rain-soaked grey of the upper campus gothics. Therefore, the Irish who flocked to BC as a birthright after graduating from BC High in Southie and Catholic Memorial in West Roxbory and St John's Prep in Danvers and Cardinal Spellman in Brockton, congregated in the vast, spacy, airy and light-filled McElroy Commons.

The first one to join our budding little clique was Dan's friend from Waltham, Zammucci. Then came Kenny Grigorian, an Armenian kid, from Winthrop, who was a high school state champion in tennis, and Victor Blanchette, from Woburn. Soon we had enough people at the same table in the morning in Lyons to get together after first class to play cards and after second class, to have lunch, and between classes, to start up the card game again. Soon we had collected all the non-Irish in the freshman class from A&S, the school of Arts and Sciences. The last to join up was Billy Michele, who came from the projects in Southie—an Irish inroad to our group. But only his mother was Irish, his father was an Italian who got to live in Southie because he was married into the Irish. The funny thing was that if you pronounced Billy's last name correctly in Italian, it came out sounding exactly like 'McKelly.'

After my tutoring session with Dan Viola at breakfast, when the others started drifting in, and the card-playing started, I would pick up and leave for the library. Cards did not interest me. Dan was the same. He would head over to Carney on the lower campus for a classroom with a blackboard where he could work out math problems he carried around in his head. I would go downstairs in Bapst Library where you could be completely isolated in a single-berth alcove entirely to yourself. Light from the outside world would come in through my own individual slit-window at my elbow. The desk was built into the alcove in front of me and had room enough to open a book and rest your elbow with the yellow hi-liter poised in your hand and nothing more. All my wire-ring notebooks from classes came from the BC bookstore in McElroy, brown covers with the school crest inscribed in black ink. I was planning ahead and looking forward to the day when I could major in English and take electives such as *John Donne and The Metaphysical Poets* with Dr Hughes and *Shakespeare,* for two semesters with the famous Dr Duhamel.

Boston College back then was a Catholic boys' school. Once a week I traveled the subway dressed in my Army uniform on the day when I had Military Science and close-order drill. Every other day I wore the school uniform, which consisted of a maroon blazer with the school crest on the breast pocket, over your heart, inscribed with the school motto, *Ever to Excel,* in English, on the bottom of the gold-embroidered crest-ring, and Latin, *Semper in Excel,* on the top half—grey woolen slacks, a white shirt, and a necktie, which shone like satin, striped diagonally in the school colors, maroon and gold. The only girls enrolled on campus were few and were all confined to the Nursing School in Cushing Hall, named after Cardinal Cushing, whose residence was behind the estate walls along Comm Ave, just before the Boston College MTA station, and diagonally opposite St Ignatius Church; or else in the School of Education, in Campion Hall.

One morning a new and final member of our burgeoning clique arrived on campus in an Alfa-Romeo from his father's car dealership in Arlington, one Lorenzo 'Don't -call-me-Larry' Martino. "You can call me Martino, all my friends do."

Martino was not interested in literature. He was not interested in math or science. Martino was interested in partying. "The college mixers? That's nowhere, man." He decided to become our benefactor by inviting us to a party, a never-ending party, which he and his six or eight girlfriends held every Saturday night (and Sunday morning) at his parents' house in Arlington, so that he could introduce us to girls. "You are a sad-looking bunch," Martino said. "I got a surplus I don't know what to do with. You think you guys could help me out with the overflow? You, Danny? Peter? Grigorian? How about Petrovich over there?"

"We are good Catholic boys," said I. "We have the prerequisite dirty minds."

Chapter 31

Something Had to Change

Nothing worked. Not the college mixers nor the parties at Martino's in Arlington.

One night I went to a mixer in McHugh Forum, on campus. The DJ was playing *Louie, Louie* by the Kingsmen, a big hit record widely reputed to be a dirty song. A girl on the dance-floor was abandoning herself to the wild music. She was throwing her long hair around and whirling to the insistent beat in a frenzy of arms and legs. I was filled with lust. I was not the only one. Many of the good and decent Mass-attending theology-studying BC boys at the mixer were forming a circle around this wanton exhibitionist and cheering, chanting and clapping. I had to go outside to gulp air and slow down my pulsating parts.

Another night I went to a party at Martino's. His parents' ranch house had an in-ground pool out back, which floodlights made to glow through the sliding glass doors and translucent drapes of his living room. I was sitting in a corner of his sofa, nursing a drink, my arm slung over the sofa-back, wondering what I was doing there. Martino was looking devilish in his budding goatee. His parents conveniently left when their son wanted to have his friends over. The liquor cabinet wasn't locked. I thought of the Alfa-Romeo parked outside in the circular drive. I didn't grow up like this. I didn't belong at a party like this.

I had one knee cocked up, and my other leg stuck out under the coffee table. A girl with narrow shoulders and straight blondish hair stepped over my leg and sat down to talk to me. She came from Malden and she was in the School of Education at BC. She knew Martino from high school and the times the girls from Malden Catholic would go to the dances offered by Arlington Catholic at the Irish-American Club in Arlington.

We made a date and I took her out one night to a movie in town. I hooked up with her at the Park Street Station. Her name was Louise and the conversation lagged. We weren't at a party and she wasn't drinking. There was nothing there, no spark, no connection, no nothing. I had to ask my Aunt Mary in Watertown if I could sack out on her couch overnight just to be in town for this date. And then I end up feeling so awkward trying to talk to her that I made sure not to repeat the mistake of asking her out again.

The whole problem was that I just missed Molly Jones terribly. I just couldn't get her out of my head. Just the idea of the closeness we once had, which I had thrown away, left a hole in my heart, made every day grey, and every night empty. I would look at a telephone and tell myself, *you know it's not going to ring . . .*

One night in my desperation I wandered down Marlborough Street looking for a party. There were something like 100,000 students living in the city of Boston, going to school at BU, Northeastern, BC, MIT, Harvard, Tufts, Emanuel, Emerson, and more who flocked to the city looking for fun from places like Salem State or Framingham Teachers' College. There must be someone for me in all this flood of young women looking for warmth. There had to be. Couples were everywhere I looked. Why was I alone?

I knew why I was alone. Because I had chosen. Not to get trapped into marriage with Molly. Not to lose my chance at college. Now I was here, and I hated myself for it.

Yet, I was particular. It had to be destiny, it had to be fate. It had to be the one girl in all this crowd who was meant for me. The night I wandered down Marlborough Street it was because I had heard that a lot of off-campus apartment-dwellers, even fraternities and sororities, held open parties on Friday and Saturday nights. I found an open front door in a brownstone. I went in. I wasn't invited and I didn't know anyone. I was by myself. Someone stuck a beer in my hand. I sat down on a stairway where people kept going up and down, climbing over me. A coed, a brunette, invited herself to sit down with me. She was from New York. She was Jewish and she went to Emerson. She was in theater and she was very dramatic. We were sitting on the stairs making out and people were going up and down, stepping over us. She stuck her tongue in my mouth and I was shocked. It's not that I was repelled, but I just didn't do that with strangers. We didn't even know each other. The next day I couldn't even remember her name.

What if I had already lost the one girl in the world, Molly Jones, who was meant for me?

Was this what I was reduced to, so desperate I'd make out with someone I didn't know, someone I didn't care for?

I could not admit to myself that I was lonely. I could not admit to myself that I missed Molly that much. But obviously I felt the lonely vibe coming off that poor girl on the stairway. So she must've felt it coming from me, too, no?

And it killed me to think that Molly was with that sailor at this very moment. Inevitably, my every day ended with me riding the trolley into town on the way Kendall Square to catch my ride home to the Valley with Slaney and my father. I would find myself weary of studying at that point in the day. I would lean my head up against the glass window at my shoulder on the streetcar. Faces would multiply in the windows across the aisle as we sped through tunnels filled with flashing, streaking lights, speeding up and slowing down, leaving and entering station after station, people coming in and getting off, a constant exchange of strangers, and sometimes, if I made eye contact, just by chance, they would look away, instantly, reflexively. They didn't want to know you. They wanted to be left alone. They were inside their own lives, focused on their own space, desirous of not touching you, while the trolley lurched and threw you together.

Molly and I had never kissed like that. Without caring, without connection, without love.

I was lost.

Something had to change. I was so stimulated by my courses and the thrill I felt at throwing myself whole-heartedly into intellectual pursuits that I felt sure I had been right to go to college, that I belonged, in the classroom, and, especially, in the library, where I could be alone. But why was there something missing, why was there a void, why did I feel momentary passing stabs of inner, grinding emptiness?

It dawned on me that whatever I did, it had to be pure, it had to be unsullied by ulterior motives, it had to be in the service of itself and itself alone. I could not go to school, like Slaney, in order to get a qualification for a good-paying job. I could not answer my father's questions and doubts about what I was going to get out of all this time and effort and expense. He was the one whose mind was made up, in his own youth, that he would get training as a carpenter's apprentice, with the ultimate goal of becoming a master-carpenter—*him*, not me. I wasn't after training or a license or a qualification—I was after knowledge.

But knowledge of what?

Whatever I did, I could never put myself through that again, that thing, whatever it was, with the girl on the stairs.

I decided that what had to change was my living at home, in the fieldstone house, in my mother's embrace, tied to my mother's apron-strings. *It was I who had to cut the cord.* I had not made a break sufficient to get me out of Spicket Falls, out of Milltown, out of the orbit of my mother, and Molly Jones. That was what was dragging me down. Until I made the split, permanent and forever, I would never be free. Until I was free I would not be happy. Loneliness would assail me until I had gotten out for good.

I got around my mother's objections fairly easily by pointing out that, in any case, the Pru was about to be finished, and Dad's job in Boston was coming to an end, whether she liked it or not, and I couldn't get stuck living at home and needing to travel to Boston daily on the train from Milltown to North Station. I tried explaining to her that as time went on, my workload of studying was increasing at school, and I needed more time, not less, to spend at the library instead of in transit. That argument made no dents in her wall of silence. She wasn't about to come out and say that her feelings were hurt, and to me, my mother's mood swings were just one more reason why I had to get out of there.

I said goodbye to Slaney, wishing him well, knowing I would miss him, as a good friend. I was not surprised to hear him say that, as long as I wouldn't be riding into Boston daily, he might as well try to find a place to get his surveyor's license closer to home. That was the difference between me and Slaney—he had to stay in Spicket Falls, because of a girl; I had to get out, because of a girl.

I threw in my lot with Nader and Rousseau. To my complete surprise, those two clunkheads, who used to ask me how to spell *commission, was it one -s- or two, no stupid, it's two s's, and two m's,* those two were going to college in Boston, Nader at Northeastern, Rousseau at Suffolk. Nader was studying math, which figured, as his big interest in life, besides screwing girls, was counting money. Just as when he used to give me a ride to Salisbury Beach, back in high school, and wanted me to pay for his gas, now he was calling me up to say he and Rousseau were getting an off-campus apartment in town, and he wanted me to join up with them to help split the rent three ways instead of two. As it was only 150 bucks a month, my share being just 50 bucks, I got together all my books and clothes and my collection of 45's and albums and moved in with them in a 3-bedroom apartment at 1387 Comm Ave at the start of sophomore year. I could afford 50 bucks a month. Over the summer after freshman year I had gotten a job busing tables at McElroy Commons on the work-study program at BC, and so I had saved up my thousand bucks again, and was ready to parsimony it out over the course of the next academic year.

Life was good again, life was easy. I had turned the page on another year. The fog was lifting. I wasn't looking for Molly Jones in every face on the subway so much anymore. Now that we three had an apartment together, the party would come to us, we didn't have to go looking for it.

I had forgotten one thing. I had forgotten all about it. It was as if it had never happened.

Yet it came back to me, one day when I was riding the trolley on the BC line and we were just passing into the tunnel leading from the light of day into the dark of the underground at Kenmore Square. The faces of my fellow-travelers were multiplying in the window-glass, and I was rocking back and forth with the sway of the Dallas-car on the rails, the explosive, popping tunnel lights in the window-reflections were streaking, morphing into the revolving mirror-lights streaking through . . . not the subway tunnel . . . but the whisky highlights of the bar-mirror at *The Stardust Lounge*.

And another day, when I was alone in the one-person alcove in the basement stacks at Bapst Library, with the light coming through the slit-window, and the autumn leaves strewn about the grass outside, at eye-level, oddly out of perspective, *the red electric guitar hanging on the guitar on the stage behind me, in the mirror in front of me.*

Suddenly it came to me all over again, that feeling.

The scene in front of me was the scene behind me.
The scene behind me was the scene in front of me.

And another day, in February, when there was snow on the ground, and ice on the Charles, and I was standing at the railing by the BU Bridge, looking downriver, and there was a flock of crows, big-shouldered black crows, standing on the ice, and they looked to me suddenly like Napoleon's army huddled in the cold shivering outside the gates of Moscow, and I felt the impulse to reach for a pen and a bar-napkin, to write down the words.

I remembered the words:

> *In the mirror on a guitar-stand*
> *Hangs the head of a maiden*
> *Who found herself lost in a land*
> *Called Aden.*

I remembered the words, but I had forgotten the impulse.
Now the impulse had returned.
What did it mean?

Chapter 32

Otherwise Known as Sheila Blake

On a balmy night early in April, in 1966, towards the middle of the spring semester of my sophomore year, I was strolling along Massachusetts Avenue, in the direction of Symphony Hall, feeling as good as the weather. It was cool enough to put my BC blazer to good use, but since I wasn't going to school on a Friday night, I dispensed with the necktie. Waves of people were sloshing back and forth on the sidewalks of Mass. Ave., all with the same idea as I had—cooped up for the winter, let's get out in the fresh air. Back at 1387, no party tonight—Dennis had his girlfriend Pauline from Spicket Falls visiting, and Benny had his current squeeze, a blonde named Rhonda, also nostalgic for the days of Penney High, spending the night, which left me free to roam the city for the evening, which suited me much better than the role of third wheel.

As I was passing an open doorway, I noticed cars pulling up to the curb, and taxis, disgorging dressed-up young people, pretty girls with their hair done, and their eager escorts battling the tides of pedestrians to make their way to what seemed to be a box-office. Curious, I stopped and looked inside. It was too dim in there to see what sort of party it was, but having nothing better to do, I ambled over to what looked like a doorman, or bouncer, to ask what was going on. He said it was a dance. "Can anyone go?"

"Anyone can go that has a dollar."

I produced a dollar and he broke off a ticket, after reaching inside the open door of the ticket-box to fetch the roll. I grabbed the ticket and proceeded to maneuver past his large frame and enter, upon which he placed a beefy hand in the middle of my chest. "You cannot go in without a necktie."

"Well, give me my money back then."

"Not to worry. I've a necktie for you right here." And reaching inside the ticket-door again, he came up with a clip-on tie. "Put this on and you'll be right as rain."

I was about to take the necktie when he snatched it back and said, "That'll be another dollar, please."

I was on the point of saying, forget the whole thing, when he said, "Look, I'm not selling you a tie for a dollar. You'll get the dollar refunded at the end of the night, when you give back the tie."

He acted as if he were explaining *Cream of Wheat* to a child who never heard of it.

Exasperated, I handed over another dollar and received the necktie, which I clipped on, demonstrably, as I went inside. My curiosity was now at thermometer pitch and I wasn't about to be denied entrance.

However, I still didn't know what I had gotten myself into. There was a dance-floor surrounded by round tables draped in white tablecloths, nearly every table full of boys and girls leaning forward on the edges of their seats, avidly conversing, trying to be heard above the noise of a live band. But what sort of band was that? They were not playing any kind of music I had ever heard. There was a drummer banging away, two guitar-players twanging electrically, and an accordian-player, playing a type of accordian I had never seen before, with buttons on the right-hand instead of a keyboard. Now I noticed a caterwauling fiddle-player, too.

I thought I had wandered mistakenly into some kind of square dance, completely out of place in the middle of a big city, least of all staid, proper Boston, and I was about to go get my money back for the clip-on tie when I saw a girl in a short dark pleated skirt and a white blouse, with long dark hair, straight down to her back, gliding across the dance floor.

Like flocks of pigeons, couples scattered to tables at the end of a number. It was as if the ocean were parting to reveal her.

I watched her cross the entire dance floor. Overhead there was a mirrored ball sending out bars of multi-colored light, spokes from a wheel. Circles of light dotted the walls and passed right through people in dizzying squadrons of purple, pink and yellow. There was a sign that said

STATE BALLROOM

but I was none the wiser for noticing it.

The spinning lights had clothed the gliding girl in an enchanted caparison of colored ribbons, floating serenely down a smooth stream.

I couldn't take my eyes off her.

There was no question now that I was leaving that hall. I had to meet that girl. I had to dance with her. I had to hold her in my arms, if only one time before I died.

She had reached her table and seated herself as I began to cross the emptied dancefloor, headed in a straight line for her table.

"Would you like to dance?" I said to her.

She turned her head sharply and her dark hair swirled like an opening fan around her white shoulders, and when she looked up at me, slightly surprised, said she, "I might."

It was only then that I noticed I had interrupted her, mid-sentence, and that there were two other girls she was sitting with, also deeply interested in what she was saying, and startled to see me.

A pair of blondes, but I hardly registered their presence. I was gazing in a deep trance at the dark-haired girl, and a smile had crept over my lips, a slightly bashful and embarrassed smile. I offered my hand and as she took it and rose from her seat, I thought she gave a sort of a smirk or something meaningful like that, quickly, to the other two, though I couldn't decipher the code.

We walked out to the center of the dance-floor, which was vacated, as if to make room for just us, and soon we were dancing, as the band on the stage sauntered leisurely into a fast country waltz, and other couples were starting to surround us. My body was spinning, my head was spinning, the lights were spinning. Mesmerized, I said, as I held her politely at arm's length, the better to gaze longingly and intently at her, the better to drink in her every feature, "What color are those eyes?"

She was not in the least put off by the question, she seemed to be quite amused. "Shy, aren't you?"

"Yes, I am. How did you know?"

"I think you're bold as brass buttons asking a girl straight off a question like that."

"But I've never seen eyes like yours before." My gaze drifted away from her eyes and lifted to her forehead, and then down around the curve of her abundant shining silkily smooth straight hair, falling down over her forehead, before it swam back and I returned to gazing deeply at her face again.

"They're hazel, if you must know."

"I must. And I must know your name, too!"

"It's Willie," she blurted out, now truly laughing at the both of us.

"Oh—is that short for Wilhelmina?"

I had read somewhere or seen in a movie this name, but never expected to encounter it in real life.

"Are you having me on?" said she.

"Do I detect an accent?"

"Indeed. I'm English, you see."

I thought how insanely wonderful this was. All the world was in love with The Beatles and and had been for two years and here I was lucky enough to meet a real British 'bird,' as they say.

"And what's your name, or is that a secret?"

"It's Nick."

"And that's short for–?"

"Short for Nick."

"Well, Nick, thanks for the dance."

"Can I have the next one, too?"

"I don't dance the fast ones, now, I'm warning you."

"I don't mind."

"You'll have to dance with Imelda and Martina if you want to dance the fast ones."

"I don't dance the fast ones, either. Who's—what's their names?"

"My friends I'm sitting with at the table."

"The blondes? They're not my type."

"You'll have to dance with them, if you're coming to the table, it's only the polite thing to do."

I was thinking *strange customs the English have.* An American girl would never ask you to dance with her girlfriends.

"Are you coming to the table then?"

As soon as we got to the table, as Willie was gesturing as if to begin introducing them, the two girls rose abruptly, grabbing their purses.

"We were just leaving," said one.

"Yes, we'll leave you two love-birds alone," said the other, hiding her face so she could giggle.

Willie looked at them with a desperate half-plea, half-vow-of-vengeance.

It was my turn to be amused. "Some friends, huh?"

I pulled out a chair for her, and she sat in a lump. "Useless, they are."

As I sat down, I said, "Well, looks like it's just us two love-birds."

"Don't be cheeky."

"I love the way you English girls talk. Talk some more like that."

We talked for the rest of the evening. We danced every slow dance that came up. I asked her every question about her that I could think of, her family, where she came from, her background, what she was doing in Boston. She wasn't a tourist and she wasn't going back home next weekend. She was working here, she had a job as a file clerk at Liberty Mutual Insurance Company, down on Stuart Street. The more I asked her about herself, the more she tried to divert the conversation to me. I told her my entire life story. She was easy to talk to. There was only one thing I held back. About halfway through the evening

I was looking at her, and I found I was saying to myself, in my mind, *My God, she's the spitting image of Molly Jones. Except for the color of her eyes.*

At the end of the evening, I asked for her phone number. I half-expected she would give me a fake number, even as she was writing it down on a slip of paper from her hand-bag. Her two friends turned out to be her roommates, Imelda and Martina. They had returned to our table, some time before, with boyfriends, also English, from their ruddy looks. I hadn't noticed. I'd been absorbed.

"How're you getting home?" said Willie.

"Oh—I'll walk. It's a nice evening. It's not that far."

"But we can give you a lift. Imelda has her car."

I thought that was a very nice thing for Willie to do.

An English bird. What luck. What would the boys think about that? Nobody I knew, except for Martino, had a foreign car, much less an English bird for a girlfriend. Visions of swinging London filled my head. And it was sheer luck that I had met her. Sheer chance that I bought a ticket. Sheer chance that the doorman had a neck-tie. Sheer chance that I saw her gliding across the floor—alone. Did she have a boyfriend? She hadn't said so—she hadn't acted as if she did—that, too, was lucky, for me. She was certainly attractive. Slender and trim. Dressed in modest but stylish fashion, an office girl going out to a dance, in a skirt that would swish, above the knee. More saucy than sexy. What was her word? *Cheeky.* Yes, that was it. I didn't know what to make of her, but if I had to I would've said *not a bird in a cage, but a bird flying free.*

Was she interested in me? If she wasn't, why had she offered me that ride home? To spend a little more time with me? In the back seat, with her roommates up front?

I certainly wanted to find out. I was certainly going to call her. But not right away. I'd have to let a decent interval go by. I didn't want her to think I was that desperate.

But I was. It was a solid year and a half since I'd felt Molly Jones put her arms around me. It was springtime, and I was young, I was in Boston, with a hundred thousand young people my age, half of them girls, they were everywhere you looked, it was 'the swinging Sixties,' in all the fanzines, *why was I alone?* I was thrilled with the success I was having at school, my grade-point average was up there, but, more than that, I was growing, expanding, I had gone into English as my major, with history for a minor, I was taking psychology and sociology, I was learning things I'd never imagined, re-making myself into an image I'd only dreamed of back in Spicket Falls, it was everything I'd always believed it would be, everything—*but I had no one to share it with.*

That phone number tucked away in my wallet in my back-pocket—I would take it out from time to time, to reassure myself I hadn't lost it, to gaze at her handwriting.

The week hadn't gone by when Thursday night came, and I thought, tomorrow will be one whole week since we met, I better call her now, before the weekend's here—what if somebody else is calling her? *What if he beats me to it?*

I held my breath as I dialed the number. I fully expected her to answer, and I had no idea what I was going to say.

Instead, the roommate picked up.

"Hi, is Willie there?"

"Who?"

"Willie."

"Who's this, may I ask?"

"It's Nick."

"Oh—." There was a pause. Then, raising her voice, she called out, "Wil-lie!"

Muffled laughter in the background. Then another voice, in the background, was calling out, loudly, "Oh, Wil-lie!–it's for yoo-oo, Wil-lie!"

There was more laughter, and the sound of the telephone receiver jangling from hand to hand. "Hello?"

"Hello, Willie?"

"Yes. Who's this?"

"It's Nick."

"Oh, hello, Nick, how're you keeping?"

"What's going on? I hear laughing in the background. Don't your roommates know your name?"

"Oh, pay them no heed."

"Well—how are you?"

"I'm fine. How's yourself? Miss me, did you?"

"Yes, I did."

"You wouldn't know it. I thought you'd never call."

"Well, I wanted to, but—. Listen, are you busy this weekend?"

"As it happens, I am. But I might fit you in. What did you have in mind?"

"I thought we might go to the library."

"Oh, the library. Yes. Indeed. The library. But it would have to be tonight, then."

"But tonight's Thursday."

"Yes. And I have work tomorrow."

"And I have to study."

"So—it's the library then."

"Yes–I thought you might like to see the campus at BC—if you've never been there."

I wanted to impress Willie by borrowing the august majesty of Boston College. I needed the backup in stature the campus and its atmosphere would provide. I didn't have money, I didn't have a car—how else was I going to impress her? I wanted her to see me as somebody important, somebody with a future.

"You'll have to pick me up, then. I've no idea where it is or how to get there."

"You don't mind if we go by the subway?"

"No. Not at all. And would you ever pick up a six-pack of beer to bring along with us?"

"Willie, we can't bring beer into the library."

"But it's such a lovely spring evening. You bring the beer, and I'll bring along a blanket."

Needless to say, I didn't do much studying that evening. We got to the campus about six-thirty, and Bapst Library would be open till ten, but instead of going inside, we spread Willie's blanket out on the lawn, at the top of the slope next to St Mary's Hall, where the Jesuits resided.

Thanks to Fr. O'Donoghue, who taught the class in *Logic* I took in freshman year, I knew all about the Budweiser truck that pulled up each morning at the loading-dock behind St Mary's Hall. It seems that the Jesuits went through a beer-truck per day, as I'd often taken notice, thereafter, of the truck returning at five in the afternoon to take away the cases of empties. Thus, it did not seem inappropriate for us to be drinking a six-pack within view of the loading-dock down the slope below us.

I told Willie the story Fr. O'Donoghue had told us in class. It seems that some time ago, early in the good father's career as an ordained Jesuit, he had been informed that a certain bishop needed a lift out to Holy Cross, in Worcester, for a high-level meeting between our Jesuits and theirs, Holy Cross being our sister-institution, and, indeed, our chief rival in the noble intercollegiate athletic wars in football and basketball, though not in hockey, where we, the Boston College Eagles, as I explained to Willie, reigned supreme over the Holy Cross Crusaders. Well, as Fr O'Donoghue had nothing better to do that particular day, he cheerfully chauffeured the bishop-in-the-back-seat fifty miles away, to the Holy Cross campus in Worcester.

The meeting went on tendentiously at great length all afternoon with Fr O'Donoghue left to sit in the limousine outside in the sweltering heat. Becoming thirsty, he went in search of liquid refreshment and, lo and behold, found the very same beer truck which delivered to the Jesuits at Boston College was doing the rounds to Holy Cross as well. The upshot of the whole adventure was that, just as the chauffeur had chauffeured the bishop-in-the-back-seat out to Worcester in the morning, the bishop chauffeured the chauffeur-in-the-back-seat back to Boston in the afternoon, the beer truck beating them to their destination in both cases. I then sang to Willie the song that Fr O'Donoghue sang to us that afternoon in class, before he dismissed us for the day. I had to summon up all my musical training in order to perform this ditty, to the tune of "O Christmas Tree."

> *Oh, Holy Cross, oh, Holy Cross,*
> *All they eat is applesauce,*
> *They eat it morning, noon and night,*
> *They even eat it when they're tight,*
> *Oh, Holy Cross, on bended knee,*
> *Kiss the arse of olde BC!*

By the time I finished this grandiloquent aria, I was quite drunk and quite smitten with my English bird.

Of course, I had every intention of falling in love with her. For that's what I was looking for. I wanted to have sex with a girl, of course, but I wasn't looking for sex, I was looking for love.

The girl I was going to lose my virginity to was the girl I loved and the girl who loved me. As long as we loved each other, then all the rest was no sin, all the rest was the consequence of our love. You see? I had the whole thing figured out.

So that night, on the blanket outside St Mary's Hall, I was testing Willie. She had to prove be the kind of girl I could fall in love with by accepting me and my school and my schoolbooks and my library.

And she was testing me. I had to be the kind of boy who would go into a liquor store and buy her a six-pack when she knew I was underage.

Each of us passed the test. She came to school with me and I got tipsy with her.

A week later, Willie and I went out to Arlington, again by MTA, to a party at Martino's house. All my BC friends, Grigorian, Viola, Zammucci, Blanchette, one by one, from time to time, drifted by with a drink in the hand to lean over and ask me confidentially, 'Where did you find her?'

Willie was holding court at one end of the sofa, while I sat on the arm jealously guarding her from the attack-wolves ranged before her on the coffee table.

Another time Willie had taken me with her, again by MTA, out to a walled estate in Brookline, across the road from *The Country Club*, where she was baby-sitting for the night, for a family called the Higginbothams. When we had gotten to know each other a little better, I brought her to my apartment at 1387 Comm Ave to meet my roommates, Rousseau and

Nader. I was showing her off, and at the same time, warning her that these two, my oldest friends, could not be trusted with innocent, guileless young ladies. "They're users. They just use girls, and when they're finished with them, throw them away."

One night Willie offered to do a load of my dirty clothes for me, at the laundromat next door to her apartment building. She was living with Imelda, the strawberry blond, and her sister, Martina, the golden blond, her two roommates, at 104 Queensberry Street, in the Fens, across Boylston Street from Fenway Park. "You can study," she told me, "while I do your wash."

I thought it was very kind of her to offer to do so, kind and considerate. Where would I find a girl like this, to do my laundry, and let me hit the books? A girl who would let you take her to a party on the MTA, way out to Arlington. A girl you didn't need a car for? Not an American girl, that's for sure. As we were leaving their apartment with the basket of laundry, Imelda, the strawberry blond, slipped and called her 'Sheila.'

I turned and said, "Okay, somebody's going to have to tell me what's going on."

The two sisters looked sideways at the floor with raised eyebrows that said, *oops*.

"All right," said Willie, "come on over to the launderette and we can talk there."

I sighed and followed her out. This had better be good.

She was silent the whole way. Unusual, for her. It must have been ten paces, at least, from her front door at 104, to the door of the laundromat. Once inside, it was loading the wash, putting the coins in, pressing the button. I was waiting. Finally, she could avoid it no longer, and turned to face me.

"Well, what did you expect me to do, give you my right name when I didn't even know you? And me, far away from home, in a foreign land, with no friends and family, all on my own."

"What is your name? Is it 'Sheila,' like Imelda said?"

"Yes."

"Sheila what?"

"Sheila Blake."

"Sounds English to me." I was a sophomore in the English Dept at Boston College and I was finally completing my introductory survey course in English literature at the end of spring semester and William Blake was, of course, one of the great English poets I had encountered in my Norton Anthology.

"It's Irish. Irish as can be. And I'm Irish if I'm a day. Born and raised. And I hope to never be anything else."

"That's good." I admit I was thinking of Molly Jones. "I was afraid you were a Protestant."

"Oh, God, no."

"When I thought you were English, I mean."

"Aren't you the clever one, anyway. Do you not know the difference between an English accent and an Irish one when you hear it?" Willie, I mean, Sheila, sat down next to me on the wooden bench behind the dryers. "Oh, that's not coming out the right way that it sounds. All I'm really trying to say is–are you great with me again?"

"What do you mean?"

"Well, when you're great with someone, it means, rather like, you know, that you're great with them."

"So, am I great with you?"

"No, listen, what I'm asking is—oh, forget it, and just give us a kiss, would you?"

I did, and then I wiped away with a gentle forefinger the tear of frustration, welling at the corner of her eye, about to burst.

Chapter 33

She Made Me Want To

It was easy to lose my virginity to Sheila Blake. She made it easy and natural. She made it fun. She made me want to. I was ready in any case. I was not in high school anymore. I was not living under my mother's roof, or her rule. It was time for me. I hadn't ruined my chances to get to college. I hadn't ruined someone else's life. I hadn't gotten Merrilee Krupp pregnant when she was fourteen. Molly Jones had found someone else. I wasn't going back to Spicket Falls. I was in college. I loved everything I was doing now. And Sheila made it all better. She was the topping on the ice cream. She was the one I was doing it all for. She was the one I wanted to share everything with. How then could I share everything, and hold myself back? Didn't making love mean that you gave yourself to someone?

I knew she liked me. She loved to talk and I could listen to her all day. She thought my eyeglasses made me look intellectual. She would steal them off my nose, put them on and parade around with one of my books open in her hand. "Amn't I gorgeous?" she would say. She would place the glasses back on my nose, and say, "How can you see through those things?" Not to be outdone, I would say, "How can you smoke Marlboros—they're filthy-nasty." But we were tolerant of our differences. We agreed that opposites attract, and we were certainly opposites. I could bury myself in a textbook, but Sheila would eventually peel it out of my hands and place herself there instead so that, rather than Erickson's *Young Luther*, I could study the green flecks and brown lily-pads floating in her hazel eyes.

One night she took me out to Southie to a place called *Ireland's 32* on Old Colony Ave, to hear an Irish band. She had invited her best friend, Ann-Marie, from Hyde Park, a girl from the office at Liberty Mutual where Sheila worked. Ann-Marie was Irish-American, the gang from the office were all fans of that music, I was the one who had never before heard *The Wild Colonial Boy*. I was not much for drinking. I tried to keep up by nursing a beer for about an hour. Ann-Marie was a very nice person, an attractive, blondish young lady with a quiet dignity who sipped a mixed drink in lady-like fashion. With her short, modest hair-do leaving her neck bare, she gave the impression that she would have fit in well in a convent, except that, instead of giving her life to Our Lord, she had a boyfriend sitting next to her. At some point in the noisy, smoky, crowded evening, Ann-Marie leaned over to me to say, "You better be very good to my friend Sheila. She is a treasure, and I love her a lot."

"I do, too, Ann-Marie." I suppose it was the atmosphere, the wine, women and song of it all, but as soon as I said it, I realized how much I really meant it, so I hastened to add, "But don't tell her I said that."

It happened about two months after I first met Sheila at the State Ballroom on Mass Ave.

We weren't in any rush. We hadn't talked about it. I think we were both waiting for it to happen. It was going to happen sooner rather than later whether we talked about it or not. I knew that inside that buttoned blouse of hers, there was a beating heart, and a lithesome, enticing, inviting woman who was only just barely beyond being a reckless girl. We had been out to see a movie at the Exeter Theater. *Dr Zhivago* was in its 48th week. We were back at Sheila's apartment, in her bedroom at the back, with the door closed, sitting up together on her bed, our backs to the bedboard, pretending to discuss the movie while we couldn't stop entwining arms and legs and passionately kissing. We were sliding down in the bed. Sheila had thrown one leg over me and I was bursting.

"Do you know what you're doing to me?"

"No. Tell me. I can feel it, you *amadaun*."

"What does that mean?"

"That's Irish for the fool that you are."

"If I'm a fool, it's because of you. And you're making me a bigger and bigger fool."

"Indeed. And what are you going to do about it?"

"Better be careful, or I'll take it out."

"Oh, do. I've never seen one. Is it like a cow's udder? I've seen plenty of them. Amn't I a farmer's daughter from the County Mayo? Oh, my God. He's as bald as Khrushchev!"

"Yeah, but he's got a beard like Abraham Lincoln."

Chapter 34

Girl From the County Mayo

What I didn't know about love would fill a library-wall of those books I was always reading.

I didn't know, for instance, that love could turn a woman all inside-out like a pillow-case. Sheila's words.

I didn't know that a man could want achingly to be inside a woman, to want to be enveloped or enfolded or surrounded or surrendered and to lose his very self in that other person. My thought.

I didn't know that love was an undiscovered country, that once you set out to visit there, that you would wish never to come back, that you would find more and more vistas, valleys, mountain peaks and river-views to explore, abandon, remember and return to, in endless fascination and ceaseless profusion.

In my case, the undiscovered country lay behind Sheila's every word or thought or glance or reflection. And that country was Ireland.

Ireland was in her speech. Ireland was in her eyes. She was the embodiment of Ireland and her every movement, from the toss of her long dark silken hair to the swish of her skirt, was the expression of Ireland.

I once ventured to vouch forth the opinion that the local Boston O'Hara's and Moriarty's, Sullivan's and Murphy's were Irish.

"They are not," said Sheila.

"What would you call them, then?"

"Anything but Irish. Certainly not Irish. They're about as Irish as you are Eye-talian, Petrovich."

"What about the Kennedys?"

"Irish once a year, on election day."

I laughed. "Don't let them hear you say that."

"I couldn't care less what the Kennedys think. You can tell them for me, K.M.R.I. A."

"What does that stand for, Sheila?"

She turned her backside to me, as she departed her bedroom, flouncing up her skirt at me, bending over to present a double-arch of white panties, calling over her shoulder, with enunciation, *"Kiss My Royal Irish Arse!"*

Riddle me this, then. Why had Sheila ever bothered to masquerade herself as English, upon our first, chance meeting? It seemed indeed a conundrum, yet it only added to the mysteriousness of her being, in the end, thoroughly Irish; and it piqued me so, it stirred my bafflement so, that I set out to study up, in my typical fashion, on all things Irish: slang, music, culture, history, by— guess what? Hitting the books.

It was the summer of 1966, after the end of my sophomore year, and I was making my annual piggy-bank run at saving up a thousand bucks to get me through the school year, this time, painting the BC football stadium, on the summer work-study program. I had discovered Lamont Library at Harvard. Their treasure-trove of culture and information was so much more extensive than what we had available in Bapst at Boston College, and the grounds and building were so much more airy and architectural, in contrast to gothic and gloomy, that again I regretted, with recriminations, and envy, that Harvard had rejected me when I applied for admission.

Still, as long as they were going to let me stroll in and out and use their rich facilities without being a student there, they nearly made it up to me. And as I applied green paint to the bleacher-seats in Alumni Field, under the hot summer sun, I consoled myself with the thought that our football team could beat theirs any day of the autumn.

Sheila said I was getting 'as brown as a nut.' That's because I was painting all day, stripped to the waist. My new friend wielding a paint brush alongside me, Algis Karelis, was not so lucky. He was an exchange student from Lithuania, tall, emaciated and red-headed, and had to keep his shirt on. He had come to the United States to study engineering. I told him he was in the wrong school at BC. But he wanted to paint bleacher seats alongside me every day so that I would help him with his English.

One night Sheila said we had to take the trolley to Brighton.

"Why? Who do we know over there?"

"I've a job of work to do, do you mind?"

"What is it?" I said, looking doubtful.

"Babby-sitting. You can bring yourself and study."

Perhaps it was true. If Sheila was occupied with a child, she might let me. In any case, at this stage, either one of us was loath to leave the room without telling the other where we were going and how long till we'd be back.

We got off in Brighton Center and began walking. We went down Market Street and turned at St Columcille's and started climbing hills. I had brought along a copy of the plays of John Synge and a novel by James Stephens called *Deirdre*. My explorations at the Lamont were providing leads and I was spending all my money on used paperbacks downstairs at the Harvard Bookstore. I had no idea where we were or where we were going, but Sheila seemed to know the way, just as she had the night she took me to Brookline to babysit the Higginbotham kids. I think she might have been enjoying making a mystery of these things, but I couldn't be sure. Perhaps she was playing a game of letting me into her secrets in her own good time, or perhaps she didn't think she was hiding anything. Maybe it was just me who thought her ways lavishly mysterious.

When we arrived finally, after much climbing, at a curvy, shady piece of this densely residential section of the city, and we were out of breath from going constantly uphill, I still didn't know where we were.

We halted in front of a house bathed in leafy shade perched high above a retaining wall with a long set of terraced steps up to the porch, a house with turrets and a single front door set back in shadow. More climbing.

At the top, Sheila rang the doorbell. The door flung open and a young lady, head tilted down to her shoulder, frantically trying to affix an ear-ring, said, "Oh, good, you're here. Come in, so, we're almost late."

We entered a dark, commodious entrance hall, with lamp-light from a room with a sofa, peeking into the darkness, and white light, far away down a hallway, coming from the back of the house.

"This is my sister Mary," said Sheila, to me, and to them, "This is the fella I was telling you about."

I say 'them' because a man rose from the sofa and came shuffling forward, extending his hand to greet me with a handshake, saying, "Very pleased to meet you, we've heard so much about you."

The frantic sister Mary was saying, "Now, Sheila, she's sleeping at the moment. Come and see, down to the room."

And she rushed Sheila away.

The man was still shaking my hand and bowing genially. His handshake was weak and his entire posture excessively deferential. "Tom Moran," he was saying, by way of apology.

It dawned on me that he was telling me his name.

I stood there speechless.

"From Galway," Tom Moran explained, unnecessarily, as he let go of my fingers, unnecessarily, as it meant little to me that he might be from Galway, wherever that was, and necessarily, as it filled in an otherwise awkward silence on the part of dumbfounded me.

Suddenly Mary was back, dragging on her coat, hustling her sister Sheila back to one side, and pulling Tom Moran away from me. "Come on, now, Tom, or we're going to be late."

"Yes, yes, coming, let me just get my coat here."

They went past me, giving me a wide berth, Mary pulling Tom by the hand, Tom apologizing, as he bowed, shuffling, "Sorry, sorry, cheerio, then."

I went into the living room and plopped myself down on the sofa.

Sheila came sauntering in, very pleased with herself.

"You could've told me," I said.

"I thought I might just—surprise you."

"'Surprised' is not the word."

Sheila whirled and threw herself off her feet practically into my lap.

"I meant to tell you, but, ah, shite, I never got round to it."

"Are there any more you have hidden away?"

"Oh, aye."

"What do you mean, eye?"

"I mean 'aye'." Nodding her head up and down. Sign language.

"You're going to have to tell me everything, Sheila. And no lying this time."

She looked at me outraged "I have never lied to you in my life!"

"Let's just say you stretched the truth–'Willie.'"

She sulked. "I thought you, of all people, Petrovich, might try and understand."

"I am trying to understand, Sheila."

She took my hand and placed her head on my shoulder. She started counting on my fingers. "Well, let's see—there was Mary, she's the oldest. You've only just met her. Then there's Bridie. She's my other sister. She lives in Jamaica Plain–."

"Jamaica Plain!"

"Did I not tell you about Bridie?"

"You meant to, but–."

"Ah, shite, I never got round to it."

"Did you actually grow up in Ireland?"

"How can you ask me that?"

"Because, so far, all your sisters are over here."

"Not all. Ann is in England."

"There's a sister Ann, in England? What's she doing in England?"

"A lot better, I imagine, than if she'd stayed back, in Mayo."

"That's where you're from. I know that. And that's in—."

"The West of Ireland, so it is."

"And what about this Galway that Tom was telling me he's from?"

"That's the next County over. Surely you can't be that ignorant."

"Excuse me, but you're the first Irish person I've ever met, other than all the Irish from Southie in the BC Band."

"They're not Irish."

"Stick to the subject, Sheila. How many more are there?"

Counting on my fingers again, she said, "This little piggie here would me my brother Pat, he's the next youngest from me. He's named after me da, Patrick Blake, who's called at home, Long Pat, as he's so tall, as opposed to my brother, Patrick Blake. And don't call him junior, he's hates that, he'll eat the head off you." Then, going on to my other hand, "And last of all, there's the babby in the house, that's my brother, Matt."

"And where are your brothers?"

"They're home, in Kilcross."

"That's your town?"

"Well, no, it wouldn't be a town, it's not that big. More like a hook in the road."

"What about your parents?"

"Home, in Mayo. My mother was Jane Loftus, now she's Jane Blake. She raised six of us. And didn't she do a smashin' job on me?"

"Smashin'. When do I get to meet the sister in Jamaica Plain—what's her name?"

"Bridie. She doesn't know about you. You're my little secret."

"She'll know now."

"No, I've sworn Mary, her lips are sealed."

"Your sister Mary looks nothing like you."

"I take after my mother, thank goodness. We have the exact same long dark straight hair. Mary and Bridie and Ann take after me Da's side of the family."

"What about your brothers."

"They're both Blakes all over, actually. Come to think of it, there's Mammy and meself, and there's the rest of them."

"Nobody else with the raven tresses of my darling Sheila?"

"Ravin', I wish."

I loved to run my fingers through her satin hair.

"Probably, I'm thinking," said Sheila, "you might meet up with my Aunt Terry and Aunt Ann and Uncle Nonie, over in Somerville, first."

"There's more?"

"That's the lot of them."

"Does your sister Mary know we're sleeping together."

"What Mary doesn't know won't hurt her. It's my own business, anyway."

"How did you get aunts and uncles over here?"

"It was in the Thirties. Things were bad at home. My mother's sisters, Ann and Theresa, and her brother, Nonie—that's short for Anthony—emigrated, so they did. Shush, now. I think I hear my little niece, Mary-Jane. Come on, Petrovich."

We went sneaking down the dark hallway, hand in hand.

Sheila picked up the baby from her crib. We took her back to the sofa in the living room with us. Sheila cradled the sleeping infant in her arms on her lap, rocking her so that she wouldn't wake up all the way, cooing a soft, wordless, melody-forsaken air from the wilds of times past in another land where wolves roamed the outer fringes of night-clothed mountains where the mythical red deer ran. I put my arm around her shoulders, and I saw Sheila Blake, in the darkened room, in the gentle glow from the lamp, in a new, ancient, mystical light.

★

May 10th, 1966, was circled on my calendar, Sheila's birthday, the first one that we spent together. We marked it with another visit to the laundromat. We were basically, by this time, inseparable. I had already forgotten how big a change had come over my life. Was it really only a matter of a few months since that night spinning under the glass globe at the State Ballroom?

They say that love at first sight happens. I say that for me it could not have happened any other way. It had to be instantaneous. It had to be unplanned. It had to be total derangement. It had to be the complete overturning of my entire universe, overnight. Sheila Blake was turning twenty. We were born in the same year, 7 months apart, and an ocean between. Already it seemed that I had known her since before she could walk. How could any rational person explain that against all odds these two people, and none other, from continents apart, separated not just by distance, but by culture and history and nationality and incompatible opposite-ness, should come together, in a cataclysmic breakdown of common sense. It was destiny. It was fate. It had to be.

But fate brings with it many strange twists.

The other fateful date circled on my calendar that May was the morning of the 26th, 6.30 AM, US Army Base, Summer Street, South Boston, the time and place where I was scheduled to undergo the Army physical for admittance into the Regular Army, the prerequisite to qualify for the Army ROTC Advanced Course. My first two years at BC, I had completed the Basic Course, and the previous summer, I had done a 50-mile hike, from the BC Campus out to Fort Devens in Ayer, MA, and back, as part of the two-week summer camp. I was looking forward to going away in July, for another camp, this time as a cadet who was scheduled to graduate in 2 years from now with a commission as a 2nd Lieutenant in the United States Army.

It was chilly out the morning of the 26th, as I stepped off the bus. It was cold in the waiting room. I was nervous standing in line. This meant a lot to me.

I flunked the physical.

Or I should say, an Army orderly slapped a blood-pressure cuff on me and got a high reading.

Two weeks later I got the notice in the mail that I was denied admittance into the Advanced Course.

I rushed over to Queensberry Street to share this disastrous news with my girl.

"I can't believe it, Sheila. There's gotta be some mistake. The Army won't take me."

"That's good," she said, putting her arms around my neck to comfort me, and kissing me sweetly.

"What do you mean, good? Oh, you don't understand. How could you? You're not an American. How do you know what it means to me?"

I should not have said this. Obtusely, I had missed the message Sheila was sending me. She didn't want me going into the Army because she didn't want to lose me. Besides, it was cruel and insensitive. *You're not an American.*

But I was all twisted up inside with the disappointment of cherished childhood dreams.

It all had to do with the image I held dearly close in my mind of my Uncle Augie landing at Omaha Beach. The war hero I grew up with. The role model I identified with. The man I wanted to be.

"I don't know why you want to go into any old Army anyway," said Sheila, as if reading my mind through the arms she had locked around my neck.

I pried her arms apart and started waving the letter. "I'm going to fight this, Sheila. They can't do this to me."

She was looking at me, clearly displeased, with her arms on her hips. "All I know is Ireland's got along very well for the last couple of thousands of years without invading anybody, Petrovich."

It was straight to the point, a reference to Vietnam.

I fought the Army's decision for that entire summer. I went first thing straight to Sgt Ryan in the ROTC offices in the bottom of Roberts Center. He said to me, "The Army doesn't make mistakes."

"But I don't have high blood pressure. I'll prove it."

I phoned home to Spicket Falls to the old horse doctor I used to have in high school, the one who drained my knee when I got that football injury and told me to use horse liniment on it. I went home on the bus for an appointment. He told me I'd have to take a series. I explained how I couldn't be away that long from my girlfriend or my job at the stadium. He told me what to do—send the readings to him. He would write it up. I felt better. I knew I could count on him. After all, he was the one who sent me back to the practice field with a knee as big as a soccer ball.

Every day painting the stadium seats with Algis Karelis, the exchange student, I was complaining about what the Army was doing to ruin my summer. "Look at me. I'm as fit as a fiddle, Algis."

"Ah," he said. "An interesting expression. May I use it?"

"In your case it would have to be 'skinny as a bean-pole.'"

"By the way, when you are going to introduce me to the girlfriend?"

"You stay away from her."

"But, my friend Nick—we be fellow Europeans. And, in addition, you know how hard it is for me to meet girl."

I took him to Queensberry Street with me one night to meet Sheila's roommates, the sisters from Kerry, Imelda and Martina. We sat around the kitchen table drinking beer. It made me morose. The Europeans at the table were finding out how much they had in common. I was suddenly the odd man out.

Chapter 35

Sheila, I Have to Go

My father called. Left an urgent message at 1387 Comm Ave. Called again. Why hadn't I called back yet? My roommate, Benny Nader, got hold of me at Sheila's.

"I have to go, Sheila. Family emergency."

She could see my face darkening as I hung up from my father. "What's happened?"

"My uncle Alek. I'm gonna have to take a trip, Sheila. My father wants me to help with the driving. I don't want him to go alone. He's just lost his brother."

It was a terrible journey. We had to stop in the Bronx to pick up my Aunt Adrienne and she sat in the back seat all the way to Pittsburgh, crying, mourning her darling brother with a six-pack of Rhiengold and a box of Kleenex. I had to listen to my father's complaints about my mother not permitting him to bring along my little brother and sister, Jack and Jill, the twins, who were now fifteen and sophomores at Jenney High. They both had summer jobs at *The Clambox,* the new fish and chips joint in what used to be a vacant lot at the corner of Elm and Woodland, back home. I was so glad I wasn't in that house any more. I felt sorry for the kids. My mother said if they went anywhere they'd lose their summer jobs. What about my father's feelings?

The whole thing was making me sick. I was so anxious to get this over with and to get back to my Sheila, to hold her in my arms and feel like it was the two of us against the world.

My poor Uncle Alek had died in the hospital in Uniontown after they cut off his leg. He had stepped on a nail down in the dark in Germantown No. 1, and it got infected. Because of his diabetes, it cost him his life. Poor old Auntie Rose hadn't called my dad or my Aunt Stasija and Uncle Mike or Aunt Adrienne because she didn't want to make them feel they had to rush down there, once he was in the hospital, because there was nothing they could do.

Life was wrong. Life was evil on the Pennsylvania Turnpike. The tunnels were endless, the tanker-trucks were barrel-assing downhill, threatening to run you off the road, my father was making me nervous as I tried to drive, he kept saying if we don't make time we're gonna be late, I kept thinking, *his brother's already dead,* the sky over the mountains was purple. We had lost another young boy who had gone away in the flush of youth to win the war by navigating C-47s over the hump to China. Where was God in all this?

Where was the god of the Jesuits of Boston College?

Where was the God of the Jumonville Cross, 60 feet tall, on top of Dunbar's Knob outside of Uniontown, visible from seven counties, three states and fifty miles away on a clear day?

THE EDUCATION OF NICHOLAS PETROVICH

There was wailing in the church at the service for my uncle at St Saba's Serbian Orthodox Church in Pershing. The professional mourners of the Serb community were there, the old women with their heads covered in black shawls who set up a keening for the dead man in the casket. They infected my aunt Adrienne with their hysteria. At the cemetery, they had to hold her back from throwing herself into the open grave on top of her dead brother's coffin.

At this horrid, spine-chilling, primitive display, I turned away my face with a disgusted expression.

My cousin Roseann saw me.

She saw my involuntary reaction and she looked right through me.

The beautiful girl to whom I wrote all those wonderful pen-pal letters sharing every childhood secret, so many years ago, then turned her face away from mine.

She had discovered that I was not who she thought I was.

She had discovered who I was.

I had lost her. I had lost her because I came from a big-city college and I did not understand or empathize with or even tolerate the customs and traditions and habitual ways of my own family members who dwelt in the valley of the shadow of the coal-mine.

I lost her because I had no pity in my heart. Only judgment. Only condemnation.

I was writing home to Sheila Blake every day that I was in Pershing. Long letters full of the details of my every day spent away from her, telling her how I felt, the doubts, the dilemmas, the queasy, agonizing, unanswerable queries floating through the perplexities of my mind.

Sheila Blake had taken the place in my heart once occupied by my beautiful cousin Roseann.

Chapter 36

The Three Faces of Jealousy

The river dives down the rocky ravine, thrashing in the open air, throwing clouds of mist up, as if dust from a dry road, dashed up by the thunder of passing horses; but then it twists and turns to pass underground, hidden, disappearing, only to emerge again, a different stream, collected, cool, quietly burbling.

As soon as I got back to Boston on the Saturday of my return I made straight for 104 Queensberry Street by two in the afternoon. I rang the intercom for Apt 4 and Sheila's voice garbled out, "Who is it?"

"Who do you think? Buzz me in."

"Oh! Nick! It's you, is it? Give us a mo. I was just in the loo. I'll unlock the door and buzz you in."

I was so, so happy to be seeing her again. The all-glass front door of the building meant you could see all the way down the brightly-lit hall to Sheila's door. I wanted to smash the glass and race down the corridor. 104 Queensbury was a Maurice Gordon building, the plaque on the wall inside the glass door informed the visitor. I had no patience for reading a notorious slumlord's statement of possession and authority just now. My foot was pumping with impatience simply from the few seconds it took for Sheila to press the button.

When she buzzed me in, I ran all the way down the length of the hall, flung open her door, and strode in. Where was she? Down the hall of her apartment I went, heading for her bedroom door, but as I passed the kitchen—there she was, sitting at the kitchen table with Algis Karelis and a half-destroyed six-pack of Carling's cans.

"Come in and sit down, Nick," said Sheila, with an impish grin. "We were just discussing erections."

"Yes," said Algis, with an unaware smile. "I didn't know Sheila was very interested in engineering. Nick—should you maybe should switch your major?"

"Algis, why don't *you* switch? To MIT, maybe? If you leave right now, you can catch a bus. You're in the wrong school, buddy. Sheila. In the bedroom, *subito*."

"What?"

"That's Italian for *'right now.'*"

"Excuse me, Algis," said Sheila, rising and pulling out her chair. "Coming," she said to me, with raised eyebrows, as I stood there fuming.

I slammed the door of her bedroom shut. She backed up against it.

"What's he doing here?"

"Oh, he just came over to visit with Martina and Imelda. But they both have fellas, you know, and they didn't fancy sitting waiting for him. So they went out shopping. I'm not in charge of them, you know."

"But you're in charge of yourself, and you have a fella, too."

"You're the one who brought him over here in the first place, Nick."

"And I'm sorry I did."

"Well, once he was here, I couldn't very well refuse him admittance, now, could I?"

"Yes, you could have."

"Oh, can't a girl have a bit of craic?"

"Didn't you stop to think he might not know that erections has two meanings?"

"You're the expert in English. Why don't you explain it to him?"

Coyly, she placed her hands behind her backside and leaned her shoulders back against the door. Sheila Blake never used makeup like other girls did. She didn't need to. Her lashes, as she looked up at me from under them, could not have been more alluring, or daring, or wet with defiance.

As I mashed her mouth with a hard kiss, as she was just closing her eyes, she was murmuring, "So, it's jealous you are, is it?"

Something was going on, deep underground, that summer of 1966. The Beatles' *I've Just Seen a Face* had been playing constantly on the radio since January. It skipped from the radio speakers through my heart straight into my head and wouldn't leave. The letters I was writing every day in Pennsylvania were lubricating my pen-hand and drawing out of me things I didn't know were buried deep inside me. The listening room at Lamont Library was letting me into the secrets of Bach's *Brandenburg Concertos*. I was finding spoken-word recordings of Carl Sandburg and Dylan Thomas that I didn't know existed. I was placing earphones on my head, for free, earphones that were beyond my pocketbook, and they invited me into a space between my temples that was waiting to be filled with words. I was developing an urge to set it all down on paper. All the things that were happening around me and inside me. All of it.

It was as if it wasn't enough to kiss Sheila, to hold her close to me, to enter inside of her, when we were making love, I had to talk to myself about it, I had to set apart time by myself to reflect the coursing of deep currents swaying me back and forth in an ocean of soaking, immersing, drowning emotions pulling me down, down, down into some earlier epoch, into some primitive undersea cave where, if only I could reach it, I would be swimming in deepest memory, floating in an ambiotic wash of ecstasy, of oblivion, of Being before Being was.

I had to break free and soar upward and propel myself toward the light till I broke the surface again, and then—write down the findings of my research, so that they would not be lost to humanity for all time.

And each time I broke the surface, when I looked up, there was the mirror at *The Stardust Lounge* staring back at me, my own face, my own reflection, lost in the glimmering tendrils of the spinning glass globe, the pen, waiting at my fingertips, the bar-napkin, an inch away, the hand, touching my shoulder, pressing on me with a touch that was somehow an imperious grip, meant to last, meant to leave me branded with red impressions, finger-marks, baked into my skin.

Who was she? Who was the woman who wielded that gripping hand? Why was she touching my shoulder? Why was she picking me out from the crowd of dancers, from the boys in the band? Was she meaning to, attempting to, possess me? *Was she the woman in the mirror, disguised as a scarlet guitar, bloody red tresses hanging down over her shoulders as she was pinioned to a guitar stand, a severed head, a lover gone mad with the jealousy of ownership?*

It was summertime and we wanted to go to the beach.

I wanted to make an expedition of it, so I selected Crane's Beach in Ipswich, knowing it to be a secluded beach without amusements, sort of the antithesis of Revere Beach. I got a car at the Low-Budget Car Rental on Boylston Street behind Fenway Park.

I had been home to Spicket Falls and seen my little brother and sister. Given my uncle's death in Pennsylvania, and the rupture between me and Roseann, in the aftermath of all that, I realized I'd been neglecting Jack and Jill, how much, how heartlessly, I'd been neglecting my own flesh and blood. So I thought this would be a good way to start to get Sheila to see me as not just an unattached, free-floating student-type who read books and hung out in libraries, but a person who had a family. Just as she did. After all, she had begun to bring me into her family circle.

And, too, there was the emptiness, the black hole, of the loss of a special kinship with a person, a first cousin, who had once filled my life and longings with the image of her face.

Jack and Jill were delighted to meet Sheila. They thought she was neat. They were thrilled to spend a beautiful summer Sunday at a quiet beach, just the four of us. Sheila couldn't have been more relaxed and outgoing with them. It reminded me of that side of her I'd glimpsed in the lamplight at her sister Mary's in Brighton; the side that embraced children with a shower of love and acceptance, the side that let out, into the light, the bright, dazzling summer light, the child in herself, that barefoot girl running through the fields.

Not so with my mother.

I hadn't thought of her. My objective that weekend was to have a good time in the company of my little brother and sister and Sheila, the girl I secretly loved. We got to the fieldstone house in Spicket Falls early in the day, I raced in to pick up the kids, pulling Sheila in the back door by the hand, quickly introduced my mother to her, and we were gone.

My mother had taken the trouble to make an elaborate show of packing beach-blankets and a wicker-hamper of sandwiches wrapped in wax-paper, a beach-ball, and a collapsible beach-umbrella, and I was out the door again in a minute-and-a-half, Sheila crying, "Cheerio, now, it was grand to meet you!"

That evening, when I dropped off the kids, I left Sheila outside in the car with the engine running.

Before I could escape again, my mother took me aside, and said, "Don't ever bring that whore into my house again."

That was unfortunate.

My face went dark with a rush of blood and I turned on my heel and left my mother standing there.

Of course, it bothered me. Of course, I was wounded. Of course, I was shattered. *But I couldn't tell Sheila.*

We drove back to Boston and I was silent. Luckily, she took no notice and chattered away happily about how much fun, or 'great craic,' as she put it, we'd had, what a wonderful day, how charming the kids were, what great weather, "nothing like back home in Belmullet, that's the beach we go to, you know, on the Atlantic Ocean it is, just the other side of us today!" Laughing at the incongruity.

By the time we got home to Queensberry Street, it became apparent that Sheila had gotten quite a severe sun-burn. Those beautiful freckles on the back of her shoulders that I liked to kiss, one by one, were fiery to the touch. I couldn't go near her for a week.

Saved. I could go away and sulk over my mother's inexplicable attitude, *that word* that stuck to my hide like a burr beneath a horse's blanket.

Chapter 37

A Shot at the Window

As time went on, it became 'time-overdue' to meet Sheila's sister Bridie, in Jamaica Plain, and, her aunts, and uncle, in Somerville.

To my utter surprise, as the only measure I had to go by was her sister Mary's husband Tom, from Headford, County Galway—Bridie's husband turned out to be an Italian from the North End of Boston named Vito. Vito Liguriano.

And a drink of Campari he was. I had to look up at him as I shook his hand in consternation. We adjourned delightedly to the front room for guy-talk as I explained how much we had in common, my mother having been born on Prince Street, in the North End.

I was not such a hit with Bridie. Again, I was completely baffled to find that this sister had lost her Irish accent altogether and converted, amazingly, to Jamaica-Plain-housewife. I wondered how and why. That certainly hadn't happened with Sheila or Mary. Bridie was pregnant with her first, and perhaps that accounted for her cool reception of me. Or could she have had some sort of visceral reaction—the way my mother seemed to have had. You would never find out from Sheila, or Bridie herself.

Vito told me he'd been in the Navy. So had my Dad. Vito told me that he was set to become an electrician, licensed, just like his sister-in-law's husband from Galway, Tom Moran. It was Tom Moran, Vito explained, who had turned him on to the benefits of membership in the IBEW.

It occurred to me, as I was sitting there thinking, that it appeared that both Sheila and I were seeking, in equal measure, the approval of our families, and their blessings on our coming together as a couple.

And I wondered at that.

Was it that we could not stand on our own feet, confident in our own powers of taste and selection and assessment of a companion? Or was it some deeply embedded craving for approval—an approval that I, and she, had never gotten, at home, in our childhoods? I could speak for myself, but how would I ever know about Sheila?

And Bridie—was she being judgmental about *me*—or was she judging her sister Sheila?

I was delighted to meet Aunt Terry, Aunt Ann, and Uncle Nonie, in Somerville. The contrast with sister Bridie was immediate. They were sociable and welcoming, definitely non-censorious. They were thoroughly Americanized, as I might have expected. They had been here since 1935, and they were never going back. In truth, they had never gone back, not even once, in all that time. In many ways, they reminded me of my own grandfather and grandmother—the same could have been said of them.

And Sheila's aunts and uncle certainly met with my preconceived stereotype of the lace-curtain Irish, right down to the doilies on the back of the cushioned seats in the parlor. Sheila's aunts, her mother's sisters, were delighted with me. They seemed to be happy for Sheila that she had found at last a lad of her own.

Unlike their other niece, Bridie, the aunts had not abandoned their Irish accents, in spite of their assimilation. And Sheila's Uncle, Anthony 'Nonie' Loftus, was the unmarried, bachelor brother who had always lived at home with his sisters—exactly as had my own Uncle Augie.

Perhaps I was becoming too comfortable in the midst of Sheila's cosseting and coddling Irish family. Perhaps Sheila was not the only one who was a long way from home. I just felt when I was at the aunts' in Somerville—that I belonged there. That I fit in.

The one who Sheila obviously took after, in this household, was her spinster Aunt, Ann Loftus, whose profession was nursing. Aunt Ann, though very conventional, had a touch of the zaniness about her. From time to time she issued forth with a comment or opinion that caused either laughter or shock, and a definite raised eyebrow from her sister Theresa.

Aunt Terry, as Sheila called her, and her husband John Geraghty, were the mildest of couples. I don't think I heard a single word from John the whole time I was in his family's midst. He must have perforce to be quite a tolerant and recessive person to preside over a household with no less than three people related to him by marriage, two of whom contributed to the mortgage payments. I did, however, see him get up and walk out of the room on occasion.

Aunt Terry was the warmest of housewives, a woman who set about busying herself to see to the visitor's comfort, and full plate of powdery, bland cookies: 'biscuits,' she called them; and of course, she served tea, in her house, as was only proper, not coffee. "Milk and sugar? One or two?" she would inquire as she wielded decorously the sugar-cube tongs. It might have been only my imagination, but I thought that Aunt Terry was quite pleased to see that niece Sheila was after all not destined to take after her own sister Ann and become an old maid.

Sheila's cousin, Charlie Geraghty, was a student at Harvard, in pre-Law. He was the son of Aunt Terry and Uncle John Geraghty. I could sit there and drink tea and eat vanilla cookies all day, and converse with Nonie, John (who remained steadfastly noncommittal) and Charlie on every topic under the sun, from American politics to Irish history, while the girls in the kitchen caught up on all the latest, puffing away on Marlboros and Newports. Even Aunt Ann, who was a nurse, and should have known better, smoked like a proverbial turf fire.

Charlie Geraghty told me about a teach-in scheduled for August at Harvard. Yes, I had noticed the postings at Lamont, on the bulletin board. To be held at Memorial Hall. Open to the public. *'The Lessons of French Indochina.'* Yes, I did think I would go.

I had begun to write. Scribblings, which I called poems. I showed them to no-one. I despaired of ever having any chance of measuring up to the standards of the poets of the Norton Anthology. I had discovered Kenneth Patchen. I picked up a copy of *The Love Poems of Kenneth Patchen* at Boylston Books, across from the Pru, for a buck: it was in the City Lights series of Pocket Poets. I sat up in bed with Sheila reading them to her. I wondered if I might ever write anything as good as a

Patchen love-lyric. I wondered if I might ever write anything good enough to be accepted by *The Stylus,* the student literary magazine at Boston College.

Sheila and I started our own personal tradition of my reading aloud to her as we sat up in bed together. It did wonders for my sense of shared intimacy. I laughed and said I hoped she didn't expect me to read my psychology textbook to her. But she thought she should get some benefit from my college education. I was terribly excited about my junior year coming up. I was going to take two semesters of Shakespeare with the world-renowned Dr Duhamel. The Metaphysical Poets with Professor Hughes. And—I was going to take Creative Writing, with one of my electives, and the teacher was going to be none other than the well-known, highly-regarded Irish short-story writer Seán Ó Faoláin. I was reading Conrad's *The Secret Sharer* to Sheila and explaining it to her, diagramming it, exactly the way I had had it presented to me in class. She said she thought I could be a good teacher, very good. I told her I had simply memorized what my teacher had told our class. She said that was very clever of me, that she could never have done that. I asked her why she didn't go to college herself. She said she was only a graduate of Gortnor Abbey in Mayo. I said why would that disqualify you? She said, "I might do, go to college, that is, we'll see." I tried to encourage her but she didn't seem too keen, and she changed the subject.

Just then there was a loud sound, very like a gunshot, or a car-backfire, but awfully close, just outside Sheila's bedroom window. There was a cry and the sound of feet running up the driveway just outside the bedroom wall. I got up and went to look out the windows. I told Sheila, "Stay back." As I looked out over the parking lot under her back windows, I couldn't see anything. I said, "Must've been a car back-firing. Don't be alarmed."

We must have been busy having sex, or reading out loud, or having sex while reading out loud, or something, and then falling deeply and satisfyingly into the sleep of innocent babes, because we heard nothing the rest of the night.

The next morning it was all over the Boston papers that the Winter Hill Gang had carried out a mob assassination on Queensberry Street in the Back Bay.

The victim had run down a driveway to try to get away, but had been caught in the back of a building.

We were sitting out in front of 104 on the low steps, the next night. Sheila didn't want to stay inside of the apartment. "I'm frightened. What if they come back?"

"They won't come back."

"What if they saw you looking out the window at them? They might want to eliminate any witnesses."

I sighed. "We'll get you out of here. We'll find you another place. You've seen too many episodes of *N.Y.P.D.*"

"I'm sick and tired of the sisters from Kerry anyway. They're oaf-ish."

"Can you stay here tonight at least?"

"I can't. I wouldn't sleep a wink."

"Come over to my place then."

"No. I don't like your roommates."

"I don't blame you. They're oaf-ish, too."

"I'll go to Mary's in Brighton."

"I hate to leave you."

"Well, walk me to Kenmore Square, so."

"I'll go with you to Mary's."

"No, you must go home. You have to study. I'll be all right at my sister's."

Chapter 38

A Time to Every Purpose

My summer-long campaign to change the mind of the United States Army had ended in failure. I went to see Sgt Ryan at the ROTC offices one last time.

"This isn't fair. I'm trying to get in and they won't let me. They made a mistake and they won't admit it. I've submitted all kinds of documentation from my own doctor, Sergeant, you know that, it was at your request, and—."

"Look," said Sgt Ryan, who by this time hated seeing my face in the door, "I'll tell you what I'm gonna do for you. As long as you can't go in as an officer, I'm willing to write a letter to your draft board in Spicket Falls and get you classified as 1-Y. That way, you can never be drafted as just an enlisted man. Fair enough?"

I gave up.

I had never even contemplated such a thing might be possible. I certainly wasn't doing this last desperate pleading encounter with the Sergeant so that I could get out of the draft.

But now it was official. The United States Army had rejected me.

Well, I was going to hold it against them. The United States Army had just recruited another student for the Anti-Vietnam War crusade.

The depth of my anger at The Establishment—my new pet word–was suddenly profound, but what I would not admit, to myself, was the depth of my hurt.

That I could be rejected by anyone for anything I went for was inconceivable to me. Hadn't I always been a straight-A student? Hadn't I always gotten everything I wanted?

And yet, Molly Jones had rejected me. Harvard University, too. Hadn't my mother, just lately, rejected my choice of the love in my life?

But it was so much easier to push on and confront the immediate crises of everyday life, namely, finding a new apartment for Sheila, than to look deeply into myself and find self-doubt and self-absorption and self-recrimination lurking there in an oily puddle.

I definitely wanted Sheila to decide on moving into an apartment with me. She had her job, I had my summer savings, we could manage, together, and end up better off, than if we were apart. And I was fed up with my own oaf-ish roommates at 1387 Comm Ave. Rousseau and Nader were leftovers from Penney High back in Spicket Falls, and the roguish charm and hoodlum reputations which long ago had initially drawn me into their orbit, were now like wings on a horse, a thing of the mythological past.

But as to our living together, Sheila wouldn't hear of it.

It was the last day at 104 Queensberry Street, and we were sitting on the low steps out front, saying our farewells to the place which had brought us so much happiness. Sheila's modest belongings, her little treasures, the big white teddy-bear I had bought her, were piled in plastic bags on the steps beside us. The bear seemed to nudge me over so that our shoulders touched.

"I'm going to miss the launderette right next door to us," said Sheila, her lower lip trembling as she was on the verge of tears.

"You know I love you," I said, "don't you?"

She turned towards me and we were so close that our foreheads touched. Her magnificent dark hair fell down around her hazel eyes. She blinked back the tears and looked at me sadly, but in deadly earnest seriousness. "Time enough for that when we're old and decrepit," said Sheila to me. "Now, when we're young and foolish, is the time to be easy."

Chapter 39

Pinky and Jeanie

Sheila found her new place through an ad in the 'Roommates Wanted' section of *The Phoenix*. I went with her to No.4 Westbourne Terrace, in Brookline, off Beacon Street, near Cleveland Circle. There we met a delightful young lady named Pinky, with whom Sheila hit it off immediately.

Pinky La Bianca was a bubbly bleach-blonde, a sweet-natured, gabby, fun-loving Italian girl from Torrington, Connecticut, a refugee from UConn, transplanted to Boston after having dropped out of school.

She was such a contrast from Sheila's old roommates. And certainly Pinky had never met anyone like Sheila. They were light and dark, Irish and American, electrically magnetic polar opposites. No longer would Sheila have to put up with county rivalries and country resentments from the West of Ireland. Pinky La Bianca wasn't about to call her a 'Culchie from Kiltimagh' behind her back. I liked Pinky because she was Italian, or Italian-American, like me (my lover had made me conscious of the distinction.) Sheila liked her because, unlike me, Pinky was girlfriend material. The first thing they planned to do was to go shopping together. And in this, it was the foreigner, Sheila Blake, who had been in Boston now for two years, who could show around the American, the newly-arrived Pinky La Bianca, to whom Boston was the first big city she'd encountered, Hartford being too small and provincial to qualify. It was a match made on Newbury Street.

I had meanwhile been making changes myself. I teamed up with a good friend from BC, Victor Blanchette, from Woburn, an out-of-towner, like me, who finally wanted to be living in town, closer to campus. It was the same transition I'd gone through two years earlier, and I liked Victor well enough to want to help him. We made the deal one day when we were studying together at Bapst Library. Vic was no scholar, but he liked to pal around with me because he said he admired my grasp of all things literary. He knew how to flatter me. The previous spring we had ventured to go see a play together, downtown at *The Wilbur Theater*, a drama called *A View From the Bridge*, by Arthur Miller.

I wanted to see this play because it featured a plot about immigrants in the 1950s in the Italian enclave of Red Hook, in Brooklyn, under the Bridge. It was a touring company from Off-Broadway in New York that brought this revival of a ten-year-old play to *The Wilbur*. It was directed by Ulu Grosbard, with the assistant director a then-unknown Dustin Hoffman.

I didn't like the play. I thought it was a hatchet-job, that Miller got the Italians all wrong. A local guy has an incestuous obsession with his orphaned niece. She's growing up and wants to wear high heels, but he forbids it. A cousin from Italy arrives, an illegal immigrant, with big dreams, and the girl falls for him. Her domineering uncle, at the turning point, kisses him full on the lips, to try to prove to the girl that the cousin is a homosexual who only wants to marry her so that he can stay in the country.

The kiss on stage horrified me. I was afraid Victor Blanchette would completely misinterpret why I had brought him to see this play.

I needn't have worried. Later, leaving, discussing the play, I could see that Victor was too stalwartly non-literary to get anything at all out of this production. I guess that's why I liked him. He was a typical BC boy who was just trying to get through school on gut courses and mistakenly took a literature survey. And he was big enough to be my bodyguard. I had found my replacement for Nader and Rousseau.

Victor and I had found an apartment in a modern-looking brick dwelling at the very peak of Parker Hill Ave in the Mission Hill neighborhood, flanking Brigham Circle. A Jewish kid from BU named Lewis Goldberg came in with us to occupy the third bedroom.

I had also taken on a new job, out at Logan Airport, loading aircraft for the *Flying Tigers* freight line. It was building me up because we had to load 80-lb boxes of ITT cable into the crawl space under the main deck in the belly of the Lockheed Electra prop-jets that the *Flying Tigers* line used in their fleet. So five nights a week I was taking the subway out to the airport to work the 4 to 11 shift.

I needed the pay-hike. I wanted to buy things for Sheila, not just a teddy bear. I knew it was going to cut down on my time at Lamont Library, but I was going into my junior year now, and coasting through Shakespeare and the Metaphysical Poets. I didn't even bother to take notes in Dr Duhamel's class. He was such a dynamic and mind-blowing teacher that all you had to do was sit there and watch him stride back and forth in front of the class, dramatizing, impersonating and undressing the plays. You didn't want to take notes because it would interrupt the show.

My classes with Seán Ó Faoláin were confirming, perhaps, reinforcing, my choice of bed-partner in Sheila. Here was a veteran of the 1920s IRA wars with the Black and Tans who made Irish history come alive before your very eyes. I raced to the bookstore to acquire all his short stories and I sat up in bed with Sheila at her new apartment reading them out loud to her, while she corrected my imitation Irish-accent on the dialogue parts. The sub-plot of the Miller play, where he accuses the illegal immigrant cousin of using marriage to his niece as simply a maneuver to stay in the country, was completely lost on me, as far as myself and Sheila were concerned. I was more and more in love with her with every day going by. As I was getting home on the streetcar so late from work at the airport, most of the time I didn't even bother to go to the apartment I was paying for over in Mission Hill. I was too tired to walk all the way up Parker Hill Ave to the top. It was so much easier to take the Beacon Street line out to Brookline and end up falling into Sheila's arms for a good, healthy sleep. And love in the morning.

Somebody new had come into our lives. It was Jeanie Anderson, from UConn. She was Pinky La Bianca's best friend from school. She came up to Boston and moved in to occupy the third bedroom at No. 4 Westbourne Terrace.

Jeanie was a tall, statuesque young woman who looked as if she had just stepped off the cover of *Vogue*. She was the female equivalent of my friends Rousseau and Nader, those self-righteous, self-absorbed, self-styled playboys whose only interest in women was to bed them and not wed them. Jeanie Anderson applied the identical logic to her boyfriends. She was coming to Boston to play the field and the field was going to be so much bigger and more exciting than the UConn campus, where she had literally used up the best and thrown away the rest. And her girlfriend Pinky needed her.

The reason, which we were not long in finding out, was that Pinky La Bianca was pregnant.

Chapter 40

What's a Petrovich?

Pregnant and unmarried, that was Pinky, and not very hopeful of being married, in the end, by the father of her child, who was one Roger Somerset, who would arrive at Westbourne Terrace each Saturday in his MG, after driving up from UConn to spend the week-end.

Roger Somerset had a matron of a mother who evidently disapproved of little Pinky La Bianca from Torrington. Roger lived at home with his mother, who was divorced from his father, in a substantial Colonial in the aristocratic Hartford suburb of Farmington, and Mrs Somerset, a scion of the Connecticut Bradleys, was very attached to young Roger. Roger Somerset was the first true dyed-in-the-wool Yankee I had met who was a mama's boy.

The first thing Roger would do when he landed on a Saturday was to call his mother to let her know he had gotten there safely. He called her 'Yes, dear,' on the phone. Roger was twenty years old and he had the physique of a country club member of 45 who had pulled his chair up to the platter of hors-d'ouerves somewhat frequently. He was pleasantly and politely bland. He was attentive to Pinky. While he was there. But then he was gone, in his MG, and, as she grew plumper and more morning-sick, Pinky's bubbly-ness was dissipating into a sad, chronic, hopeless despondency.

"I'm going to lose him because I'm becoming such a frowse." As time went by, after Roger's departure each Sunday late-afternoon, in his MG, the rest of us would spend the week trying to cheer up poor Pinky.

Meanwhile, Jeanie Anderson would be carrying on her latest affair behind the closed door of her bedroom at the back.

Each morning we would all meet at the kitchen table. Sheila and I would emerge from behind the door of her room. Pinky would usually be cooking breakfast for everyone. Sometimes it would be Jeanie, or even me. Sheila claimed she didn't know how to boil water because the woman in the village who had the recipe died. Everyone laughed and Sheila was permanently exempted from cooking any meals. Sheila would grab an English muffin or Boston Cream and be off to work at Liberty Mutual. Jeanie would take a lift from her latest beau downtown to her job behind the desk at the Ritz-Carlton. That would leave me to sit with Pinky until it was time for my first class.

Pinky wasn't working. Roger Somerset was supporting her through her time of trial. Or I should say Roger's mother. Or maybe Roger's trust fund. I really had no idea, but I knew that Roger was planning never to work at all, or, if that failed, becoming a lawyer. I was fond of Pinky. I thought it was terrible what she was going through. I tried to be supportive, but, privately, I was saying to Sheila every night, "Poor Pinky. Could you ever see yourself an unwed mother, Sheila? How can Roger Somerset be such an insensitive bastard? What's going to happen to Pinky, and the baby, when the baby comes?"

Sheila's approach to helping Pinky was altogether opposite mine. Instead of the earnest, sympathetic male friend, Sheila was playing the dodgy Irish girlfriend. Her entire objective was to make Pinky laugh. "Pinky, he's a dead sod, that one, that Roger. Why don't you tell him just to eff off once and for all. He's as thick as shite and only half as handy. He's as useless as a member of the Labor Party in a London hoor-house. You couldn't light a fire off him if he gave a blue fart and you with the match in your cupped hands. If I were you, the next time he tries his tricks, I'd just tell him, straight off, why don't you go and Roger yourself in the corner?"

She never failed to crack up Pinky.

"There. That's better. Isn't laughter the best medicine in the end? Be sure, now, you don't break your face."

Sheila made a running joke out of my name. Soon, every time I made an appearance, one or another of them, Jeanie, Pinky, or Sheila, would stop in the middle of the floor, a glass in one hand and a milk carton in the other, or holding a basket of laundry, or carrying a bowl of peeled potatoes, and ask me, idiotically, with head cocked to one side, and eyes crossed, "What's a Petrovich?"

They would never fail to erupt into peals of hilarity, as I stood there sheepishly. "No, it's not an extinct reptile."

Chapter 41

Life Doesn't Come in a Bottle

This Petrovich was trying mightily to break into print in *The Stylus* and get at least one poem accepted before graduation. This Petrovich was becoming enthralled with the colors and hues of Debussy's impressionistic palate in Dr Peloquin's Music Appreciation course. This young apprentice scribbler Petrovich was devouring the stories in Hemingway's *In Our Time* and churning out 50-page masterpieces of his own time to turn into a bemused Seán Proinsias Ó Faoláin as classroom assignments in creative writing. This young cautious and conservative product of the Eisenhower Fifties Petrovich was imbibing the mother's milk of left-wing pacifism and turning rapidly into a contentious Sixties alienated existentialist proto-rebel. San Francisco was beckoning and *Sgt Pepper's Lonely Hearts Club Band* was embarking on the summer of Love. I was working too hard out at *Flying Tigers Lines* to pass up the chance to shoplift a steak or two or some nice thick pork-chops at the Star Market on Beacon Street. It was the era of the poor student struggling to survive in the American arena of excess and waste. Wasn't

I entitled to a free lunch like everybody else? Why did I have to pay for that book when I could just slip it into my pocket? Everywhere I looked around me, the world was wrong, and it started with the President Johnsons and didn't end until it reached all the way over to the Roger Somersets.

One Saturday when I came home from the library to Westbourne Terrace expecting to relax a little and find some peace and quiet in the company of my beloved Sheila Blake, instead I stumbled into an emergency when I found Pinky and Jeanie and Roger at their wits' end trying to cope with a deranged Sheila, who was, evidently, flipping out.

I came in the door hearing a commotion in our bedroom, hers and mine, the first one on the right after the parlor, and I found them sweating and shouting trying to hold her down on our bed. She was writhing and thrashing, uttering imprecations and curses, and refusing to be controlled. I looked desperately at Pinky for some explanation. Pinky said, "She keeps saying her father's dying in Ireland, she knows it, and she can't reach him."

I leaned over close to her face. "Sheila, if you don't stop this, I'm going to have to get you to a hospital."

She knew it was me. "No! No!" she cried. "Don't do that. I'll stop. I'll be good."

But she didn't.

I rushed out to the parlor and called her sister Bridie in Jamaica Plain on the phone.

"Bridie, have you had any news of your parents at home?"

"No. Why?"

"Nevermind."

I went back and told Sheila, "Bridie says no news of your dad and mum, and that's to be taken as no news is good news."

"Ah, ye fookin' gobshite, it's nothin' to do with Mammy, it's me Da's dyin'!"

She started in then threatening to throw herself out the window if we didn't let her up, and I said, beside myself, "Roger, can I use your car?"

It took the four of us, one on each arm and leg, to carry her out of the apartment, through the front door, and down the long steps of Westbourne Terrace to the MG parked at the curb of the circular drive. It took all of our combined might to get her jammed into the tiny backseat space, designed only to fit small children and camera-bags, as she struggled against us. Jeanie Anderson climbed into the passenger seat to hold her down, and Roger got the convertible top up and fastened as I started it up.

We got to the front door of St Elizabeth's Emergency Room in Brighton, Jeanie and I, Pinky and Roger pulling up in a taxi, and by that time, Sheila had calmed down enough for Jeanie and I to walk her inside through the automatic doors, holding onto one arm each. At least she was helping us by using the power of her own legs. But a look of utter panic came over her and she sagged in our arms as she realized we had really got her to the hospital and she was about to face a doctor.

"No, no, I'm all right, now, you can take me home now, please don't make me."

There was such a desperate pleading look on her face that we took pity on her, and we brought her back to the apartment.

Afterwards, I said to Pinky, "It was like turning off a switch. She got inside the doors and she was herself again." I looked at Jeanie, and Jeanie nodded.

The four of us surrounded Sheila on the sofa, on both sides, Roger and me in front of her on the coffee table. She slouched back, exhausted, absolutely drained. Pinky went and turned the TV on, low, just to restore some sense of normalcy to all of us after going through all this.

Gradually, Sheila fell into a deep sleep, and we picked her up and put her to bed.

The phone rang and it was her sister Mary calling.

"No, no," I said, "everything's all right." To myself I was saying, *I should have called Mary—why did I ever call Bridie?* "Is everything fine at home, Mary?"

When I said 'at home,' it was understood I meant in Ireland. "Yes, yes. Is everything fine here?"

"Yes, yes."

I held Sheila close all through the night, but she was as limp as a dishrag.

The next morning was Sunday and I crept out to the kitchen to find Pinky sitting at the table. Sheila had been sleeping the sleep of the dead all night. Only then did it occur to me that she might have passed out rather than simply fallen asleep. I looked blankly at Pinky from the middle of this troubling thought.

"Look what I found," she said, as she turned to open the door under the sink. She pulled out a fifth of vodka, three-quarters empty.

"Do you think that was it?"

"What else could it be?"

"Christ—I thought she was having a full-scale nervous breakdown. Pinky, where were you when all this was happening?"

"The three of us were out doing the groceries for the week and we found her raving, like you saw her, when we got back,

Nick. Then you walked in the door, thank God. She wouldn't listen to us."

I took this episode as testimony of Sheila's tenacious attachment to her home, her past, her family and her roots. And her mother and father. Especially her father. He was the one she had feared was dying.

But I was shaken to my foundations. What did I know of the immigrant soul? Had I ever been exiled? Had I ever lost my country?

I wondered what it was about Ireland that made so many of her sons and daughters so fiercely bonded to her soil and her spirit that eruptions like this could come out of the deep mountain of their love of home?

I didn't blame Sheila for what had happened. I didn't blame it on the bottle of vodka. That was a symptom, not a cause. All this time I had known her, Sheila Blake had been masquerading as one thing and another. To begin with, right from the start, as an English person. As a heedless young rebellious girl, just out for 'the craic.' As a file clerk in a standardized American insurance office. As a dutiful sister who minded the child so the sister and brother-in-law could have a night out. As the girlfriend of a college boy.

Yes, what about that last one?

Had I ever really known Sheila Blake? Would I ever?

A couple of Saturdays later we were waiting at a streetcar stop outside BU; Sheila looked up at me, with her chin on my chest. "I must go home, for a fortnight, at least. Will you miss me, if I do?"

If I had ever doubted that I loved her, if I had ever asked myself whether my feelings were real and lasting, honest and true, and not some kind of self-deception, some fool's gold, some counterfeit coin, in that moment, I doubted no more. The awful thought of losing her felt like tremors beneath the surface of the earth. "Are you coming back to me?" I whispered.

She was whispering, too, lifting her chin, putting her cheek next to mine, breathing into my ear. "If I come back, Nicky—I'm not coming back unless you're going to marry me."

"Sheila, you know how I feel about you. I love you. So—if you love me, you'll come back to me."

"No, Nick. I have to know now."

So it was not enough that I loved her. Sheila needed something more. A promise. A commitment.

Yet she had never said to me those words I longed to hear.

I held her close to me, there, at that streetcar stop, outside BU, and I stroked her silky, long raven hair. "Listen, my love. If you come back to me, I will marry you. Because then I will know that you love me."

Chapter 42

The Summer of '68

She was gone, and I might never see her again. I had vowed that this time was going to be different. I was not going to let the girl get away this time, as I did with Molly Jones. I was not going to put myself through the agony of feeling the loss of a special closeness with my cousin Roseann, through my own stupidity, again. Yet, I was powerless, against the call of home, the pull of *Ireland,* to keep Sheila Blake with me. *'If I come back,'* she'd said. *If.* To overcome that *If* would take a very large and powerful desire, a desire bigger than the need to be home again, to be with the 'old ones' again. Sheila's love for *me* would have to be that large, that 'grand.' It was me against a whole country. It was me against history and culture and inclination. It was me against a childhood among her own flesh and blood. It was me against a permanent separation from her mother. It was me against the thought of never seeing her father again.

And what did I know of Sheila's love for her 'Da,' as she called him—or his love of her? If my cousin Roseann could stop talking to me, could have a permanent rupture with me, could freeze me out of her life, because of a face I made at her father's graveside, what in the world would Sheila be like if she ever lost her Da? The thought scared me. What did I know about a Daddy's girl? About as much as I knew about a mother's love for her son, that's what.

I sat there gazing at the snapshot in my wallet. In this photo, which I had taken of her, Sheila Blake was dressed in a red tartan outfit from a Newbury Street boutique called *No Rest for Bridget*. She was posing for the camera, big smile breaking into a laugh, arms out, like balancing wings, the ailerons of her hands turned palm upward, open to the sky, black pocket book dangling from one wrist; on her head, matching her jacket and mini-skirt, a red tartan pillbox hat; lithe and supple knee-high black leather boots, and the sinuous, long dark silken hair cascading over her shoulders. *I wanted her back. God help me, but I wanted her back.*

After two weeks of staring at the telephone that would not ring; after a 'fortnight,' as Sheila would have said, of abandoning her bedroom on Westbourne Terrace in favor of returning to my own place on Parker Hill Ave. (I could not bear sleeping in 'our bed' without her); after persuading myself that I would never see her again (after all, what hope was there of receiving a letter from her? the time, as yet, had been too short)(and if she could not write, why would she not telephone, to tell me she was thinking of me, to say that she missed me? People made transatlantic calls!) After going back and forth interminably, wondering why she had to leave at all, wondering most of all, why she just couldn't say the words; and not knowing why that was, resigning myself to never knowing why, realizing that the only way I would ever know would be if Sheila came back to me—the phone rang. "Sheila? Oh—thank God."

"Nick, get hold of yourself," she told me. Then my Sheila lowered her voice to a breathless, teasing, intimate whisper. "You knew I'd be back."

The wedding was arranged for a Saturday, August the 3rd, 1968.

Sheila Blake and I were to be married at St Gabriel's Monastery in Brighton. The day arrived and I found myself on a high hill with all of Boston spread out below the cliff at my feet, a high blue unclouded sky up above. It was the perfect day and the perfect setting for a wedding.

Pinky La Bianca was Sheila's Maid of Honor. Jeanie Anderson was a bridesmaid along with Ann-Marie from Liberty Mutual and Sheila's two sisters, Mary and Bridie. The ex-'flatmates,' as Sheila called them, the two blond siblings from Kerry, Imelda and Martina, were nowhere to be seen. Sheila's sister Mary's child, Mary-Jane, just beginning to walk, was an adorable flower-girl. All my cousins and aunts and uncles were invited.

Two weeks previously Sheila and I and all the other guests, from my side of the family, anyway, had attended a wedding at Sacred Heart on Mt Auburn Street in Watertown, in which my cousin Tony Laverna, the other graduate of Boston College in our family, was married to a Scottish lass named Loretta Cunningham, a nurse who came from Glasgow. Tony's bride Loretta had come out here recruited by Sancta Maria Hospital in Cambridge.

My mother, Gerry Petrovich, was invited, of course, to both weddings. At first, she let it be known to me that she was not coming to mine, but then, on the day itself, she showed up in all her finery, wearing a flamingo-pink designer-hat glowing with a flowering profusion of synthetic pink tendrils that looked as if they'd been baked in the Dryer Room on the 5th floor of Malden Mills: the mother of the bridegroom recalling her own youthful days as a maven of fashion.

My mother had let herself be persuaded to attend by her sister, Mary Laverna, during the course of her own son's wedding to Loretta Cunningham, and only after putting up a show of resistance.

My father arrived looking dapper in lemon-yellow slacks, a white coat, a pink carnation, and a red bow-tie. It made me think of him and his brother Alek, the coal-miners, who always got slicked up like legitimate gentlemen when they were going out to a dance. It was saddening to me to think that neither Uncle Alek nor Uncle Augie had survived to see this day come for me.

But then, Sheila's parents, who were still with us, had stayed home in Ireland, and the bride was to be given away by her brother-in-law from Galway, Tom Moran.

Our wedding was scheduled for 11 AM sharp that Saturday morning. Eleven-oh-five came and I was waiting at the altar, peering all the way down the aisle to the open front doors of the church, which, from the interior, seemed a blinding splash of sunshine. I kept waiting for Sheila to emerge from the sunburst.

At eleven-ten the priest informed me that he had another wedding to perform at twelve.

I went down the aisle, having to pass my mother in the first aisle who gave me a grim look of *I told you so.*

Contrary to all custom, then, I was waiting outside in the sunshine on the top step of the church at eleven-fifteen, and I was worried to death.

I had taken a student loan out for a thousand dollars to pay for Sheila's wedding gown and the wedding reception for all the guests, once I found out the bank didn't monitor what you spent the money on.

We had gone shopping for Sheila's wedding gown together, along with Pinky and Jean.

Pinky had had her baby, a bouncing boy, which she named Roger, in the hope that Roger Somerset was going to make her legal. He did not do that, but he wasn't about to miss our wedding and a free meal at the Fenway Commonwealth Hotel, next door to BU on Comm Ave., where we were having the reception.

Jeanie was coming to the wedding stag. She had a blow-out with her latest beau the night before, and it was a shouting, crying, jaggedly emotional affair, our farewell to all the good times on Westbourne Terrace.

They were all standing there with me, on the top step, staring at the rows of automobiles in the parking area, all shined up by the guests who came to celebrate a wedding.

Pinky was just saying to me, "You think she's gonna show?"

I loved Pinky at that moment for her anxious sympathy. It was so like her. I felt so bad for her. Sheila and I both adored the baby Roger. Pinky had put him down with a nanny-service for this one day, just to be there for us. I was so angry at Roger Somerset.

Yet I myself was about to be doused, in front of all my guests, family and friends, too, in red and purple shame-faced embarrassment.

I could count on somebody like Vic Blanchette, or my cousin Linda, to buck me up, but I could hear in the back of my mind the hooting holler coming out of Benny Nader and

Dennis Rousseau, both of whom I'd invited, even though both of them had warned me not to marry Sheila as, they maintained, we fought like cats and dogs.

Then suddenly we saw a dark blur of automobile race over the top of the crest by the monastery-house, make a careening loop, and come to a squealing stop at the bottom of the steps.

In the back seat of Tom Moran's car, looking up at me, scarlet-in-the-temples, was my bride.

From the top step I watched Sheila climbing out in her tear-stained face and tear-stained veil, wearing the beautiful lace-bodiced ivory-white gown we'd found, and fell in love with, at Bonwit-Teller's on Newbury Street.

When she got to the top step, her hand shot out and gripped mine in a death-claw of emotion.

I would have to hold her up or she was going to collapse. "That brother-in-law of mine, he's as slow as Paddy's donkey, I could murder him!"

The story came tumbling out of her while Pinky, who had gotten some tissues out of the ever-prepared Jeanie's handbag, tried her best to dry Sheila's tears, and Jeanie with her brush and pencil from her makeup kit, tried to fix her eyes—those tender hazel eyes and long dark lashes which Sheila never needed to or bothered to apply eye-liner to, or anything else, except for this one, special day when she let them persuade her to make an exception.

And now her mascara was ruined and it was all Tom Moran's fault.

On the way to St Gabriel's, Tom had had a minor collision with an elderly Jewish man from Brookline, whom he softly rear-ended, a mere nudge, no more, at the stoplights at Comm Ave. and Chestnut Hill Ave.

The elderly Jewish man had insisted on blocking all the traffic to exchange insurance papers.

The bride was crying in the back seat. Passersby were stopping to sympathize and encourage her, saying things like, "Oh, what a beautiful bride! Such a pretty veil! Don't cry! Oh, my, she's late for her wedding, is that it? Yes, yes, I'd be crying, too, poor thing!"

And Sheila, with horns honking, and drivers desperately trying to pass them before the light changed again, in front of all the hand-wringing onlookers, was rolling down the window in the wilting August heat to call out to her brother-in-law, who was leaning over signing documents on the hood of the car, "Tom Moran, for the love of God! Would you ever hurry on!"

And so, Sheila and I, like Tony and Loretta, were married, in that summer of 1968, that summer following the Tet Offensive, that summer after Johnson told the nation that he could not and would not run for re-election.

In April, after the assassination of Martin Luther King on a balcony in Memphis, for the first time in my life I turned out for a public protest in the streets, that very night, when crowds gathered in the twilight for a memorial candlelight vigil on Boston Common.

In June, we lost another favorite son of Massachusetts, Bobby Kennedy, in a kitchen in Los Angeles, again, like his brother John, in a death by gunfire.

In July, and in August, Sheila and I, and Tony and Loretta, and all young, hopeful people the world over, from Paris to Plainville, all those who pursued their plans for the good life, in peace and in peril, were getting married; true believers, putting their faith in forever, they were stretching out grasping fingers to try to clutch, in a passing moment, a future for love, in a world gone permanently mad with death, war, violence and destruction.

Chapter 43

Snake in the Grass

Our honeymoon in a rented car began with a trip up the coast to Portsmouth, New Hampshire. Fortunately, Sheila had her regular two-weeks of paid summer vacation off from work at Liberty. We stayed the first night in a seaside motel, and then headed north to Conway.

"I'm sorry, it's not Bermuda, I know, it's not Hawaii, but I thought you might want to see something of the country you've never seen before, Sheila."

"I'll wager I've seen more of the country than you have, Mr Petrovich."

"How is that? Where have you ever been?"

"Have you never been to Nova Scotia?"

"When did you go to Nova Scotia?"

"I had a life before ever I met you, you know."

"Why did you go there?"

"Because they told me it was the nearest thing to home. And it did indeed remind me very much of Mayo and the West."

"And when did you go there?"

"When I had my holidays from Liberty Mutual. I went for a fortnight and it was lovely. The people are so much like the people at home."

I looked at her across the car seat as I was driving. "Why is it, Sheila Blake—I mean, Sheila Petrovich, sorry—why is it that I'm always finding out things about you that I never knew before?"

"Well, you wouldn't want to know everything, now would you? Where would be the mystery in that?"

In Conway, we went to a photography studio, looking to buy film. I had a new Kodak camera and I was set on memorializing our honeymoon. I pictured us as two prosperous oldsters in our dotage poring over our wedding pictures and honeymoon snapshots, reminiscing. We let ourselves in the glass door of the studio as no one seemed to be around. I wandered off gazing at easels while Sheila did the same on the other side of the room, which let in a great deal of light coming from floor-to-ceiling plate-glass walls. The photographer appeared, brushing aside a green curtain, emerging—from a dark room? He clearly did not notice me there at all. His eyes followed Sheila around the glass walls. He became very still and a slight smile of surprise crept over his countenance and he was careful not to make a noise that would disturb her, holding onto the green curtain so that it would not swish. He wished to watch her unbeknownst. Perhaps, being a photographer, he was a true voyeur. I went to the cash-register counter and made a noise on the glass case with the little box of 110 film. He came over behind the counter and his eyes never left her. He rang up the sale and completely ignored me while Sheila joined me at my side. The photographer said to her, "Have you ever posed to have your picture taken by professionals?"

"No," Sheila said, embarrassed.

The man handed her a business-card from a tiny vee-stand on the countertop. "Call me when you're ready to. I'd love to take your picture."

Outside, as we walked away on a wooden sidewalk, I burst into laughter, quite amazed at myself. I was taking the incident as an unprovoked, unrehearsed, absolute confirmation of the staggering beauty Sheila possessed, a thing of which she was completely unconscious. "Sheila, he saw you as a covergirl model or something."

"Oh, don't be ridiculous, Nicky."

"I swear! Did you see the look on his face?"

"I did. He was undressing me with his eyes. I'm certainly not taking my clothes off for him, or any man, to take my picture."

"But, honey, that's not the only kind of modeling they do. Did you ever consider that you could have a career for yourself in the pages of something like *Vogue* or *Mademoiselle?*"

"No, I have not." Sheila turned to face me squarely. "Let me tell you something, Mr. Petrovich. When I was a girl, my mother never wanted me to think I was pretty."

I suddenly knew why Sheila had left home.

"She said that a girl who thought she was pretty soon went on to knowing that she was pretty, so. And when that happened, she'd never be happy again."

I thought it was very sad that her mother had done that to her. But, knowing her sisters, knowing that Sheila was so different from them, knowing that she had said it was her mother she took after, I could see it. Her mother had been talking from her own experience, and what had happened to her, she wanted to save her daughter from.

The next day we were in Franconia Notch, and we took a side road, off the beaten path, in our rented car, and we came to an old stone wall, a relic of the seventeenth century, to be sure, the kind of stone wall that populated that part of the country, and populated, as well, the poems of Robert Frost. I wanted to stop and take a picture of Sheila sitting on the stone wall, "For our honeymoon album," I said. "You won't have to take your clothes off," I laughed.

Reluctantly, she posed for me, leaning her backside on the stone wall, feet on the ground, legs crossed at the ankles, arms crossed over her chest, a look of wicked promise on her pouty lips.

Suddenly, a very, very large black snake came tumbling over the stone wall, just at her hip.

Sheila shrieked and leapt into my arms, upsetting the Kodak caught by the strap around my neck. "Mother of God, did you see that—that—thing!"

I was crude enough to laugh at her. "Sheila!–what kind of a country girl are you?"

"There are no snakes in my country, I'll have you know. Oh, can we ever, please, get back to the city? Snakes on the ground, snakes on the wall, snakes on two legs! Oh, it's horrid!"

Chapter 44

A Death in Vietnam

Back in the city, no sooner had we settled in to domestic bliss in a basement flat on Beacon Street near the Public Garden, following the honeymoon, than Tom Moran came looking for us on a Friday night.

"There's been a message, you see," said Tom "and I couldn't ring you up."

"Yes, Tom," said Sheila, "we're going to be here only three weeks—."

"Then we're headed for Rhode Island," said I, with bright anticipation.

"Is that the plan?" said Tom.

"—so there's no point in having a phone put in," Sheila continued.

"And we'd rather be alone, in any case," I added putting my arms around Sheila from behind, peeking at Tom with my chin on her shoulder.

"What's the big attraction in Rhode Island?" said Tom, amiably, ever curious, always on the point of a chat and a cup of tea.

"Narragansett Bay," I said, winking.

"Tom—the message?" said Sheila, who had no patience for the man.

Tom was just seating himself and he said, "Right—the message."

"I'm going to grad school, Tom." I said.

"We won't be seeing the two of you, then."

"Tom!" said Sheila.

"Yeah, what was so important you had to run down here?" I said.

"Well, I don't know, but, you see, you're to call your father."

"It couldn't wait?" I said, not relishing the prospect of my father unexpectedly intruding upon our life together.

"Apparently. But that was the only message—I know nothing more, only that I'm to tell you to call."

"Must be a phone booth around here somewhere," I said, releasing Sheila to head for our lone bedroom to look for change on top of the dresser. She followed me and blocked my exit, crossing her arms.

"I know, I know," I said, softly.

"Don't encourage him." Under her breath, eyebrows knit.

In the sitting room, I said, "Back in a flash," and dashed out the door and up the three steps to the parking lot, glimpsing Sheila through the basement window, looking furious at me.

I walked back from the phone booth on Beacon Street in a cloud of despondency, slowly, with my head down and my hands in my pockets.

I took the three steps down from the parking lot and entered the little flat. I had no idea what I was going to tell them, or how to put it.

"Tom," I said with a sigh, "would you take Sheila back with you, to your house?" And to Sheila I said, "It's just for tonight, honey, or maybe tomorrow night, too, I don't know. But I don't want to leave you here alone. I have to catch a bus back to Spicket Falls, tonight. I have to go to a wake tomorrow."

"What happened?" said Sheila, thinking the worst. I knew that she couldn't accept the idea of anyone dying, and I knew that she thought it was my mother.

I looked at her glumly. "Jimmy Dillard was killed in Vietnam. The wake is tomorrow. All the boys from the old neighborhood are gonna be there. I have to be there, too. I don't want to, but I have to. I'm lucky I found out in time. Can you forgive me, babe, just this once? I'll feel better knowing you're staying with your sister. I'll be back by Sunday, I promise. I just have to do this alone."

On the bus to Milltown I had plenty of time to be alone. There were other passengers but the bus was not filled. There were other passengers but they weren't going where I was going. Whatever they were doing on that bus, in their private universes, they weren't going to a destination filled with doubt, a date with recriminations, a rendezvous with death.

But wasn't that where we all were going? Wasn't I going there, too? Eventually. Not now. This wasn't supposed to be happening now. Jimmy was supposed to be coming home alive. Why was I going home alive, and he was coming home dead?

The war. The answer was: the war.

Every empty seat on that bus was occupied. By the ghost of Jimmy Dillard. Sitting next to my thoughts.

This wasn't supposed to happen. Jimmy Dillard wasn't supposed to be dead at 21. It was a preventable death. Why hadn't we prevented it?

Why hadn't we all done more to prevent this? Why had we all turned our backs on him, the kids in the neighborhood? We knew he had lost his father in the Korean War, we knew him as the only boy growing up in the neighborhood without a dad at home. Why weren't we better friends to him? Why did everybody leave him alone, to face his life alone? Why, in the cliquish days of Jenney High, when Jimmy drifted off to seek someone among the bikers and the hoods, anyone, to like him, to accept him, some gang where he fit in, some group where it was okay to stick your pack of butts on your shoulder under your tee-shirt sleeve, why didn't we go after him, to pull him back, to let him know we cared about him, and that he belonged with us?

Why hadn't I?

Instead, I had rejected him. I had pushed his face into the bricks and made him bleed. I had made him walk away, staggered by the thought that somebody he thought was his friend could do this to him.

So, at Jimmy's wake, I was overcome with guilt.

He had never spoken to me again, and I couldn't blame him. Indeed, I just wrote him off.

And now it was too late to tell him that I loved him. For that's what it was, love. Love between two sixth-grade boys who were lonely and needed a friend. Who reached out to each other in hope. Who reeled back from the rejection, the slap in the face, the blood on the cheek, the humiliation. *Which would never have stung so keenly, so deeply, if the love had not been there before it.*

How could I say to him now—*Jimmy, I'm sorry.*

I intended to hurt him that day, and I did. And he was hurt so badly that he never came back.

He never came back any more than his father had come back from Korea. He just kept going all the way to his own destruction. And who knew how much the loss of his father determined what happened to him? He must have grown up with stories his mother told him about his dad.

Maybe he worshipped his dad as a lost hero, someone to live up to, to emulate. In the same way that I did with my Uncle Augie, especially after he passed on. Why else, when it came to his time, did Jimmy join up? Was he trying to put the disaster of high school behind him? Trying to make something of himself?

And what about poor Jimmy's mother, Mrs Dillard? Imagine losing your husband in one war and your only son in the next . . .

The wake was held at the Dewhirst Funeral Home on Broadway in Spicket Falls. I walked in and the first thing I noticed was the Marine Honor Guard flanking the closed casket.

Mrs Dillard was seated alone in a straight-back chair off to the side. The room was full of flowers. I went to pay my respects to her, but she didn't recognize me. She seemed to be slumped, with her shoulders down, withdrawn into some interior place within herself, while her body stood in for her, performing ritual handshakes with strangers. I was thinking of the time she had Jimmy invite me over and she cooked a dinner of meat and potatoes with gravy for her son's friend, but clearly she did not remember that.

The Perrault brothers were there, Ronnie and Ray Robillard, Jimmy's next door neighbor, Bonnie Jo Mazzeo, the girl from across Glenwood Ave from Jimmy's back door, Carol Clapp, Steven Morelli, the son of Mario Morelli, Sharon McCoy, Frankie Fidelio and Jerry Ellsworth and Corinne and Brian Beauschene, all people I hadn't seen in years, but they remembered me, and asked about the wedding ring on my hand. "No one you would know," I said. "She's not from around here."

I didn't want to make small talk. I just wanted to be depressed and then get out of there. It was reminding me intensely of why I left Spicket Falls to begin with.

I asked Frankie Fidelio, "Why the Marines?"

"Jimmy was in the Navy. Oh—you didn't know?"

Immediately, I thought then, *he didn't want to die*—he was trying to avoid what happened to his dad in Korea. *For his mother's sake.*

"Frankie," I said, "how could he have got killed in Vietnam *in the Navy?*"

Frankie touched his forehead and lowered his voice yet again. We were huddled in a corner, both of us trying to make sure Mrs Dillard didn't notice us talking about her son or hear anything we were saying.

"Nick," said Frankie, out of the side of his mouth, "he was on board a carrier called the *USS Intrepid*. My dad says it was a left-over from World War II. Somehow, nobody knows how, Jimmy fell off the rear deck and got chewed up in the propeller blades. That's why the Marines said it had to be a closed casket. They don't want his mother to see him carved up like that."

Part 4

SOUTH COUNTY

Chapter 45

Love on 250 Dollars a Month

South County, Rhode Island, was the flattest place I had ever seen. It seemed there were no hills at all for miles around.

When Sheila and I first set foot on campus in Kingston, we went straight for the Student Housing office. Given our budget, they directed us to the most economical place we could live, Narragansett, which was twelve miles east and south.

There we found a tidy little sky-blue-painted one-bedroom cottage in Duncan Park, just steps off Route 107. Mr Duncan rented his cottages to students for nine months, and then, by the week, in summer tourist season, to vacationers, for a lot more. We were lucky enough to be able to live in his little tourist patch for a hundred bucks a month, considering that the teaching-assistantship I had been awarded for grad school carried a stipend of only 250 dollars a month.

My mother, to my utter surprise, stepped in and took charge of our moving. She organized my father to drive us all in his Jeep station wagon and made it into a family expedition so that even my brother and sister, Jack and Jill, could come along. Jack curled up on the pillows and bedding in the back, Sheila and Jill and I were in the back seat, making room for dresses and coats under our feet, and my mother was up front with Dad driving.

Was this the same woman who had called my beloved a whore and vowed not to attend our wedding?

Now that Sheila and I were properly married in a church, she had reversed course entirely. When we got to the campus and she had to wait while we went into the Housing Office, Mrs Gerry Petrovich was the model of patience. Afterwards, she bought everybody lunch at a restaurant in Peacedale, on the way to Narragansett, and, not stinting us in the least, had brought along a week's worth of home-cooked Italian dishes she had prepared herself to get us through our first week. She thought the little blue-clapboard cottage we picked out was the perfect love-nest for newly-weds. She promised to be back the very next weekend with more supplies. I decided that if I lived to be a hundred, I would never understand women.

We were so happy to be left alone, Sheila and I, when they had gone. No mother-in-law, no brother-in-law—we could hide out in a place where nobody would ever find us. Our first night alone in our own place, months and months ahead of us to make a life. My bride and I dived under the bed-covers to make sweet love.

That very Monday morning I was scheduled to start classes at school, twelve miles away. We were on a squeezed-tight schedule since Sheila had worked till the very last possible Friday at Liberty because we needed the money. When Sunday morning arrived, the nearest coffee-shop, Mr Duncan said, was about a mile away, at the beach, straight east, over there, or else, four miles north on Rhode Island 107.

Sheila and I were used to going everywhere we needed to go by subway or bus, on the MTA. But this wasn't Boston anymore, and we had neglected to figure that into our plans. I had no idea how I was going to get to campus every day for classes twelve miles away. I had my usual thousand bucks a year saved up for school, but all the loan money we used to get married, plus the money we received from wedding-guests, was gone on honeymoon motel rooms, fancy dinners, and film for the camera. With only 250 bucks a month coming in from my stipend, and Sheila needing to find a job, we were going to have to make it last.

Sheila didn't fancy walking the mile to the beach. She said she was knackered from love-making and from luxuriating, sleeping-in late, on her first weekend away from Liberty, so—why don't we hitch a ride? We went out to Route 107, put our backs to the north, and stuck out our thumbs.

I should say that I was very confident that we would find a ride without much trouble, since I put Sheila out in front of me. But I was still surprised that the very first vehicle that came nosing out of a side-street stopped immediately to offer us a lift.

It was a young man, our age, coming from the direction of the water; a sandy-haired guy, with a beard, a flannel lumberman's shirt, and a southern accent.

We didn't notice how tall he was till we got to the coffee-shop and he stepped out and came around the battered nose of his '57 Chevy pick-up truck.

"Now there's no need to discuss it any further," said Robbie MacDuff, of the North Carolina MacDuffs, and he squinted at us with his sun-weathered blue eyes. "I'll pick you up Monday morning, 7 am sharp. Don't worry about it. You're going my way, Nick. I'll be glad for the company. We're probably gonna end up in the same classes, anyway."

That's who Robbie MacDuff was. He picked you up thumbing and inside of four miles in his truck, he was your friend for life.

I looked at Sheila. "Is this the Luck of the Irish I've always heard about?"

We had made a new beginning. It was just as well the land was flat around Narragansett. It made for wider horizons, which matched what was going on in my mind: a broadening, a pushing-out from the cocoon, an awakening. If I could have quantified it with calipers, measured it with electrodes, or calculated it on a slide-rule, I might have said I was exploding.

We had landed in an off-campus beach community of graduate students. The talk all around you was of mind-expanding, of consciousness-raising. It was everywhere from *Sgt Pepper* to Carlos Castaneda. But what was happening to me was an almost palpable, physical sensation of rapid-ring-growth, like a redwood adding centuries in the span of one autumn.

I was leaving behind everything I had been at Boston College. Suddenly, I was unfettered by religion or the need to be bound by a code of behavior, and it was liberating. I had slipped through a side door into a secular world. At the University of Rhode Island, there was no St Ignatius, no Pope, no God.

I had been through four years of undergraduate studies, but not in a public university. Here in Kingston, the campus was open to the world, we were on the edge of Narragansett Bay, the ocean was flooding in. It was not a cloistered enclave like Boston College. Here you did not feel a wall between you and real life. Every motion of the sea of change going on in the wider world seeped through the open doors of URI. There were no Gothic buildings reminding you of the medieval roots of Catholic philosophy. Instead, here there were stout New England granite white-brocaded Colonial-style edifices on the point of being transformed into revolutionary bastions of Liberty. The quadrangle in Kingston was an open-air assembly area just waiting for anti-war orators to take up the baton of speech-making. No such open rebellion against the status-quo had existed at Boston College, even in this tumultuous year of '68.

However, back in Boston, in the spring of that eventful year, I had followed up my first foray into the streets, at the time candlelight vigil on Boston Common for the slain Dr. King, by attending a rally held by Bernadette Devlin, leader of the civil rights marchers in Ireland, also on the Boston Common.

Why not? Was Boston not the birthplace of American freedom? Were not Bernadette Devlin and her followers living the philosophy of Dr King, fomenting his creed, traversing in his footsteps? Where else should they come to seek the aid and understanding of the world community but to the place where Revolution first rang? Wasn't I a citizen of Boston, and of the world? Was I not molded by that milieu, born out of that cloth?

My biggest job that fall was *not to forget* Jimmy Dillard and his death in the war, not to put him behind me, as I was doing with Boston College and all my friends and teachers there, to whom I hardly ever gave a thought anymore, but to channel all that grief and anger and guilt I felt on the afternoon of Jimmy's wake into something productive.

If I could do that, then maybe in some small way, Jimmy did not die in vain. If I could use his death to motivate just one person, me, then maybe Jimmy Dillard would not have sacrificed his life for nothing.

Already, at the time of Bernadette's visit, I had stepped up to the table in Boston Common and signed up for *Irish Northern Aid*. Was that not in service of my dearly beloved wife's native land?

I went to meetings in the North End of Boston, where my own mother was born, where Paul Revere once lived and worked, and where I met others like myself who, although Americans, sympathized with the cause of Irish civil rights.

But America was my country. If I were so ready to commit to Irish Northern Aid, could I do less than that in the cause of saving the lives of young American servicemen like Jimmy Dillard? *Especially since in my own personal case I was exempt from the draft?* Did that not confer on me a freedom of action I might not otherwise have had?

Now, when I was no longer in Boston, and beyond the reach of the ivory-tower quiescence of the BC campus, now was the time to step up to the table and join The Movement to end the war in Vietnam.

In South County, Rhode Island, I was a long way from Boston, and at the University of Rhode Island, I was a long way from Boston College—and the Army ROTC.

Chapter 46

Marshall Andrews

Marshall Andrews was a tiny man who pulled himself up in front of people to his full height of five foot three inches. He was 67 years old and he was a survivor of the *Titanic*. His daughter, Ellen Andrews, towered over him as she introduced him. After escaping the infamous maiden voyage in a lifeboat at the age of 11, her father had gone on to become an artist in his adult life.

Ellen was telling us this at an exhibition of her father's drawings, watercolors, oils and acrylics. Rowboats in the weeds and dunes of Narragansett Bay were in his pictures, but no lifeboats, no *Titanic*. Nevertheless, that was the only thing people wanted to ask him about. Ellen could have advertised the exhibition as *Titanic Survivor On Display*.

Marshall was a lovable guy, and Ellen, his daughter, though divorced, was devoted to *amour*, and believed in sexual liberation and scented candles. She was the doyenne of the local literary, artistic, and photographic circles. She gathered round her the likes of Gary Wheeling, the Director of the University Arts Center, Khachig Khachatorian, the Writer-in-Residence, and Thom Bell, the undergraduate campus bohemian who staged the *Bogart and Bacall Revival* every Friday at lunch-time, on the Quad. The *Revival* was a ritual in which Thom Bell and fellow campus hippies arranged themselves in a circle on the grass to surreptitiously pass a pregnant joint while reciting the racecourse dialogue from *The Big Sleep*.

Nobody knew what Khachatorian was writing, or what Richmond did besides interior-decorate his house in Peacedale, or whether Thom Bell, in his 7th year as an undergrad, intended to graduate or not, but all wanted nevertheless to be admitted into Ellen Andrews' charmed circle.

Her salons were held at her house in Westerly. She did the cooking and everyone marvelled over her steamed sea-weed. Robbie MacDuff and I were acolytes, having joined the staff of the campus literary rag, which was called *Perspective*. Robbie became the Editor-in-Chief. I joined the staff because I did not want to repeat my mistake at Boston College and be frozen out of publication. I had learned how to play the game. My little poems had to see print. In the meantime, I became the Editor of *The Grad Side*, the campus newspaper for graduate students, since no one else seemed to want the job, and it would allow me to editorialize about the war.

My first target for darts and barbs, as a convinced Massachusetts Kennedy-Democrat, still in mourning over the loss of Jack and Bobby, was Richard Nixon, a man I loathed with a visceral vehemence. Previously rejected by the fickle American electorate, Nixon was now mounting a resurrection from political Hades as—amazingly, impossibly—the Republican candidate for President.

The showdown was coming in November, and the Democrats had disastrously nominated Hubert Humphrey after George McGovern joined the race late. The fatally flawed

Democratic Convention in Chicago failed to nominate Eugene McCarthy but succeeded in provoking the Chicago Police to charge Yippie protestors, led by Abbie Hoffman and Jerry Rubin, in Grant Park, with flailing nightsticks, in a classic definition of a police riot, which resulted in hundreds of injuries and 668 arrests of peaceful anti-war demonstrators exercising their constitutional rights to assembly and free speech.

My prose glittered in high dudgeon in the columns of *The Grad Side* as I battled the reactionary tide which I feared was about to swallow the nation.

Robbie MacDuff and I first met Russell Sage, who was devoted to Ellen Andrews, at her house in Westerly. Russell came from East Providence. He was a philosophy major, two years older than Robbie and I, and we promptly signed him up to be the third man in our triumvirate by acquiring his astute services as business-manager of *Perspective*. Though he was older than we were, Russell was still an undergrad because he was a veteran who had spent four years in the Coast Guard. However, as a man of the world, he had been stationed not only at nearby Point Judith Lighthouse, but also in far-off Japan, and thus, he added ballast to our beer-soaked, tippy canoe.

One of our favorite meeting-grounds, besides Ellen's in Westerly, was Iggy Palmissano's Pizza House on Route 108, on the way up to the campus. Russell had a house in Peacedale with his wife and baby son; Robbie was actively looking for love, but dating a picture-perfect young dance-major from New York, a cheerful blonde named Cathy; and for the next two years Robbie and Russell and I basically ran the small contingent of campus radicals from the bar at Iggy's, with help from Liam

McCarthy (no relation to Eugene) from New Haven and Larry Lyman, from the SUNY campus at Binghamton. Russell Sage leant weight and solidity to our collective anti-war endeavors as he was a veteran-against-the-war. In recognition of that status emeritus, I never called him 'Russ,' only Russell. Both he and Robbie were six-footers, and dwarfed me in the middle. Our meetings at Ellen's house in Westerly were genially presided over by our figurehead, our guru, our mentor, our very own Bilbo Baggins—Marshall Andrews.

Chapter 47

The Honest Truth

I had two sections of Freshman Composition to teach that year as a grad-assistant, and together with my own course-work, plus papers I was bringing home to correct, I was more than busy. Poor Sheila. She no longer had Pinky and Jeanie to turn to for amusement and she was trapped in a little beach cottage with me constantly shushing her because I had to work at the kitchen table late into the night. I was taking *The American Transcendentalists* with Dr Foster and *The Irish Renaissance* with the English Dept Chairman, Dr O'Toole. "You've made a grass widow out of me before my time," was Sheila's comment.

I eventually relented and got my mother to bring us a portable TV set on wheels on one of her weekend provisions-runs. I claimed I could work in the kitchen while Sheila watched her shows on the couch under the picture window in the living room—but as this beach cottage living space was organized on the open floor plan, there was no wall between the two, only the front door, and a flimsy lattice for decoration, so Sheila had to keep the volume down.

Having proceeded from undergraduate pre-requisites to English-major concentration, and then progressed to focusing solely on the great writers in grad school, I now had a career in mind, the next logical step in the progression, a career as a teacher. But secretly I was banking on publishing as a poet.

My models on campus were our English Dept professors who worked the creative rather than scholarly side of the street. Nancy Cotter was a short-story writer, like Seán Ó Faoláin at BC. Paul Petersen was a poet. Of course, I bought their books. "It never hurts to sidle up to the turf fire for inspiration," said I to the missus. (Obviously, I was picking up expressions from my adorable Irish housemate.) "Maybe you can get yourself lit on fire," said Sheila, archly.

Nevertheless, I was convinced that this was my future. I was literally in the thrall of the great books. I considered myself the luckiest man alive to be able to spend my life reading the Authors of Western Culture. Especially now since, because of Sheila, I had discovered the writers of the Irish Renaissance, and I could ignore the Ezra Pounds and T.S. Eliots and Prufrocks of urban alienation. I would much rather arise and go now to the Lake Isle of Innisfree. Was I not immersed in nature by the wilderness atmospherics of South County?

I hadn't picked up my squeeze-box in more than four years. I didn't miss practicing half-an-hour every day with my mother pointing out my mistakes, but once in a while I'd go looking for a piano room at school where I could sit for a minute and pick out the minor-key nostalgia of *Come Back to Sorrento* on the right hand. It didn't feel the same without the breathlessness of the accordian.

But the die was cast. It was the written word for me. Literary analysis, the convoluted textual breakdown of the New Critics, was to me anathema. Might as well go back to the

Jesuitical counting of angels on the head of a pin. A scholar I was not cut out to be. I needed the wide open spaces of spontaneous bop prosody. I needed the romantic call of visionary mysticism in Yeats. Deep in my bones, which is to say, my buried self, (another borrowing: Matthew Arnold?) I was convinced with a singular monomania that ink-drippings from my pen were destined to one day be called immortal.

And—after four years of undergraduate time spent in classrooms with sometimes outstanding teachers—I was convinced I knew how to teach by sheer osmosis. All I had to do was to repeat what I'd heard, and act like they had. Nothing to it. My students were, improbably, only a little younger than I was. Made no difference. It was a snap. Nor did I have any need for courses such as *Education Psychology* or *Theory of Learning and Teaching*, or such evident time-wasters as *Education and Public Policy* (running your finger down the list of the School of Education courses at URI.) Back at BC, and even here, I had had the best of role models in the classrooms I sat in, and I was nothing if not a medieval monk when it came to being a copyist. Just ask Jerry Bellanti.

Poor Sheila. She had to put up with me shushing her. But—I needed her, too. Just as she had back in Boston, she enchanted everyone who met her. She was my charm-offensive. It did me no disservice introducing her to O'Toole, the Department Chairman. I thought it was the smartest thing I had ever thought of doing, to start an academic future by marrying her. She was the woman who had made a made a man out of me. I was proud to be seen with her around campus. At faculty receptions, at professors' house-parties, at Ellen Andrews soirees, she was the one people just gravitated round to. I was reading with intense fervor and delight things like *The Ginger Man*, by JP Donleavy, *Borstal Boy* by Brendan Behan, the *Collected Poems of WB Yeats*—Sheila was my Caitlin Thomas, she was my Maud Gonne, she was my Nora Barnacle.

By the end of September, she was 'with child.'

She cried and cried.

My Sheila was distraught. She could barely push out the words between trembling lips. "My life is over! I hate you!"

I was appalled. This was not the reaction I anticipated, all my previous life long. Becoming a father was something aspirational to me. It meant I would stand on a stage with the beloved grandfather of my memories. I had pictured it, believed in it, foreseen it, entirely differently, this moment of revelation, this announcement, this discovery a lifetime's wish coming true at last. Every man in love wants his beloved to want his child. None of them expect her to reject him in that supreme moment.

All I could do was sit on the couch with Sheila and try to put my arms around her to comfort her. But she wouldn't let me. Her shoulders were shaking so violently I thought she would hurt herself. "Don't touch me! You're a fooking asshole!"

Sheila had never been a stranger around the F-word. If anything, she taught her girlfriends Pinky and Jeanie back in Westbourne Terrace that it was perfectly acceptable in a jaunty, breezy, liberated way that they were sure was terribly hip and—European. Delightedly, they even adopted her pronunciation—'fooking!' as in 'the rock group's manager got them a good booking.'

They went tumbling around the apartment emitting wild guffaws, crying "What's a fooking Petrovich?"

Now, to my eternal chagrin, I was learning that a fooking Petrovich was a fooking asshole. With a capital 'A.'

Gingerly, I attempted to touch her, trying not to burn my fingers.

"Oh, go play with yourself in the corner, why don't you!"

We slept together in our bridal bed that night on wet pillows and I was helplessly and hopelessly convinced that I had ruined not just Sheila's life, but my own.

In the morning, she turned to me and said tenderly, "I'm sorry. Poor Nicky. Can you ever forgive me?"

That was how I discovered that my darling Sheila, my sweetheart, my own, was into make-up sex.

And afterwards, when I rolled away and, lying on my back, threw my head on the pillow and my forearm across my forehead, she sweetly snuggled up to my shoulder and breathed into my ear, "Did you enjoy yourself, then?"

"I did. Oh, I did."

"It's just that I was so looking forward to having some time to spend with you, Nicky, just the two of us, and now our chance is gone."

Sheila Blake was deadly to the male ego. She would stab you in the heart, and then kiss the boo-boo, and make it better.

"I'm going to get big as a house and you'll stop loving me."

"I will never stop loving you, Sheila." I looked at her sadly, and, I thought, sympathetically, as I admitted to myself, out loud, "That's the honest truth."

Chapter 48

The Darling Month of May

That winter, as our baby grew inside Sheila, a winter-shorn, naked birch tree grew leaves inside of me. The stone walls of South County, settling into the sandy soil for three centuries now, trooped across the white lines of my notebook pages, placing stone after stone in a line of thought until the world was connected in a network of sentences from horizon to horizon, from dawn to dusk. The sentences recoiled and broke themselves apart, like the waves of the Atlantic breaking open on the rocks of Point Judith. The fragments turned into poems, snatches of lyricism rescued from the bare, flat cattail-waving marshes of the Pond behind our house, where the winter wind skidded puddles across the sheen of water. Seagulls perched on telephone wires in the barren winter wind. Those wires carried Sheila's voice to her distant sisters in Boston, Mary and Bridie, as all three sisters were having babies at the same time. Sheila found a friend close by to sit with her through the long days while she was being pregnant, and I was twelve miles away on campus in Kingston, teaching classes, taking classes, and dwelling in the library with my notebooks and the *Duino Elegies*.

Sheila's friend was Tina Gomez, a young Dominican girl our own age, who moved in next door in Duncan Park when her husband, Pedro, who was a U.S. Marine, was assigned to guard duty temporarily at the Quonset Naval Base nearby. Pedro had just returned from Khe Sanh, but he knew he was going back. He wasn't dead yet, he joked, but it was only a matter of time. We got through the winter on his gallows humor. Pedro had a car he used to commute to work every day and together, on the weekends, we'd go shopping for groceries at Almacs in Wakefield. Every day I rode to school and back in Robbie MacDuff's pick-up truck and we discussed everything political, literary, musical and military, all that was distantly impinging on the slender shade of the leaf-shedding local trees.

To our horror, it turned out *Nixon's The One*. Between election-day and the new year of 1969, Thanksgiving and Christmas fell without snow. Sheila and I were getting along fine on 250 dollars a month. Sirloin steak at Almac's was 99 cents a pound. My mother was arriving with supplies every couple of weekends. The plastic Christmas Tree in the living room and the bassinet in the bedroom we owed to her. Sheila's sisters were too occupied to come visiting but they were only a long distance phone call away. My mother and father, in their absence, provided the nurturing family around us. Robbie MacDuff and Cathy and the Gomez couple shared our Thanksgiving and Christmas libations. Life was blooming in the infertile waste of winter.

Though, sometimes, I found myself feeling profoundly sorry for Sheila, as her own mother was so very far away.

Daily I was discovering new joys of stirring satisfaction among the great writers. I was stepping on winter puddles and cracking the frozen ice into starbursts of tangled skeins. I was reading Erich Fromm in the pages of *The Art of Loving*, Viktor Frankl in *Man's Search for Meaning*. R.D. Laing was another author who jumped of the shelf of the URI bookstore and flew into my hand with *The Divided Self*. Just as the ice-puddles cracked, I was cracking open, and new gestations were being born within me. I was in sympathetic pregnancy with Sheila. She was carrying our baby and I was carrying the new world for our baby to be born into.

Still, Sheila was getting bored, sitting around pregnant, while I charged ahead, self-absorbed in books and classes. Somehow she heard of a fellow countrywoman in the area. I don't know how she did it. She must have used Irish radar.

There was a pub down on the water, in Matunuck, about four miles distant from our house, called *The Joyce Family Pub*. And a girl our age from County Tipp behind the bar there, so we heard. Sheila got Robbie MacDuff, who was never known to be late for a beer, to drive us over there. The girl behind the bar turned out to be Nuala Mulroy, and the two of them hit it off famously. Sheila was hired on the spot, as Mr Joyce, the owner, said she'd add a spot more of local flavor and could tend bar and hide her stomach while freeing up Nuala to wait on tables instead of doing double duty, as she was at the moment. Great craic was therefore had by all, none more so than Sheila, who finally had seen her way out of "a flippin' muddle. And a few bob to spend on baubles for myself won't hurt my aching arse, mind you." Nuala Mulroy promised her rashers and eggs for lunch, if she liked, or bangers and mash if she preferred, perhaps on a rotating basis, seeing as Sheila was eating for two?

But it was a struggle with us, for me, trying to get Sheila to stop smoking. Tina Gomez wasn't helping, as she smoked, too. The bartending at the pub wasn't helping. I felt Sheila was getting the best of American-style care from Dr Williams, our obstetrician/pediatrician, whose office was next door to Almacs in Wakefield. He was constantly lecturing Sheila on the dangers to the baby of her cigarettes. Finally, I took out a five-dollar bill and, with Sheila's matches, held it up and set it on fire, saying, "This is what you're doing to our money."

I didn't want to do it, but I was getting desperate. I was hoping against hope that this shock tactic would work. I was in a reality-warp where nothing seemed so outrageous to me that it would be impossible. Think of it. A new world was being born inside that baby. I knew I was being cruel, but I took the risk. Dr Williams had frightened me, and by this time I had figured out just how fragile life on this planet is.

Sheila behaved after that. At least, I think she did. I wasn't there all day every day, so how could I ever be sure? And then there was *The Joyce Family Pub,* with the cigarette machine in the corner.

Since I didn't smoke, I thought it was easy to just stop. Just make up your mind and do it. The power of will-power. I didn't see smoking as an addiction, just a bad habit.

And I was planning such a brilliant future for our brilliant baby, a boy, who was going to be named Daniel, our own Daniel Petrovich, our own biblical lion, our own 'Danny Boy,' a chip off the old Eastern bloc. Already I was planning to use the new kit I had found on sale at the URI bookstore, which offered phonics flash cards in a red box and advocated that parents teach their child to read starting at age two and three. This system was developed by educators who came by their wisdom from the early days of Lyndon Johnson's *Head Start* Program. The more I learned the more research I did. Now that I was a teacher myself, all the more reason why I should start to delve into educating myself on Education. Soon I had become an Early Literacy advocate for young Daniel before he was even born.

On a Saturday in February, we ventured out in the howling wind to watch a winter storm batter the Lighthouse at Point Judith. We got too near the rocks and came home laughing and soaked in sea-water. We stripped and dried off and huddled in a blanket on the couch, with the drapes drawn across the picture windows we had in both kitchen and living room, and the front door locked, and I put my head down on Sheila's belly with my ear pressed close to listen for the baby kicking. I showed him phonics flash cards and told Sheila he could see them from inside the womb, he was that smart. "Indeed," said she, "he's a budding genius, with a fool for a father, dripping water on the throw-rug. What's a poor girl to do but put up with the both of ye?"

If I thought I'd acquired a guilt-complex when Sheila first announced she was pregnant, that was nothing compared to the day she went into labor.

It started when we got up on a Thursday morning for breakfast. The days of morning sickness were long gone, but this day, Sheila felt the first sign as queasiness. Then she proclaimed she was going into labor, right now, she knew it–"I think." Her due date was still about six or seven days away, but counting the months, we knew it could be anytime now, as we were in the 40th week, we thought.

We started walking Sheila in a circle in the living room, round and round the coffee-table, and timing the intervals, as we'd been taught in pre-natal classes. The first two or three were 20 minutes or longer, when Robbie walked in the door to pick me up for classes.

"Go away!" Sheila shouted.

"Is it time?" said Robbie, raising his eyebrows, wide-eyed, rubbing his hands together. "Okay. Let's go. Got the truck right here."

"I'm not going anywhere, you eedjit."

Robbie promised to be straight back after his early class, and to make my excuses for me, and true to his word, he came flying back in at about eleven-fifteen. Only to be sent away again by Sheila, who said the intervals were only down to 17 minutes at this point.

At half past twelve noon, Russell Sage, having heard the news at school from Robbie, came puffing in, only to be told he was acting the ninny by Sheila, and would he ever please just disappear himself, she'd go when she was ready and not before.

Russell was followed at 1.30 by Tina and Pedro, who had got home for lunch from the Naval Base, then at 2.30 by Ellen Andrews, all in a proper matronly fizz, who had heard the news on the phone from her sycophant, Russell.

All were sent away by Sheila who gave out with a lecture. "Don't you know that it's the first babby that takes the longest to come? I could be here for days! And I'll be damned if I go to that hospital, only to be sent away for giving in to the pains too early. I won't have them saying I was in a panic."

At 4.30, I thought I was going to faint walking her in circles, as the labor pangs were hitting her so hard she was doubling over, and I had to strain against her tensed arm-muscles to hold her up while we staggered through another ring around the coffee-table. I was sweating, I was nervous, I was the one in a panic. The intervals were down to nine minutes, when she announced, "Call Nuala Mulroy. She can help me bathe. I'm not going to that hospital till I have me bath."

But Nuala couldn't get way from the pub, and I helped Sheila into the tub, and helped her to wash and get out again, praying that she wouldn't slip and fall. I was picturing having to deliver the baby right then and there in the bathroom myself.

At five-thirty Robbie MacDuff came back in and insisted we go now.

"If you don't remove your shadow from my door I'm going to banjax you, so help me God." cried Sheila.

"You see what I'm up against?" I said to Robbie, throwing my hands up. "It's just like when I tried to get her to quit smoking!"

"I did quit, you bastard! You made me! Jesus!—I wish I had one now!"

"Why are you two fighting?"

"You'd deny a scrap of a lick of a bone to Father Doolin's dyin' dog, you would!"

"You're supposed to be happy, you're having a baby!"

"GO A-WAY, MacDuff!"

Robbie said he'd go get a pizza at the beach stand and be right back, don't go anywhere.

"Is he codding me?" said Sheila, looking up at me as she doubled over, hanging off my arm. "Where would I be going like this?"

I was afraid she was going over the edge, losing her senses.

The next set of pangs were only five minutes apart.

"All right," said Sheila. "The doctor said we could go now, when the intervals were only down to five minutes."

"Can we go now?" said I, idiotically. "It's the month of May, you know, and we'll only have light till about seven-thirty–."

"We're going, we're going. Help me down the steps."
"How are we going to get there?"
"We'll have to stick out our thumb."
"Where is everybody? All day they've been coming in and out, except right when you need them."

Somehow, don't ask me how, we had managed to make our way out of Duncan Park to the far side of the road on 107, to the sandy ditch at the side of the northbound lane, to stick out our thumbs, thinking that, since we'd been here since September, and everyone who lived here knew us from school, we were bound to get a quick pick-up from one of our own friends.

But no, it was a total stranger who saw a disheveled man holding up a pregnant woman in a maternity dress by the side of the road, who stopped.

"Oh, my God," he said. "Get in, quick."

We fell back against the back seat as he sped off, spinning up sand, and he reached at least seventy by the time we got to the traffic circle outside of Almac's.

Sheila was having a bad patch of pain, and exclaiming, while the man took the traffic circle on two wheels, yelling, "Please, please, don't have the baby in my car!"

Our daughter was born at 7.20 AM the next morning, Friday, the 16th of May, 1969, at the South County Hospital in Wakefield, Rhode Island.

I stayed in the labor room with Sheila until the very last moment when an agitated nurse in a surgical mask escorted me out and shut the door in my face, with a look of 'good riddance.'

Chapter 49

Culchies, Jackeens and Ignorant Yanks

"Oh, my God, there's a Culchie in the bed!"

It was six-fifteen on Saturday morning at the hospital when the priest came into the room to give communion to the new mother. Sheila cranked open one eye to examine him head to foot. It was a member of the clergy, all right. "You must be a Dublin Jackeen. They've no couth at all."

"I am from Dublin, I admit it."

"How did you find me?"

"Nuala Mulroy."

"I'll wring her neck, like Sunday's chicken."

"Father Lally," he said, sticking his hand out to me, as I sat in the chair. "You must be the proud Papa. Oh, don't get up." He was making himself comfortable on the side of the bed. "I came to give you communion, Missus—and a bit of a slaggin' match I thought might make you feel at home."

"You're very welcome, I'm sure. I'm happy to give as good as I get."

"And how's the child?"

"Perfect. Has all her fingers and toes."

"Ah, Mayo, God help us."

"Indeed."

Sheila was sitting up and arranging herself by this time, when Father Lally asked, "And what's the babby's name?"—imitating the way he thought Culchies spoke.

"She hasn't any name as yet," said Sheila. "We were expecting a boy. At least himself was. I hope he's not too disappointed."

"Sheila!" from my corner.

"It's his own fault, anyway, the nurse was telling me. Something to do with X's & Y's. I don't understand it myself, but, there you go, that's the way of Mother Nature in the modern world."

Father Lally looked at me kindly and said, "Do you mind if I make a suggestion?"

"Not at all."

And after slipping the wafer to Sheila, he began a long story short about the old-time Irish *fili* of the 18th century, who travelled from place to place reciting the traditional tales from times past, going back even, he said, to the mythological cycles of the pagan times, before even St Patrick, and composing their own poems, too. "And in those days of the Penal Code, when Irish was forbidden to be spoken, and even the mass had to be celebrated under a bush, it was the custom of the country that the bards would carry the latest news of the struggle against the foreign foe, from town to town, from Big House to Big House. They were the newspapers of the day, so to speak, and they developed what they called a vision poem, or, in Irish, an *Aisling*, in which the poet would meet a lovely lady in a silver wood, she being the spirit of Ireland. And she would tell the poet of her troubles. And nowadays many people, at least at home they do, they call their daughters by the name of Aisling, it's become a very popular name, actually."

I leaned forward, fascinated, my ever-present notebook in my hand, pen ready, and seeing this, Father Lally spelled it for me. "But, mind you, it's pronounced 'Ash-leen.'" Sheila might be a Culchie, but I was an ignorant Yank.

And, taking good notes, as was my habit, I asked again for his short version of what the name meant.

And Father Lally said, "You might say–'a beautiful dream I had last night, who came to me in the form of a woman.'"

And that was how our daughter got her name.

"What do you think?" I said to Sheila.

"Suit yourself, Mr Petrovich."

I went home that evening, haunted by the story Father Lally had given, a gift, to me. After a full day at the hospital, with all our friends trooping in and out, after all the phone-calling to all our long-distance relatives, on both sides, I was glad finally to have a moment to myself.

As I pulled up a chair at the kitchen table, darkness was falling beyond the picture windows; the kitchen was glaring with white light, spreading a halo in a half-moon across the patch of lawn outside. A mood settled over me.

I picked up the pen and opened the notebook and began to write. The lines came easily, as quick as thought itself. I could not write them down fast enough. I could not race ahead of the lines, for fear of losing the last thought before this. My hand could not write fast enough, for fear of the next rhyme-word evaporating before I could get it down, fixed and fastened, on paper.

I was in the throes of a mysterious process that defies analysis. One might call it composing. One might say that it compares to daVinci sketching helicopters, a pure figment of imagination, divorced from reality, a thing of the mind only. One might say that Verdi was hearing in his head an aria impossible to sing, that Renoir was feathering onto canvas the brushstrokes of impressionistic roses that no one ever saw.

I myself, in the midst of the act, was certain beyond any doubt that I felt another hand moving mine, another mind thinking for me; that nowhere under heaven could I have created these lines, these stanzas, alone, of my own volition, by myself.

I wrote at the kitchen table for three nights, while Sheila and the baby, Aisling, were staying in the hospital, and I was alone. Being alone, I was open to all the deepest emotions stirring inside me, washing over me, like breakers on the beach. The elemental experience of becoming a father was changing me with every pen-stroke I laid down.

Outside, in the night, in the darkness, the heart of the ocean waited, the waves of the Bay beat in rhythm, a breathing immensity.

I realized at once that Aisling herself, our child, was my greatest creation, not this poem.

And yet, I felt compelled to set it all down in words.

And I was conscious of the presence of another person— no, three of them. Yes, a trinity of women. My mother, my wife and my daughter. All born in the month of May, within 8 days of each other, under the sign of the bull.

All this I stuffed into the poem, as furiously fast as I could, before the words escaped, got loose, vaporized.

Everything fell into a preset pattern. It was a 6-line stanza form I had read in William Butler Yeats—four rhymed lines in a quatrain, followed by a couplet. Over the course of three nights these stanzas marched down the blue lines of a URI notebook in formation.

When it was done, I thought it was easily the best thing I had ever written, and I gave it the title Father Lally had given me, "A Beautiful Dream I Had Last Night Who Came to Me in the Form of a Woman."

As I sat there, in the white light at the kitchen table, and looked up to see my own reflection, swimming in the dark in the picture window, the three women in the poem, my mother, my wife and my daughter, all coalesced into one scarlet face, hanging on a guitar stand on the tiny, low stage in *The Stardust Lounge.*

Chapter 50

Catch You Later, Man

My life had been taken over by a female presence, a personage whom I dubbed 'The Muse.'

I was not the first to do so, and my feeling, or guess, was that *She* came from a birthplace somewhere around the Mediterranean basin, somewhere around two or three thousand years ago, or earlier. In any event, this invisible woman had put her hand on my shoulder. From that moment to this she had grown her shadow inside of me, ever more expansive, until with Aisling's birth, she occupied my whole being. Not just the trinity from the *'Beautiful Dream'* poem, but all the women who lived and loved, gave birth and died, from all of history and pre-history, in their countless numbers, had come to camp inside me, as if I were an undiscovered island in the Aegean which they had been searching for and finally found.

Ah, yes. There I was, shorn of my male powers, dressed in a dress, at last, Achilles in the camp of the women . . .

And *She* stood on the shore, a shadow, on this island in the sea. And the island, the sea, and the shadow were inside of me.

Meanwhile, Sheila and the baby came home. Normal living in everyday reality resumed, never having lapsed, not really, and resumed soon. My new contention with Sheila was not over smoking but breast-feeding, which I favored, but she, and my mother, did not. However, I was going to have the perfect infant, raise the perfect child, and be the perfect father, and even teach Aisling to read by the time she was three, and so, I got my way. Not without protest and upset and consternation.

Sheila, while rocking Aisling in her lap, had taken up again with the ancient, fierce cooing over the baby, that wordless, tuneless singsong, which I had first heard come out of the depths of her being with her sister's baby, Mary-Jane.

This chant came out of the wilds of Ireland from Druid times. It was another manifestation of The Muse's presence in the house. No one could teach a modern woman how to do this. Sheila herself, as a child, had heard her own mother cooing this tuneless singing over her infant brother Martin as he lay his head in his mother's lap. The ancient music was imprinted then, somewhere in the deep, unconscious being of Sheila Blake, who was now, in her turn, a mother herself.

At school I had seen a posting in the English Dept on the bulletin board inviting writers to submit their poems to a publisher in New York City called Dr Deeds. I sent off the 'Beautiful Dream' poem and thought no more about it.

I was getting busy. We had to move, as Mr Duncan was about to begin summer beach rentals and needed the house. Robbie MacDuff found us a new place right next door to his on Sewall

Road in Narragansett. We were actually that much closer to the beach, and didn't have to cross 107 anymore.

I also needed money. Fortunately, for me, Russell Sage was a friend who was instilled with the entrepreneurial spirit and he came up with the idea that we should team up into a two-man house-painting crew.

All I had to do was to show up for work in the morning. Russell found all the contacts and made all the deals to paint houses. There was plenty of that kind of work in South County along the shore because of the salt and wind. We started with Dr Cotter from the English Dept. Hers was the first house we did. It went from there. Soon I was pulling down 500 bucks a week, and so was Russell, even a cut more, since he was the brains of the operation. I was happy to follow along and collect the table scraps without having to bother my head about business details. I needed to keep space free for The Muse.

However, it was delightful, and, surprisingly, inspiring, to be up on the ladder in the open air all summer, with Russell crying, "Slap it on! We gotta get this one done by Thursday, so we can start the Do-little place on Friday, she's ringing my phone off the hook." "Do-little" was his name for the Smallwood lady who was our next project.

We were never bored on our two-man crew as we discussed and debated Hegel, Kant and Kierkegaard up on those ladders. With a wife and child at home in Peacedale, Russell needed the money as much as I did. He was full of wild ideas for making substantial bucks while at the same time enlightening the world and pursuing the fine arts. When we graduated, in about a year's time, said Russell, he was going to start a magazine up in Providence, his home-town, and I was going to be his literary editor. As I slapped paint on those lines of clapboards, lines of poetry were appearing in my head.

The next upset at home was the rolling-over-the-baby-in-the-bed crisis.

This turned out to be a sort of watered-down repeat of the 'my-father-in-Ireland-is-dying' episode, only without the fifth of vodka under the sink.

Sheila decided that the crib my mother had bought her wouldn't do, nothing would do but to bring the baby to sleep in bed with us at night, the way she remembered her mother had done, at home.

We did this, and as soon as Sheila dozed off, she woke with a start, jumped upright in the bed, and started crying, "What if I roll over in the bed during the night while I'm sleeping and smother her!" She looked at me, horror-stricken. "I'd wake up in the morning and find the poor thing dead!"

Nothing would do now but to put the 'babby' back in the crib. However, the child had to be placed on her back so that she couldn't roll over and smother herself. But, then, she had to be changed to sleeping on her stomach, because, what if she swallowed her own drool and choked herself? This went on all night.

Luckily for us, Aisling turned out to be the most pleasant and placid baby in history. She never was 'colicky,' she never gave any trouble. She even slept peacefully all through the movie one night when we took her with us in the bassinet up to campus to see *Che!*

Within a month of sending off the *'Beautiful Dream'* poem, I got my SASE back from one Raymond Deeds, the editor of

Dr Deeds Press. He wanted me to come to New York immediately as he was going to publish the poem as a broadside to be distributed free on the streets of New York, and he wanted me to do a poetry reading, the next Saturday, at his pub, to launch the poem.

The lights came on. The circuit had been closed. I was going to New York. I now had recognition as a poet. Recognition, readings, money.

"Sheila, this is fantastic. It's a career step for me. Can you imagine—New York? This means I will have a track record as a published academic when it's time to go for my doctorate."

Sheila was happy for me, but she was also disconsolate. Ellen Andrews and Nuala Mulroy had warned me about watching for signs of the post-partum blues. I couldn't be sure, but I think she had it. I didn't want to leave her and the baby, but she insisted I should go. Fortunately, Robbie MacDuff was right next door, to keep her company, and I planned to make it a quick-hit trip and be back on Monday so I could go painting with Russell again and keep the big bucks rolling in.

I went by train to the city. It was most stimulating to find myself strolling down a street near Penn Station. In my folly, in my egotistical fancy, I was picturing myself as the dude on the cover of Dylan's *Freewheelin'* album. The poetry reading was held every Saturday afternoon at two, down in the back of Dr Deeds' Pub at the corner of 72nd Street and 2nd Avenue. Raymond Deeds turned out to be a large teddy-bear of a man who tended bar at Dr Deeds and was also the owner of the pub. He dressed in flower-print shirts, as he came from Hawaii, and his pub was Waikiki-themed.

I met Ray Deeds at the bar when I walked in and introduced myself. I only had one beer, just to take the edge off, as I was nervous and didn't want to slur my words. It was my first time in New York since I went to the Bronx with my Dad to pick up Aunt Adrienne on the way to Uncle Alek's funeral. How many years ago was that? I was thinking about it as I wandered down to the back to set up for the reading and passed the chalkboard where Ray had written '*Nicholas Petrovich, 2 PM.*' I took my seat and leaned into the microphone on the tavern-table and spread out my little poems. I read them with as much enthusiasm, emphasis and gusto as I could muster,

> *Aisling, my daughter, my own, in the light*
> *of day, with all your might, sing of the way*
> *of those who live untroubled by the night,*
> *to all the children who come to you, say,*
>   *here is the flower, and here is the thorn,*
>   *a woman and a child, suffering to be born . . .*

but I couldn't connect with the audience. They kept their heads down, barely noticed, ate their sandwiches and talked, drank their mixed drinks, and talked, right through my reading. I thought I was a disaster, but Ray said I was fine. "Hey, this is New York, they're into their own heads, I want you back in about six weeks again, when you gonna come out to my place on Long Island?"

I was among strangers. Raymond Deeds, my only friend. I was miserable spending two days away from Sheila and the baby.

One day on campus I happened to be at the Student Union and bumped into Agnes, one of my students from Freshman Comp, back in the spring.

"You've changed," she said, as I walked past her table without noticing her. "What's happened to you?"

"Oh, Agnes. I didn't see you there. How are you?"

"Sit down, sit down, I wanna hear all about it."

"Oh, Agnes, I don't know, I should get going." But then, it came to me that there was something I wanted to ask her. "Okay. Just for a minute."

Agnes was a brash, outspoken, cynical put-down artist who I remembered from class as being difficult. A tough girl from Cranston. "Mr Petrovich, you're growing your hair!"

"Call me Nick, please, Agnes."

"See! There you go! You *have* changed."

"Is it these painter's overalls I'm wearing? No? I guess not. Well, it must be the baby coming along, you know. "

"I know, I know. It was before the end of semester. How is she?"

"She's great, Agnes. I gotta tell you. We're so lucky, she's a perfect kid. She's made such a difference to me. I'm so happy."

"So that's what it is—you're happy."

Something in the way she said that, nodding, tilting her head—I leaned over. "Agnes, can I ask you something? What was I doing wrong with you, the kids in class? Especially you—I felt if I could just have gotten through to you, I would've been accomplishing something. As it was, I felt like I wasn't get through to anybody. Just a bunch of bored, dis-interested kids, don't know why you're there."

Her eyes narrowed. "You really wanna know?"

"Yes." I looked at her, my nightmare, and honestly, I said, "Yes, I do."

"You were uptight, Nick. You walked into class in that 3-piece pin-striped suit and tie of yours—"

"That was my wedding reception suit that I wore on my honeymoon."

"—and you were going through the motions."

"I was just repeating everything my professors had said to me."

"And where were *you*, in that scene? Nowhere. You were hiding. Behind that mask. Doing an impersonation. Nick—ya gotta loosen up. Let it all hang out. Grow your hair. *Get real.*"

I looked at her for what seemed like a long while, and saw someone there, in her eyes, I had never seen before. Not 'difficult Agnes,' but a completely different person. Finally, I rose, and said, "I gotta go. But—thank you."

Big smile. "Catch you later, man."

Chapter 51

David and Susan

I decided I was going to change everything I was doing. Or The Muse decided for me. Or events in the world intervened. It was hard to decipher any cause-and-effect links in the chain as everything in the mirror over the bar seemed to be alive in the melting transformations of the spinning ball of mirrors.

Was it precisely at the moment when we saw on television that something monumental, ground-breaking, epoch-making was going on at Woodstock? We had just finished watching Apollo 11 landing on the moon, and now this. Could things get more earth-shattering?

Woodstock. I was content to not be there. I didn't feel I was missing anything. I had everything, and everyone, I wanted in the little house with the tall steps on Sewall Road next door to Robbie MacDuff's place. Gary Wheeling was moving on to the confined space of the next square empty canvas. I was moving on to the next rectangular blank page. Within those boundaries we were making microcosmic compositions of the macrocosm beyond the borders. We were outside the edges. Marshall Drew was still surviving in that rocking lifeboat at the age of eleven. I was diving deeply into the mind of A.S. Neill, in the pages of *Summerhill,* gaining insights, seeing children and students as something completely new, not tin men to be stuffed with the straw of knowledge, but independent seekers who could be trusted to find their own truth because they possessed, and were possessed by, their innate goodness, their unstained selves, and their motivation came from the rotary engine of their uninhibited curiosity. The same place that landed Neil Armstrong on the moon. The same place that drove all those half a million to Woodstock.

Larry Lyman, who came to us originally from SUNY-Binghamton, was the first to return from Woodstock. He glided around the English Dept office, raving. We flocked to his house for the party and the celebration and the narration. He passed a joint around to me. Although I had never smoked anything in my life, I let my friends turn me on. At first, feeling nothing, all I could do was choke and sputter. But then a feeling of immense satisfaction came over me, and I was hearing things, seeing faces, laughter bubbled up out of me, hunger. I could feel my hair growing. Touching Sheila, my fingertips were alive with sensation and tenderness.

I was changing in the mirror before my own eyes. Growing and developing, and the tendrils of all the interconnected undersea formations in the aquarium over the bar were growing octopus links from the one central fundamental red heart. I was floating, one of the fish, one of the sea-monsters, one of the creatures of the depths, the Little Red Book of the Revolution was waiting in the waving weeds for me to grasp.

THE EDUCATION OF NICHOLAS PETROVICH

I stepped on board the interstate bus with *Washington, DC* flipped up by the driver into the destination window on the forehead of the walrus. Why must you go? my Sheila asked. Stay here with us so I won't be afraid. I said that if it were her country, she might do the same, I knew she would. Stay home with the baby and watch on television, just as we did with Woodstock. I'll be thinking of you every minute I'm gone. I'm doing this for our little one, so that someday she will have a country to live in that will be at peace.

All the hopes and dreams of half a million anti-war souls boarded that bus. I understand that all this is out of sequence, but then, everything was happening at once. You arrive on the first day of classes in September and you tell the students, no more military formation of ranks and rows of desks in the room, get up, rise up, and put them all in a circle. We will face each other. We are all equal. No one person in this room is the repository of wisdom. No one person wields the baton of knowledge. We will learn from each other. We will learn together. We will not be taught. Open your notebooks and write. You are all A-students. Write the way you speak. You have been speaking the language, and making yourself understood, for a long time. *Go with the flow.* Get out of your own way. Don't erect artificial barriers of sentence construction and paragraph composition, to become a roadblock to the stream of your thought. Vocabulary. If you need a word, go and find it. Your assignment is to bring back what you have written to the next class and share it. If you need a book, or want to introduce us to something, make it your contribution to the family.

Marshall McLuhan said "The medium is the message." What does that mean? Don't worry about what the administration put into the syllabus. You are the syllabus. Speak. Listen. Hear. No raising hands. I am not your leader. I am one of you. Martha wants to be called Marty. Are you listening? Marty has brought a record to class today. Let us all listen. We will lie on our backs on the floor in a circle with our feet touching and listen to The Moody Blues, *On The Threshold of a Dream*. Marty is a beautiful young woman and she has opened our ears by opening her heart to us. There is no shame in making a mistake. Next time you will get it right. Everything can be erased, everything can be over-dubbed. Practice will make you perfect. Keep practicing. That's why they call it a practicing doctor. You laugh when I say, but don't get on that airplane with a pilot who's only practicing. We gotta be real, people. This is a rock. That is a window. The window will break. Reality is the rock we stand on. Don't ignore the realities, but don't let them interfere with your vision. It takes many broken egg-shells to make a Revolution.

I returned from Washington with my baseball jacket soaked in tear gas. I had to throw it away. I cherished that jacket. I won it when our team won the league championship when I was fifteen. But I had to throw it away. We cannot cling to the used-up objects of the past, we cannot let them drag us down, when we are building a new world. In January, it will be 1970. *Does that mean the Sixties will be over?*

By April, in the spring semester, I was the most radicalized teacher on campus. I was popular. People were talking about my classes. They were coming to sit in, for no credit, to see what was going on. My hair had grown out, big, bushy and curly and dark. I'd gotten a pair of gold-rimmed granny-glasses.

People pointed me out. "There goes Jerry Garcia." Thom Bell, with his *Rocky's Revival* pageants, on the quad, on Fridays, at lunchtime, was the only person on campus crazier than I was. Like me, he had updated. No more Bogie and Bacall, he was now reviving Rocky Racoon.

One day, at the beginning of May, when Aisling was, amazingly, already almost a year old, and it seemed so many things had changed, I rented a yellow school bus, and everyone in my two sections of Freshman Comp climbed on board as I took them out to the Naval Base at Quonset. The overflow followed in their own cars.

We didn't try to enter the base. We just descended from the bus and crossed the grass to the chain-linked fence and spread out, a long line of people, feet planted, peering at the Naval Base inside through the fence topped with barbed-wire. Eventually, armed men in uniform came out to stand on the other side of the fence, but they just watched us, they didn't tell us to move or try to make us go away. They might have been wondering what we thought we were doing, or they might have been instructed not to bother us, so that this wouldn't turn into an incident. One of the students finally spoke up, asking me, "What are we doing here?"

"Good question," I said. "I just thought you might like to see what the Military-Industrial Complex looks like."

We left the Naval Base and proceeded on the school bus out to Jamestown Island, in the Bay.

There was an old Civil War-era fort half-buried in the grassy hillocks and dunes of the island, with magazines and powder-rooms and gun-turrets built out of concrete.

Eugene Christy

I saw two students, Susan and David, who had been a couple for a while now, sitting on a wall, watching the sunset.

I took out my notebook and wrote this down, for practice. (There were no cross-outs. It just went the way it came.)

It was almost evening, on the first day of May.
We went to the fort, on the island in the Bay.
Abandoned turrets dating from the Civil War
Aimed their dead artillery at the Newport shore.

I saw them in the distance, sitting on a wall,
David and Susan, wrapped in a shawl,
A pair of silhouettes, dark and slight,
Holding on, holding on in the twilight.

It is too late now to promise a return.
We are the lessons we could not learn.
Let the guns remain silent in the haunted fort,
While we go to the Captain and make our report.

Chapter 52

The 4th of May

Four days later, on the 4th of May, 1970, four students were shot and killed by the National Guard at Kent State in Ohio.

The image of the girl kneeling with her arms spread over the downed and dying student by the curb on the pavement by the tree and the grass appeared on the front page of the Providence Journal the next morning and sped around the newsstands of South County, the nation, and the world.

That day Robbie MacDuff and Russell Sage and Liam McCarthy and I met Larry Lyman at the *Perspective* office upstairs in the Student Union. Having heard that campuses all over the country were going out in protest, we discussed our situation. There was no argument. We all had been active for the entire past year in anti-war work on campus. We were going to take URI out on strike, too.

For the next two weeks, till the end of the semester, we took over the student union building as our base. Liam McCarthy was our best speaker. We held rallies on the quad daily. Hundreds of students trooped in and out of the Student Union every day, organizing, mimeographing, phone-calling, making signs. Fortunately, the faculty went out with us, and the governor of Rhode Island was persuaded that we had no intention of burning anything down and that police and soldiers were not necessary. Many of the phone calls we got were from anxious parents worried about their kids, trying to help, calling their state reps and senators, begging for hands-off. Nobody wanted a repeat of Kent State or Jackson State at our school. Instead, we held seminars and teach-ins and history classes; something was going on in every spare room in the Student Union, all day and night, every day. It seemed like ages ago since I'd first attended a lecture at Harvard, '*The Lessons of French Indochina.*' The rallies on the quad were outdoor teach-ins, a parade of students and professors to the microphone stand on the platform to testify, instruct and learn. No regular classes were held. I didn't go home to Narragansett for two weeks. Neither did Robbie, Russell or Liam. Nobody was arrested, penalized or prevented from graduating. This wasn't Mississippi or Ohio. This wasn't Nixon's Silent Majority-country. We were one of 242 campuses around the nation who had gone out on strike.

It was springtime, the sky was blue, the birds were singing, it was Sheila's birthday, Aisling was turning a year old, the sun was shining, the war went on.

Part 5

MILLTOWN

Chapter 53

Leaves of Grass

I thought that I had escaped forever the clutches of Milltown. But now, for the second time in my life, that derelict, downtrodden city reached out to suck me under, and this time, I would find no spell of romance cast by smokestacks on the horizon, stone dams holding back rivers, or frothing waterfalls, as once I did when I was nine and ten years old.

This time I was a grown man with a wife and child dependent on me, a grown man with no job, no money, and no place to live: in short, the usual unemployed, directionless, young, over-qualified, under-prepared liberal arts masters' degree graduate pseudo-hippie, who, after six years' absence, locked away in an ivory tower, drifts back to the grinding streets of Milltown as a last resort, only because he has family there to fall back on.

How I ever let this happen to me is easy to explain. The first step probably took place as early as my senior year at Boston

College. At that time, worn out from heavy lifting and long hours at the airport, Sheila had hooked me up with a job at the insurance company where she worked, Liberty Mutual. In the print department, I learned how to operate an offset-printing press to churn out all the forms the company used. When I wrote a letter to the head of the company criticizing the investment of company funds in apartheid South Africa, they called me in and offered me a job, to start as a trainee salesman.

At a time when my graduating BC cohorts from the School of Business Administration were fielding job offers, this was the one and only time a company ever tried to recruit me. I said no thanks, I'm going to grad school, for English, not bothering to explain to an insurance executive that I wanted to write poetry.

Then when I was in graduate school, instead of wooing professors in order to obtain letters of reference to apply for Phd programs, I thumbed my nose at them and violated every rule of behavior regulating the performance of graduate teaching assistants, sure that I was right, radical and progressive, and that they were wrong, right wing, and retrogressive.

Then, instead of planning to find a place to live, a decent job, and a logical next step to my life, as soon as the school semester ended, the strike against the Establishment I was fomenting ended also, and I ran off to spend a week in Long Island, at the invitation of my editor, Ray Deeds, in his little grass hut, where we smoked weed, drank beer, ate pizza and played the role of alienated young Sixties hippie word-smiths, fancying ourselves (my God, I was starting to talk like Sheila!) the literati of mind-altering poetics: self-appointed legends before our time.

Next I hitch-hiked my way to Roanoke, Virginia, to spend two weeks at Hollins College attending a literary conference under the tutelage of James Dickey, George Garrett and Larry

McMurtry. Of course, I arrived with no money to pay the tuition or fees, but of course, that didn't matter at all, as everyone was completely charmed by my insouciant bravado, and fed and watered and partied me just as if I had been one of the paying suckers.

Thus I was able to add to my resume the line, 'Studied under James Dickey, author of *Deliverance*, and Larry McMurtry, author of *The Last Picture Show*,' neither of which facts would help me to get a job bagging groceries at the Grand Union.

At this point, operating an offset-printing press was still the only practical skill I had acquired, unless my stint at Logan Airport could be said to qualify me for an unskilled-laborer job humping TV sets in a warehouse.

It was July 1st, 1970, and we had to leave our house on Sewall Road in Narragansett. So did Robbie MacDuff next door, as summer tourist season was now underway. Rob said he had been accepted into the BU Theological Seminary up in Boston, to start in the fall.

Unlike me, Robbie had no draft deferment, but like me, he opposed the war. Being the son of a North Carolina preacher, he was serious about his religious inclinations, and serious about being a pacifist. I supported his agenda wholeheartedly. He told me he didn't know anyone in Boston and didn't have a place to live, so I hooked him up with Billy Michele, in Southie, my old BC classmate.

I loaned Rod my last fifty bucks, since he was broke too, and he would have to give something to Billy to room with him in a flat in the Old Colony Road projects. Then I called my mother.

I called my mother in Spicket Falls and told her Sheila and the baby and I were coming home. I piled everything we owned, books and blankets and beach-buckets with little toy shovels, into the solid white hard-top '61 Olds I called 'The Ghost,' which I had bought with house-painting money the summer before, for 150 bucks, when Aisling was born, thinking we really need a car of our own now, we have a baby: one of the few concessions to practical necessity I made in two years in South County.

Motorizing up the highway heading for the interstate in that V-8 'monstah,' relaxing back into the red naugahyde bench seat in the front, with Sheila and the baby feeling the wind rush in the open windows, I was thinking, *I wonder if you could radicalize the working class in a place like Milltown, the way we did the campus?* Wouldn't that be a worthwhile experiment? If we could generate anti-war demonstrations in a place like that, if we could *'c'mon people now, smile on your brother, everybody get together try to love one another, right now . . .'*

The shock of un-recognition was like a hard slap. In six years away, while I went forward, Milltown went backwards. The magnificent old Post Office at the corner of Broadway and Essex Street was gone, a drive-thru McDonald's in its place. Movie-house Row, just to the north, with the neon brightness of *The Modern, The Astor, The Palace* and *The Broadway* queued up to invite the imagination—gone, like Rita Hayworth's youthful allure. Of the Essex Street five-and-tens, which used to include *Kresge's* and *W.T. Grant's*, only *Woolworth's* was left. The *Lauriat's* bookshop I used to haunt when I was in high school, dreaming over paperbacks of Stendhal and Thomas Hardy—there was a rumor that it might re-open in the new mall in, of all places, Spicket Falls.

Yes, that little country town of no more than 12,000 or so people that I remembered from fifth grade was now swelling with white flight from Milltown. When I was growing up there, you could identify the major ethnic groups in the city as the French, the English, the Irish, the Italians and the Syrians. The Greeks all lived upriver in Lowell. Now, Milltown had become home to a wave of Dominican emigration from New York City, and the character of the city was said, by the old-timers, to be forever altered.

The Italian neighborhood, centered on Common Street and the Sacred Heart Church in the shadow of the Everett Mills, had shrunk, and Hispanic shops were making inroads—Chiara Cheese was gone, and only Tripoli Bakery was still there to remind you of the old times. The Italian Festa of the Three Saints, Alfio, Filadelfo and Cirino, which used to attract thousands to Common Street every September to pin dollar-bills on the statue of the Virgin as it was carried through the streets on the shoulders of the men of the Society, was now a shadow of a vestige of its old glory.

In Spicket Falls, the quaint old redbrick Town Hall with its twin cream-colored columns flanking the front door had been replaced. A brand-new, modernistic, low-riding monolith housing the town offices, and the Police Station as well, on a landscaped campus of its own, opened at a new location opposite the Nevins Library, with stoplights added outside that were never there before,

The last job I had held in the place where I spent my teenage years was in the Dryer Room at Malden Mills. Now it was one of the few places around where Dominicans could get hired, and all the jobs were taken.

Why didn't the government do something about this eyesore of a city, where poverty was endemic and cast a pall over generations of residents, instead of spending America's wealth in a far-distant rice-paddy, blowing up billions of dollars bombing peasants' grass-roofed huts?

I promised my mother we weren't going to stay. It was just for the time being. I reminded her that now, in the fieldstone house on Elm Street in Spicket Falls, we were going to have three generations of the family under the one roof for the first time since I was a toddler and we were living on Payson Street in Revere.

I then retired to the parlor and shut the door, to close out the noise of the television coming from the den. For two weeks I laid on the sofa, stretched out in the shade from the front verandah, cooling off from the summer heat while I read through the entire span of Whitman's *Leaves of Grass,* a pleasure which I had postponed from graduate school until such time arrived in my life where I didn't have to write a term paper, but could read for the sheer ecstasy of reading.

I would read a few poems, lean my head back on the couch-cushion, blow smoke out the open window from my last bogarted joint, and reflect on what an uncannily accurate prophesy of our pot-smoking Sixties counter-culture Whitman's title, *Leaves of Grass,* made, chuckle to myself, and nod off to sleep with the book propped open on my chest so I wouldn't lose my place.

By August, I was answering questions about when I intended to leave the house and go looking for a job. And they were coming not only from my mother, and my father, but also from unspoken reproachful looks from Sheila, as she held the baby in her arms. Not to mention Jack and Jill, my brother and sister—who somehow, while I was away, unbeknownst to me, had grown up, and even graduated high school. *How did that happen?*

I knew I was related to my father because, like him, I was thoroughly content, when out of work, to sit at home and wait for the phone to ring, with that magic call from the Union Hall to start Monday morning at such and such jobsite.

This was a way of life down in mining country, imbibed in Dad's youth, and therefore, impossible to eradicate from his bloodstream. I could see the outlines of it in Uncle Mike Kowalcyzk as well. But it was worse in my case, as I was inoculated by DNA. It was an acceptance and indeed embrace of nonchalant loafing that infuriated my mother. In my case, however, there was no union hall carrying my name on the rolls, and I couldn't collect unemployment, as Dad might, and did, whenever he was out of work, since my brilliant career as a college teacher on a grad assistant's stipend did not qualify for anything practical such as social security deductions.

What nobody seemed to understand was that I was very diligent, and busy, pursuing my poetry career. I was firing off long letters of arcane literary ruminations to my editor in New York, Ray Deeds, as well as carrying on voluminous correspondence with people I had met at the Hollins College Literary Conference, mailing them off to such faraway cultural outposts as Toronto, Denver, Montreal and St. Paul.

It also seemed absolutely essential during what was left of this summer to use my time wisely to commune with the spirit of Walt Whitman. To do this it was most useful to recline on the sofa with my feet up. Not only did this cause blood to rush to my head, (I had unfortunately run out of both weed and money) but also it induced one to close one's eyes. This was crucial because to truly absorb such a long work as *Leaves of Grass* it was best to bite off small chunks and take one's time to digest them. You wanted to savor the morsels at the banquet, not inhale them like a vacuum-cleaner. To best achieve this I developed a method of reading just a few lines, then placing the open book face-down on my chest, and closing my eyes. Anyone in the house looking on might have thought I was sleeping, but I was not. I was letting those long lines filter themselves into my brain until I felt the moment of enlightenment turn on with a gentle glow of–comprehension, understanding, indeed, awakening. Upon this zen moment, I would open my eyes again, read another digestible amount, and repeat the procedure. And so it went until Walt and I were as one mind, universal and true, *the soul of America.*

And did not Brother Walt himself enshrine in his sacred upanishads the creed of loafing?

> *I loafe and invite my soul,*
> *I loafe and lean, observing a spear of summer grass . . .*

Chapter 54

Chickie and Phil

This did not mean that I was going to apply for welfare. Such an idea was several levels beneath my dignity. No one from our family, that I ever knew of, had ever sunk that low—unless it was Uncle Mike, back before he departed Fayette County and emigrated to Milltown to demolish the Wood Mill.

So I called my union hall—in my case, the Massachusetts Division of Employment and Training, commonly known as the Unemployment Office, which was located in Milltown, on the north bank of the Merrimack, only yards downriver from the Falls and the Broadway bridge. This low-rise one-story brick edifice was squatting in a parking lot dotted with chunks of un-repaired frost-heaved tar from the previous six winters, a parking lot flanked by scrub-grass and tall weeds along the riverbank.

Curiously, it also basked in the shadow of that old cast-iron railroad trestle upon which I had ventured to cross the river, on foot, precariously balancing, not looking down, when first I came to Milltown, so many years ago, a memory which now bubbled up, proving I had never really forgotten the tingling thrill of that childhood escapade.

An attractive young lady named Leslie had me take a seat at her desk after calling my number.

Looking over my application, she then perused her computer screen, after inserting a microfiche.

I marveled at this state-of-the-art technology, and calculated that it was about time the power of the establishment did something for me besides driving me to rebel against the military-industrial complex.

Though I was loathe to leave the immediate vicinity of the chance to chat with the lovely, ash-blond, long-legged Leslie, I was quickly referred to a job interview, on the fifth floor of the Bay State Building, at the corner of the Milltown Common where Milltown Street and Common Street intersect.

I departed, reminding myself that I was already married.

Let it not be said that my master's degree never even got me a job. Over-qualified as I was, and although it was a social work position, I filled a quota: they were hiring an unemployed statistic.

The organization was a Johnson-era poverty-program called the Community Action Council. A man named Chickie LoPino, an Italian, like me, hired me on the spot. He was second in command to a fellow named Phil LaRiviere, who was the head of the CAC, the initials by which Chickie referred to the organization. The CAC was an umbrella designation that covered a number of programs funded by federal dollars ranging from things like Head Start to the Fuel Assistance Program. Chickie wanted me to fill a vacancy in the CETA Program Intake office, which involved aiding and assisting new arrivals in the city to apply for and become enrolled in the Federal Comprehensive Employment and Training Act (CETA) programs such as the Job Corps and Neighborhood Youth Corps, which were designed to help the unemployed, underemployed and disadvantaged.

Chickie called Phil in to meet me. They both were enthused by what they took to be my expertise in English because they had big plans for me to take on grant-writing for the CAC, to help them secure federal funding for the many new program-ideas they had to expand the Milltown CAC.

I could not believe my luck. I had just been taken on by a pair of back-slappers who came from the old school of the city's ethnic groups, the French and the Italians—the Canucks and the Wops—two guys who were locals, and to me, obviously owed their positions to political connections, since neither one had degrees or backgrounds in social work.

That work-load they left to the professionals while they themselves wined and dined the city's business community and political apparatus and newspaper guardians, to grease the round, rotating mechanisms of support for the CAC. I was now one of the professionals that they counted on to do the grunt-work.

I could not believe my luck. Old Brother Walt had come through for me with his gospel of loafing.

Stop this day and night with me and you shall possess the origin of all poems,
You shall possess the good of the earth and sun . . .

Chapter 55

Eddie Domani

Now I could begin to test my hypothesis, that if we could bring the anti-war organizing from the campus to the nitty-gritty streets of the working-class city, we could bring the war home, and thereby, end it.

But where to begin?

I had been away six years. In that time, Milltown had changed, but I had changed, too.

Despite the pervasive gloom of grief that filled the room at the Dewhirst Funeral Home when the body of Jimmy Dillard lay there in a closed casket guarded by Marines, I did not think of any of the kids from the old neighborhood as anti-war material. *Kids?* What was I thinking of? None of us were kids anymore. If I couldn't talk to them when I was in high school, how would I be able to communicate with them now?

It wasn't just them—it was me. On the quad in Kingston, I was set down amongst equals, and I spoke freely, without condescending, since I knew they'd all been in the same courses I had, that we shared an equivalent intellectual footing. Knowing me, if I opened my mouth to the old gang, I would only be forcing myself, and I would end up talking down to them—from my superior height? I had to face it. Since the day I first set foot in Milltown, at nine years of age, I'd been the definition of an interloper: one who intrudes on the domain of others.

Then I saw a notice in the local newspaper, the *Eagle-Tribune*, which I now recognized to be a notorious Republican rag. It was buried mid-week on page 11 in the *Things to Do* section alongside the items for the upcoming Fall Arts and Crafts Fair and the Suicide Hotline.

> *Catholic Social Action Convocation*
> *Meeting on the Feast of St Cyprian*
> *Saturday, Sept 16th, 10 am*
> *St Basil's Seminary, Spicket Falls*
> *Public Invited*

To my astonishment, the Seminary turned out to be hidden in a grove of trees, doubly hiding inside the vast crenellated castle-walls of the Searles Estate. Growing up in Spicket Falls, I had been aware of the Castle Gate, and had even heard that this gate had once belonged to Napoleon Bonaparte, though I doubted that. The only other thing I was certain of was that Presentation of Mary Academy housed a Catholic girls' high school in several buildings right behind the main gate.

When I went to the meeting and evinced amazement, one of the monks kindly explained that Mr Searles, who built the Castle and the extensive walls, had been an architect, born in Spicket Falls in 1841. He went to San Francisco in the 1880s to design and build a mansion for the wife of a certain Mr Hopkins, who happened to own the Union Pacific Railroad. When Hopkins died in 1887, leaving all his fortune to his widow, Searles married the widow and brought her back to his home—Spicket Falls. When she died four years later, her fortune passed to him.

Searles adored the 16th century castle architecture he'd visited in Stanton-Harcort, in England, the home of his ancestral family. He copied it when he built his own Castle and estate walls, and when he died in 1920, the Hopkins railroad fortune had grown to 100 million dollars, making him the richest man in Massachusetts. "St Cyprian, of course, whose feast-day we celebrate today," the kindly monk hastened to add, "was a rich man of the 3rd century AD, who, after his conversion, became Bishop of Carthage, in North Africa, and donated his entire fortune to the poor."

We were standing in the foyer of the chapel of St Basil's, which was a Tudor-styled mansion made of heavy, dark wood, hidden in an evergreen grove next to a swan-pond. The Seminary had the air of a gingerbread house in forest of hooded elves.

Not more than a few streets away, you crossed the line into Milltown, where the tenement district began. Where the poor lived.

The man I met at that meeting was a devout Catholic layperson named Eddie Domani. Our first connection was a shared Italian background, which I inferred from his last name when he approached me to introduce himself. He was a tall, slender, handsome gentleman, a good deal older than me, I thought, from the grey tingeing the temples of his jet-black hair. He seemed as curious about me as I was about him. After the meeting, we walked out together to our cars parked under the evergreens.

Eddie Domani shook his head. "I don't expect much social action to be coming out of this gang, meeting here once a month. It's so hard to get cloistered clergy to move their heads over to where us lay people live."

It seemed to me this new acquaintance was a restive Catholic, who somewhere along the line had become disenchanted with the Church. Perhaps, like myself. "Where did you go to college, Ed?"

"Who, me? You got the wrong guy. I went to the US Navy school of swabbing decks. How is it you're Italian, if I may ask?"

"My mother's name is LaStoria."

"You're kidding me."

"No. Why?"

"The LaStorias who had the factory at the Oxford Mills?"

"Yeah. Why?"

"My wife Audrey is one of the stitchers who worked for Gene LaStoria."

For the next six months all our anti-war activities were fomented at Ed and Audrey's kitchen table on Alder Street in Milltown, one block north of Park Street, the most notorious slum in the city.

Ed and Audrey had six children, some of whom were almost as old as I was. Their teenage daughter Sophia was an enthusiastic supporter. She drew in some of her closest girlfriends from Milltown high school, rebellious girls who wore peace-symbol earrings and liked to chant "All we are say-ing, is Give Peace a Chance" at rallies. They brought along their boyfriends, who couldn't stand letting them out of their sight.

Ed worked at Western Electric in North Andover and was a staunch union member at a plant where they had Department of Defense contracts, and there was a certain element to the left of center among his union brothers who followed him into our activities.

Ed also knew all the musicians in town, as he was a jazz drummer going way back to his youth in the late 1940s on the South Side of Chicago. We knew all the same people from Milltown Music on Common Street, Mario Morelli, Roland Moore, Frankie Cahn, and Jerry Bellanti, who fortunately had made it back alive from his stint in the Army.

Music turned out then to be another common passion between Ed and me. Ed encouraged me to get out my old squeeze-box, which I hadn't touched in six years, and start practicing again, and soon we were doing gigs as a trio at the British Club in South Milltown, with myself, Eddie on drums and Roland Moore on guitar, and we were playing everything from *Lullaby of Birdland* to *I Left My Heart in San Francisco*.

This gave us the idea to start going around the city putting on pancake breakfasts and bean suppers. Milltown was dotted with social clubs all over town. These were often linked to the city ethnic groups, but also they were a place where you could still sit at the bar and get a 10-cent glass of beer in 1970. So we did the rounds of the social clubs that way and began raising money.

The city was full of cheap, empty storefront space, and soon we opened a street-level place right next door to Rainbow Lane, the tie-dye and water-pipe emporium at the corner of Park Street and Broadway. Our storefront was a desk, a table and a telephone, with anti-war posters on the walls and in the windows, and a hand-lettered sign above the entrance that read

Merrimack Valley Peace Action Consortium

Eddie and I stood across the street, in the deep late-afternoon shadow thrown by the Arlington Mills, to look at our handiwork.

"I like it," I said. "'Consortium' gives the idea that it's more than one group, and—."

"It spells Merrimack Valley PAC," said Eddie, completing my thought, "which kinda rolls off the tongue, sounds good."

It wasn't long before we were attracting interest from student activist groups at Merrimack College in North Andover and Phillips Academy in Andover. Our first black member was Tmolura Braxton, the son of a preacher from Jamaica, an immigrant who came, like so many others, in the long history of the city of mills, to start a new life in Milltown. Another valuable member joined our group in the person of Pat Scannell, a transplant from Philadelphia. He was a Vietnam veteran and he brought along local members of the *Vietnam Veterans Against the War.*

Pat Scannell was a vocal anti-war activist and he gave us credibility. He was a terrific speaker in the open air in front of a microphone. He reminded me very much of Liam McCarthy, whom we used to feature at the rallies on the quad down in Kingston.

In Milltown, we planned our rallies in October and November of 1970 to be held on the Milltown Common, across the street from where I worked at the Bay State Building.

Eddie Domani was a moderating influence on the rest of us. Also, he was nervous about the kind of rioting we'd all seen on television in recent years in Washington, Detroit and Los Angeles, sometimes in proximity of anti-war protest, as in the case of the Trial of the Chicago Seven.

"I don't want any SDS coming here to take advantage of what we've built up. I have to live in this town and raise my kids here, you know. And Milltown has a long history of getting their hides up against what they like to call 'outside agitators.'"

This was news to me, interesting, though. Eddie Domani was versed in local history that I was totally unaware of. "Nick, where have you been living all your life, under a rock? Ever hear of 1912?"

"No."

"The Bread and Roses Strike?"

"What are you talking about?"

"Hey—sorry–I forgot—this is America—why should I expect they teach you kids the real history of the country in school?"

Chapter 56

I Dreamed I Saw Joe Hill Last Night

Audrey Domani had an album called *Live at Woodstock* which she placed on the turntable in her parlor on Alder Street. Eddie wanted me to hear a track, and Joan Baez came on, singing 'Joe Hill.'

> *I dreamed I saw Joe Hill last night*
> *Alive as you or me*
> *Says I, but Joe you're ten years dead,*
> *I never died, said he*
> *I never died, said he . . .*

"Joe Hill was here in Milltown, singing and playing his guitar from the same bandstand we use for our rallies on the Common," said Eddie, "did you know that?"

"Tell me. Who was Joe Hill?"

"You'd probably think of him as a folksinger. But he was long, long before Bob Dylan or Pete Seeger or any of them. Even Woody Guthrie. Joe Hill was an organizer for the union, and the union was the I.W.W. They called them the Wobblies. Long before your time or mine. But if you want, I'll take you around to Garden Street to meet an old Italian friend of mine, Angelo Del Carmine. He was six years old when they sent him and a couple of hundred other kids out of town to sympathizers in New York City, to save them from starvation. There's old-timers still around like Angelo, Nick, who were in the Strike—it's almost sixty years ago, now, but still, that's within living memory."

Eddie and Audrey and I, with their daughter Sophia, stayed up long into the night discussing the lost history of the place where I grew up.

I went home troubled. I somehow felt guilty that I had lived a large part of my life in and around a city of which I was only now finding out, at the age of 23, I knew nothing.

I did what I always did. I went to the library. I started by retracing my steps back to the branch library on Winthrop Ave, across the street from my first school in Milltown, the Packard—which had now been converted into a pharmacy, with a parking lot full of cars in place of the 4th grade girls I remembered playing jump-rope at recess.

Wasn't this the way it always happened? *They paved over paradise and put up a parking lot.* And in the process eradicated all trace of what used to be.

The branch library had nothing at all on the 1912 Strike. The librarian advised me to try the main branch.

I went up to the corner of Hampshire Street and Haverhill Street in North Milltown where I remembered the old brownstone pile of the main city library used to be, across from the Gothic magnificence of St Mary's Church, the biggest Irish parish in the city. The library was now a day-care center. They sent me to the new library, just opened, across from Milltown High School on Milltown Street.

To my utter astonishment, there I found a modern glass-and-concrete building that looked exactly as if it had been plucked from Harvard Yard and set down by helicopter in the middle of Milltown.

The story of the Bread and Roses Strike, I now found, had been written in New York City, and what few books there were, had been published there by reputable publishers, but, during the Depression, when unions were strong, and the left-wing culture-mavens of the Thirties were carrying out writing and research projects on the Federal dollar through WPA arts projects, and you had to piece together the story for yourself by looking up histories of American Labor or the I.W.W. and biographies of people like Elizabeth Gurley Flynn.

There was basically nothing that told the story of the Strike itself. I turned to the newspapers of the day, available on microfiche, but there I found very slanted, biased reportage that focused on violent incidents and courtroom trials, even in the pages of *The Boston Globe* of 1912 and 1913—not to mention our local right-wing Republican rag, the *Eagle-Trib.*

When I got back to Eddie, I had the story filled in, blocked out, and memorized.

Flashback: (movie interrupted, a digression to fill in the backstory.)

Eugene Christy

In the dead of winter, 1912, for sixty-three days, twenty to thirty thousand Milltown millworkers, led by women, since most of the mill-hands were teenage girls and married mothers, had gone out on strike, braving the cold and snow. The mill-owners, led by William Wood, owner of the Wood Mill, (the same mill my Uncle Mike Kowalcyzk had demolitioned) had cut their pay by thirty-two cents a week, which represented three loaves of bread for the family.

It was a sudden, flash walk-out that started on the morning of January 11 at the Everett Mills, but spread quickly through every mill in the city. The Wobblies had a small contingent of members among these workers, but they immediately called in union officials from New York City, Joe Ettor and Arturo Giovanitti, already familiar with the city, to organize 23 ethnic groups, all with different languages, ranging from the English to the Irish and on through the Italians, Poles, Germans, Lithuanians, French-Canadians, and Syrians.

These 'outside agitators,' so-called by the mill-owners and their hired enforcers, organized a Strike Committee with representatives of every group. They brought in Elizabeth Gurley Flynn because they recognized the prominence of women in the origins of the strike, and because, in one of the most severe recent winters, there was real fear of starvation, especially among the old, the sick and the children. The national leadership of the Wobblies soon recognized that the President of the Union, Big Bill Haywood, would have to come to Milltown. Along with him came Joe Hill, the veteran songwriter and cartoonist of the Wobblies.

Two shipments of strikers' children were sent out of the city from the main Milltown railroad station (on Parker Street, on the south bank of the Merrimack; I had passed it a million times as a kid, on my way to cross the river on the Casey bridge, to go to W.T. Grant's, or maybe the Warner Theater, to see a show, never knowing what had happened there.)

The strikers' children, 6-year-old Angelo Del Carmine among them, were shipped out from the Milltown railroad station to sympathetic families in Cleveland, Ohio and Rochester, NY, Paterson, NJ, and elsewhere, but the third attempt to do so was attacked by the Milltown mounted police at the railroad station, during which assault pregnant women were billy-clubbed to the ground.

The Mayor of Milltown had long previously called out the local militia, and now the Governor of Massachusetts sent in state troops with bayonets drawn.

On a dark night, a striker named Annie LoPizzo was gunned down in the snow at the corner of Garden Street and Union Street. The authorities immediately arrested Ettor and Giovannitti and charged them with her murder. These two were arrested even though, at the time when the shots rang out, in the dark and the snow, they were at an indoor meeting *three miles away.*

They were jailed and their case became a worldwide *cause célèbre.* Demonstrations were held in Helsinki and Rome. Joe Hill came out with a song about Elizabeth Gurley Flynn called *'Rebel Girl,'* and another one called *'John Golden and the Milltown Strike,'* set to the tune of *'A Little Talk with Jesus.'* The authorities declared martial law and sent another 22 companies of state militia to Milltown to patrol the streets and enforce a curfew.

In spite of everything, and improbably, the Strike ended in victory, 63 days after it began, but only after a 14-year-old girl named Carmella Teoli had testified before Congress in Washington about how she had been scalped by a machine in the Everett Mills.

It was a dramatic tale full of pathos and anger.

I said to Eddie, "We have to write about this. This should be a movie. People have heard of Sacco and Vanzetti, but what about Ettor and Giovannitti? The story's never been told."

I had learned that my friend Eddie Domani was a self-educated man who was not just a union member, a father of six, an anti-war activist, and a musician, but who also painted and wrote poetry.

"How is it," I said to Eddie, "that I was in the Milltown school system and they never told me about this?"

"They didn't want you to know, Nick. You know what happened after the strike was over? The workers lost all the concessions that William Wood made to end the Strike. There were layoffs and shutdowns, people lost their jobs, especially when the economy went down after the war ended in 1918. Inflation went up in the Roaring Twenties and then there was the Red Scare that put the fear of God into politics. In Milltown, they started something called the 'God and Country Parade,' on Labor Day, of all things, and that went on for years and years because they were so scared shitless that the reputation of the city had been forever ruined by those uppity workers and they could no longer attract investment capital to the city. Then, after 1945, after they won another war on the backs of the people, they shut down all the mills for good and went South. Avoided the whole scenario. Wiped the slate clean. Escaped the unions for the right-to-work South. *Erased your history.*"

"Is that what's going to happen to us, too, Eddie? Will future generations know nothing of what we're doing here today, on Milltown Common, to fight against the war?"

Chapter 57

Thanksgiving and Forgiveness

Thanksgiving Day, 1970. Six months since Kent State and Jackson State, the Cambodian Invasion, the nationwide campus 'Strike against the War.' It seemed that nothing had changed, and yet, everything had changed.

My mother went all-out on her traditional Thanksgiving Day repast, with the Italian minastera-soup followed by the lasagna course followed by the 23-lb turkey with her uncanny vinegar-bread stuffing and the sides of mashed potatoes, yams, broccoli-limone, steamed cauliflower, and her inimitable home-made gravy, which she pored over on the stove, adding delicate increments of flour to the pan-scrapings while steadily stirring.

As always, she was the last one to sit down, and the last one to let anyone near her stove to help. Still, I could tell that something of the pleasure she took, in the old days, when the children were small, some of the light in her eyes at a house-full of her sisters and brothers and nieces and nephews, had gone out of the holiday.

It used to be that only on two or three special holidays a year did she open her dining room, and then it was filled with small, collapsible tables for all the little ones, separate from the grown-ups at her big table.

Now the only child at her Thanksgiving table was her little granddaughter Aisling, already a year and six months old, and, toddling around, babbling nonsense syllables and her first words, the apple of my eye.

I had much to be thankful for. Yet the war went on. It was a day of mixed blessings. I was busier than I ever could have conceived of back in South County, when all I had to worry about were two sections of freshman composition to teach and a student union to take over.

Now I was up to my neck in grant-writing, playing gigs with Eddie's trio at the local social clubs, trying to keep my desk clear with all the paperwork and interviewing involved with the Intake Program I was running at the Bay State Building; constant meetings with LoPino and LaRiviere and the rest of the staff at the CAC; and trying to manage weekends away in New York State, as Ray Deeds, down in the city, had arranged for myself and his stable of poets and writers to perform live readings to audiences on campuses in the SUNY system.

I had made tedious, high-speed overnight Saturday-Sunday trips to Cortland State, Albany and Binghamton, scurrying back home again in time to be at work on Monday morning.

Then there was my obsessive preoccupation with anti-war work, as if the fate of the nation depended on me.

I hardly ever saw poor Sheila anymore, nor did we have a minute to ourselves, alone, in the fieldstone house. My brother and sister, Jack and Jill, had graduated from Jenney High back in June, and I had missed everything, their proms, their graduation ceremonies, because I was all wrapped up in my own life, in my writing, in my trips to Long Island and Virginia, in my wife and baby and family, in a thousand pressing, urgent, minute-to-minute instant-dramas of anti-war organizing. *No sooner did I open a can of soup than it was boiling over on the stove.*

It was unforgivable of me, yet my sister Jill had forgiven me.

I had missed the last six years of her growing up, those crucial problem-years of the high school girl with the black-plastic-rimmed pointy eyeglasses. That was my sister who looked up at me out of her high-school yearbook photo. She had given me a folder holding her picture, a folder which allowed you to stand her picture up on top of your dresser.

On the blank-leaf side she had filled in the entire page in her flowing, slanting-upwards script with expressions of her love and caring, admiration and pride, in what she wistfully called her 'Big Brother.' And there was the yearning which is ever-present in the teenager leaving high school.

And where had Big Brother been during all this time? Absent. Out of touch. Neglectful. Inconsiderate. Selfish. All the things I had vowed never to be.

And yet, she had forgiven me. She found it thrilling to be an Auntie. She adored little Aisling and went out of her way trying to be of help to Sheila and me. Nothing phased Jill from burping to diaper-changing. She would sit and play with the baby for an hour straight, and look up smiling. In my little sister I could see the same maternal instinct that thrummed through every fiber of my mother or my wife. And as much as I pondered it, as much as I wished to put it down in writing, the understanding, the appreciation remained beyond me, a mystery incomprehensible to the male mind, pre-occupied as it is with stupid pride and obstreperous navel-gazing.

The kind of feeling I got from Jill I did not get from her twin, my brother Jack. There everything was shaded to the opposite. There was an edginess there, a kind of stand-offish-ness, as if Jack took me as some kind of rival, who had returned home to occupy the spotlight that he had become accustomed to belonging to him. No longer was he the sole subject of his mother's catering ways. No longer was it obvious that his mother preferred him to his twin sister. Now he had to split time with his mother's first-born.

And his relationship with our Dad also was different than mine.

No longer was I "No.1 Son," to use the phrase Dad had long-ago borrowed from the Charlie Chan movies. I had simply turned out not to Dad's liking at all. I had turned out wrong. Jack was much more the son Dad wanted, the son who took up the hammer and nail in his footsteps, the son who inherited the carpenter gene. Where the hell had I come from? What in the world did I mean spouting poetry?

I knew that I didn't belong in this fieldstone house anymore, no more than I had belonged in it when I first came to Spicket Falls. I was an outlaw in my own family. I was the interloper.

Sheila knew it, too. The longer we stayed in my mother's house, the more difficult it became for her. She picked up on all the nuances, all the cues. The tensions and the silences bothered her intensely. She missed her girlfriends, Pinky and Jeanie, even the Gomez girl in South County. She even missed the year she was pregnant, when we were alone together, independent days in our little beach-house, when we could do as we bloody-well pleased.

Here in the midst of a home-life between family members who had a history going back to infancy, a history that did not include her, she missed her own mammy and da, her own brothers and sister, far away in Ireland and England, even her two sisters far away in Boston. Any weekend when I wasn't on the road to New York or attending meetings at the Merrimack Valley PAC, Sheila wanted me to drive her and the baby in 'The Ghost' (I still had the old V-8 '61 Oldsmobile) down to her sisters' houses in the suburbs, thirty miles south. Mary and Tom Moran now had two children, Mary-Jane and John, and they had moved from renting in Brighton to a house they bought on Dwinnell Street in West Roxbury. Bridie and Vito Liguriano now had two daughters, Carol-Anne and Jennifer, and they too had moved, leaving Jamaica Plain to settle in a new house of their own at Wollaston Beach in Quincy.

As soon as we stepped into Bridie's or Mary's house with Aisling in our arms, I could feel the sigh of relief coming from Sheila. She was among her own again.

Who could blame her? Evidently, marrying an electrician was the way to go. What was I doing for her? Making Sheila have to share and divide and debate child-rearing practices with my know-it-all mother, in my mother's kitchen, was not the way, exactly, to make her happy.

Yet we loved each other, and because we did, we overlooked imperfections in one another, and did not make an issue out of politics, literature, or love—or Eddie Domani.

Sometimes I longed for the slower pace of campus life, the bucolic setting of South County.

I avoided any topics that I knew we disagreed on, such as Nixon, or the war, with Tom or Vito, my brothers-in-law through marriage. I stuck to those beautiful babies we were making with three wonderful sisters.

I found I could talk to my brother Jack if the subject was the Red Sox or the Celtics. We avoided the lousy Patriots. Bobby Orr and the Bruins were hot. There we were on safe ground. Strictly, we avoided religion, politics and anything to do with The Beatles vs Three Dog Night.

I sometimes felt so distracted and pulled in directions that I couldn't piece together any threads that would align themselves to compose whole cloth. I often despaired of writing anything, and instead felt my own soul slipping away from me, along with all the grand projects I had planned upon acquiring a master's degree.

Our baby Aisling was now no longer an infant, but a year and seven months old, when Christmas came around in 1970, and she was a delight to the whole household on Elm Street. Not since my sister Jill stood still for a half second on the stairway in her footie-pajamas, on the way downstairs to the tree in the den, to have her snapshot taken, had the fieldstone house seen such undiluted joy of the season. And Aisling was still too young to really know what was going on, so the gift-giving and present-opening showered on her was more fun and excitement for the grownups in the house than it was for 'The Child,' as Sheila called her.

In so many ways it was a season in our lives which seemed to testify that the older you get, the more you cling to earlier days, days of sunniness and hope, and treasured memories.

I was most proud of Sheila. As we sat on the Christmas sofa in the den together, crowded around my mother's cherished photo albums, showing black-and-white pages of mountains of presents piled under gloriously-tinselled-and-starred Christmas trees, I wondered if it pained her at all to have missed such things in her own childhood.

I knew that she had grown up in a farm family of six in the west of Ireland, but what did I really know? What was that like for her? In their house had she been the object of abundant gift-giving, as these old snapshots seemed to take for granted, or had there been want and deprivation? How would I ever know, since I didn't dare even to bring it up.

Yet Sheila did not begrudge any of us our happiness. There was not such a bone in her body. Nor had she ever seemed to evince any feeling that she had ever gone through a deprived childhood. In fact, whenever she brought it up of her own accord, she seemed to cover those days with a patina of reminiscence that made it glow with a lost perfection, unmatched, unexcelled—never to be regretted. Certainly not. If anything, it was the sort of childhood she would wish own Aisling might have.

That was why the new year of 1971, as it was approaching, seemed to hold so much promise for Sheila and me. Whenever we had a moment together to ourselves in the fieldstone house when we could stand there and gaze upon our sleeping child in her crib, it made us embrace each other, arms around waists, and look into each other's eyes with such tenderness and love, to see what we had created together, that it was daunting to think that there could be this much emotion in the world.

And that was why, in the middle of January, when an evening came with a bit of a January thaw in the midst of a New England winter, and Sheila pulled on her coat and asked me to come outside to take a walk with her, I went gladly with her, happy that she asked.

Hand in hand we started away from the back porch down Glenwood Avenue past the Perrault's snowed-under basketball court, past the Dolan's white house with the low hedges opposite the vacant lot, approaching the crest of the hill on Glenwood at the corner of Durrell Street where Mrs Dillard's lonely two-family waited still for her Jimmy who was never going to be coming home again. All the scenes of my own adolescence which I had forgotten, but which were—still there.

Down the hill we went hand in hand, past the Clapp's house, and Paul Lamond's on the corner of Hazel Street, where we entered the path that led over the brook through the snow-littered bare-branched patch of woods and swamp that led to the schoolyard behind the Ebenezer Parker—where once, in February, we used to shovel off the basepaths so we could choose up sides and play ball, unwilling to wait for summer.

We sat on the fire-escape behind the school nearest the closest ballfield and I put my arm around her as Sheila shivered, pulling her close.

"Cold?"

"Not really. You can keep me warm."

"Could be worse. At least it's up to 42."

Sheila shivered again. "I don't think in Ireland I can ever remember it going below about 40 in the winter. I mean, a day like this. I never know if my Celsius translates, you know?"

"So this suits you, does it?"

She looked at me, but didn't answer. Instead, she said, "I miss you."

"Sheila!"

She put her forehead against mine.

"I didn't know."

"Can I have my Nicky back?"

"What can I do?"

"Do you think we could get a place of our own?"

"Has my mother been nasty with you?"

"I don't think she's trying to be. I just think it's hard for her to tolerate me."

"She loves that baby."

"She's my babby, too. Our child."

"Okay, honey. I think you're right. I think it's time we moved. I think's it's long past the time. Why didn't you bring this up before, Sheila?"

"Oh. You know. The holidays, love."

Chapter 58

The War Comes Home

To promise to leave the fieldstone house was easy, but to actually do it, not so much. I was hesitant to come right out with a big announcement for fear of my mother's reaction. Ever since I'd come home from Rhode Island, we'd had two cars in the driveway, a novelty in our history. Neither Uncle Augie nor my mother had ever had a driver's license. We had to keep the cars off the street in winter, for the plows. My Dad was not about to give up his privilege of parking his Jeep in the garage, so The Ghost, my '61 Olds, was blocking the driveway behind him. As usual, he was working a jobsite in Tewksbury, or Burlington, or Billerica, or Haverhill, wherever the Union Hall sent him, always a commute. I had to get up early to move my car.

Since I was up early, I would see my mother getting bundled up to trudge out to the top of Elm Street and cross over Haverhill Street to wait at the bus stop opposite the Hillside Market. The days when her brother Gene would pick her up in the morning to drive her to work at the shop at the Oxford

Mills were long gone. While I was away for six years, she was working for Papagallo's at the Everett Mills in Milltown, where her father, long, long ago, had been the factory manager, in the late forties. One day it finally occurred to me to say, "Ma, the car's already warmed up—I can drive you to work in the morning, you know. I have to go to Milltown anyway."

"Thank you very much. I've gotten along very well without you for all these years."

I took this as a no. I knew better than to ask again. My mother had her ways of letting you know exactly how she felt. Sheila knew. Behind her words, I heard her saying, *this is how I paid for your tuition at BC while you were taking Sheila out to the movies.* It hurt me every time I passed that bus-stop to see my mother still standing there in the cold, with her mittens and knit-cap, still waiting for the bus, and I had to pass her by. She was almost 56 years old and still making under three dollars an hour, on piecework as a stitcher. Now I knew why she had failed to show up at my graduation from Boston College, and sent her sister Mary from Watertown in her stead, and why my photos of the occasion showed my Aunt standing next to me proudly, and not my mother.

And then, the next thing you know, we have Aisling, at South County Hospital, and my mother is ferrying herself, loaded down with big boxes of Pampers, which we couldn't afford, on weekends, driving Dad batty in his Jeep with her co-piloting. I never in my life would ever understand women.

The end of February was arriving and the twins were turning nineteen, and their birthday party coming up gave me yet another excuse for not being ready to move out quite yet.

That, and the fact that, on my take-home of 325 bucks a week from the CAC, it wasn't exactly easy to save up the security deposit money we needed. On top of a security deposit, some landlords were demanding three months in advance, at rents of 500 and 600 a month for a two-bedroom apartment, on a second or third floor, or in a brick complex, like the Lowell Arms on Lowell Street.

Nor did I want to confess to Sheila that I'd loaned 500 bucks to Hector Fernandez, my assistant at my office, who translated for me on interviews. Hector had come to me very awkwardly, feeling forced to beg for money. He was desperate to fly his sick sister up from the Dominican and get her in the hospital at the Milltown General.

How could I say no to the poor guy? That was one of the reasons I hadn't proposed moving out myself, before Sheila ever did.

I knew what it was like to be broke. When we returned from Rhode Island, I was stone cold broke, so broke that I had to hitch-hike to that literary conference in Roanoke because I didn't have the scratch for the bus ticket.

And once we were re-settled in the fieldstone house, I couldn't offer to give my mother a little something for expenses, since I didn't have a job yet.

And now, I still hadn't seen Hector pay back any of that 500 dollar loan. Every week was a new excuse. He worked for me, so I didn't want to press. It would only make everything so much more impossible around the office. I was very good at my own area of expertise, having no trouble reclining on the sofa to read old loafer Whitman; but with household finances, or sums of money above two bucks, I was clueless. Somebody had whispered in my ear, *All You Need is Love* . . .

Finally, I had found the Uniondale Apartments. They had a one-bedroom unit available in a decent-looking redbrick complex wedged into a hillside next door to the Mt Carmel Church and parochial school in the middle of Spicket Falls, only a block from the fire station and the Oxford Mills.

Perhaps the landlord only wanted two months rent in advance because the parking lot beside the building was so steeply inclined that people didn't want to live there. How would they ever get it plowed out in the wintertime? That, and the fact that the view from our bedroom window, and living room window, as well, would look out across Union Street at a Civil War cemetery.

I told Sheila it was an historical location. In any case, it was sight more decent than the top floor of a triple-decker on the Broadway side of Tower Hill in Milltown.

In spite of these high-finance dilemmas, I managed to buy birthday presents for Jack and Jill. Books, naturally. I found them at the new Lauriat's, at the new Mall, which was now finally opened in Spicket Falls, with a special exit, which had never been there before, from Route 213, which had never been there before. I'd been away too long. I'd missed too many birthdays. How would I ever make up for it? Jill was getting *The Mists of Avalon* by Marion Zimmer Bradley, because she was a devotee of the King Arthur tales. Jack was getting *The Curse of the Bambino*, by Dan Shaughnessy, the Globe sportswriter. Would that be enough?

I was quite happy that evening to arrive in the den for the twins' birthday party with my gifts. I thought I'd done well in picking them out to suit their interests. I knew that my mother would be taking care of things such as: one birthday cake, but with double candles, plus ice cream.

We all knew that Ma never allowed for our friends to attend these affairs, as we were growing up—it was strictly family circle only. Dad's presence was hardly necessary, but, of course he was there, probably with a new wrench or drill-bit set for Jack, and God knows what for Jill, probably something plastic. Mister Sensitive he was not.

Sheila had Aisling on her knee on the sofa, ready to explain to her yet another set of weird grownup rituals that she could not be expected to comprehend just as yet. Dad had his ever-present fire going in the fireplace. Ma would be sad and woebegone; she would be thinking of how her brother Augie wasn't here to celebrate with us; how she was getting older, day by day; how, as the years went by, she was, more and more, kicked to the curbstone. I myself was picking this occasion, with everyone gathered, to lie in wait for the appropriate moment to spring my big announcement about moving out.

But my brother Jack beat me to it with a big announcement of his own.

"Ma—Dad—I guess I gotta tell you sometime, but—Roland Perrault and me have enlisted, and we're going in the Army on the buddy system."

"Oh!" said Dad, jumping up from Uncle Augie's recliner, nearly spilling his plate of birthday cake on the floor. "Congratulations, Jack!"

When I heard that coming out of my father's mouth, I lost it.

"Whaddya mean, congratulations! Are you outta your mind!"

My father only looked at me open-mouthed with cake crumbs on his lips.

"Don't you know this is a death sentence for your son!" I cried. "Haven't we already lost one kid from this very neighborhood in Vietnam, and seen him come home in a box! What the hell are you people thinking?"

I did not spare my mother as I looked around the room with this accusation. "What is your son to you?–just–just–cannon fodder! Yeah, yeah, send him off to the Army, they'll make a man outta him!"

My little brother Jack then said, "Nick, why don't you just shut the fuck up!"

I saw Ma's face turn deadly black and she moved to crawl away from the room when she heard her beloved Jack utter the word *f-u-c-k*.

I turned on Jack. "What do you think I've been fighting for all these months! Don't you know it was to save you!"

"Oh, you can talk, all right, Nick. You're nice and safe with your little draft deferment on the side. But I turned 18 this time last year, and I had to go down to the Spicket Falls town hall and register. I'm not so lucky as you. So—what did you expect me to do?—sit around and wait to get drafted? I ain't getting anyplace as it is working at *The Clambox*, I can tell you that. I gotta think of my future."

"You're not going to have any future!" I exploded.

Now my father intervened. "Don't you dare talk to your brother like that!"

He made a move toward me with the plate of cake still in his hand, but I was enraged. I pushed him in the middle of his chest, and somehow, the cake and the plate went flying one way, and he went flying and staggering and stumbling backwards over Uncle Augie's recliner, when the back of his knees hit the seat. As he lost his balance and fell, the whole recliner tipped backward up against my mother's built-in bookcase with the hardbound sets of John Steinbeck and Lloyd Douglas. Then the stubby back legs of the recliner skidded out, and the chairback ended up flat on the floor, and all the books came tumbling off the shelf, spilling all over my father, lying on his back on the seatback on the floor, after knocking over the firescreen with one leg.

I looked at what I had done, stunned.

Jill was crying, and moaning, "Oh, this is awful!"

And all I could think of was that she was a part of condemning her own twin brother to being hunted down by Viet Cong because she was dating her brother's best friend, Roland, and they were going in together on this crazy buddy system, which was just a scheme on behalf of the military-industrial complex to make it more palatable to our generation to impale themselves on a flagstaff from Iwo Jima.

She must have known all about it, and she hadn't said anything to me, and probably she thought she was in love with this kid Roland, and probably she supported the whole thing because it was what Jack wanted, and Roland, too, and how could she, *she* go against her own twin, and—*Oh, God!*

I ran from the room, barely conscious that Sheila was trying to save herself, and 'The Child,' by escaping up the stairs to our bedroom at the top, Aisling wailing with fright.

I fled from the den into the kitchen.

And there was my mother, slumped at the table, as I made for the back door, muttering at my back as I went by, "Nice birthday party."

Chapter 59

Nixon Strikes

Spring began for me that year of 1971 on March the 1st when we moved into the Uniondale Apartments.

It was as if the Civil War headstones across the street had risen up from their tents to form up for the new campaign.

The nation divided was in my head. All I had to do was to lift the white shade on the un-curtained window in our bedroom to know my life had changed forever.

I was completely estranged from anything which had gone before that could be considered normal. Everything now came down to Sheila and me and The Child, and whether or not we had the money to put enough gas into The Ghost to get where we were going.

At least Sheila was still with me. It was hard on her trying to comprehend me and what I had done and why I had put her and Aisling and everyone else through such turmoil. But she knew enough not to bring it up with me. Whether that meant she understood, or was just afraid, I didn't know or care, because all I could think of was to be single-mindedly focused on ending the war which had done this to me, my brother, and my family.

Our first spring protest on the Milltown Common was a disappointment. People who had flocked to our support back in the previous fall were slow to return. Nixon had brought home 25,000 troops from Vietnam, and he kept promising that victory was just around the corner. Kissinger, at the Paris peace talks, was still arguing about the shape of the table. Cold, rainy weather did not help, nor did the frozen ground. The war now was just a fact of life. It had always been there and always would be. We pushed it aside and lived around it. Even I went to my dutiful desk everyday at the Bay State building and did my chores. Did I have any choice? No. I had dependents, that's what I had. Playing guitar from the bandstand on the Common where Joe Hill had once stood to sing out *'Rebel Girl'* was just a gesture from my Vietnam Vet friend Pat Scannell. We could play Country Joe's *'Feel Like I'm Fixin' to Die'* Vietnam Rag all we wanted, it was just 'blowin' in the wind.'

I stood there in the dank March chill on the frozen Common and despaired as I looked around at the few stragglers. What did it matter what I did?

But the people came back in April, with the improvement in the weather. We were now a tradition. We were now expected to be there in the summer concert season, our own local, mini-Woodstock. You could bring your girl and your blanket and your baby-stroller and bottle of wine and picnic basket and a couple of joints, lay out on the grass and gaze at the clouds going by. Set your watch by the fifteenth of every month on the

Milltown Common for the protest. As long as we had to have the war, at least we'd have music from the bandstand.

Our father-figure from the Merrimack Valley PAC office, Eddie Domani, politely ignored the pot-heads and spread his wisdom of poetry and peace. Eddie and I had grown closer in the wake of my troubles. He was now like a mentor to me, and where I couldn't turn to Sheila for useful advice, or even to unburden myself, I could talk to Eddie. He advised me to leave the bridge open instead of burning it down. He advised me that when one door closes, another opens. He didn't question or condemn me. He knew I could do that for myself. Eddie was the one who forgave me.

In May and June, the protests were larger, and we were getting press coverage in the local Republican rag, which I now called the '*Eagle-Flea-gle*.' The Boston papers took no notice, although every time a derelict 3-decker burned down in Milltown, they were on it. But the photographers from the local press were now there on a regular basis. We could see them standing on the margins of the crowd, maintaining their professional distance, taking their pictures. They would stroll languorously in circles around the edges, like shepherds with their flock, looking for interesting signs, new and different head-bands, protean beatniks, extra-long-haired hippies, and soon we'd see the pictures in the papers.

Sheila came dutifully and while I ran busily hither and yon as if I were someone important, I knew she and the child were there, and I had family with me. It was on one of these occasions when I returned to our blanket just to spend some time with her that she first brought up an idea we hadn't discussed before.

"I've been thinking lately of going home this summer."

"Really."

"Just for a fortnight or so, maybe. What do you think? Have we the money for Aer Lingus?"

"I don't know. I suppose we could muster it up, as long as the rent is paid. Why? What were you thinking?"

"Well, it's just that mam and dad, you know, have never yet met up with their new granddaughter, and I rather wish they could, you know, before they pop off or something."

I knew exactly how Sheila felt. I felt the same way, precisely, when Aisling was born—I wanted my parents to be proud of me and happy to welcome our child into the family.

So, how could I ever deprive Sheila of the same satisfaction? It still pained me that her parents had not attended our wedding. Even though I knew they hadn't attended the weddings of Sheila's sisters Mary and Bridie, either. After all, my own cousin Tony in Watertown had married a girl from Glasgow, and her mother managed to cross over from Scotland for the wedding.

"Now that Aisling's turned two years of age, don't you think it would be all right for her to travel in the airliner? Aer Lingus has never been known to have a crash, so it's quite dependable, you know. It's like taking the shuttle-bus to Jamaica Plain. And the old ones are not getting any younger. Last summer they had Mary's John and Mary-Jane over, and I'm told they were thrilled with them. Wouldn't it be grand for them to have the same chance with our Aisling?"

"Of course you're going to go, darling." I leaned over and we kissed sweetly. "Just as long as you come back to me when your holiday's over."

"Will you not come with us, Mr Petrovich?"

"I wish I could, Sheila. Oh, how I wish I could. But—it's not just a question of the money. It's all this here. I just can't get away right now. Someday. I promise."

I would be keeping that promise a lot sooner than I knew then.

After our protest on the Common in July, our biggest gathering yet, in spite of the hot, beach weather, or maybe because of it, Chickie LoPino called me into his office at the Bay State Building.

"Sit down," he said.

That sounded ominous, as he was standing when he said it, and not sitting down himself, but pacing.

Reaching down into a desk drawer, he pulled out a handful of enlarged, black-and-white glossy photos.

"Is that you?"

I looked over them and instantly saw myself on the Milltown Common.

"Where did you get these?"

"The FBI's been in to pay me a visit."

So—*not all those photographers were from the Flea-gle.*

"What I do on my own time is no business of yours, Chickie. I'm exercising my God-given Constitutional rights as a U.S. Citizen, that's all I'm doing, and I have every right, and nothing you can do or say's gonna stop me."

"Do you know who you draw your salary from?"

"What's that got to do with anything?"

"You draw your salary from the US government you're protesting against every month on the Milltown Common, that's who. And if you ask me, you're a goddam disgrace, and I'm not about to be embarrassed by you."

"What are you, LoPino, a fucking Republican?"

"I'm a goddam law-abiding citizen—."

"I know you live up across the line in New Hampshire. You're a suburbanite. You don't even live in Milltown. What the fuck are you doing running poverty programs in the inner city?"

"Oh, you're right about that, Nicky-baby. I am running this program. And as long as I am, I'm not receiving any more visits from the FBI at this desk. So you just get down to your office, Mr Petrovich, and clean out your desk. You're gone!"

"Does Phil LaRiviere know you're doing this?"

"Oh, don't you worry about that. Phil knows better than not to back up his second-in-command."

"You haven't heard the last of this from me, Chickie."

"Look. Just get out of my office. And don't be here at five o'clock or you can walk out in handcuffs courtesy of the Milltown Police."

When I got home early to the Uniondale Apartments, Sheila could tell I was furious, and tied in knots, with just one look at my thundercloud brow.

"Fucking Chickie LoPino fired me, Sheila."

"Why? What happened?"

"The FBI, that's what."

I grabbed the telephone.

"I gotta talk to Eddie. What's his number? Jesus, I just can't think right now."

When I got through, Eddie advised me to calm down and take it slow and tell him everything. I told him I knew where all the bodies were buried on Chickie and Phil. I told him I wasn't going to take this lying down. I told him how many grants I had written for those two, and how every time I got them another program funded, they always instructed me to write them in for a grand or two in the budgets of the new ones for 'supervisory responsibilities,' so that The Director of the CAC and the Deputy Director were getting literally tens of thousands a year padded onto their base salaries, while doing little to nothing besides appearing, in name only, at the top of the letterhead. They were making a mockery of the poverty programs and using them to line their own pockets. Phil was running for mayor and expected me to show up at his spaghetti dinners and work the phones for him so he could exercise his political ambitions while he fired me for exercising my political rights, and I wasn't about to take this lying down. Eddie said to calm down, I was repeating myself, and going way too fast, he'd make a call to a reporter friend at the Eagle-Tribune for me, and get back to me.

I put the receiver back on the hook and said to Sheila, "You're still going home, but I may be going with you."

In the end, I sent Sheila and Aisling on ahead of me. I told them I would follow in two weeks or maybe a month at the most. In the Yellow Pages, I looked up a day-laborer agency called *Jobfinders* down on Essex Street and signed on. I was used to getting through a year at college by saving up a thousand bucks by the end of the summer. I figured that was all I needed to get through a year in Ireland, as long as I pinched pennies and had a place to stay, which, thanks to Sheila, I would. I told *Jobfinders* I was an experienced house-painter, but they sent me out on lawn-care jobs and warehouse temping five days at a time and one time they sent me over to the Milltown Airport to stand there with a shovel in my hand while a backhoe dug a trench for a pipe-laying. I held back the rent due on August 1st at the Uniondale Apts. I added that to my kitty, 500 bucks, so I was halfway there. I didn't care about breaking any year's lease. I would be gone.

I went to the interview Eddie set up for me with his friend-reporter at the Eagle-Trib, but the guy was skeptical at best and, moreover, mistrustful. He blew me off as a disgruntled guy who got fired and not much of a whistle-blower. I didn't care anymore. I was gone. I was through with this filthy country, its stench of corruption, that creep Nixon and his war-mongering mongrel semi-Nazi war-criminal attack-dog, Kissinger.

Eddie advised me to go see my mother before I left. He told me no matter how I felt right now, I'd regret it the rest of my days if I didn't. He told me bluntly she was the one who had given me life and she deserved that much respect from me.

I had sold my car to get 100 bucks out of it, but I didn't know what to do with my squeeze-box. I would never sell that—but I could hardly take it with me. Where would I leave it? It gave me a good excuse to drop in back at the fieldstone house on Elm Street.

I tossed the accordian case up on one shoulder and walked the two, two-and-a-half, three miles, or whatever it was, from Union Street all the way to Elm Street, switching the box from one shoulder to the other, walking wearily the same way I used to go, in the other direction, full of anticipation in my cleats and uniform, on the way to play ball with the Ingalls at the Pelham Street Playstead.

My mother was sitting at the kitchen table when I came in through the back door with the accordian by the handle of its case. I sat it down upright on the floor. She glanced at me, and it, and then looked away, putting her chin in her hand. I could see she was going to give me the silent treatment. My dad was in the den with the TV on low, nursing his hurt feelings.

"Ma, I gotta leave this here. Where I'm going I can't take it with me. You may not believe this, but, you bought this for me when I was ten years old, and it's meant a lot to me. Well. That's all."

As I went out the door, I looked back and said, "If I don't come back, you'll know I'm dead."

I don't know what made me say that. I was leaving my mother sitting there with one son in boot camp on his way to Vietnam and another leaving for Ireland.

As I was walking away down Glenwood, thinking of paying one last visit to the Ebenezer Parker schoolyard, one last walk down the path through the woods, my sister came tumbling out of the house running after me.

"Where ya going, big brother? Can I come?"

I looked down at my sister Jill and threw my arm around her. "I'm going to Chicago to see a man about a horse."

"What?" she laughed.

"Uncle Augie once said that to me when I went running after him—no, you can't come with me."

"Let's go up to the beach! We'll take the Jeep. I have a license now, you know. I can drive, you know."

"You've got a hell of a nerve growing up while I was away. Is the old man still sore at me?"

"He's getting over it. He's given up on you!"

"You sure he won't raise hell?"

"I'll get the keys. Wait here a minute."

I stood right there in the middle of Glenwood outside Jimmy Dillard's house till she came driving by to pick me up.

"Move over," I said. "I'll drive."

We took the newly-completed Rte 213 over to the newly-completed Rte 495, which now hooked up with Rte 95 and the New Hampshire Thruway to take you all the way from Milltown past Haverhill and Newburyport up to Hampton Beach.

We sat on the sand and talked about love, my sister and me.

"Are you really serious about this guy, Roland Perrault?"

"I'm just waiting for him to get back and then, probably, I will marry him. Surprised? I'm his reason to get home safe."

"Then—you know how I feel about getting back to my little girl Aisling and her mother."

I left my sister sitting there wiggling her toes in the sand of Hampton Beach and walked down by myself to the water's edge.

I gazed out across the cold grey Atlantic waters just warming up in August and the twilight gathering on the distant horizon, beyond which, somewhere out there, were my wife and daughter.

So far away that my baby girl Aisling was truly *'A Beautiful Dream I Had Last Night.'*

I missed Sheila badly.

I was conscious then of having turned my back on America.

I could feel it there, behind me, stretching all the way to the Pacific.

I wished I could penetrate the darkness of the future, now foreclosing on the eastern rim of the world. But all I could see was the vision of Sheila and Aisling, and the place where they were dwelling at this moment. And that place, that island, was a place I had come to believe was the holiest and most sacred and visionary place I could want to escape to. Knowing the words of the music, and the power of the poems, and the stories of the books and the illuminated manuscripts of her saints and scholars and writers and rebels, I called it, in my own mind, *the Isle of the Blest.*

Eugene Christy

Quintet, five novels telling the saga of Antonio LaStoria and his descendants through three generations in America from 1899 to 1972, to be published by Adelaide Books, New York, in 2020 and 2021.

About the Author

Eugene Christy is a novelist, poet and musician currently enjoying retirement in his home in the Berkshires. His maternal grandparents Antonio Scioscia and Giuseppina Fabrizio came from Alta Villa Irpina, near Avellino, in the South of Italy. He has studied under Sean O'Faolain, James Dickey, and Larry McMurtry. Appearing as Gene Christy, he was previously known around the Berkshires as the singer-songwriter and accordian-player who led The Dossers, the Irish-themed pub-band trio featuring Bill Morrison and Rick Marquis. His current project, six years in the making, is called The Twentieth Century

www.ingramcontent.com/pod-product-compliance
Lightning Source LLC
Chambersburg PA
CBHW021437070526
44577CB00002B/194